Madaline

Madaline

LOVE AND SURVIVAL IN
ANTEBELLUM NEW ORLEANS

Edited by Dell Upton

The University of Georgia Press   *Athens and London*

Library of Congress Cataloging in Publication Data

Edwards, Madaline Selima, 1816–1854.
Madaline : love and survival in antebellum New
Orleans / edited by Dell Upton.
p.   cm.
Includes bibliographical references and index.
ISBN 0-8203-1758-6 (alk. paper)
1. Edwards, Madaline Selima, 1816–1854.   2. New
Orleans (La.)—Biography.   3. San Francisco (Calif.)—
Biography.   4. Women—Louisiana—New Orleans—
Biography.   5. Women pioneers—California—San
Francisco—Biography.   6. Pioneers—California—San
Francisco—Biography.   I. Upton, Dell.   II. Title.
CT275.E357   1996
976.3'3505'092—dc20   95-14156
[B]

British Library Cataloging in Publication Data available

In memory of

S. K.,

J. O'D.,

and

B. Z.

Contents

Illustrations

Preface

The remarkable life of Madaline Selima Edwards ended abruptly on August 20, 1854, at her house on Telegraph Hill in San Francisco. She was in her thirty-eighth year, one of many Forty-niners who sought and failed to find a better life in the Golden State and were soon forgotten. Even her grave in the potter's field of the city's Yerba Buena Cemetery disappeared within a few years of her death, when the graveyard was removed to make way for a new city hall. Yet, through a series of fortunate accidents, a handful of letters, two diaries, and two books of miscellanies, all written in New Orleans in the mid-1840s, survive as memorials of an engaging personality and an expressive voice. These documents tell the story of a turbulent love affair that was the emotional center of an equally tumultuous life.

Although few of the "events" of traditional histories intrude on these pages, Edwards's writings speak eloquently of decisions, emotions, and judgments. They record the contingencies of everyday life, some momentous and others incidental, and the struggles of a mind and heart laboring to make sense of them. Although she was a singular woman, living on the fringes of southern urban society outside a conventional middle-class domestic setting, Edwards was constrained by nineteenth-century religious and gender ideologies. She accepted standard moral pieties in principle but understood the pain and injustice they inflicted in practice. In a society that demanded domestic stability and female dependence on male bounty, Madaline Edwards found stability elusive and bounty scarce. She was a woman on her own and often alone, both dependent and independent in exactly the wrong ways. Yet she lived in a manner that preserved a tenuous self-respect. This is her tale, a fragmentary, sometimes enigmatic, but always moving testimony to a life lived and a life imagined.

As Madaline Edwards saw it, her story was about choices: about the consequences of those we make and our ability to choose even when circumstances seem most constraining. She made difficult choices, and when the consequences were dire, she made even more difficult choices to deal with them. In the face of the glib talk of "resistance" and "subversion" current in social history scholarship and cultural criticism, Edwards reminds us that it is a more common human experience simply to get by, hoping for small forward steps rather than enormous leaps and usually achieving neither. She never denied responsibility for her own choices, and she never stopped getting by, no matter how severe the setback. Often her tone is painful, and occasionally it is desperate, but behind it stood a woman who was tougher than she pretended to be, who knew her mind, understood her possibilities, and was fiercely determined to make the most of both. She always thought that she could make her life better.

Madaline Edwards's tale is a powerful story powerfully told, and it spoke to me at a particularly dramatic time in my own life. She seized my imagination, and her spirit helped shape my responses to my own circumstances. Yet her story might not have come down to us at all, but for a series of accidents.

As her affair with her married lover, Charles William Bradbury, foundered, Edwards asked him for "an order by which I can get the things you took charge of for me," including her letters, writing books, and diaries, along with a miniature portrait of Bradbury. Still, she was ambivalent about reclaiming them: "My MS.S books I wrote with the sole hope and belief that they would be yours. . . . Little did I think when penning the most of those pages, a day was so close at hand when you would spurn them and me. Your name occurs so oft in them that I cannot well leave them to another."[1] Finally she demanded their return, but Bradbury never gave them back to her. Edwards left Louisiana in June 1849.

There is no certain evidence of the papers' fate after 1847, but the circumstantial evidence of Edwards's words and Bradbury's life suggests a plausible hypothesis. I suspect that the papers resided in a safe in Bradbury's office at the Royal Insurance Company, along with odds and ends of his own youthful correspondence, and that they remained there after his death in 1880, of no use to the agency and forgotten until the building, or the safe, or the contents of it, were cleaned out in the twentieth century.[2]

By some means, Meigs O. Frost of Lafitte, Louisiana, gained possession of the papers. Possibly he bought them as incidental parts of the contents of the building or office. In any case, the Frost family recognized the importance of Edwards's story and in 1954 donated the papers to the Southern Historical Collection at the University of North Carolina at Chapel Hill. It is ironic, given the history recounted here, that Edwards's writings, packaged with a few odd scraps of Bradbury's, are cataloged as the Charles W. Bradbury Papers.[3]

In the fall of 1992 I stumbled across the Bradbury Papers. Friends in Raleigh suggested that the Southern Historical Collection might hold leads for my projected book on the urban cultural landscape of antebellum New Orleans. The collection's catalog entry described Madaline Edwards as the mistress of insurance agent Charles Bradbury. Thinking I might find something racy, I turned to the papers themselves. There I discovered something much more remarkable.

Edwards's words were so compelling that I decided immediately to try to publish her work, but when I traveled to New Orleans to trace her history, I encountered the kinds of frustration one might expect in researching a nineteenth-century woman who was of no account in the eyes of record-keeping officialdom. There was no reason to expect that I would uncover anything substantial about her, and for a week I could find no evidence that she had even existed. I began to imagine that the papers were forgeries. Finally I turned up an item in some school board minutes that noted Edwards's dismissal from her teacher's post, and the story began to unfold. Striking coincidences at difficult points in the research made it possible for me to go forward and strengthened my determination to tell Edwards's story. It seemed fated.

Try as I might, I couldn't discover what had happened to Edwards after Bradbury left her in 1847. I surveyed every New Orleans death record from 1840 to 1905. I looked in the Alabama census, since her father lived in Mobile. I scanned reference books containing death records for Alabama, Mississippi, and Tennessee, all states where Edwards had lived. Then, standing among the genealogical shelves of the New Orleans Public Library, I remembered a passing reference to California in one of her last letters. There on the shelf next to me was the 1850 California census index. Perhaps she had moved to San Francisco during the Gold Rush? This was another dead end, for the San Francisco census for 1850 had burned. Paging through the other county listings — more from frustration than hope — I discovered Madaline Edwards, aged thirty (not quite accurate), born in Tennessee, living in Sacramento County! After I returned home to California, a halfhearted glance at an 1850 San Francisco directory turned up her name again. Edwards had remained in Sacramento long enough to be enumerated there in June 1850, rather than in San Francisco, whose census has not survived. Then she moved to San Francisco in time to appear in a directory published in September of the same year. The city's second directory was compiled during her brief return visit to New Orleans, so she is absent from it. She lived long enough (by a month) to appear in the third San Francisco directory, issued in the summer of 1854. The pages had fallen out of the Sutro Library's copy of this rare directory, up to the one with her name on it. From a chance encounter in a North Carolina archive, I had caught up with Madaline Edwards a few miles from my own doorstep.

Acknowledgments

I found Madaline Edwards's papers and began to edit them during a year's leave devoted to another project, on the antebellum urban cultural landscape of New Orleans and Philadelphia. That leave was funded by a fellowship from the John Simon Guggenheim Memorial Foundation and by sabbatical funds from the University of California, Berkeley. Their welcome support has now done double duty.

I am grateful to the Southern Historical Collection at the University of North Carolina at Chapel Hill and to SHC Reference Assistant John E. White for permission to publish these documents and for arranging the microfilming. In Louisiana, I was ably assisted by John Magill, Stan Ritchey, Pamela Arsenault, and Jon Kukla of the Historic New Orleans Collection; Wilbur Menary and Joan Caldwell of Tulane University Library; Beatriz Owsley at the University of New Orleans Archives; and the staffs of the New Orleans Public Library, the Louisiana State Museum, and the Louisiana and Lower Mississippi Valley Collection of Louisiana State University Library. Outside the Pelican State, the Mississippi Division of Archives and History, the Tennessee State Library, the Missouri Historical Society, the California State Library, the San Francisco History Room of the San Francisco Public Library, the Sutro Library, San Francisco, and the Bancroft Library, University of California, Berkeley, were equally helpful.

Malcolm Call was the first to confirm my enthusiasm for Madaline Edwards's work, and he has been patient during the delays that life imposes on scholarship. Zeynep Kezer has been a brilliant and imaginative colleague. Her contribution goes far beyond that of a mere research assistant, as she knows, and it has been a privilege to work with her. Elizabeth Byrne and Kathryn Wayne of the Environmental Design Library at the University of California, Berkeley, in turn made Zeynep's job much easier. Rowena Olegario ably searched the R. G. Dun and Company Collection at Harvard University for me. Larry McDonald of the San Francisco City Planning Department as well as friends and colleagues Bob Alexander, Cathy Davidson, Jenny Franchot, Mike Grossberg, Greg Hise, Alice Kaplan, Barbara Melosh, Mary Ryan, Eric Sandweiss, and Katherine Snyder provided timely leads and suggestions. The members of the Bay Area Seminar on Early American History and Culture made suggestions early in the project, and my old and valued friends among the Berkeley Americanists—Paul Groth, Dick Hutson, Larry Levine, Margaretta Lovell, Don McQuade, and Chris Rosen— gave the Introduction close scrutiny that made it better. The press's outside readers examined the whole work even more closely, and Catherine Clinton, in particular, went far beyond a reader's duties and made major substantive suggestions for which I am deeply grateful.

I was delighted that Madaline Edwards intrigued my friends as much as she did me. Catherine and John Bishir first steered me to the Southern Historical Collection and entertained me, in all senses of the word, while I worked there. Bob Reimers tolerated a very long residence in his house that made the Louisiana research possible as well as fun. Barbara Carson, Cary Carson, Tom Carter, Edward Chappell, Betsy Cromley, Jim Deetz, Henry Glassie, Paul Groth, Marlene Heck, Kathi Kern, Anna Kevorkian, Ellina Kevorkian, Karen Kevorkian, Raffi Kevorkian, Soseh Kevorkian, Margaretta Lovell, Jean McMann, Orlando Ridout V, Stephen Tobriner, and John Vlach offered vital support of many sorts. My love and thanks go to them all.

Finally, authors rightly delight in acknowledging professional mentors and current friends and colleagues. This work, about a woman who was intensely concerned with personal histories and storytelling, influences and choices, gives me an opportunity to thank two early teachers who first showed me the pleasures of history, Joseph Lombardi and David Strauss. Whatever I have become as a historian I owe to them.

A Note on the Text

Madaline Edwards's diaries for 1844 and 1845 form the skeleton of this book. I have bracketed them with the letters that chronicle the beginning and end of her affair with Charles Bradbury, and I have interpolated selected essays and poems from her writing books along with occasional supporting texts such as newspaper articles, public documents, and entries from other people's diaries that illuminate her story.

Judging from the relative absence of interlineations and strikethroughs and the relative frequency of omitted words, Edwards's surviving works are most likely fair copies made from drafts. Thus the texts are clean and generally very legible. Edwards's spelling follows contemporary conventions; I have not altered those words that do not. Her punctuation, however, was idiosyncratic. Commas, periods, semicolons, and dashes were used almost interchangeably where they were used at all. Her capitalization was equally erratic. She favored long, run-on sentences and essays with few paragraph breaks. I have tried to preserve the flow of her thought and her voice, but I have silently added a few commas and periods for clarity. Otherwise all my additions appear in brackets.

Madaline Edwards refers to most people in her diaries by initials and a few by nicknames. I have supplied names where I could. Several recurrent characters, though, I have identified only at their first appearance and in passages that would otherwise be difficult to follow. They are

B., Bud, Henry Josephus, Josephus	Henry Joseph Budington, a friend
C., Ch.	Charles William Bradbury, Edwards's lover
Mr. C.	The Reverend Theodore Clapp, Edwards's pastor

J., J.A.B.	James Anson Bradbury, Charles Bradbury's brother
Dr. R.	James Ritchie, Edwards's physician
S., Mr. S.	A longtime suitor known only as Sayre or Sayres
Mr. S't	Another suitor, known only as Mr. Scott

Introduction

For most of her short life Madaline Selima Cage Elliott Edwards was a woman on her own and on the move. Between her marriage in 1831 and her death less than a quarter of a century later, she lived in Tennessee, Mississippi, Alabama, Louisiana, and California. As the penniless veteran of two failed marriages and the mistress of a married man, she was denied a recognized place in a society that made none for women without money and without the protection of husbands, fathers, or brothers. As a woman fascinated by words, she understandably turned to books and writing to help construct, reveal, and sometimes conceal a self.

In Madaline Edwards's diaries and letters, we read of the social being, the woman struggling to earn a living and to find fulfillment in a love affair on the social and urban fringes of New Orleans. In all her writings she worked to construct a tale that would make sense of her experience, give it a moral, redeem it. As she shaped the story of her life, Edwards tried on a variety of identities that might define a place for her, if not in the world's mind then at least in her own. She described ill-starred efforts to play her roles as daughter, niece, wife, mother, and schoolteacher acceptably. She earned a modest but erratic living as a teacher of painting and gained satisfaction and some repute, if no money, as an author. At times she fantasized about other callings, as astronomer,

1

missionary, and even soldier, occupations that fascinated her or that she thought suited her temperament but that she believed were closed to her.[1]

The intersection of Madaline Edwards's daily life and imaginative life in her writings elicits from modern readers the "interest," or empathy for recognizable fellow beings, that nineteenth-century critics attributed to the best novels. In her work we detect a common human dilemma, that of an ordinary person caught between "should" and "is," between the demands of society and the exigencies of personal circumstances. Edwards lived her life within social and moral structures that in many instances she painfully acknowledged to be appropriate and even just. Yet her "situation," as she called it, constantly demonstrated their limitations. When she was caught between contradictory dicta or trapped by those that seemed unfair, she questioned assumptions that most of her contemporaries accepted without thought. Edwards challenged the constraints of received moral and social precepts and of middle-class notions of gender and gentility by evoking other, equally common, precepts derived from Enlightenment religion and nineteenth-century popular literature.[2]

Edwards's predicament is less surprising than her detailed, explicit firsthand commentary on it, which offers a rare personal assessment of the life of a nineteenth-century woman at odds with her society. For that reason, Edwards is of interest not only to general readers but also to scholars who wish to understand the relationship between social structures and the people who live them. In recent years many anthropologists, archaeologists, sociologists, and geographers have turned back to the personal, recognizing that the grand structures of society are frameworks within which particular lives are conducted. These scholars seek to avoid accounts of structures so overarching that they stultify individual action as well as romantic interpretations of personal action that ignore the defining role of social context. In his work on the Pacific Islands, for example, the anthropologist Marshall Sahlins depicts the networks of social rules, beliefs, and values—the ought-tos of our existence, the setting within which we frame our expectations of our lives and surroundings—but he also shows that these structures are placed at risk every time people act. Structure is tested in action, stretched, warped, and sometimes broken and cast aside.[3]

Sahlins calls the process of testing and modifying structure "history." Oddly, though, historians have been less openly interested in the problem of personal agency in a social context. When they have considered individual actions, they have traditionally examined the actions of great men (and, less often, of women) relatively divorced from social structure. Since the 1960s historians have democratized the field, opening it up to include ordinary men and women like Madaline Edwards. Yet they have tended to speak more of entire social groups and grand patterns, leaving no room for the good and bad human choices that nineteenth-century critics thought created "interest" in a good story and that attracted readers to older great-man history.[4]

For historians, then, Edwards's writings are valuable for their explicit juxtaposition of structure and individual action. She analyzed her own actions in the light of her social milieu, weighing the claims of self and society carefully. At the same time, her work was often self-consciously literary—not great literature, certainly, but a revealing effort to pour daily life into the molds of popular culture. In this respect, it illuminates the meaning of reading to ordinary people, a problem that has fascinated literary scholars in recent years.

A Choice and Its Consequences

Madaline Edwards wrote these diaries, letters, poems, and essays as a young woman aged twenty-six to thirty years old. By her own description, she was then five feet seven inches tall, weighed about 145 pounds, and was "well proportioned so I'm told." She had a high forehead and "large and full green eye[s]." "I sometimes paint but not my face," she added.[5]

Edwards had already lived a life that would have been eventful for someone twice her age. Clues to her history are scattered throughout her writings, and to the extent that her words can be confirmed by other documents, there is no reason to suspect that she misrepresented or distorted biographical facts, although her interpretations of them varied from time to time. The story she told was a strikingly familiar one, of a powerful but unforgiving family, of parents unable to control their own lives, and of a daughter similarly unable to establish a satisfying life or personal relationships.

Selima Madaline Cage (she would later reverse her first and middle names) was born on December 28, 1816, in Sumner County, Tennessee, to Lofton Cage (born 1783) and Naomi (or Nabury) Gillespie Cage. She was the third child, after a brother who died as a young adult when Madaline was thirteen years old and a beloved sister, Eliza, who is mentioned frequently in Madaline's writings. A younger brother, Albert, and a younger sister, Fanny, played much smaller roles in her life.[6]

Madaline's family were leaders of the Sumner County community where she grew up. Her paternal grandfather was William Cage, a Virginia native and a major in the American Revolution. An early colonist in Tennessee, he settled at Cage's Bend on the Cumberland River before 1791. Major Cage was an active politician who had been the treasurer of the state of Franklin (the predecessor of the present state of Tennessee) and a county magistrate. After serving as county sheriff, Cage passed the office on to two of his sons in succession. One, William Cage Jr., probably the uncle who raised Madaline, was a merchant and land speculator in partnership with James Winchester. Together they founded the town of Cairo, where they were the principal merchants and owners of the first steamboat based in the town.[7]

As the daughter of one of Sumner County's leading families, Madaline was a privileged child. She attended the female academy and the dancing academy at Gallatin, the county seat. For much of her childhood she lived with her uncle at the "ancestral homestead" (which was not much more than twenty-five years old when she was born), her grandfather's house adjacent to the family burying ground at Cage's Bend. There the child Madaline "loved (for I was a tomboy) to go in the fields and ride home in the carts loaded with the grain of the field and throw up the fodder and hays, but more than all the other joys dearest to me was the one of taking my book and steal[ing] away from all my companions." Her uncle's well-stocked library whetted this appetite for reading. As a young woman she was "daily accustomed to hear the violin and flute together and was ever in motion to dance."[8]

In her essays Edwards reminisces about rural beauties, beloved relatives, and the joys of the old homeplace. Yet these scenes of childhood idylls and of the genteel upbringing of a young woman destined for a comfortable life owe as much to the clichés of popular literature as to her own experience. They contrast sharply with the specifics of Cage family life that she reported.

Although she was descended from local gentry, Madaline Edwards was the child of a broken marriage, separated from her siblings and left to Cage family care soon after she started school. She rarely saw her parents until she was an adult. As late as 1844 Madaline had not met her brother Albert, who was then twenty-four years old. The separation from her immediate family was a bitter one that remained with her throughout her life. "I have never known a Mothers *love* and parental care and Oh! what have I not lost," she lamented. When Naomi died in 1844 Madaline wrote of her as "an unnatural Mother yet I am her child and it is natural to drop a tear to her memory." By this time her parents were divorced, and her father had remarried and moved to Mobile.[9]

The entire extended Cage family were to Edwards's mind a hard-bitten, judgmental lot who held highly restrictive notions of a young woman's path. Despite Madaline's love of books, her uncle pulled her out of school before she was fourteen years old, "having given me the rudiments of an english education." After she had moved to New Orleans, the Cages pursued her, mostly to torment her, as she saw it. They could muster little tolerance or understanding for their female relative's misfortunes, owing in part to their strict Methodist views. After an early misadventure, or the appearance of one, her uncle, she said, "ruined me upon a charge of which I was as clear as my angel babe before Gods throne." One day in 1845 Madaline encountered "an uncle and five cousins who are not my friends. . . . they deem me pollution."[10]

Raised in such a family, can it be any surprise that an unhappy, de-

fiant, but confused Madaline chose to marry a few days after her fourteenth birthday? She wed Dempsey Elliott on January 2, 1831, which
she later called "the most unfortunate day of my life." In her autobiographical "Tale of Real Life," Edwards claimed that pity for her hapless
suitor had overridden a powerful, instinctive sense of impending disaster. She noted defensively that "as I had no Father, Mother or brother
to please in this union I did not conceive that the world had a right
to judge," but the opposite may have been true. Nine years after the
couple married and three years after they separated, Madaline's husband, Dempsey Elliott, and her father, Lofton Cage, were next-door
neighbors and business associates in Mobile. This simple fact, gleaned
from the United States Census for 1840, makes one wonder how long
husband and father had known each other, and whether the girl had
been pressured to marry a parental friend.[11]

Soon after the wedding, Dempsey and Madaline moved to the small
college town of Clinton, Mississippi, just outside Jackson. According to
the "Tale of Real Life," Madaline missed her friends and soon regretted
her marriage to an untutored man who was ill equipped either to support his wife or to introduce the intellectually ambitious young woman
to the town's lettered society. Three children—an unnamed boy, Mary
Jane, and William—were born and died in Clinton during the five or six
years of the couple's Mississippi sojourn. The two oldest children died
within a few days of each other, probably during an epidemic of scarlet
fever, a disease from which their mother also suffered. The couple then
moved to New Orleans, where a fourth child, Isabella, was born.[12]

Around 1837 Madaline and Dempsey Elliott separated. In her "Tale,"
Edwards described her former husband as "a steady, industrious, and
honourable man," "kind and devoted," a man who loved his infant
daughter and who reluctantly left their home at his wife's insistence.
She forced him to leave because he had lost heart and refused to work
to support his family, but she promised reconciliation if he changed his
attitude, Edwards wrote. In other essays, however, she implied that he
had been unfaithful or that she was simply tired of him. "I had often
thought of a separation and wished for it," she admitted, "but the fear

of the opinion of the world that makes and keeps so many in misery" had stopped her, so that she had "lived my best years with a bad choice doomed to bear the penalty of my sad choice unpitied but not unblamed."[13]

At the age of twenty, Edwards now faced the problem of supporting herself. She had begun to sell her paintings before she and Dempsey separated. Now she supplemented that income by teaching at the New Orleans Female Orphan Asylum. Teaching was a recurrent occupation throughout her residence in New Orleans, but this stint was short-lived. Soon after she began work, she resigned to care for the mortally ill Isabella, who died when she was about nineteen months old.

The story of Edwards's life in Clinton and New Orleans until she met her lover Charles William Bradbury is undocumented except in the "Tale." She moved back to her uncle's house in Tennessee during this period, where she took up with another "E," probably the Edwards from whom she took her preferred surname. She returned with him to New Orleans. Again Madaline knew the bargain was a bad one, brought on by her own circumstances and by her sense of pity for a man. Again an inner voice warned her against an impending mistake but was unable to dissuade her from making it. "Wants too numerous to relate sometime after again brought me under the necessity of giving my hand to one that I must have loved better than I did the former although had I been left free to choose would not have been my choice. And here again my benevolence caused my misery." Since she had returned to her uncle's house to live, these wants were not financial. Instead, the stern regime of the Cages was probably too much for a woman already branded as a failure for having left her marriage, and she could not stand to remain there.

I have found no evidence that Edwards ever formally divorced Dempsey Elliott. Although some recent historians argue that divorce was easier to obtain in the antebellum South than is sometimes supposed, others note the reluctance of some southern courts to grant women divorces even under the most extreme abuse. In either case, it is unlikely that one would have been available to a woman in Madaline's straitened circumstances. Yet she married the otherwise unidentified and unknown Edwards and nursed him through yellow fever, then pursued him to Red River (the region around Alexandria, Louisiana) and Alabama after she found out that he too was already married. All we know of the end of this relationship is dramatically related in the "Tale of Real Life." [14]

During the years between her separation from Dempsey Elliott and her encounter with Charles Bradbury in New Orleans, Madaline Edwards circulated among her family, staying at her uncle's house in Tennessee, her sister Eliza Coleman's house in Jackson, Mississippi, and her father's house in Mobile, Alabama, before returning to New Orleans in 1842 or 1843.[15] These years were evidently eventful ones, and Madaline did more than languish in her relatives' homes. This must have been the time when she knew F.G., "the young man who brought me to my ruin when he was assuming the garb of friend in Vicksburg." We know nothing more of the incident. We know little more about the way that Edwards and Bradbury met. Neither party ever described the encounter, but the words of both suggest that the circumstances were less than genteel. When Bradbury first met Edwards, he admitted, he was sexually attracted to her: "It was the *Animal* that first prompted me to seek an interview with you, for then I was as ignorant, as the child unborn, of your identity." He learned she was a deeply religious woman who imagined herself unworthy to attend worship services or even to pray. Put simply, he then seduced her by taking her to church. Here the Edwards letters and diaries published in this book take over the story.[16]

An Available Woman?

Madaline Edwards's gender was the defining circumstance of her life. The differences between women's and men's powers, possibilities, and responsibilities, the disparate standards to which men and women were held in her era, in her city, and in her social world, governed her daily life, shaped her understanding of her past, and colored her assessment of her future. Because she had no acceptable relationship with a man, Madaline Edwards was on her own. Although she often fantasized about living entirely alone, that was impossible. Because she was a woman on her own, she could not support herself and was forced to rely on the assistance of men. Edwards's male partners and acquaintances were exempt from the moral censure and inability to make a living that her gender inflicted on her.

When Madaline Edwards decided to rectify her first, poor choice of a mate, she became a woman on her own. Everything else followed from that action, which, first and finally, "ruined" her. "Were moral laws so constructed that a fallen female might reinstate herself by any penance that life could endure however severe how gladly would I embrace it," she wrote, but she knew that "this cannot be." Unable to make a respectable alliance, she was faced with the prospect of living with her uncle or her father or of allying herself with men who would not scruple at her "fallen" character, such as the bigamous Edwards or the philandering Bradbury.[17]

Nineteenth-century America had little room for women not under the protection of fathers, husbands, or brothers. Legally, single women enjoyed the same rights as men to own property and earn money, and some women were able to make substantial livings on their own. Such careers, however, were unusual, and they contradicted customary notions of female public passivity. It required great force of character or great economic need for a woman to act publicly on her own. In the South this was particularly true. As Elizabeth Fox-Genovese has noted, both single women and opportunities for them were rarer there than elsewhere in the United States.[18]

Edwards's opportunities to support herself were limited by her status as a woman with a broken marriage. She tried all the avenues available to respectable females: she taught painting and sold her own works, she took in needlework, and she taught children. These were suitable occupations for women, it was sometimes argued, because they accorded with women's physiological makeup, as refined but relatively weak beings who bore and nurtured children.[19] Painting, sewing, and teaching evoked customary elements of women's education and women's domestic duties. Furthermore, they allowed women to work privately.

Edwards did needlework at her own home and at her clients' residences and gave painting lessons and taught school in her own home as well. Even teaching in a school, as she did at the Female Orphan Asylum and later at the Marshall School, was not really "public work," since teachers worked in a controlled setting where they met only children and where they were supervised by a male school board and a male principal. These men saw to it that teachers did not stray from the moral paths laid out for women.[20]

Yet as nineteenth-century observers as well as modern historians have pointed out, it was nearly impossible for women to earn an adequate living by these respectable means. Work was difficult for Edwards to come by, and when she did find it she often had trouble getting paid. More than once she complained that "all my debtors seem not to pity me in the least for I can not get a dime."[21]

Edwards's sewing accounts show that even in the best of circumstances she could not make enough to subsist. Long hours of hard sewing in December 1844 brought in $14.50 for the month. In January and February 1845 she made $16.50 a month, but only $8.20 in March. Her best month was July, when she made $19.50, but then she broke her arm. The next month she needed $72.00 from Bradbury to help her get by.[22] During her brief career as a public-school teacher, she made $35.00 a month.

There were many demands on this income. Just as gendered limits constrained what she might do to earn money, so class and racial limits controlled what she might do for herself. After a shortage of food, she complained most often about lacking money to pay a laundress. When she thought she was pregnant, Bradbury hired a slave, Maria, to help her. Edwards had to feed and clothe the young girl and was sometimes unable to do so. The situation might have been worse. Her mortgage required an eight-hundred-dollar payment in one year, which would clearly have been impossible had Bradbury, who held the note, forced her to pay. Renting the same house, according to the award a New Orleans district court made to her in 1853, would have cost her twenty-eight dollars per month.[23]

Alone, without the assistance of a family and without an independent fortune or income, Edwards and women like here depended on male assistance. Frequently Edwards's diary entries record gifts of food, money, and clothing from Bradbury. Many of her other male friends extended occasional assistance. She received gifts of money and goods from her admirers Mr. Scott and Mr. Sayre, from Bradbury's brother James, and from the brothers' friend Henry J. Budington.

During the years of her liaison with Charles Bradbury, Madaline Edwards never forgot her economic dependence, which was a recurrent source of tension between the lovers as his fortunes rose and fell. In one of her first surviving letters, she asked for a loan but acknowledged "that you have lately had to spend much money and that times are dull in your business and that it will look to you as though I intend to make a practice of this, but it shall be the last time." A year later she "took a good cry" after one of Bradbury's visits, "for I felt bad and have not a cent to spend and he did not offer me any and I could not ask."[24]

Edwards was probably correct in believing that Bradbury's financial problems finally ended their affair. Although the relationship had been strained for years as a result of her desperation and his own fear of discovery, he did not break it off until after she lost her teaching position in 1847 and seemed unable to find any other way to support herself.

Bradbury's exasperation was obvious. After Edwards was fired, he wrote that "I determined to propose to you to muster your little means together, and with the aid of one or two friends, commence a small retail establishment by which I then believed, and do still believe, that you could make a support, and perhaps realise a handsome little living for old age. But this scheme did not seem to meet favor in your mind. I was then prompted to make the other proposition, which you have now rejected."[25]

Bradbury was irritated by Edwards's apparent refusal of genuine offers of assistance. She thought he was searching for an excuse to cut her off. He had accused her of infidelity, she said, when his real problem was that she had become a financial burden. In a clear-eyed assessment notably different from her earlier praise of his unfailing generosity, she observed that "I have ever noticed one thing. If men neglect their wives, that is extend to them no pecuniary assistance, or, if men do not treat their mistresses as they had once been able to do," they cover their embarrassment by accusing the women of faithlessness, as Bradbury had done. His real reason, she had no doubt, was "that you no longer extended to me the means of living."[26]

It was a revealing exchange. In Bradbury's eyes, Edwards's only bond to him was money. In hers, emotional attachment was paramount, for despite her financial need, she turned down several suitors to remain with him. Now she was desperate, her arm broken and badly healed and her job lost, and she felt victimized by his charges. She believed that she had made good-faith efforts to free herself from his largess and would have tried harder had she known his predicament: "Have I called on you for means? Have I ever grumbled. No, often have I wanted a dime so much that I would resolve to ask you, but my heart or pride would fail me, and I would eat stale bread and sometimes none until I could get a trifle for my sewing."[27]

The conflict touched on undercurrents that ran powerfully, if not always visibly, through many aspects of Edwards's life, for economic dependence had metaphorical and social as well as monetary dimensions in antebellum New Orleans. Many of her social relationships incorporated an element of exchange or transaction that, in the nineteenth-century gendered context, evoked prostitution. There is no evidence that Edwards turned to prostitution at any time in her life, yet it was a subtext of her self-conception and a specter that could easily be raised against her. The letters and diaries are full of allusions to it. Throughout her affair with Charles Bradbury, arguments often provoked words that made Edwards's heart ache: "Before he left one little question caused me intense pain." On other occasions, her Bradbury "laid his first charge against me" or "began some jesting words which I feared was half in earnest, which with my gloomy feelings ended in tears." A visit from her suitor Mr. Sayre provoked "an evening of misery for me" when Charley found him there. "He did not intend to wound me but an unguarded word did it all." The contexts of these remarks imply that

Bradbury had accused her of prostitution. Eventually he was more direct, charging her with "mercenary" behavior. After she was fired from the public schools, Edwards turned the charge around, warning Bradbury that her circumstances "left [her] no hope but that of abandoning [her] self to a life that [she] detested."[28]

Prostitution was more than an insult or a threat to the numerous, usually unnamed, casual male visitors who found their way to Edwards's house. Common male beliefs about the relationships between men, women, and money allowed them to assume her availability. The attentions of these men were always unwanted and usually hurtful. Some taunted her openly. "Slandered and abused by one too low to notice" one day, on another she was "accosted by a stranger on my return [from church] who mortified my feelings much in offering the language though chaste he did." Even friends took advantage of her vulnerability, as happened the day she took a walk with Sayre, "to avoid an insult." These men required repeated demonstrations of "firmness" to discourage them.[29]

Ironically, Madaline Edwards's unsuitability for respectable marriage made her world overwhelmingly masculine. The diaries are filled with references to her male friends and even suitors. Bradbury's male friends and relatives were often found at her house as well. At times when tensions between Edwards and Bradbury relaxed, these social occasions took on a friendly, appealing tone, as Edwards and her men friends chatted, joked, read aloud, combed one another's hair, and took walks. Such lighthearted gatherings permitted a male-female sociability that was more informal than that found in polite society. At the same time they depended on the less appealing asymmetry of gender roles that colored all of Edwards's existence. The money nexus as well as the loneliness occasioned by her social stigma encouraged her to open her home to these men even when she preferred to be alone. The power of their money gave them a freedom to associate with women like her, whom they believed to be beneath them, while they remained unstained in their own minds.

Although the evidence is sparse, apparently the men who enjoyed themselves at Edwards's house were mostly business and professional men, mostly young, not wealthy but no longer junior clerks either, and mostly single. They tended to work in the "American district" downtown and to dabble in real-estate speculation at the developing upriver edge of the city where they resided. For example, the New York–born Henry J. Budington (ca. 1814–76), the "Bud" or "Henry Josephus" of the diaries, was "employed in commerce" in 1840. He may have been between marriages at the time Edwards wrote, for according to census records one woman between twenty and thirty years of age lived in his household in 1840, yet in 1850 his wife, Margaret, was only twenty-four years old. In the mid-1840s Budington owned three lots in the city, but by 1850 he had accumulated real-estate holdings worth ten thousand dollars.[30]

Charles Bradbury's brother James (ca. 1816–71) lived alternately in New Orleans and Terrebonne Parish and was a physician later in his life. Like Budington, he owned some New Orleans real estate, although his dealings are difficult to separate from his brother's, since the two regularly bought and sold land for and to each other.[31]

Edwards's most prominent acquaintance, and the one with whom she had the most casual connection, was the exception to this pattern. Dr. John Leonard Riddell (1807–65) owned the house next door to hers. A well-known scientist, professor of chemistry at the Medical College of Louisiana, public lecturer, physician, melter and refiner at the United States Mint, and New Orleans postmaster by appointment of his friends John Tyler and William Henry Harrison, Riddell was an active real-estate speculator. He owned nearly thirty parcels in all parts of the city during the mid-1840s. Two of them were assessed at fourteen thousand dollars in 1843. Riddell described himself in 1846 as "moderately independent. If living at the north, I should consider myself rich with my present means."[32]

Like his brother and his friend Henry Budington, Charles Bradbury was an aspiring businessman who believed a prosperous future lay before him. Bradbury was perhaps a year older than Edwards, having been born in central New York on May 9, 1815 or 1816. His parents immi-

Dr. John Leonard Riddell. Courtesy Rudolph Matas Medical Library,
Tulane University School of Medicine.

grated to the Ohio River Valley in 1821, where his older brother Cornelius had already established himself in 1819. During Charley's young manhood, Cornelius, then the effective head of the family, was a flour merchant in Cincinnati. Other siblings lived nearby in Madison, Indiana, where one of them ran a flour mill and a sawmill. Young Charles Bradbury moved to New Orleans in 1835.[33]

In his new home, Bradbury set out to make his fortune, following Cornelius's advice to find placement in "one of the first houses . . . with steady & active employment, giving entire satisfaction to your employers." He wrote to James Waller Breedlove, president of the Atchafalaya Railroad and Bank, and obtained a job there.[34]

After leaving the bank, Bradbury worked for the Royal Insurance Company, whose offices were on Camp Street in downtown New Orleans. In 1840 he bought a house at the corner of Bacchus (Baronne) and Erato streets, then on the edge of the city, and lived there for the rest of his life. Bradbury had already begun to buy real estate, a common nineteenth-century route to an independent existence and retirement from active business. During the time he knew Madaline Edwards, Bradbury owned as many as six parcels, including his own house and hers. Yet he was constantly mortgaging and redeeming the properties to raise cash, perhaps to finance business projects of his own, for he never achieved the fortune he sought. Instead, his lifelong pattern was to set up badly capitalized, short-lived manufacturing businesses, then to return to insurance clerking when they failed. During the 1850s, for example, he purchased an interest in the patent for a new cottonseed-oil manufacturing process, but two factories failed. After another period of clerking and a brief stint in the Confederate Army, he tried cottonseed-oil manufacturing again and apparently failed once more. When Bradbury died, his estate consisted of only his house.[35]

Bradbury's double character as sexual adventurer and pedantic moralist is evident in Edwards's writings. His own papers show that he became expert at using women to his advantage early in life. When he left Cincinnati, Bradbury left behind a brokenhearted sweetheart, Helen Hart, who wrote to him in a semiliterate version of the same pleading tone that characterized many of Edwards's writings. On the steamboat trip downriver, he made the acquaintance of a Mrs. Ellis, and through her fell in with the young women on the boat. "Several evenings I sat out upon the guards & plaid the flute for the ladies and they sang while I plaid." [36]

Bradbury's interest in women was long-standing, wide-ranging, and rarely as innocent as on the steamboat journey. While Charles wrote letters full of pious moralizing to his older brother Cornelius, the ones he exchanged with his brother Marcus were much racier. "I do not know how my old dulcena M.F.P. comes on more than [what] Beck Wilson said," wrote Marcus to Charley. "She joined the Methodist Church lately and intends to reform her old ways some or Make it a cloke to cover her hypocracy and cockollogy as her mother does before her for she is so full of it it must come out." [37]

In Louisiana, Charley sought his fortune in business, but also by another time-honored means: he courted a well-to-do young widow, Mary Ann Taylor Hamilton, whom he married in the Reverend Theodore Clapp's First Congregational Church on February 12, 1837. When he learned of Charley's plans, Cornelius was enraged, believing, probably with justice, that his younger brother aimed to take advantage of a woman's vulnerability to enrich himself. Cornelius sent a blistering letter that characterized his brother in terms that seem appropriate to his behavior a decade later as well:

You say on 25 Mar. that she is a young Girl, O.B. [a Mr. O'Brien] says, she is a Widow — with 2 Children. . . . I am really astonished, not however at your folly & madness, but that a woman having the reputation of common sense should so far forget her self & dignity, as for one moment to have sanctioned any advances from You, (a lad in your teens) which could be construed by you as meeting with her approval or sanction. A widow to[o], said to be rich[,] true, but what signifies that to you, I know that with you, that is the moving string, the ground attraction. What signifies her fortune to you, do you suppose that her money is to be at your controul? No Sir if

she has any, she will understand your motive & your rations in the
article you will find very soon meeted out to you. Suppose she dies,
where is her fortune? Not at your Controul I guarantee—and where
is our gentleman then? A Widower—a poor Gentleman—a poor
Widower—out of business, out of funds—out of employment—out
of habits of business & out upon the World[.] I am truly sorry, that
I have an occasion to talk so lightly of the good sense & prudence of
any worthy woman, as far as one moment to suppose she could be
found so destitute of all these qualities [in] risking herself with you,
at this Period of your lifetime[.] With yourself your doings & actions, I have some early impressions, & well know that an opportunity is only wanted, to do just so foolish a thing. . . . Marry and your
fate is seal'd. You never rise in the World if at this time & under
the circumstances. There is time for all things. Think of this.[38]

Cornelius was not offended that Charley planned to enrich himself
by marrying but thought he was too young to do it well. He had not
established a secure financial base for himself, so he was dependent on
his wife's money. Consequently he had exposed himself to her whims.
Cornelius passed along his wife Sarah's observation "that she had [not]
thought you among all the Bradburys were one who would be willing to
place your dependence for daily supper upon a woman—who would at
every application for the needful pettishly enquire what you wanted of
it & be constantly throwing it up into your face, that she had no desire
to support you &c &c." Cornelius thus placed in a woman's mouth a
critical statement of the relationship between men, women, and money:
whoever controlled the money controlled the relationship, and it ought
to be the man who did so. To place oneself at a woman's mercy was to
risk one's whole future. On the other hand, to have one's own money
was to be able to chart one's own course and others'. It was a lesson
young Charley learned well.[39]

Charles Bradbury's friends repeatedly tried to tell Madaline Edwards
that he was an adventurer, but she would not hear it. During Bradbury's
extended trip north in the summer of 1844, Henry Budington, Edwards

wrote, "talked of my beloved C. . . . He asked me if I would be jealous if I knew he was kissing some other woman." Just before Bradbury's return, Budington tried again, telling her "a great deal I wished not to hear." Edwards's suitor Mr. Sayre also had uncomplimentary things to say about his rival's conduct. Bradbury himself may have revealed something in December 1844, when "we had some unusual conversation and although I felt very unhappy at some of his confessions yet I stifled my emotions for once and did not let him see my pain." [40]

As evidence of one man's failings, Bradbury's behavior was unremarkable. It is more meaningful when we place it within the larger patterns of male sociability and extramarital male-female relationships that we glimpse in Edwards's writings. The Edwards-Bradbury affair opens a new window on sexuality in a city that had long been renowned for its "immorality."

Men in antebellum New Orleans enjoyed a range of possibilities for sexual relationships with women outside marriage. Brothels were common, and for a time in the 1850s prostitutes were licensed. Nor was New Orleans a stranger to the kinds of furtive, ephemeral, exploitative sexual connections between white men and their slaves that occurred throughout the South. Among the city's elite white society, particularly among the Creoles, extramarital alliances between white men and free black or mixed-race women were relatively common and relatively open, even though they were illegal. In some instances, these relationships were stable and long-lasting, families in every sense but the legal one. [41]

Jean Boze, a French émigré, commented on several such households formed among the acquaintances of his patron and correspondent Henri de Ste. Gême, who had fathered several mixed-race children himself. According to Boze, some wealthy Creoles had two or even three separate households. In 1831, for example, Boze mentioned a M. Sauvinet, who was building a house in the Faubourg Marigny for his second mistress, a native of Saint Domingue, and their two minor children. Sauvinet's first lover, Lize Thuet, remained in the house he had built for her. The next year Boze reported the death of Barthélemy Macarty, who had formed two families in addition to his legal white family "du premier

lit." Macarty left money to have his sons by his first mistress, Luce, educated in the North. When Luce was middle-aged, Macarty had started
a third family with her daughter Cécé, to whom, it was rumored, he
bequeathed $130,000. In the process, he disinherited his white family.
Although such bequests were usually successfully challenged by white
heirs, the relationships that prompted them necessitated no loss of respectability in white Creole eyes. When sugar planter Pierre Caselar
died, he left many "enfans naturels de couleur" but was nevertheless
"keenly mourned by society on account of his widely recognized pro-
bity and his humanitarian acts."[42]

The stable, open relationships of the Creole polygamists and the fleet-
ing intercourse of brothel patrons and slave-owning rapists violated the
public morality of New Orleans's American residents and the political platform of the business community. Since the second decade of
the nineteenth century, for example, business leaders had pushed ordinances against bawds and bawdy houses through the city council, and
they made the suppression of prostitution a part of their 1852 campaign
to reunite the city, which ethnic animosities had caused to be divided
into three semi-independent "municipalities" in 1837. Yet the life in
and around Madaline Edwards's house reveals a fourth scenario of illicit
male-female relationships among New Orleans's Americans, who were
no more upright, but only more secretive, than their Creole neighbors.[43]

The purchase of Madaline Edwards's house, a joint project of Charles
Bradbury, his brother James, and their friend Henry Budington, is emblematic of the labored secretiveness that extramarital affairs required
in respectable American circles. Budington bought the property from
John Craig and Joseph Stanley on November 2, 1843, for eight hundred dollars. A month later he sold it for nine hundred dollars to Jim,
"now absent," with Charley acting as his attorney. Jim in turn conveyed
the house to Charley, and Charley mortgaged it to Madaline for eight
hundred dollars plus a two-hundred-dollar down payment. The entire
series of transactions was an elaborate blind to disguise Charley's purchase of the house for his lover, but the arrangement was advantageous
to James Bradbury and Henry Budington as well. Edwards's house was

just six blocks down Bacchus Street from Charley's and served as their boys' club, a male refuge where they gathered to socialize. In addition, Budington used Edwards's home to meet a woman named Adelle, who eventually broke off the affair and returned his presents, but not before she had borne their child at Edwards's house.[44]

In many respects Madaline Edwards's and Charles Bradbury's affair was as much a joint project of the three male friends as the house purchase. To be sure, Henry Budington and James Bradbury were true friends of Edwards. They spent many evenings in her company, reading and talking. They helped her when her lover was away, and they tried to protect her from his worst behavior. Not only did they warn her against relying too much on Charles, but when Edwards sued him to overturn the foreclosure on her mortgage, James testified against his brother. Mostly, though, their help was directed toward facilitating and concealing the relationship on Charles's behalf.

Edwards's own affair with Charles Bradbury and that between Henry Budington and Adelle were only two of several such liaisons, and possible liaisons, within Edwards's circle. John Leonard Riddell, a casual acquaintance, was the lover of Ann Hennefin during these years. He had two sons by Hennefin, and the birth and baptism of one of them, "christened by his mother John William Riddell," were among the rare personal events to intrude in his lengthy scientific diaries. Riddell never named Hennefin in his diaries or alluded to her in any other context. In fact, in 1846, on the tenth anniversary of his first marriage, he wrote that "my wife lived three years and a half to a day. Six years and a half therefore have I been a widower. Thus advances time. I doubt not it might have been better, if I had married again in the mean time." Six months later, on December 1, he wed Angelica Eugenia Brown. Both wives and their children were buried in the Riddell family tomb in the Girod Street Cemetery, but not Ann Hennefin or her sons.[45]

While the affairs of Bradbury, Budington, and Riddell were concealed from respectable notice, they were obviously well known among the confederates. By virtue of her "situation," Edwards was one of these confederates, privy to this knowledge, but she was also an object of it, an available woman prey to men on the make. On one notable occasion, she "had some very unwelcome visitors," one of whom "took the pains to tell me . . . my character was lost and I could make it no worse by doing as he would persuade me." It was an encounter that drove home the duplicitous nature of such relationships in the city's anglophone society, for while this visitor tried to seduce her, Edwards noted without further explanation, "that very mans wife was in a great measure the cause of my ruin." [46]

Edwards's encounter with James Waller Breedlove, which precipitated the final break with Charley, illustrates the nexus of money, power, and gender in her life. The Virginia-born Breedlove (ca. 1790–1867) was a longtime friend of Andrew Jackson and a conspicuous figure in New Orleans politics and business life. In addition to serving as the president of the Atchafalaya Railroad and Bank, he was a commission merchant and had been Mexican consul, collector of the Port of New Orleans, and first president of the New Orleans Temperance Society. When he entered Edwards's life, he was still a prominent public figure but had fallen on hard times. A credit agent reported in 1847 that he had "small means" and in 1848 added that he "had some difficulty in settling his [accounts] wh[ich] were deficient." [47]

Charles Bradbury may have introduced Breedlove, his first New Orleans employer, to Edwards in November 1845. Once again she found herself caught between the public and private morality of New Orleans's American community. Breedlove's wife, Maria Ellen Winchester, became Madaline's friend and defender; she was almost certainly the subject of the poems of November 17 and November 20 addressed "to Mary." They were followed by the diary notation "There is a benevolent lady who has learned that I am M and has taken it into her head she can elevate me to the standing her kind wishes alone dictate and I am in torture about the unpleasant feelings it may create on her husbands part." [48]

Edwards was right to be apprehensive. Maria's husband had begun to make visits of his own. "JB was here this evening and I do not wonder if he will make his visits fewer for he so often leaves me in tears," she wrote the day after her comment on Maria's friendship. He was there again a few days later. The next November he was still pressing his attentions on her, "determined by his visits to carry out the worlds suspicion though I remain innocent." Madaline complained to Charley, "I will no longer keep you ignorant that he is pressing a certain point."[49]

By that time Edwards was Breedlove's employee, for he was a member of the Second Municipality School Board and had been appointed to the board's new Committee on Teachers just as Edwards was being hired to teach at the Marshall School, in October 1846. The pressure intensified. "I told him today that I would rather he would dismiss me from the School than to hold me under obligations I could not fulfil," she wrote in November.[50]

In January 1847 the school board turned its attention to Edwards. A committee was appointed "to investigate the rumors in relation to Mrs Edwards . . . as well as to her conduct as a lady; as to her treatment of the Scholars." Twelve days later the board dismissed her. The Edwards-Bradbury letters reveal that the board had examined her relationship to Breedlove, not Bradbury. Yet Edwards believed that Breedlove had sabotaged her, and she "curse[d] ten fold the circumstances that led him to damn instead of befriending me." If he betrayed her, Breedlove did it remarkably coolly and duplicitously. He was the only board member to vote against dismissing her, and he was one of three (out of twelve) to vote against paying her only one month's salary for the three she had worked. Six years later Breedlove testified on Edwards's behalf in her lawsuit against Bradbury.[51]

More likely, Charley was the informer. Two people told Edwards that he "had you put out of the schools in order to make you feel your dependance." Bradbury denied it vehemently: such an action would have made him "too base even to be called a man." However, he had "fears of Breedlove," whom he suspected of trying to win Edwards's affections away from him. This would have injured Bradbury's male pride more than his heart, since he had lost interest in her by this time. Charley had secured Madaline's position by lobbying Joseph A. Maybin, another school board member. Since Maybin introduced the resolutions calling for her dismissal and for docking her pay, Bradbury may have decided to thwart Breedlove's plans by intervening with Maybin again.[52]

Edwards's misfortune did not deter Breedlove or Bradbury. After she was fired, the banker offered to buy her a slave and to take care of all her needs, "if I would say he might visit me occasionally." Bradbury pretended that the school board's charges against her were true and used them as a pretext to break off the relationship. Thus Edwards was caught between the amorous rivalries of a patron and his protégé, trapped by the demands of a suitor who was also an employer. She could only "curse the day I ever entered that school or saw B[reedlove]."[53]

A Lover's Ethic

Madaline Edwards understood the matrix of men, women, and money in nineteenth-century New Orleans, and she recognized the double standard by which men and women were judged, but she drew different conclusions from her knowledge than most of her male acquaintances did. They believed she was an available woman. She thought of herself as a woman who had made mistakes but whose moral trajectory was upward toward respectability, even though she acknowledged that others might never see her that way.

True, money forced Edwards to rely on Bradbury, and this colored her feelings for him. One July night in 1844, when her lover was far away to the north, "I dreamed twice of seeing my dear Charley. One time I thought he filled my lap with gold, which did not make me half so glad as the sight of him." Financial need forced her to endure and to excuse many more slights than she might otherwise have done. Still, she genuinely loved him, and in her view they were moving toward a morally if not a socially legitimate relationship. This is the only way to understand the astonishing testaments she left in her diary and writing book when she thought she might die in childbirth. Edwards took it for granted that if she died Bradbury would acknowledge their child as his own, raise it, and teach it about its mother. These assumptions spoke less of naïveté than of the intensity of her desire for a stable, lifelong bond. She believed that their love had been sealed when Bradbury placed "a plain gold ring" on her finger one day in 1844 and she vowed to wear it for the rest of her life. Edwards's faith in the future and rightness of the alliance allowed her to reject determined, eligible suitors, most notably the otherwise unidentified R.P. Although she obviously returned R.P.'s affection, when he said "serious things" to her she ruefully turned him down, despite Bradbury's own advice to accept the proposal.[54]

Edwards's interpretation of her actions marked the moral distance she had traveled from the teenage girl who married out of anger and pity. The young wife who developed the courage to part with an indolent husband was still horrified to find that her second partner was already married. The mature Edwards entered the affair with the married Bradbury with her eyes open, goaded as always by her precarious situation, yet she still felt a need to define an ethical basis for the relationship. She could do so because, occasionally and dimly, the older, less naive Madaline glimpsed the cracks and ill-fitting joints of the moral structure she was expected to inhabit. She acknowledged the sanctity of Bradbury's marriage, the primacy of his responsibility to his wife, and Mary Ann Bradbury's moral superiority to herself. From one point of view, she admitted that Charley's actions might be construed as "acting a faithless part by [his] wife," but she preferred to describe her own relationship with him as a charitable one. She was helpless and ignorant; he was a man acting on "the noble wish of your heart to raise the oppressed and deserted being who once shone as fair as the dear one by your side."[55]

Against the obligations of marriage, however, Edwards set the claims of love. "My love is deeper than hers," she wrote in the same letter. The power of her love sanctioned condescension toward Mary Ann Bradbury and toward wives in general. "Doubtless [Mary Ann] loves you with all the force of her nature," she told Bradbury, but it could not be as intense as her own love for him. On occasion Edwards even gave him flowers to take to his sick wife, a gesture that was kind, that recognized his marital bond, but that was also a kind of covert jibe directed at an unsuspecting spouse.[56]

Desperately wanting Bradbury without feeling free to disparage his marriage, Edwards imagined a kind of polygamy, represented by the plain gold ring and exposed in her vivid dreams. In one dream she found herself at the Bradburys' table: "His wife seemed much pleased with me and I did not feel unjust towards her." In another she, not Mary Ann, found herself embracing Charley at the Last Judgment. "Mrs B passed by us in that position but did not seem the least displeased." Yet she also dreamed, presciently, that her lover had "resolved to act paltroon no longer" and had abandoned her.[57]

Most often, Edwards's condescension and fantasy succumbed to jealousy and bitterness. Chance encounters with the Bradburys always brought a "mind . . . full of torture" or "a flash of bitter feeling": "I strive against it yet I am human." She vented her anger in a long essay on husbands and wives that blamed marital troubles on women's self-absorption and their inability to subordinate their trivial whims to their husbands' serious worries.[58]

Madaline Edwards salved her conscience by cloaking herself in conventional gender stereotypes. Men were to be strong but courtly; women were naturally weak and yielding. Just as Charley was concerned to portray himself in a manly light, so Madaline expected men to act in that manner. In the autobiographical "Tale of Real Life" she dismissed both her husbands as "womanish," meaning, respectively, evasive and timid. In the same story, she attributed her downfall in part to her pity for the two men. By being womanish, they were unworthy of her regard, but as a woman she could not help pitying them. At the same time, she possessed a powerful inner voice—an intuition—that warned against these and other disasters, but she was too womanish to resist them.

In depicting herself in this way, Edwards echoed the argument made in a pamphlet given to her by her suitor Mr. Sayre. In *Woman Physiologically Considered,* the phrenologist Alexander Walker argued that women's "sensibility and observing faculties are great; [their] reasoning faculties are small." Women were naturally intuitive. They could grasp any situation instantly, but lacking powers of reason or strength, they were unable to analyze the situations they understood intuitively or to act on their intuitions. "Extreme sensibility is the great characteristic of her mental system, but it is at the same time the very basis of all instinctive action. Feebleness equally characterizes her locomotive system." The instinctive sensibilities of women impelled them, among other things, to a great capacity for pity, and it also made them feel emotions deeply and helplessly that men might not even notice.[59]

Although couched in the jargon of phrenology, Walker's arguments recapitulated common nineteenth-century views of women's capacities. There is no evidence that his pamphlet was a direct inspiration for Edwards's self-portrayal. Of the many books that she mentioned in her diary, this is one of the few that she simply noted without any comment on its contents or even an indication of whether she had read it, so the gift may say more about Sayre's attitudes than her own. Still, it suited Edwards to adopt this common caricature of women's abilities from time to time. She bowed to Bradbury's manly wisdom, for "he had strove so hard to lead my mind to higher aims, as he may term it." In return, he gladly played the pedant. One January evening in 1845 "we agreed to adopt another mode to improve our minds. I made a grammatical error and he reproved me for it."[60]

In short, Edwards took advantage of the inconsistencies in conventional gender roles to shape an individualized moral universe for herself. Her ethical sphere, like her contemporaries', emphasized lifelong male-female relationships, but it gave primacy to love and charity over legal ties. It acknowledged some traditional claims for men's strength and women's weakness, then used them to reverse the double standard, offering more moral leeway to women than to men. None of the elements of this morality were novel, but Edwards's synthesis of them was idiosyncratic.[61]

A Woman's Creed

The theme of judgment permeated Edwards's writings. She thought that she was constantly being judged. Her personal morality provided a platform from which she assessed her own failings and a set of ground rules for acknowledging responsibility for her actions and accepting judgment. Edwards developed a strong sense of who had a right to judge her (and an equally strong conviction that she had no right to condemn or judge others). She rejected "the stern decrees of society" when they were applied by hypocrites. She declined to be judged by her family, by "some dashing ladies" too frivolous to take seriously, or by people who had no claims on her. So she obtained a restraining order against a Mrs. R.'s "language," which had caused "a good cry." In a tougher mood, she "had quite a farce" with someone who saw Charley leave her house and wished that "persons who accidently become acquainted with me would let me act as I please."[62]

On the same principles, Edwards freely submitted her actions and her character to be judged by her friends and acquaintances, particularly by men, and most of all by Bradbury. She "told M^{rs} W my position" and was relieved that they remained friends. She was delighted that Mr. H. "is highly pleased that I am to be a mother. Approves and encourages my love for the father though unknown to him." She was grateful to be "forgiven" for her way of life by her cousin Jack, and she dreamed of "full forgiveness" from a younger brother she had never met.[63]

Nevertheless, Edwards understandably sought ways to mitigate judgment. Her pose as a woman too weak to avoid choices she knew were wrong or to resist temptation and coercion by stronger men or unfair social structures was a strategy for doing so.

The essays "Woman" and "Man," written in response to a pair of sermons preached by Theodore Clapp in April and May 1844, vividly capture the ambivalence of Edwards's moral position. Clapp's sermons were based on familiar nineteenth-century conventions of morality and gender, of passive women and active men, spiritual females and worldly males. Edwards listened to the sermon "Woman" skeptically. She admitted her own errors as usual and accepted her exclusion from the role of "angelic wife or mother," and indeed from social reconciliation of any sort. But she objected to Clapp's notion that "women create their own sorrows" (a jibe that Bradbury repeated at the end of their relationship), arguing instead that others had "dug the grave" of her happiness. As a woman, she was prey to the bad-intentioned, but she had also been rescued by the good-intentioned. Although rejected by polite society, Edwards argued that she had been redeemed by God and Charles Bradbury. Consequently, she did not hear Clapp's sermon as a condemnation of her own ways: she had owned and transcended her sins. Instead, it was a warning to the "[un]reflecting and prosperous part of my sex" who might unthinkingly fall into the errors that had ruined her.[64]

Edwards's reaction to the sermon on men was much more emotional. When the pastor denounced men who seduced women, she burst into tears in church as she recalled her own seduction. She fixed her eyes on Charley, who was sitting across the church with Mary Ann, and she desperately hoped that he would not take Clapp's words so to heart that he would abandon her. But then Edwards returned to her moral confidence. She had erred, she knew, but there was no reason for her to hear these things. She believed that God wanted her to be happy and that his purpose was not served by reminders of things she could not change.[65]

As Edwards's essays suggest, her sense of the hypocrisy and imbalance of power inherent in nineteenth-century gender relations mitigated her guilt and at times encouraged a moral condescension similar to the emotional condescension she sometimes expressed toward Mary Ann Bradbury. She took great comfort in the belief that she had transcended her errors: respectable people needed the preacher's warnings more than she did.

If judgment was one great theme of her writing, another was redemption. Men were the cause of Edwards's downfall, and they were the agents of her redemption. At times she seemed to have difficulty distinguishing Christ, Charles Bradbury, and her pastor, Theodore Clapp, for she wrote of all three using language steeped in Christian metaphors of grace and unmerited salvation. Sometimes Charley was an evangelist, sometimes a savior. He had "spoke[n] words that acted like magic upon me. He said I had a heart too good for such a life. He said I could yet be a better and happier woman. He pointed to me a minister whose blest admonitions and promises would tranquilize my wounded spirit, and by his kind and eloquent reasoning induced me to hope I was not lost." Charley was her "adored preserver," sent by God to save her, but his "friendship is not based upon my virtue and moral goodness." Edwards admired Clapp as greatly as she did Bradbury, for the same reason: he offered her hope. "God alone knows how I venerate and bless that man." Trapped in a world controlled by men, she turned to men to save her.[66]

Edwards was attracted to Theodore Clapp by his forceful and kindly personality and perhaps because he, too, fit uneasily into the confines of conventional belief. A Massachusetts-born clergyman, Clapp (1792–1866) had come to New Orleans in 1822 to replace the popular pastor of the First Presbyterian Church, Sylvester Larned, who had died of yellow fever. He quickly established himself as an equally popular preacher, but during the first decade of his service his theology drifted toward antitrinitarian principles. He was tried for heresy and expelled from the Presbyterian ministry in 1833. A group of theological traditionalists, including Edwards's school board persecutor Joseph Maybin, withdrew to form a new Presbyterian congregation. Clapp carried on in the old building, and his church flourished owing to his vivid preaching, his energetic ecumenicism in a polyglot city, and the patronage of the wealthy merchant-philanthropist Judah Touro, who paid off the building's mortgage.[67]

At Clapp's church Madaline Edwards found a pastor and a congregation that welcomed outsiders. Because the church set aside an entire gallery for those from outside New Orleans and from other city churches, it was known as the Strangers' Church. The minister's impassioned preaching, which so engrossed Edwards, was compelling enough that it attracted even those who rejected his doctrine. The diarist Luther Tower frequently attended Clapp's services, even though he dismissed the sermons as "original without head or tail discourses" or "strange." Yet Edwards thought that to hear other preachers after Theodore Clapp was "like drinking slops after the richest wines."[68]

Clapp's popularity owed as much to his social ministry as to his public performances. He was famous for his steadfast presence in the city during its many yellow fever and cholera epidemics, when most other clergymen fled. He also preached religious ecumenism in an era when Protestants had little tolerance for other beliefs. Clapp praised his Jew-

The Reverend Theodore Clapp, pastor of the First Congregational Church in New Orleans. Courtesy The Historic New Orleans Collection.

St. Charles Hotel, New Orleans. Daguerreotype by Thomas M. Easterly, ca. 1845–47. This shows downtown New Orleans during Madaline Edwards's residence in the city. Immediately behind the hotel, the social and business center of English-speaking New Orleans, the spire of Clapp's church is visible. Courtesy Missouri Historical Society.

ish patron, Judah Touro, as a man who better exemplified Christian charity than most of his Christian neighbors, and he wrote at length about the salutary moral leadership of the Roman Catholic Church. On the most volatile social issue — slavery — he modified his opinions to suit the cherished principles of New Orleans's white leaders.[69]

Parson Clapp was "eminently a social man," according to the historian of his church, and more than anything he "enjoyed the society of his fellowmen, young and old, always ready to interest himself in their pleasures and troubles, their occupations and undertakings, touching elbows with the people in the labors and commonplaces of their daily lives." He assisted supplicants in finding homes for children and jobs and even made small loans to them. "His counsel reached the flotsam of a great city," memoirist Eliza Ripley recalled. Madaline Edwards was among this mass of humanity. After nearly two years of listening to him from the pews, she finally met him. "Though our conversation was short and my feelings so overcam[e] me yet I found him the same kind and dear being that he is in the pulpit. I told him many of my errors but he said all was not lost to one who wished to return." Later Clapp offered advice to Edwards on obtaining a new job after she was dismissed from the schools, and on the disposal of her house when she moved to California.[70]

The preacher's personal ministry was a comfort to Edwards, but his teaching was more important to her, for it helped her to define her own moral universe. It is easy to understand why his doctrine appealed to her. In the winter of 1833–34, during the time he was expelled from the Presbyterian clergy for antitrinitarianism, Clapp came to question the doctrines of original sin and eternal damnation. He concluded that there was no such thing as absolute or eternal evil, and thus no such thing as eternal punishment. They were inconsistent with the nature of God's justice as he understood it. Good was to be found in the most degraded people, a point that Edwards took personally. Original sin and predestination implied a capricious God and removed free will from humanity, for if people could do nothing but evil, how could they be responsible? This was a familiar Arminian argument that Edwards embraced enthusiastically. Like Clapp, she believed that people were responsible for their own sins. However, they sometimes made errors for excusable reasons, such as ignorance or diminished capacity (which was sometimes the product of "inferior phrenological developments," according to Clapp). Though these errors were still sins, their seriousness was mitigated. Sin demanded punishment, but it would take place in this life. Clapp denied the existence of hell, arguing that sinners create their own hell on earth. After death, God's free grace would save everyone.[71]

Clapp's doctrine enabled Edwards to understand her unhappiness as a consequence of her errors, while allowing her to hope that she would eventually be freed. In fatalistic moods, she wrote off her life and waited for death. On more cheerful occasions, she echoed Clapp's claim that people are made for happiness.

Edwards sought happiness in the wonders of divine creation and the glimpses they offered of future bliss, for the minister insisted not only on personal responsibility but also on the autonomy of personal judgment. Hearing a Clapp sermon on mercy, she "gloried in the emphasis he placed on 'I *will not* be cheated out of my opinion.' " She avidly devoured religious books, mostly rationalist treatises on natural religion derived from the Enlightenment tradition, which served her in the way that devotional tracts did orthodox Christians. She read them over and over, extracting lessons for her life.[72]

Edwards explored deist writers such as Constantin-François Volney, whose *Law of Nature* she read twice and to whom she steered a friend, "a catholic of the old irish school," but her two favorite authors in 1844 and 1845 were Thomas Dick and George Combe. Dick was an astronomer who, "connected with Mr Clapp's preaching has unfolded to my mind a new world and induce[d] me to hope though lost in this world yet there is another home for me." He aimed "to illustrate the harmony which subsists between the system of nature and the system of revelation." It was a point that Edwards made repeatedly in her essays on nature and religion: glimpses of the heavens "increased my conception of the Deity," she said. Echoing the natural theologians of the seventeenth and eighteenth centuries, she wrote that "the right study of nature is of itself sufficient to lead the heart to God," although "it needs the bible to support and confirm the conceptions it may have formed." Still, if it were necessary to choose between the Bible and nature, only the latter was indispensable.[73]

Combe was a moral philosopher who claimed the rationalist heritage of the Scottish Common Sense philosophers Francis Hutcheson, Adam Smith, Thomas Reid, Dugald Stewart, and Thomas Brown, which he elaborated "with the aid of the new lights afforded by Phrenology." He argued that God had made the world in such a way that it was capable of being understood by human powers. Thus "the Divine Spirit, revealed in Scripture as a power influencing the human mind," acted through natural laws. "Nature is religion," and "a knowledge of the natural laws is destined to exercise a vast influence in rendering men capable of appreciating and practising Christianity."[74]

Madaline Edwards's devotional reading convinced her that God might be discovered through scientific knowledge: the more one knew of the natural world, the more one approached divinity. In Combe's work she read that "knowledge is truly power; and it is highly important to human beings to become acquainted with the constitution and relations of every object around them." Her pursuit of knowledge turned her against both orthodox theology and popular religious beliefs. "I never could comprehend how three persons could exist in one and be separate, yet one and the same," she wrote of the Trinity. She rejected the popular notion of heaven, "a golden City paved with jewels in which God sits enthroned while it is the duty and only employment of his angels to bow down before him and sing his praises with golden harps," preferring instead to imagine a realm of eternal rest and spiritual peace "where the A b C we have learned of God and his attributes will go on to higher and higher grades." In the afterlife the knowledge we accumulate on earth will vastly expand, as will our capacity to understand and the portion of creation with which we are familiar, she was convinced. "In a future world we will commence just where we leave off in this, and . . . the more intellect and knowledge we imbibe in this world the more our happiness is increased even here and we are fitted for a higher state of bliss in that far off home to which we are approaching."[75]

Edwards's religious inquiries had unexpected consequences: they tended to undercut the sense of helplessness that her "situation" and her relationship with Bradbury promoted, as well as the feminine passivity that she often affected. Edwards's religious convictions buttressed her personal moral universe, leaving room for an independence of mind and an intellectual adventurousness that was at odds with conventional views of women's capacity. Even as she acted a stereotypically feminine role, Edwards educated herself to exercise her own judgment. As a counterbalance to the rhetoric of the female sinner rescued by charitable men, she found a theology that offered redemption to a woman on her own.

Madaline Edwards's independence of mind and her curiosity led her through a wide range of reading as she explored issues that were male provinces and that were often declared to be beyond women's understanding. To each she brought the critical moral sense and intellectual independence that had been shaped by her life experience.

In 1844, for example, a presidential election and a heated debate over Texas annexation drew her attention to politics. In some respects, her political views were colored by what historian Suzanne Lebsock has called the "personalism" of women's concerns. She leaned toward Whig politics because Bradbury was a Whig. She supported the annexation of Texas because Bradbury owned land there and because a beloved cousin, John Coffee Hays, was a founder of the Texas Rangers. Yet her politics were more than simple affirmations of her menfolks' vested interests. She followed political issues carefully, reading tracts, speeches, and treaties and expressing points of view that were often at odds with those of her friends and with the politics of the parties she preferred. Edwards's political opinions and her right to them were accepted by her male friends, who argued with her and teased her about them. She bet her physician Dr. James Ritchie, a Democrat, that Texas would be annexed, while Henry Budington brought her Democratic newspapers "for he knows I am a whig." [76]

Throughout the 1844 presidential campaign, Edwards supported Henry Clay, and she was disappointed when he lost the election. Yet she rejected Clay's opposition to Texas annexation. Instead, she read and applauded Democratic politician Robert J. Walker's widely distributed and enormously influential pamphlet, which advocated annexation as a way to end slavery in the United States. Walker also argued that unless the United States took Texas, New Orleans might fall under British domination, a view that found wide support in the Crescent City. In addition to supporting the Democratic Party's position on annexation, Edwards was attracted to the politics of the new Native American Party and eventually published her poems and essays in New Orleans's nativist newspaper.[77]

Edwards's personal experience gave her moral and emotional insight into important political issues even when she did not discuss them in the explicitly political language of her day. She never enunciated her views on slavery or race, for example, but they were on her mind (and Bradbury's, who once "nodded and dreamed he was in England hearing a discourse on slavery"). Edwards lived in a slaveholding society, and most of her male acquaintances owned slaves, including Bradbury, Budington, Riddell, her father, and her estranged husband, Dempsey Elliott. Her revered pastor Theodore Clapp arrived in New Orleans as an abolitionist but ultimately became an ardent defender of slavery. Edwards was happy to employ slaves when she could. In one of her first surviving letters, she mentioned a desire to buy one, and she was gratified when Charley hired a slave girl, Maria, to assist her. Yet some of her favorite authors opposed slavery on practical or moral grounds. Not only did Walker's pamphlet on Texas advocate the end of slavery (or it claimed to), but Combe's *Constitution of Man,* which Madaline read at least three times, contained a violent attack on slavery in the United States as "a heinous moral transgression."[78]

Most likely Edwards took the personalist course of "unsteady complicity" that Lebsock has described. She did not oppose her slave-owning friends and relatives on principle, but her moral sense and her own sad experience promoted a predilection to view free and enslaved blacks sympathetically. She recognized African Americans as kindred spirits, at least in the sense that she thought they were usually unfairly judged. A striking passage in her testament asked Bradbury to teach their child "that it should never utter a word of detraction against the poorest African and where it was compelled to do so or remain silent, to always choose the latter." These passages hint that Edwards understood the oppressive nature of slavery and was uncomfortable with it. Her empathy allowed her to relate to the few blacks she encountered as human beings. She was sad to lose Maria's company when the girl's term was up, and she ran charitable errands for a poor black woman. This act of kindness stands out in a society that most often denied poor free people of color much assistance and instead treated them as quasicriminals.[79]

Edwards understood that even in a so-called free society the benefits of freedom were denied to many by their circumstances. Metaphors connecting her own situation with that of all sorts of trapped beings, from caged birds to convicts and slaves, pervade her poems and essays. A diary entry and essay on the celebrations of July 4, 1844, developed this theme at greatest length. She had always celebrated the American republic in the abstract, Edwards wrote, but "I felt that though I was included among the free-born Americans never had a 4th of July dawned on me as free and independent until this morning." Before then "I was more than a slave in bondage, for I was a slave to the worst of misfortunes and a football for the heartless. Now I am *free* and surely no liberated convict feels the contrast more forcibly."[80]

An Imagined Life

Madaline Edwards's insights never led her to an outwardly radical politics. Instead they turned her inward to a personal morality that often transcended the pieties of her upbringing and her era and gave her room to make a life and a self. This is what I mean when I write of the tension between structure and action.

In truth, Edwards fashioned several different selves in life and in words. They were linked by her determination to take charge—however helpless she liked to think herself—to shape the ways others perceived her, and to guide her own fortunes as much as possible.

Self-education—building the knowledge that she believed drew the individual closer to God—was central to Edwards's self-creation. Like many educated women of her era, she had been a voracious reader in her childhood. In the prevailing nineteenth-century view, reading was an appropriate pastime for women until they married. Then their hearts and minds were supposed to turn to their husbands and families. This expectation frustrated many antebellum women writers. Edwards confronted it as soon as she was married, when, according to her autobiographical "Tale of Real Life," her husband's limitations thwarted her own intellectual development. During the twelve years between her marriage and the beginning of her affair with Bradbury, her reading may have been sacrificed to the turmoil of births, deaths, and marital difficulty. By the time of the first letter to Charley, though, she had taken advantage of her single status and particularly of her isolation from urban life to return wholeheartedly to her studies.[81]

Madaline Edwards was an active and critical reader, careful to distinguish her own views even from those of her favorite writers. As a reader and a writer, she was intellectually engaged, a conscious, even if self-deprecating, participant in the public world of culture. She identified with the community of women authors, and when Bradbury remarked that no one could believe that a woman had written her published works, she found it "very strange when such abler pens are daily used by females too. But so it is," she added, perhaps surprised by "Dear C's" obtuseness.[82]

Partly by her own choice and partly as a consequence of Charley's attempt to "model" her, Madaline cast her literary net widely. As with so many of her contemporaries, novels were the centerpiece of her reading. In the mid-1840s the European domestic novelists Sarah Stickney Ellis and Frederika Bremer were her favorites, but passing references show that she was familiar with Lydia Sigourney, Felicia Hemans, Hans Christian Andersen, and Washington Irving.[83]

In 1844 and 1845 about half the books Edwards read were novels. She gave nearly as much time to theological and scientific works such as Combe's and Dick's and to political tracts during the 1844 election season. She read the ancient Jewish historian Flavius Josephus, Milton's *Paradise Lost,* and Alexander Pope's poems, and she read part of the New Testament every day.

Whatever Edwards's momentary interests, Lord Byron was the center of her literary consciousness. She quoted him frequently (with enough minor errors to indicate that she wrote from memory) and alluded to him even more often. To her mind, the poet's literary value was often lost to sight, even by "our dear Minister" Theodore Clapp, through the public's obsession with his "immoral" personal life. Edwards devoted an entire essay to defending Byron's morals from unjust condemnation and his poetry from oblivion. Her view of the poet was consistent with her religious convictions, particularly with her belief that one might transcend previous sins and achieve a kind of moral peace in the face of society's disdain. Edwards recognized the connection with her own life and identified deeply with Byron. She pointed out the providential resemblance between the circumstances of her own marriage and his and, more to the point, the similarity of their temperaments: "There is so much congeniality between his melancholy and my own that I never tire of poring over some of his productions," she wrote. For Madaline Edwards, the juxtaposition of Byron's life and his literary greatness inspired confidence in her own writing.[84]

Left to her own spiritual and moral resources, Edwards had "to make a friend of my pen, to commune with for I have had no one else." She was a writer before Bradbury gave her a diary and a notebook, but his gift was an excuse to devote herself even more energetically to her literary calling. Edwards tried to write every day, and she took it upon herself to submit poems and essays to the *Native American.* More than that, she used writing as an indispensable tool for analyzing her identity. In her powerful personal essays and poems, "the pen was called into requisition to unfold my sad tale."[85]

Although we respond easily to the intense emotion of Edwards's writing, to the strength of her voice, and to the simple facts of her life, it is obvious that her work is neither a naive nor an unfiltered record of experience (if any writing ever is). She created a character, "Mad," who presented her author as she wished to be seen, within the constraints of certain assumptions about writing and about her readers.

Edwards's literary works presumed the ever-present Charles Bradbury as her principal audience. He encouraged her to write, and he read and commented on her work. She wanted him to return to it after her death, to remind him of her existence and of her love for him. The diaries, essays, and poems depicted the gendered relationship of dominance and subordination that Charley clearly expected the couple to play out. They were her ultimate act of submission to his judgment and made the case for the good heart that lay behind her failings: "I know when these come up before you that no force of imagination could convey to you what I feel, but all I ask is your charity for my many faults."[86] Occasionally, Edwards imagined that others would read her private words after her death, but these readers were only of passing interest to her. She did want outsiders to read and like her published writings, but even there Charley's approbation meant the most to her. Since all her readers' expectations were as gender-bound as Bradbury's, gender conventions colored her publications. Like many women writers, Edwards took for granted the male point of view as normative, as her dismissive comments on silly, conventional "females" show. She conceived literary authority as dominantly male and deferred to it, submitting her "scribbling in Prose or Poetry" for publication assuming that it would be rejected. She was grateful when the editor of the *Native American* gave her "free use of his paper." But while she sought to distance herself from other women, Edwards stuck close to the mainstream of women's occasional writing in her poems and essays, flirting with male correspondents, composing religious meditations and nature sketches, and in general playing the female.[87]

In both public and private writings, then, Edwards felt constrained to cast her views in gendered terms acceptable to herself and to her readers. This is not to say that she was insincere, but that she never conceived her writing as pure self-revelation. Instead, it was self-justification and self-defense, and most of all self-definition. In the end

her ambivalence about being judged guided her hand. By concealing
herself, she could deflect unwanted judgment; by revealing a carefully
constructed persona, she invited judgment on her own terms. She was
at once deferential and elusive, a conventional woman because her un-
conventionality was concealed.[88]

Edwards's many names are an important key to the layering of fragmentary identities that was her most important strategy for concealment. Many nineteenth-century women writers cloaked their ambivalence about exposure and the contradictions of going public to support
private values behind a curtain of anonymity. As Mary Kelley has noted,
"the woman surfaced as a published writer, but she surfaced in disguise.
The writer was a woman, but the published work was not ascribed to
her. These women had not stepped beyond the bounds of their homes;
only their works had, and anonymously at that." This reticence was an
element of Edwards's work. Her use of the initial M in her publications
nodded to propriety, particularly since many of her writings bantered
playfully with pseudonymous male counterparts, such as "Coelebs,"
with whom she exchanged humorous poems about marriage and courtship. Edwards's anonymity had another dimension. Whereas Kelley's
novelists were afraid their publications would taint their private purity,
Edwards was afraid that her private notoriety would taint her public
innocence, that readers would discover that the flirtatious M was the
tainted Madaline, even though she could not help alluding to her faults
on occasion.[89]

Edwards's name play began long before she had published a word.
Selima Madaline Cage added the surname Elliott after her first marriage
and probably acquired the name Edwards from her bigamous second
husband. By the time she began her diary in 1844, she had reversed
her first and middle names and called herself Madaline S. Edwards, the
name she preferred for the rest of her life. She may have continued to be
known to her friends and acquaintances in New Orleans as Mrs. Elliott,
though.[90] In her legal battles with Charles Bradbury in 1849 and 1853,
she was Mrs. S. M. Cage, widow of Dempsey Elliott. She signed her
personal letters Mad and her published writings M. When she died in

San Francisco the *Wide West* reported that she was "well known as the Madeline of the New Orleans *Delta* and *Picayune*."[91] Although the information was probably supplied by her cousin John Coffee Hays, the report misspelled her name and attributed her writings to the wrong newspapers.

Had she known of them, those errors might have pleased Edwards, for they added more layers of uncertainty to her identity. The difficulties that others had in getting her names right were emblematic of her opacity and even invisibility to her neighbors, but also of her success in concealing herself. In choosing and changing her names, she shaped the self she wished to be. No one else could discover anything that she wished hidden. To a newspaper poet, W.A.P., she wrote,

> The truth I boast will not allow;
> That you should undeceived be
> You have not seen M I avow
> Some one has April-fooled thee.[92]

Edwards's reading, particularly her reading of fiction, provided the models for her self-concealment and her self-revelation, which were carefully and consciously literary. The literary transformation of experience is clearest in her autobiographical story "A Tale of Real Life." To mid-nineteenth-century readers, a tale was a narrated story with a relatively simple plot. In her tale, Edwards chose the very common narrative device of a conversation between a main character, Justine, and her long-lost friend Sarah K.[93]

In its combination of revelation and concealment, "A Tale of Real Life" is aptly titled. It is real, and it is a tale. It is Edwards's true story, an account of the things that happened to her, but, more important, also of her strategies for survival. Yet she never allows us to be comfortable in what we are reading. This is a "tale," a fictional type, but "a tale founded on facts": "The only fiction I shall borrow is that the conversation never will take place that I shall here represent, but those parts that shall be called up as having passed between myself and friend in happier days are true." That is, the central event of the story—the conversation—is a fiction, but its substance is real. Sarah's name is real, but her presence is imaginary. The "Tale" is Edwards's story, but she chooses to take the pseudonym Justine. The sites of the episodes and the names of the players are disguised with initials, and the events are reduced to their emotional essences. We learn of events only as much as is necessary to set the stage for emotional drama. Justine is a woman whose being is reduced to emotive states and whose actions and motivations, as we are given to understand them, consequently arise from raw emotion. There is no need to describe her meeting with the Bradbury figure because only his effect on her emotional well-being is relevant to the tale. Yet Edwards writes that the tale "will easily be perceived to contain a few of the incidents of my own life." The "Tale" is inscribed in the writing book, intended for Charley, though with the added thought that later generations might see it. Nevertheless, "what inducement there was to write it is alone known to myself." Having said this, Edwards immediately revealed the inducement: she wrote her "Tale" in the hope that "one far away"—Bradbury—and "one dear object"—her unborn child—might read it, and she wrote as well to occupy her mind and to make her grateful "to my God and my dear C" when he had gone north and seemed to have forgotten her.[94]

This playful elision of fact and fantasy conceals more significant reversals, for the meanings of "A Tale of Real Life" depend on our understanding of the conventions of several genres of mid-nineteenth-century fiction. Edwards made her way in literature by exploiting the peculiarities and contradictions of novelistic convention, as in real life she exploited the vagaries of social convention.

As a straightforward narrative of early happiness transformed into adult sorrow through misguided choices, culminating in rescue, the "Tale" falls into the genre that literary historian Nina Baym has labeled a moral fable, a plot type that "arranges events in an order that displays the ineluctable operations of a principle; although settings may be real, they are rather implied than represented. Action and character are schematized according to the principle being illustrated." In addition, the "Tale," like many of Edwards's other discussions of her life, evoked those early nineteenth-century novels that historians refer to as seduction novels: a helpless female is betrayed by men, gives in to her sexual passion, and is punished by death or, in Justine's case, social death. By eliding aspects of her own background in the "Tale"—her family's power, her privileged upbringing—Edwards could cast herself in the role of the poor, orphaned heroine, thrown by misfortune to the world's mercy, or mercilessness. Alliance with the wrong man had "ruined" her, alliance with the right one—the unnamed Bradbury—rescued her. She was restored to a kind of happiness, but one that was sadder, wiser, and more knowing than the innocent happiness of her childhood. Justine was no longer Eve: she had become Mary Magdalene.[95]

Justine is a woman out of control, completely dominated by her passions, in need of a male rescuer. Our understanding of Edwards's message, however, is transformed when we call to mind a third mid-nineteenth-century narrative formula that lurks behind the "Tale" and that surfaces more visibly in Edwards's other writings. In the so-called domestic novel, a heroine overcomes her misfortunes by developing her inner strengths: "Helped occasionally by people in her community, the heroine also called on God for strength as she mustered her own internal resources."[96] Justine is an antitype of this heroine. Her helplessness resonates with an unexpected twist on the literary stereotypes of gender that Edwards employs. Yes, Justine falls because she is weak and passive, but her weakness and passivity are manifested in an interesting way: most of her wrong moves are made in performance of her womanly role. Whenever she listens to the voices of her family, her friends, her society, she comes to grief. She rejects a man who would have been a good husband because she has unrealistically romantic views of love. To marry the man she is expected to would be disastrous, she knows. Nevertheless, she marries one who fills socially accepted criteria of eligibility, and she does so out of pity, an emotion that nineteenth-century writers like Alexander Walker thought natural to women. Similarly, Justine's union with her second husband springs from pity for his misfortunes and a charitable desire to nurse him through a dangerous illness. Her socially poisonous separation from her first husband is prompted by a mother's desire to protect her child's welfare. On the surface, then, all her choices are the right ones. Her fatal weakness is to follow others' standards, rather than the promptings of her own best judgment. Had she been more attentive to her inner voice, she would have been a happier woman, but in acceding to the norms of her society, she finds herself transgressing its most sacred standards of women's behavior. Thus the "Tale," cast as a seduction novel, is really a kind of anti–domestic novel: the woman without inner strength and self-reliance comes to grief. Doing right did her wrong.

Because Madaline Edwards wrote her personal history partly for her own benefit, and partly for Charles Bradbury's, the domestic and seduction models are held in unresolved tension in her telling. Justine is a type of the "Mad" we encounter in the diaries, in some of the letters to Bradbury, and in the early essays, the Mad who was present whenever Charley appeared on the page. But there was a second Mad who was very different, whose lineage can be traced to the domestic novel. This was the Mad who inhabited many of the contemplative essays and the religious writings, where Edwards presented herself as a person who, through dint of self-discipline and study, had rescued herself morally, one who no longer needed the sermonizers' warnings as happier but less aware women did.

In fact, Madaline Edwards enacted her life in ways that were closer to those of the domestic novel's heroine than the seduction novel's victim. Although the tone of many of her writings is despairing and occasionally self-pitying, her actions were those of a woman not afraid to take decisive action. To free herself of the burden of Dempsey Elliott, to break off the marriage at a time when, legally, even violence was not always seen as a sufficient cause for divorce, must have taken great courage in a twenty-year-old woman. So her immigration to California, during which she was alone as usual and with few economic resources, and her return from California to press her lawsuit against Bradbury were beyond the physical and spiritual resources of most women—or men—in the nineteenth century.

Linking these defining incidents was a life of less dramatic but equally determined action. The account in the "Tale of Real Life" of nursing Mr. Edwards, when Madaline had "to sew for my very life for the means to keep him alive," is of a piece with her reports of daily life in the diary. For over a year she struggled through a long false pregnancy that masked a serious illness. Through the entire time of the diaries, she was ill with headaches and fevers for several days of every month. She also suffered a bout of malaria and a horrifying experience with a broken arm that never set or healed properly because her treatment was left until after her male companion's was completed. Despite these setbacks, Edwards refused to become an invalid. She worked diligently to support herself and walked all over the city on business. She negotiated her boundary dispute with Dr. Riddell and took legal action in two separate instances in 1844 and 1845, one time to press an unexplained lawsuit, and on another occasion to obtain a restraining order to "stop the slander of Mrs R."[97]

Literary historian Felicity Nussbaum has argued that "it is the spaces between the cultural constructions of the female and the articulation of individual selves and their lived experience, between cultural assignments of gender and the individual's translation of them into text, that a discussion of women's autobiographical writing can be helpful."[98] Nussbaum's words recall the structure-action tension with which this essay began. The contrast between Madaline Edwards's conduct of her life and her presentation of it are remarkable. The structures of antebellum social thought, particularly those of gender and religion, offered Edwards multiple frameworks for interpreting her experience, but they were inadequate as means for projecting action. Justine's history in "A Tale of Real Life" is an extended moral fable of the dilemma of a woman on her own in antebellum New Orleans. To follow the dictates of society was to invite disaster, but to contravene them offered the same unhappy fate. Edwards's history is different in a small but important way. However difficult her life, she relished her right to make choices. Her strength of mind led her to thread a personal history through the cracks and disjunctures of social practice and moral rules. Convention caused her anguish, but it could not control her. Unlike Justine or Mad, Madaline S. Edwards was able to shape her own destiny by changing her life and by reimagining it in her writings.

CHAPTER ONE

A Better and Happier Woman

lone and miserable in New Orleans in the summer of 1843, the twenty-six-year-old Madaline Edwards fell in love with Charles W. Bradbury, a married man who seduced her through kindness. The passionate letters Edwards wrote to Bradbury in the fall of 1843 radiated love and gratitude that shaded over into desperation and optimism tempered by ambivalence toward the dim but threatening presence of Bradbury's wife, Mary Ann. No response from Bradbury remains. Although this is an accident of survival, it is an appropriate emblem of the emotional distance he maintained throughout the affair.

Madaline to Charley, early fall 1843

My own Beloved Charley

With feelings of burning gratitude, and a heart gushing with the purest affection, I have seated myself to give vent to a portion on paper. Short as has been our acquaintance yet to me it has been replete with bliss such as is seldom permitted to mix with the dregs of misery that have long filled my cup. That these happy hours have been oerclouded with tears and dimmed with sighs when you were not by to witness you will not wonder, at least *would* not were it in my power to convey to your mind what I have experienced. Could you but know how often I have thought my griefs were coming to a close, and that my almost crushed heart would again be warmed into life and then witness with what force the cup untasted has been hurled from my lips. Could you see the half of these scenes you would not wonder that I tremble whenever I pass one happy hour not knowing how soon it will be succeeded by deeper misery and bitter disappointments than all the preceeding, and I generally take one such hour as the harbinger of some additional sorrow. By nature blest with the happiest cast of mind, the most contented disposition being ever termed the light-hearted happy one, it is not *natural* in me [to] look forward to or anticipate sorrows but they have so crowded themselves on my path and made themselves my daily companions that it has become second nature to miss them if absent even for an hour. That I have often confided and been deceived is but too natural to suppose from the position in which I am now placed contrasted with the one I once occupied, and although this be unknown to you yet I believe *you* do me the justice to see some vestages of it in my acts. That I may be again placing myself in a position to mourn over my deep affections for one so far above me and beyond my enjoying only in a clandestine manner would be the wish of the majority did they but know it I am too well aware, and judging by the past I might dread all our bliss as the light side of the picture which would soon be rendered appalling by the gloomy backgrounds of dissappointments which would soon present themselves; that such is the case in part I admit. Your heart beloved is too good to cause a fellow being a pang and I know you do not design ever to add another drop to my cup but to drain to the bottom the bitter contents, and run it over with happiness. That such is your wish and your aim I firmly believe. The more I analyze your dear disposition, the more I see of your exalted benevolence and purity of motive the more I bless my fate that I have even known you thus late, even though our acquaintance should terminate forever. The purity of your character will be to me a subject of study and contrast between the many I have met and may still meet and though parted forever it will afford me pleasure to know I could not have had the power to make myself the misanthrope I once prayed to be for then I should have lost the dear pleasure of knowing the earth yet held one so good, so noble. But you are united to one for life, one who is pure and on whom the world dare not frown, and when a few more days throw you together and in your mind you contrast her with your poor lost Mad will you not turn from me with disgust, and wonder that you ever became thus entangled, will you not abandon the noble wish of your heart to raise the oppressed and deserted being who once shone as fair as the dear one by your side? Will you not say to yourself, I am acting a faithless part by my wife and I will at once break all off with Mad for faith broken to her will not condemn me in my own eyes and is no more than she has often felt from others & has still a right to look for. These things I do not believe you will say or feel if so only in part. If these should not arise may not another should the fact reach the ears of her you love. Cast me from your mind forever for sooner than give her a pang of jealousy to embitter her happy days, thereby rendering my dear Charles miserable, I would live the unblest outcast that I am and never behold thy dear face again, and this to me would be the greatest of punishments; but never in my life have I sought, or even wished to erect my happiness or interest on the downfall of another. The partner of your bosom no doubt loves you with all the intensity she is capable of feeling. She loves you with that pure confiding love feeling herself your equal and that she receives no more from you than she has a right to claim. My love is deeper than hers. I love with the fervour of one who has lost all she ever had to love, and lost alas! that which could make her love worth possessing; with the intensity of one clinging to the object with the dread of loosing it for ever, with the reverential feeling of gratitude for being permitted to love one so far above me, and for the kindness and respect rec'd from you to the one who is deserted by all that once composed the world in which once she lived. My love is not the less pure for being embodied in such a shrine for I believe the heart and soul have not the controul of the outer flesh; but still one hours love, one low-breathed sigh, one tear [paper torn] the wife of thy bosom would be worth all the years of deep devotion and oceans of [torn] that Mad could give to thee, therefore do not endanger the loss one tithe of her love for all my premeditated happiness. I have refused to be made happy since I have been thus situated in life because I could not bear that any one could ever say that I was so selfish as to throw a mantle of shame over another life in order to screen myself somewhat, and could I willingly cause one I love so much to wish at some future day he never had beheld me. The stern decrees of society and pretended morals of the gazing, prying multitude impose much on those who would do good and many a noble act has been lost from that fact. The man who is daily taxing his wits how he can oppress the poor, the man who is lucky at the gaming table, the man who puts on his long face and his cloak of reli[gi]on on Sabbath, and does all manner of evil in the week would not be condemned by the many who would highly censure the noble heart that would seek the bed of sickness to administer comfort where lay the wreck of what was once as fair in fame as the wife of their bosoms and but for such as themselves might still have been. I do not say this to extenuate my own errors or to console myself with the belief that I merit the kindness I sometimes receive, far from it. I feel that I do not and that is one reason my gratitude is so deep. I say but little but I feel much. Weigh every thing dear Charles before you act and if consistent with your own happiness and one others you can so far trust me as worthy and you will assist to place me in a more happy condition Oh! Charley undying gratitude on my part and a blest reward in Heaven will be your recompense. But if on the other hand after you leave me and reflect ca[l]mly and then regret, do not I implore you to hesitate in telling me so at once, for it will make me love you not one drop the less. I have not loved you for the wish you manifested towards me but for yourself alone, from the fact of having met one so congenial in soul and sentiment, one who is so superior in nobleness of heart and purpose to the moving throng that I can but worship your character. Forgive this scroll [scrawl] and when each moment is bearing you farther from poor Mad sit down and read it and at least give me your pity if no more. I shall ever look on the hours I have spent with you as the happiest I have seen since the pure spirits of my blest babes left me here to mourn and such thoughts make me fear they *will* not *can* not last. God grant otherwise. I trust if we are here doomed to part I will see you after death and know you too. There will be no Heaven to me unless. May God ever protect you my dear, dear Charley. Oh! do not forget me midst all your happy hours! but give one sigh to poor Mad.

Madaline to Charley, October 9, 1843. Here Edwards raises the money issue that eventually stifled her relationship with Bradbury.

My Dear Beloved C.   Monday Morning
   You will think I presume upon the privilege given me very soon, and probably [am] making an excuse to see you. However much I wish to see you (and God knows it can not be more) my honour would not permit me thus to trifle with your request, and thereby endanger your interest. I regret exceedingly that circumstances compel me to call on some one at this time for a small assistance and as I have applied to one who took the occasion to insult me for so doing although I had a right to do so, I know one thing in asking you I run no risk of a reproach or insult, but feeling as I do towards you and being fearful that you do *not* know those feelings I am sorry to ask another favour at those hands which have already bestowed so many. Could I feel less towards you than I do I would not be at this time so destitute, but it happens when others come and I contrast you and them I dismiss them, and others have imposed on me. I am now in need of $1.50 for my board and the same to pay some washing and if you will let me have it I will call on you no more, for I am now sick, and cannot go out or I would go to the Bank and try them to let me have $15 or 20 on the faith of my box for I am in debt for a part of my rent. I have in that box $300 which I am saving to try and buy me a servant but I will not hoard it up there and impose thus on the only friend I have on earth. It is ungenerous and ungreatful but I trus[t] you will forgive it, for I have tried hard to get something from those who should befriend me, and all I receive is an insult or sneer. I have even tried to get some sewing but cannot, and I am much mortified that I call on you this early after your return and if I had any thing I could soak I would not do it. I hate to take my box out but if you say I can get any on it by letting it remain, I will do so as soon as I get well enough to go out.
   My Dear Love you do not know, you can *never* know how I think of

you, and long to see you each night as formerly and with what bitter tears but these of resignation I submit. Why? because I know it is for your good, and I could sell every moment of peace on earth to procure, any pleasure for you. Misery is ever to be my doom on earth and it matters not how much. Better perhaps not to love than to be thus miserable from it, but yet I *could* not I *would* not resign it with all its pain. It is useless to write, it is useless to weep or to think as I do, but *memory* cannot be controuled nor feelings such as mine subdued. Beloved one do not come if there is the least danger to arise from it. No Charley do not let a wish or a want of mine cause you to do an act that you might reflect on afterwards, for as dearly as I love you as much as I would undergo to see you, yet I do not wish you to run any risk for me, for there is one whose momentarily happiness is worth more to you than that of all my life and if hers is lessened so is yours, and therefore act as your own judgment dictates. It appears like an age since I saw you and Oh how much I have suffered since I saw you in body as well as mind. *Do* not think me mean in this request dear Charley I beg you. I am aware that you have lately had to spend much money and that times are dull in your business and that it will look to you as though I intend to make a practice of this, but it shall be the last time.

Believe me ever your poor but affectionate —
God bless you Loved one forever

Madaline to Charley, October 12, 1843

My Own Beloved

I am tired trying to work and as to reading with only *one thought* in my mind would be folly for thyself is that one thought and I sit down to commune with you as it were on paper. How blest, how happy must Mrs B. be if she loves you as I do, to await the dinner hour for your appearance, to greet thee with a smile and kiss of affection, to bid you farewell with the full assurance of meeting again in a few hours. These scenes from repetition may loose their weight with her but never could, now with me. I do not reproach her in saying so, for doubtless she loves you with all the force of her nature, and had I been thine when care and sorrow, when the world and its knowledge were strangers to me I might have loved you with all my soul, but that love would not have been what it now is, and it only remains for her to feel what I have felt, to see what I have seen and to *prove* what I have (which God grant she never will) in order to love you with that *deep intense* feeling that alone can be *felt* for tell or shew it I never can. The day is thy time of buisness and as pleasant as it would be to me to see you through the day yet to her I would yield those hours, could I by any magic secure to myself the other twelve. To sit by thy side in the calm moonlight, with thee to gaze on the stars and from thy dear lips to derive instruction, to link arm in arm and wander alone where other eyes could not mark us, to admire and love the same objects, and being with thee objects, places and scenery would have charms for me unnoticed without thee, to ramble thus for hours, to return home and if time and season permitted to sit down by a cheerful fireside while you would read some work to me that would teach me to lift my thoughts and mind above the dying things of this life, that would confirm my unutterable hope that when I leave you here dear Charley that I shall meet you above those planets we love to gaze upon, and that there I can love you unreproached. After this pleasing task was over, to take a social meal and return to rest then with thy loved head pillowed on my breast and my hand clasped in thine, would I forget that ever I was unblest. If this *could* be my happy lot Oh! would not I be too happy. Do not my ever loved one, do not censure me for permitting such thoughts to occupy my mind, for I cannot help it. I work all day and at night I set myself by the window to reflect, the moon shines so lovely and inviting that it woos my hours there to think ten thousand things of the only one I love and I think now his cares for the day are over and he seeks rest and pleasure and I am selfish enough to wish the task mine to administer [to] you each eve all the little indearments of my heart. I *cannot* help loving you as I do then do not blame me for wishing for an unjust thing towards the one that never did me any injury and the one my dear Charley loves, but I *do* wish that I could see you every night if no more.

Beloved Charley Will you grant me one request? If it will not interfere with your intent to come here tomorrow Thursday as soon after breakfast as you can and stay until your dinner hour. It will be pleasure to see you only one moment but do not come merely because I ask it just to say I cannot stay but a little while Mad, because I want you to stay a long time. Oh, I want to see you so much. Do come if you can the door will be open and no one here. Dearest, dearest Charley I shall look for you.

Thine ever while life lasts, and *thine* beyond the tomb

Adieu, Adieu

Madaline to Charley, November 10, 1843

My Beloved

Pardon this (I hope last) appeal to your forgiveness in this I fear very unpleasant manner to you, for I never address you of late but I fancy you are not well pleased at me, and I had concluded never to force my sentiments on your notice again in this manner, but as the painful state of mind in which you last found, and left me calls for some acknowledgement, and explanation, and as the time allotted me in your company is always so short that I dare not steal therefrom a moment I would otherwise give to the fulness of my love and happiness while gazing on the face and clasping the hand that gives a magic to every moment; and to think I so embittered one of those sweet moments of my existence by giving vent to feelings over which I can have no controul added to the conviction that I have thereby lost some of the favour I gloried in possessing has given me feelings that no stoic could feel without having his faith shaken as to the validity of his doctrine. Again, My Love when I sum up in my mind many things I would say to you, I glance over the catalogue and so condense them that I imagine they can be said when we meet and leave me room to cariss and to love, but when we meet (generally) my heart feels so bouyant, one caress so care-absorbing that I forget all the array of words and reasons I had so earnestly thought of and am *more than willing*, when I can to banish all care and live a whole life in the few moments of bliss I spend with you. There are persons who can use their tongues fluently and their hearts a stranger to their words. There are others who can command no words and write their thoughts powerfully.

There are others who can *feel* all the depths of love, all the torturings of concience, all the degradation on which they are looked, all the pent-up feelings of desertion, the heart-rending, soul-destroying conviction of their ruin, and yet too the benevolence and soul-ennobling qualities that *might* have been turned to some noble purpose. These and many others they can deeply, intensely, *feel* and *endure* without the power or gift to express them in either way and this is just my situation for I can even express myself more clearly on paper than in words, from the fact of never having been blest with one congenial spirit who possessed knowledge to impart where I possessed understanding and willingness to receive. But like one groping in the dark, I have read until my soul would expand and yearn for such a guide that could satisfy the silent emotions those volumes had imparted but could not fill, and I have tried in writing to conjure up that spirit that I have so much felt the want of and thus by degrees have learned to transfer to the spotless sheet a small portion of the many oceans of thought that has flooded through a once spotless heart (at least of guilt) and in the same manner have I tried to forget the simple effusions of those days in penning lines that the next moment was effaced with tears, and wherever there has been one kind enough to listen to my errors and my sorrows it has been so far off that the pen was called into requisition to unfold my sad tale. I have hereby learned to make a friend of my pen, to commune with for I have had no one else, and from the fact that my lips have ever been kept sealed and though my pen was sometimes employed, yet the heart, the heart, has had its gleams of sun shine and rain bows of hope, and its many, yes very many dark clouds of sorrow and despair its cord rending desertions, and scalding tears, while even the pen was no participant of sensations that my heart alone can enshrine. Under such feelings I am often lost in a whirl of hopeless ideas from which no reasoning of mine is able to extricate me; and to *know* from those internal aspiring[s] that we were ordained for something loftier than words can express and to see that by one misdeed all is eternally lost to us, *this* beloved Charley is itself food for many tears I shed for which many can condemn me but none feel. If I could for once open the recesses of my heart and show to you the secrets

of my nature, the aspirations, the upward, onward craving feelings for
which I have no name, and see them crushed down, pent up, suffocated
in the resivours of that heart (by nature good) but now destroyed by the
opinion of the world, sanctioned by the soul-blighting conviction that
my conduct has justified that decree! Oh! Love could you see all this and
know that by this I have to abandon these once bright hopes and would
cling to one so intensely loved as thou art, as the only being on earth who
could call forth any thing good out of the chaos of my soul, and then
to feel the bitter cold waters of separation roll over my ardent feelings
in the benevolence of your noble soul, you would say weep Mad for it is
all that is left you in this world of sorrow. Do not my own Love (as you
intimated last evening) think that I imbibe romance from those or any
books you can give me. No dear for all the romance that is in my nature
is inherent and I can trace its recollections to happy school day hours,
but what has romance to do with misery? My years are now matured
and though I love the beautiful, the wild, the grand and good of all Gods
works yet the[y] are feelings of reverence and were in my nature as far
back as memory will carry me, and not drank in from fiction. You would
perhaps infer after reading this far that I imagine to myself that I can
write. Oh Charley if you knew how hopeless I look upon every effort I
make to write, and after my best effort how humiliating it is to know that
such depths of feelings lies in my soul while I can command no words
to bring them forth, but at the same time I believe I can write better
upon any subject than I can converse and upon one in which my feelings are much concerned being so sensitive I can never express the half
I wish. In writing I can do as over this lay down my pen and weep tears
unseen or unknown to others and for this reason I have often troubled
you, but more particularly as I have above stated because we so seldom
meet that I wish not to loose one moment of moments so dear to me.
The fear that by such a step as last evenings will lead you to make those
visits fewer and then not from choice but a desire to add to my pleasure, together with the conviction that you think me less amiable than
before, more unjust and unreasonable has caused me bitter anguish today but Oh Beloved Charley do forgive me and I will make no promise
but I will do my best to make it the last time I act so before you. It was

these fears that acted so upon me at our parting knowing I had to leave you to think of me as you thought best without the time to beg even for forgiveness. Oh! what a creature I am no one but yourself could in time fathom, for even in all the agony of my feelings last night there was one but one little word had it have fallen from your lips would have silenced the tumult of my breast and gave such happiness to my wounded spirit as all the vocabulary beside could not afford, but ah I had better not dwell on it or my brain will again become maddened. What gave rise to such a tide in your feelings ask you? I had looked for you fed upon the bliss I should enjoy in your company, hoped and feared until conviction forced itself upon me it must be ever thus, doomed to disappointments in every path you tread through life. Thought is a quick traveller. I ran over all the past, the dark vista before me, my longing aspirations to be what I never can. I felt that I once had a mind that was gone to decay in the prime of life, and I felt like all the world and all it could ever be would mount in the scale were you put in the other with the assurance that you could be my guide my teacher for the future and that you would feel for me and for the deep stream of adoration that poured itself from my soul for you, that you would not spurn the humble office of raising me from my ruined state. Read this not superficially for I wish you to divine my *meaning* in some passages for I cannot express what I wish you to catch and then such a desolation swept through my soul as I sat in the twilight thinking that I had no loved voice to hear, no loved hand to press and I *felt* it must always be so and in the agony of my feelings I burst into tears. I thought I would not let you see that such was the fact for when you came in I dashed back the tears and in my heart tried to be calm, but so seldom is my ear greeted with the words of sympathy and kindness that it but redoubles the emotion to receive it, and yet is so dear coming from one we love. Forgive me and do not think me ungreatful for all your efforts to make me happy. You said Love you could make me hate you. *No* you could not and if you had the power to call up the aid of Demons to assist in this magic you would not do it although my temporal peace might rest on it. Let me love you and let me *hope* that my happiness is dear to you and you will be the means of making all the good of me that I ever dare to look forward to and though it will be the

glow worm striving to eclipse the mid day sun yet I will hence owe all
that may be good in me to your influence and efforts. Already have I felt
from you and the books you have given me, at times a new life spring up
in me, and at times a ray of hope will dart across my mind that I may
be able some day to make you feel a little proud of your modelling. You
have it in your power more than you ever dreamed of to make me a part
at least of what you wish, to that end how can you blame me when I weep
over the fate that tears me from the sweet intercourse I would share with
you by which you could learn me and the failings with the few virtues
out of which you could mould a being you might not blush to own at
least in that world to which we are hastening. Were we together more
my love, my admiration for you would lead me to do all I could and tax
my ability to do all you could wish to make thyself or me good or happy.
Do not mistake me in these wishes; I would not tear you from another if
I could to give her pain and promote my happiness. I only mourn over
what could never be and if I could feel that when seated by her side you
sometimes thought of me and wished it were so that you could slip out
and whisper a consoling word in the ear of one who loves you so much,
Oh you do not know how happy it could make me for I am one who
takes the *will* for the deed so much. Oh Life without love is not life atal
and *you* cannot realize nor comprehend what I mean in saying this for
you have never proved the reverse. To love so passionately as I do and
know not only that I am not loved but that [it] is an impossibility that I
ever *can* be loved by that one is more than enough to keep the stream of
agonizing life-destroying tears ever flowing. Then *do not* Oh! for pity do
not think me unjust and simple for these I do not merit in loving one so
noble, and for the reasons above never destroy my love for you if it could
be done, for if you do destroy the foundation on which I am endeavouring to start life afresh and if that is once swept from under me adieu
to all my wishes and resolves. *Forgive* your poor Mads faults and errors.
Bear with me and make me by your noble forbearance and amiable disposition what no force no wrangling could ever make me. For the Love
I bear you I *will* try to be more deserving of your dear Friendship.

God ever bless You.

CHAPTER TWO

My Own Cottage Home

O

n December 1843 Bradbury purchased a house on Bacchus (Baronne) Street for Edwards. It stood six blocks from his own, near what was then the edge of urban settlement, just beyond the city line in the old city of Lafayette. The one-story frame house had a separate kitchen and cistern, a gallery, and a yard large enough for an extensive garden.[1] Madaline's first entry in her Writing Book, a blank book that Charley gave her, celebrated her new cottage.[2]

Dec 14.th [1843] Night

I have now inhabited my new home two days, and with feelings no one could realize but those who have been so situated and possessing the same feelings by nature as myself have I taken charge of what I have never possessed in life *an own Home.* These sensations arise from more causes than one. There are emotions of joy, gratitude, and strange to couple with these bitter remorse; were it not for the last I could now be Oh! so happy! Could he who is the cause of this blest change in my life fathom the deepest recess of my heart he would find towards him feelings too full of meaning to be translated to words. I bless God that he was fated to cross my path and I bless the Minister[3] from whose hallowed life and upright walk he has been led to improve or extend the noble, the benevolent desires of his heart, that heart by nature so good so pure and I bless him, I adore him for the independence, the sympathy and exalted traits of his character that have operated so favourable upon my miserable life. My joy and gratitude may in a measure be conceived, but Ah! who can unbar the soul and see the wound **Remorse** can make. Were I now what I have been I could feel that I was not altogether unworthy of some kind feeling from my fellow mortals, but as it is I feel so degraded in my own mind that when I think of all the noble one has done for me my heart recoils at what I have been and I know the unalterable rules of society will never award to me a higher place than the one I now occupy; but with this follows a balm of consolation and humility, and not revenge prompts me to express it: I will for the *future* merit the approbation of my Preserver. He shall see that his exalted kindness shall not be abused, that he shall often feel a thrill of joy, that none will share as he thinks I have saved and redeemed one greatful being from infamy and when seated alone in my Cottage Home enjoying the fruits of his gift, isolated though I am from all the world; I will feel less remorse as I think *he* alone knows me and believes me just from the 12 th of this month at least.

My heart will swell with gratitude as I rise step by step in my own estimation, and as I see he feels an interest for the creature of his own reclaiming, my ambition will be to prove to him he was not mistaken in believing me what he thought. There is another glorious and consoling reflection, that will often light up my soul when clouds of Remorse hover o'er it is that *life* is not long and that God who so loves a good action can also forgive a bad one, that he is not like his creatures, that he will yet claim the poor out-cast as his child and will forgive all the past, and in that blest world I will live forever with my adored preserver, yes I say *more* than Preserver for he has saved me from all that can degrade us here, he has saved me from treating [treading] the road of degradation to the extent to which too many go, and from which I might not have had moral courage or foresight to shun. Yet a little while more in my dear little Cottage Home and I trust he will believe me what he could hope of me and it will be the pride of my life to be all he will wish me to be.

In thinking so much of him it may not be thought I think as much as I should of the Giver of all good gifts, but it is not so. I never think of his

Madaline's diaries and writing books. Courtesy The Southern Historical
Collection, University of North Carolina at Chapel Hill.

bounty but I thank my God for the gift of such a friend and my heart heaves with reverence as I think how approvingly our Maker looks down on this noble deed of his, and I know it will be a star in his crown above that will outshine the many that compose it, because the more lost the object the more meritorious the action and Deity gives more weight to it than if done to one of the wealthy and respectable.

For years I have dared not pray, now for the last two nights I could thank God and I trust truly, that my lot was so changed that I could venture to approach him without my acts giving the lie to my words. I can now say give me a *better* heart and bless Oh bless my dear friend forever. My candle is near out and I will close my scroll and retire to my bed, the third night in my Cottage Home, feeling though now alone I have one dear friend on earth and that we have a mutual on[e] in Heaven.

Madaline Edwards was "degraded" and outcast, she says, until her spiritual worth was recognized by Bradbury, who introduced the deeply religious young woman to the Reverend Theodore Clapp. The way she describes her encounter with the two men reveals her religious psychology in striking terms. Her words and phrases recall traditional evangelical language and evoke the story of the Good Shepherd as well as metaphors of wise fathers and errant children. The ambiguity of Edwards's language, particularly her pronoun references, conflates Bradbury, Clapp, Christ, and God the Father, even as she equates her earthly rescue with spiritual salvation.[4]

Saturday Night Dec 23rd [1843]

My weeks work is done and I sit down by my cheerful fire, alone, but not lonely, for I feel so cheerful, so glad and content that I feel not solitary. I think of the change that has taken place in the last few days and my heart leaps for joy, and overflows with gratitude to my adored preserver. I feel so calm away from the heartless throng that I would not again mix therein on no terms. My days on earth may not be many but now I have the blest consolation that they will not end in the degradation that has obscured some of my best days of life, now I can look forward with hope, while before I saw nothing on which to lean, nothing to hope for nor any one to say I will guide you to a better life. Some would jest, others would say you have my sympathies and pass on perhaps forgetting the next hour the tears they had seen wrung from my breast by calling up associations, and misfortunes. But at last came one whose soul was true, who saw that I had a soul tuned to higher joys than such degradation. He spoke words that acted like magic upon me. He said I had a heart too good for such a life. He said I could yet be a better and happier woman. He pointed to me a minister [Clapp] whose blest admonitions and promises would tranquilize my wounded spirit, and by his kind and eloquent reasoning induced me to hope I was not lost, that I had not sunk too low to be an object of interest to one so noble and good, that he was my friend and that was joy to my disponding heart. He saw what others *would* not see: my desire to be a better person. He did not stop to weigh arguments and to sum up improbabilities, but he determined to act upon his own impressions, and he has done so, given to me a home, to insure to me that I should not be under the dire necessity to live as I abhored. He has done more than this in giving me his confidence, in believing me when I say to him I will now reform, in this he does an act my heart alone can appreciate, and it will be the guiding star that will lead me on to a higher and better destiny and one at which I trust he will never blush in this world and will rejoice with me when he hears in that blest world, "Come up higher, and still higher, for thou hast saved and brought back one of my lost ones." Yes his reward above will be great, for our God judges not as men judge, and he will give him his due and I bless my God that his justice makes such a provision, for an act done in secret, from such pure motives, for were it done to be lauded about as an act of charity in his eyes it would lose its rewards. When I sit down and ponder on the past I feel so thankful that I am so blest and others so much more deserving, without such a friend, that I am vain enough to think I am one of Gods favourites, for he directs all good acts, he must have sent my best Preserver to save me. I know how greatful I should be to him as my Father who still pities [h]is erring child and to him for such a dear friend and I hope he will hear my nightly prayer to give to C. more wealth for he will use it to his glory.[5] Having been so long without the joy of feeling that I was dear to any one, that my interest was any one else's, or that my situation ever caused any one a pang, and now to know there is one who feels a solicitude and desire for my welfare. Oh! it makes me joyful and I lie down with peace in my breast thanking God first and then him that I have so much to enjoy and I try each day to be content with less. My dearest Father give to C all the blessings he so well deserves in my own hope and aspiration. I will lay aside my pen and go to my bed of repose and to rest sweetly under the roof of my Cottage Home, and the eye of my ever guardian Father above.

N.O. [New Orleans]

Clapp's sermons were common subjects of Edwards's essays. The habit of taking notes on sermons stretches back at least to the time of the Puritans, but Madaline did not restrict herself to recording Clapp's thoughts. She listened critically, commented on points with which she disagreed, and discussed the evolution of her own theological understanding. This essay reveals another side of Edwards's religious life. The evangelical emotionalism of her personality was balanced by a strong dose of rationalism. Her rejection of the orthodox Christian doctrine of the Trinity, like the views on eternal life, damnation, phrenology, and natural religion that pervade her writings, was strongly influenced by Enlightenment critiques of Christianity.[6]

Sabbath Dec 24th [1843]

I have just returned from church where I heard that great and good man the Rev Mr Clapp deliver a sermon on a subject that has ever perplexed my mind and he so fully satisfied me upon it not only from his reasoning and proof but from the same ideas on a limited scale having ever existed in my heart in defiance of all I have heard to the contrary. His text is "there is but one God" and he so ably and forcibly shewed the relation between that God and his son and that relation separate in itself yet so near allied to the insurance of our happiness that one will not avail without both. He so fully proved that Jesus Christ was not the same *as* the Father but his created son who was once mortal as we are (sin excepted) where as God himself is, nor ever was created by existing eternally, then how could the son be the same as the Father who was the Author of his being. I have but very recently heard a Universalist minister and until this day never had my mind at ease upon that subject and ever since I have been capable of reading and trying to judge for myself I have been more perplexed upon the subject of the Trinity than any one passage in scripture, for although expounded to my hearing so often by different denominations yet I never could comprehend how three persons could exist in one and be separate, yet one and the same, for the reading scripture tells us Jesus called on his Father and says why hast thou forsaken me. It tells us he prays to the Father for the cup to pass from him if it is possible but not my will but thine be done. Now if he was in the Father and the Father in him it must have been hypocrisy to pray thus. If I may be pardoned the expression of the thought that has long lain in my bosom, it is that God as he so calls himself is our Father and Jesus is as our brother who so loved us that he was willing to die for our redemption therein shewing how he loved us. I have ever felt when I wished to address a prayer that if there was a sin in not including the God head or three in my aspirations that I was ever guilty. I have conjectured upon this theme until I have turned away from my own thoughts confused and unhappy. Now my mind is fixed and I feel that I would not have lost the hearing of that sermon for a great deal. Indeed I bless the day I ever heard that man preach not from the liberality of his doctrine only after death but the good it is calculated to produce upon the mind while here. He has created within me a new life, new joys, new hopes and new determinations and I believe from his sermons I shall be enabled to feel resigned to a long life here (if Gods will) whereas before nothing but fear prevented suicide. I believe he will teach me that even *I* have a destiny to fill and that I am watched from above with the same solicitude to one who stood far higher in the scale of mortal popularity. He teaches me though I have greatly erred yet even at some future day I may be as others say saved, but he gives us the bright side of our Redeemer that prompts the heart at once to love and not to fear, abject fear that paralyzes all our better efforts, and he teac[h]es us the day *will come* (not may) that I too will be received into my Saviours love and the happy home of the blest. When I think of the change already wrought in my feelings and determinations since hearing that man preach I am lost in gratitude to the one who lead me to hear him and who is my Saviour here in leading me to a Saviour on high. It was gratifying to my mind to hear a man so gifted, a man with such towering intellect, such powers of imagination, such brilliant genius, such stores of knowledge and such treasures of memory, pass such an eulogy on Dr Channing. In speaking of his coinciding with his views (Mr Clapps) respective the Trinity he said, "I would rather be the author of one of his sermons than all that has been written in a Century," and this coming from such a man as Clapp in an encomium that might swell any heart with pride in which such a spark existed. Each day convinces me of late that there is much in this world of ours worth living for and this beautiful, blest sabbath confirms my belief the more and I trust that my heart will expand and my views become clearer under the influence of the Sermons I hope yet to hear from that dear man, and that by the aid of My Father above I will never cease to bless the day I saw my dear friend C and heard the good Mr Clapp.

Charley gave Madaline a blank diary and composition book, along with a scrapbook that has not survived, to encourage her to "improve her mind." It took her a while to form the habit of writing in a diary, so there are no regular entries until March 1844. Before then, many of the entries comment on current and historical events; they were clearly copied from newspapers and books and may have been inserted later to fill out the blank pages. Only a few of these incidental entries are included here, to give a sense of their character.

Monday, January 1, 1844. The new year finds me enjoying one blessing that no preceeding one ever has, it finds me in my own comfortable and happy home with only one thing lacking to make me, I may say completely happy, that is denied me but I will not throw away the bliss thats in my cup only lamenting the loss of that.

Jan. 2. The Anniversary of the most unfortunate day of my life, my Marriage. My presentiments then have been more than realized. I launched my bark upon the waters of expectation and it has been wrecked sadly wrecked, the cargo lost the wreck till late all abandoned.

Jan. 8. This morning all here is music and noise. While doubtless the old Hero of N.O. is silently and solemnly reflecting upon the day we celebrate with such triumph.[7] In the Hermitage perhaps he is musing upon the clash of arms the rolling drum the groans of the dying and the shout of victory that fell upon his ears here in 1815 and he feels that his feet have trod these shores the last time yet when he goes down to the silent tomb thousands will echo his name and his deeds.

Jan. 12. How animated and happy have I been today while reading Dicks works upon astronomy, how sublime his views of the countless worlds that float in space, how beautiful his ideas of the Supreme Being who made them, and how holy it is to feel the influence of such hopes excited thereby to feel that ere long the little we can know about them will be magnified to a knowledge that will ever increase.[8]

Jan. 13. Steamer Lexington burnt 1840 the loss of lives 140.

Jan. 19. American independence acknowledged by Great Britain in 1783.

Jan. 30. Laid out my flower parterre and I promise myself much real felicity in planting and nursing my flowers for they will ever constitute one of the greatest enjoyments in life.

Jan. 31. Set out white rose and a number of other kinds sent me from Miss.

Feb. 6. The Sun 880,000 miles in diameter / turns on its axis in 25 days 10 hours.

Mercury distant from the sun 37,000,000. / revolves around the sun in 88 days / his diameter 3200 miles. on its axis 24 hr 5 min

Venu[9]

Feb. 17. Conception I *Think.*[10]

Feb. 22. While the guns are booming and the bells are pealing, while all the City are celebrating this great anniversary I am quietly reflecting upon the noble but modest, the great but unpretending, the loved and unstained Washington whom no Country has failed to award merit and goodness to and who doubtless has had fewer enemies than any publick man that ever trod our earth.

Liberty he gained us, freedom he bequeathed us may we ever appreciate it.

Feb. 23. My Eldest sisters birth day. It tells of a time when its return brought joy around the fireside of our child hoods home, and now it but numbers years of anguish, care and sorrow, but it is ever thus with mortals joys. Though far away from thee Eliza perhaps too forever yet I ever remember thy birth day.

Mar. 1. Birth day of my little William my third child, buried in Clinton Miss.

Mar. 5. Birth day of my Mary Jane my second child, born and buried in Clinton Miss.

Mar. 6. Crocket killed in 1836 at the Alamo Texas.

Sun. Mar. 10. Heard Rev Mr Clapp preach upon the ceremony of taking the Sacrement an able and pointed discourse. Staid and saw the sacrament administered. In the evening taken very sick and no one came.

Very sick all night wished Henry Josephus would come but did not.[11]

From the Daily Picayune:

STATE LEGISLATURE.—After the reading of the journals yesterday, Mr. Winchester introduced resolutions charging Judge Elliott with gross malfeasance in office—malfeasance which called for his impeachment; they further demanded that a committee be appointed to prepare the articles of impeachment. After some remarks in opposition from Mr. Selby, and in explanation from Mr. Wilson, the resolutions were passed by a very large majority.[12]

Mar. 11. The Committee report on the case of Judge Elliott of Lafayette, which results in his dismission from Office, which would have been well had it been sooner as his rascality has caused the Whigs defeat in the election of Senator.

Heard some one walk in the front room and getting to my room door who should it be but Henry Josephus. Was very glad to see him although in bed sick. Brought me morning papers.

C came and appeared cold set me to crying from which I could not refrain. Left me so. Took a letter for me to M^r C[lapp].

Mar. 12. Expecially warm, like a midsummer day. Saw the specimens of the style of painting termed Grecian, think it very pretty indeed. Would like much to acquire the art. Melancholy all day. C came at night and reflections came up again filled with tears. He strove to quiet them but all in vain, like the summer rain they would flow.

He is kind and true and I should not thus weep.

Bought one half cord of wood. gave $2.12 ½.

Mar. 13. Recd a letter giving intelligence of my poor ill-fated Mother. Her errors will now rest in the tomb with her, and although she was an unnatural Mother yet I am her child and it is natural to drop a tear to her memory.

Noon. Rainy and gloomy. Sewed down in town all day and rode up in the Car.[13] Found my flower pots well beat with the rain. C came and found that I had at length dried my tears and met him as my heart is ever wont with a smile.

Planet Herschel discovered 1[smeared] 1781.

Mar. 14. Sewed a good deal and read some. Worked in my garden.

Night. Read a good deal in Dicks works and found much to study upon.

Pulled a sweet monthly rose, the first fruits of my garden.

Mar. 15. Raining incessantly yet I ventured out and got wet, felt the effects in a violent head ache all day. Came home in the rain, wet feet, bathed them and went to bed. C came and completely restored health and spirits, spent two happy hours and parted. Gave him a sweet rose for Mrs B[radbury].

Andrew Jackson born 1767.

Mar. 16. Cold and raw, pitied my poor flowers and did all I could to cheer them by placing them in the sun. Night is cold with lovely star light, covered up my flowers fearing frost.

Had C & B[udington] to pass an hour with to night. Just left so all alone I sit in the corner while not even a cricket will chirp me com-pany—ah-ha—yes there is the musketoes melody.

My fire is almost out—my eyes are too and I will go to rest as well as other *insects.*

From the Daily Picayune:

Rev. Mr. CLAPP will preach in his Church This Morning, 17th March, at 11 o'clock, on the subject of "Total Abstinence from all Intoxicating Liquors." The public generally are invited to attend. "Thoughts that breathe and words that burn"—pathos that will thrill every soul, and eloquence that will carry conviction to every mind—may be anticipated on the occasion.[14]

Sun. Mar. 17. Frost last night, but a lovely sunny morning that ushers in the great day among the Irish population St Patricks day. 9 oclock heard that great and good man Mr Clapp preach a sermon on total ab-stinence. Remarked that 14 year this month in that same pulpit he de-livered his first sermon on the same subject, and that he was ridiculed at his attempts but that he had lived to see it spread in every land. The Washington total abstinence banner was unfurled in the church. A very large concourse were assembled. Night. Agony and tears. Saw C pass this evening and would not stop nor speak to me. I cannot read atal.

In her Writing Book, Madaline wrote of her loneliness.[15]

How natural for sorrow to seek relief from some source, and Oh how prone we are to seek it in any other form than through supplication to him who can give consolation for ever[y] sorrow. My heart is almost bursting, my eyes are as wells and to forget these pangs or to give them rest I have sat down to try to write. These are trifles "as light as air" in appearances that will "harrow up our souls" wring from our eyes the scalding tears, and lacerates the very chords of our hearts. Sometimes I am wondered at and in particular by him whose opinion I value more than that of the world, for feelings that come over me and in which it is thought I indulge. Could he, could others analyze the feelings implanted within my breast by nature, could their force and bearing be realized, with this conviction could they trace my path from happy youthful days through all its changes, could they *feel* my position they would not wonder, they would not condemn, but pity me that feelings so sensitive should ever have been allied with so many misfortunes and sorrows. The more my gratitude is called forth, the more I realize the blest change in my life, the more I enjoy, the more my tears will often flow and others cannot tell why. It is that I feel the want of some congenial spirit to complete the charm of their joys, it is that as much as I love solitude yet take a person who never leaves his home or his village and by law prescribe to him those limits and see if he will not yearn to go beyond, so with my self. I love to be alone, I love to sit for hours and dwell upon my own thoughts, gloomy or not, but when I *feel* that compulsion dictates this, *thought* quicker than lightning flashes back, and looms over the present and pierces into the future. I see myself surrounded with blessings and comforts that could make me completely happy had I one to give that zest to them that an affectionate idolizing nature demands. I reflect that the deadly sirocco of shame has withered all that once gave life a charm, has blighted hopes that once leaped in my heart, has crushed noble resolves and sunk my once elevated spirits. I look around and see others with fewer temporary enjoyments, yet all

possess a tie that endears them to life. I think of what a different fate
mine might have been and worse than all that it is never to be amended,
that the future long or short is all blighted. I feel and see the censure of
the world, I turn within and I find there no approval.

And under these sensations I sit down and weep until life is to me
a thing of no moment. I am far from being naturally melancholy but
when a cloud of gloom should overspread my face, when a tear should
start to my eye, did the kind voice of sympathy or affection salute my
ear, could I look in the eyes of one congenial soul and read there that I
was *loved,* lean upon that arm and feel it would sustain and protect me
and *know* within my own breast that virtue and merit won and would retain those sentiments, then the sigh and the tear would soon yield place
to smiles and hope. But such is not nor ever can be the case. Who can
wonder that I shed such bitter tears, cut off from the world with such
feelings, for while we are mortals we need mortal comforts and consolation. I do not repine or murmur at the world that such is my destiny,
but the pang to feel it *is* so and that it is *just* is more than I can bear up
under with fortitude. As much as I wish to use, for I have so much to be
greatful to God for, so much to bless one being for, that I am ashamed
to do or say anything that looks like repining. God knows I had rather
bear all my sorrows with an accumulation than to exchange my feelings
for those too callous to feel their own or others griefs. Yes I had rather
weep out my existence than live it five times over without sen[s]ibilities;
but still I would not weep and be sad for fear my best, my only friend
will think I am repining and not so happy as I should be, and as I am
when I can keep back the past. He has done all he can do to make me
happy but *Fate* has willed the one thing that could make me blest is beyond his controul, and I must drink my lonely tears and feel my own
heart rending pangs while others share his smiles and witness his joys.
God grant they may increase as long as life lasts. Who could blame me if
they could know how much my nature demands affection and interest.
I have no one to speak to, to divirt my mind from care, no one to sit or
walk with, no one [to] enjoy all the beauties of nature and life with, no
one to tell my griefs or few joys to only as momentary, and yet my very

soul was made for such enjoyment. With such a spirit as his I could be led in realization of beauties and sublimities of a higher order than this world can give and it is in this alone I so much feel the want of a congenial spirit. It is not to pluck the few flowers of earthly happiness that might cling to [my] path. Although not sought yet [they] would not be despised, but higher, nobler views would be my aim.

Dear C perhaps these lines may meet your eye when the hand that now weeps for happiness denied me with you, may slumber in the dust. These lines I see I unconciously marked with my tears, and those tears were not mechanical but from my very soul. Pity me but do not think me unjust, for all your kindness for my gratitude and love for you are far more powerful than all my misery, and those feelings will live with me in Eternity be it happy or otherwise. I intend these humble pages to be read by no one while I live and to you I leave them. I know when these come up before you that no force of imagination could convey to you what I feel, but all I ask is your charity for my many faults.

March 17 1844

Mar. 18. Went down in the City, recd a letter from my Father saw some old friends; brought home some frames for paintings, got some Dahlia bulbs and other flowers as a present. Engaged to take lessons in the style of Grecian painting. Got a little sewing. C came to see me at night, felt my spirits restored, but much damped at his mashing his thumb in the gate turned him very sick. Brought me some papers, just read them find news favourable to the annexation of Texas to the U.S. See from the papers cheering news as to Clays being our next President. God grant it.

Mar. 19. Framed some paintings early this morning. Mr A brought me some fine dahlias and set them in the ground for me.[16]

Sewed until 11 oclock then walked out to get an orphan boy in whom I feel much interest to take a situation I had procured for him. Came home, sewed until 5. Took him down to Dr S. gave him some good advice. Doct seemed pleased with him and engaged him. Came home and sewed until 11 oclock and now I will go to bed for I feel very unwell.

C sent me some groceries to day of which I am much pleased.

Mar. 20. Got my little hoe and rake fixed. Tried them a little in the garden this morning.

Noon. Took a lesson in Grecian painting.

Had solicitations to give lessons in drawing and water colours.

Night. Saw C. Spent two happy hours with him. Brought me some morning papers in which I find a most touching and beautiful letter from Jno Hamilton of SC. in reply to the Clay Club soliciting his attendance at the reception of H Clay.[17] He confirms my hope that C[lay] will be our next president.

Mar. 21. Watered and worked my plants. Took a painting lesson and made a pair pants. Read the first part of Walker of Miss speech or address on the annexation of Texas.[18] Find it much to the purpose and very able. Night. Had the pleasure of seeing C and B here together, just left. Well now for the reading—Ah No! for there is some one.

Mar. 22. Early this morning read another portion of Walkers address.

Went to market, then took a lesson came home and made pickles, souse &c. Scoured and worked pretty hard. Feel tired but am not done yet. Hope C will come to night want to see him. Finished my first piece in Grecian painting and C thinks it beautiful and that is compensation enough for any pains.

Venus and Jupiter nearer than at any time this season.

Mar. 23. Painted, sewed and walked until night, passed two happy hours with C. brought me a paper fruit and so forth. Read the conclusion of Walkers address, think [it] sound logical reasoning as well as exhibits the immense trouble he has been at to acquire correct information from records, and no small degree of personal observations. Think it will have great influence upon the annexation of Texas to the U.S. and that speedily.

Heigh-ho I am almost asleep so farewell pen.

Sun. Mar. 24. Rose early, watered my flowers, read a portion of Dicks Christian philosophy. PM. Just returned from Church, heard the Rev Mr Clapp preach upon the pernicious practice so prevalent of slander and falsehood. The subject was a copious one and it was in the hands of one who well understood all its bearings and he displayed them with force and reason. Beautiful indeed were his remarks upon the equality of mankind and that no being on earth was so degraded in whom there was not some moral excellence and it only remained to be developed by kindness from some fellow being. Touching were his sentiments up[on] the grovelling, unhappy disposition of envy. Appropriate the quotation from ancient history of the envious man who could not live if his neighbors statue stood in his view, so in order to destroy it he availed himself of the secret night to demolish it, and met the reward of the deed, was crushed beneath it as it fell from the pedestal. Happy his illustration of the life and death of the ever to be remembered Copernicus. I trust that sermon will not be forgotten by me soon.

Mar. 25. Rose at day light, worked in my garden until 8, then took a lesson in painting, came home and varnished all my furniture, watered my flowers and sat down to await the visit of one so dear. His hour passed and I gave him out with a heart ready to burst, excused him in my own breast, but grieved not the less, but at last he came. Oh how glad I was. Just left.

Mar. 26. Took a lesson, bought a pair of shoes, came home to work. At night Josephus came and passed an hour or two very plesently with him. Next to C he is my best friend on earth and I shall ever appreciate his goodness. He brought me some *democratic* papers for he knows I am a whig.

Mar. 27. Rained last night quite hard, which put my garden in good order to set out plants which I did. I feel quite unwell which in addition to the rain prevents my taking my painting lesson which I regret.

Night. Have watched for C until I knew he would not come, felt so lonely and disappointed that I sat down and wept until I am totally unfit for reading or any thing so I will try in slumber to forget that which must make me ever unhappy.

Mar. 28. Feel very bad this morning after my mental suffering last night. Read a good deal in Dicks Christian philosophy went to my painting to day from there to D^r S, got a little sewing to do.

Evening. Mr A[dams] gave me some more dahlias and some plants
called gamunds. Find I have got a tulip open, am very proud of it. Got
muddy and am much displeased at my walk.

C came and brought me the 2ⁿᵈ No of the pictorial Bible.[19] He was
not well; feel very sorry to see anything ail him.

1802. Pallas discovered by Dʳ Olbers of Bremen.[20]

Mar. 29. Did not take a lesson to day for I was painting a map of Gal-
veston for C just done it. Hope he will like it. Am very tired.

C came was much pleased with the map. Brought me a paper.

1807. Vesta discovered by Dʳ Olbers of Bremen.

Mar. 30. Cold, cold, this morning, has even misted a little snow. But
not too cold to prevent my taking my painting lesson. Finished a landscape which C is very much pleased with.

Worked pretty hard to day and feel tired so I will go to bed and read
the paper C brought me.

Sun. Mar. 31. Clear but very windy and cold. I wish to hear Mr C
preach to day so I think I must go.

My poor flowers look drooping to day and well they may for it was so
cold last night I pitied them.

2 oclock. Just returned from church. Heard a beautiful discourse
upon the abuse of property, apparently an inappropriate theme for the
pulpit, but Mr C plainly shewed otherwise. Night. Have had Henry Josephus, Dʳ R[itchie] and Mr B to visit me to day.[21] Have all left and I am
now quietly alone. Mrs R has just given me a little dog. Hope he will
be sharp.

Apr. 1. A combination of circumstances have made me very miserable
to day. I have wept until I am sick.

Madaline described parting with Charley in her Writing Book.[22]

I feel as if my heart could burst. C has just left me and perhaps we
meet no more on earth. One circumstance is now pending that may ere
Tomorrows sun sets leave me again in this wide world without a friend
or adviser. Oh God grant he may not be taken from this world so soon,

for he will yet do much good in addition to all he has done. Oh spare him to be the star that will guide me to thee. He is my all in life take him not away. Strip me of all else even to the necessaries of life and I will be content if he but live. My brain is almost on fire at the dread thought. It must not be. It cannot be that we will meet no more. Oh dred thought. Oh holy *hope* now I need thy aid.

April 1st N Orleans. 1844

Apr. 2. Rose very unwell. Took my lesson and passed the balance of the day at Dr S. Went shopping, and got a letter from M^r C.

Night. C came and we took a lovely moon light walk. Long will I remember it. It reminded me of some happy walks during our first acquaintance. Came home, he wrote a memento in my scrap book.[23] Bud came and we had a social evening. After C left we talked and read until near 11 oclock.

T Jefferson born 1743.[24]

Apr. 3. Finished a piece of painting; sewed until sun set then watered my flowers. C came and brought me some pens and daily papers. Josephus came too and brought me some papers and presented me with a beautiful parasol. Two dear friends are these two to me.

Apr. 4. Had my washing done to day. C gave me money to pay for it. Have been almost crazy with the head ache all day.

Just had a couple of gentlemen to pay me a visit.

Harrison died 1841.

Apr. 5. Took a walk this morning and came home to work. While busy sewing, Mr S[ayre] one of the gentlemen here yesterday came in with a piece of the wedding cake of the other Mr H.[25] I wish them much real happiness.

Night. Been down in the City and feel much fatigued. C and B were here, just left, brought me papers, which I will now go and peruse.

Apr. 6. Before day light was up; picked all the grass out of my garden and then put my house in complete order. Then attended to my cooking to avoid the same on the sabbath. Had a very unpleasant visit from one I once esteemed as a dear female friend. We parted without hostile or any reconciled feelings on my part. Mr S. came and brought me a lovely bunch of flowers for which I am very greatful. Dear C came to night brought me some apples. God ever bless him. C gave me five dollars in gold.

Judge Elliott dismissed from Office.[26]

Sun. Apr. 7. Lovely day; read until 7. Wrote until near 8 when Josephus came up and for want of better partook of a cold breakfast with me. Gave me money to get a gutter for my house. A dear good friend he is.

Went to church to day and heard a glorious sermon on the Devil. Crowded house and very warm. Read until late in the evening when Mr S came with flowers for me and took a long walk with me. We had a long and animated conversation, returned and sat with me until 9 and then at parting pointed out some particular stars to me, and so I am disappointed in a long night reading for I am tired and sleepy.

Apr. 8. The birth day of my youngest sister [Fanny Cage], and also of my last child, my dear Isabella who was born and buried in this place.

Henry Josephus was here before 7 oclock, took a glass of milk and left.

Took a lesson to day. Went down in the City, and spent the balance of the day, came home and had the pleasure of Cs company until 8. Did not get home in time to water my flowers.

Apr. 9. Looks cloudy, but still I watered my garden well, for we have had a long dry spell and it needs water. Was up before day light in my garden.

Took another lesson, came home and found a trunk of clothes of Henry's. Knit and read until near sun set and watered my garden.

Night. Sat down to write, heard the gate open got up to see and behold it was C. Quite unexpected by me but more than welcome to my glad heart.

Apr. 10. Henry J took breakfast with me by 7 oclock then went out to do a days work. Came home very tired. Will not see my C. tonight

High ho—will compose and read some then go to bed.

Apr. 11. Bonaparte abdicated in 1814.

Feel very unwell this morning but still attended to my flowers. Josephus came.

PM. Just returned from the City and got a little sprinkled.

C came at night and I went nearly home with him.

Apr. 12. This day I have been in my own house four months and Oh how pleasantly has the time passed since. C asked me how much I would ask to return to that I left. Little does he know my heart if he deems worlds could tempt me. To him I owe all, all.

Got breakfast for Josephus and he disappointed me.

PM. Took a long walk with M^r S and got some pea poles sat with me in *door* until 8 oclock. Josephus has just gone and I am *going*—to bed.

Apr. 13. Worked very hard to day but with it came the pleasure of seeing my house and garden very neat.

C came at night and looked more cheerful than of late. We eat some blackbery pie, the first we have had. Bud came and met him here, brought me some presents for which I am very greatful but he will not let me say so. We read the papers until 10. And now for sleep the soother of all toil or care.

Sun. Apr. 14. Beautiful balmy morning. Oh I think of C now in bed and wish he were with me to enjoy the glorious breeze sweeping over my little garden so softly. I have been finishing the latter part of Dick's works.

I will go and hear Mr C preach to day. PM. Heard Mr Clapp preach upon the absurd doctrine of parents sins being visited upon their children and vica versa.

Josephus came as soon as I got home took a cold dinner with me. While here my cousin J.C. came and tried to prevail on me to leave the City.[27] Breath spent in vain. Mr S. spent the evening with me and walked with me to M^{rs} C's and back.

Apr. 15. My Father sent my dog and some guinea pigs over and I went this morning before day light after them. Went down in the City, came home with a violent head ache from the sun.

Had some visitors this evening. Night. C came and we had some straw berries together. Brought me a paper.

Apr. 16. Heigh ho I am so tired I can scarce sit. I have been baking and pickling all the morning to get to send C. and B. some. If they derive any pleasure from them I will be amply compensated for my labour.

Shakespear born in 1564.

Night. A soft, gentle rain is now saving me the pleasure of watering my flowers. Hope it will rain enough to fill my unfortunate cistern.

Had a back gate made to day.

Apr. 17. Dr Franklin died in 1790.

At day light I was in my garden planting flowers for I saw we would have rain. The moon changed at 11 oclock and at 12 we had a tremendous shower; how refreshing it was. Mr S brought me a lovely magnolia and loaned me Walker on women to read.[28] Dear C came at night and I gave him the first sweet cluster rose that grew in my garden.

Apr. 18. Went down to the green house and got some plants, sewed some and read some.

Josephus came at night very melancholy.

Apr. 19. Nothing new to day, but a new moon tonight by the light of which C and myself took a lovely walk down the Canal.[29] Oh how pleasant to walk and convers[e] with him.

C brought me the NY Herald in which I see a great move among the new sect of Native Americans and though their policy I think the right one yet I am much afraid it will be the only barrier to Henry Clays election.

Apr. 20. Josephus came early this morning.

Did a good days work then went down in the City, to Dr S. As I came home met C.

Night. Dear C has spent an hour with me and brought me a beautiful fan and some garden seed. How kind he ever is. Walked part of the way home with him.

Sun. Apr. 21. Welcome lovely sabbath morn. I was watering my flowers long before it was light. How can persons sleep such beautiful mornings. My morning work is done and I will now read until church time. Read two chapters in my pictorial bible.

PM. Just returned from church. Mr C delivered a learned and argumentative discourse upon faith.

Mr S spent an hour with me this evening and we then walked out to the Jewish burying ground.[30]

Apr. 22. Nothing new, only saw Mr E who would have pleased me better had he staid away.

C came this evening and we passed a pleasant evening together.

Bought me some white sand and lathes to day.

The treaty for the annexation of Texas to our Union recd in the Senate.

Apr. 23. Had my washing done to day.

C came at night and eat supper with me, and B came and took him away. So I read their papers and then went to bed.

Apr. 24. Slept but little last night for the musketoes bit me so that I was awake a great deal. Awoke this morning quite unwell but was up before light at work in my garden.

Have this day finished reading Dr Dicks works on religion philosophy &c &c and am much gratified that it was ever put in my hands.

C made me a present of Coombe on the constitution of man of which I know I shall be pleased.[31]

Apr. 25. Sewed all day.

Saw C to night and will now read some before I go to bed.

Felt a sensation that I think will unfold for me a new destiny.[32]

Apr. 26. I am not well and have too much to do to write any.

Apr. 27. C & B brought me some papers last night in which I see the president has given his sanction to the annexation of Texas and it is highly probable before this, the Senate has done the same.

I hope so.

Sun. Apr. 28. Went to church to day and heard Mr C preach upon the duties and privileges of woman in which he not only lauded her above price but above the fixed stars. Just as I got to my gate it began to rain and we had a lovely shower.

Have been taking down some astronomical points for C.

Mr S came and walked with me to get some ice cream. He is gone and now I must finish my composition.

In April and May 1844 Theodore Clapp preached paired sermons, "Woman" and "Man," built around common nineteenth-century clichés of gender. In

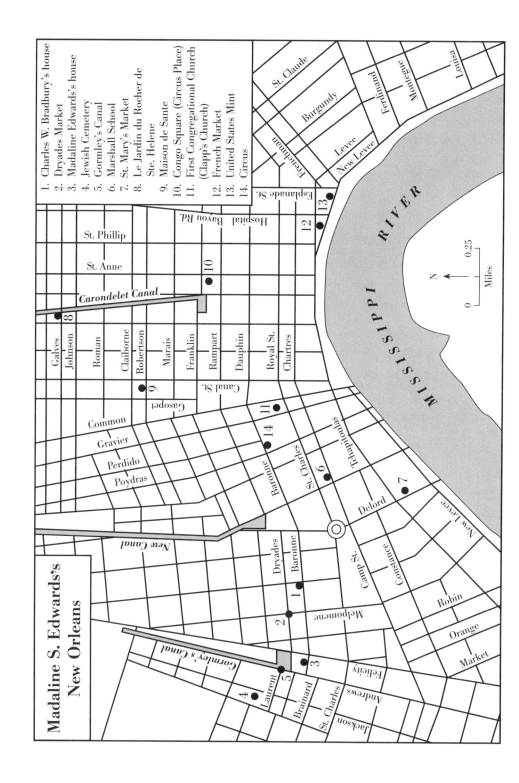

Madaline S. Edwards's
New Orleans

1. Charles W. Bradbury's house
2. Dryades Market
3. Madaline Edwards's house
4. Jewish Cemetery
5. Gormley's Canal
6. Marshall School
7. St. Mary's Market
8. Le Jardin du Rocher de Ste. Helene
9. Maison de Sante
10. Congo Square (Circus Place)
11. First Congregational Church (Clapp's Church)
12. French Market
13. United States Mint
14. Circus

MISSISSIPPI RIVER

N

0   0.25
Miles

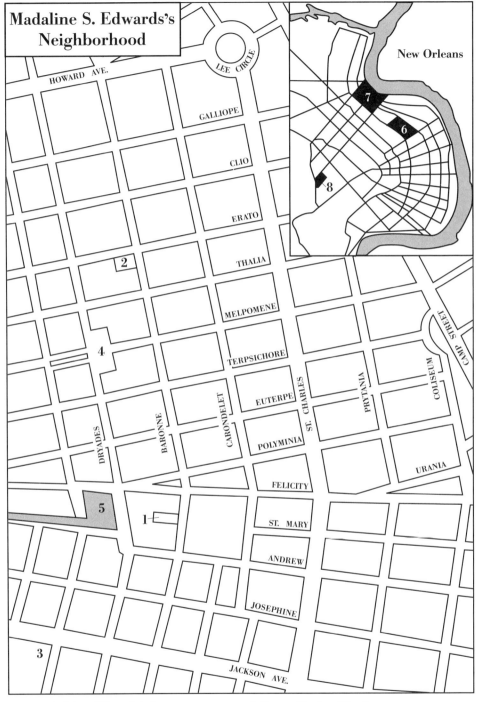

Madaline S. Edwards's
Neighborhood

HOWARD AVE.

LEE CIRCLE

GALLIOPE

CLIO

ERATO

THALIA

MELPOMENE

TERPSICHORE

EUTERPE

POLYMINIA

FELICITY

ST. MARY

ANDREW

JOSEPHINE

JACKSON AVE.

DRYADES

BARONNE

CARONDELET

ST. CHARLES

PRYTANIA

COLISEUM

CAMP STREET

URANIA

New Orleans

7

6

8

2

4

5

1

3

1. Madaline Edwards's house
2. Charles W. Bradbury's house
3. Jewish Cemetery
4. Dryades Market
5. Gormley's Canal (turning basin)

6. Lower Garden District:
   Madaline Edwards's neighborhood
7. Vieux Carre
8. Firemen's Cemetery (Cypress Grove)

the first, he stressed purity as the highest moral value in a woman and blamed women for their own sorrows. He spoke about women as mothers whose natural domain was the home. Edwards's response was confused. She accepted the minister's claims as a matter of education and habit, but her heart and her experience told her there was more to the story, that she was not entirely to blame for her predicament. In an essay she gave a novel twist to the standard metaphor of the home as a refuge that counteracted the immorality of the world at large. Her home was a refuge from the world's moralist hypocrisy. By the end, she had deflected Clapp's moral judgment away from her own life and toward those secure, well-off women who were not as self-aware as she.[33]

Woman

Heard Mr C preach to day upon the duties and privileges of woman and although the sermon was beautiful in the extreme, sublime in the highest degree, thrilling and touching, yet to me it had one barb that pierced my inmost soul, and hath a sting that will reach the grave if it goes not beyond. He said "unless woman was pure and immaculate she was a curse to all who knew her." Now it is not my nature to console myself with the errors of others being a palliation for mine. How many, or how few will come up to this standard is not for me to decide but enough for my woe I know that I am not one. Then who can blame and reprove me when the tide of memory comes rushing in bearing the past, the present and future, when I see in perspective a long vista of years that must only be spent in grief over the past, and blushes for the slight and contempt that past but too justly merits. The past has now and will eternally alienate from me all those high and noble spirits with whom I could commune and from whose lips I could hear the sweet tones of affection, whose sympathies would be the sweetest cordial, whose appro-bation would be the noblest incentive to excite me to be in part at least the angelic wife or mother he so beautifully painted to day. True it is I now possess the friendship of one of the noblest spirits of earth, yet that friendship is not based upon my virtue and moral goodness and conse-quently I fear its superstructure is destined to fall, while my imperish-

able desire clings to the being who has saved me from the lowest degradation to feel at least that it were worth an age of sin an[d] guilt to know
he had pitied me if his kindlier feelings can go no farther. I would not be
a misanthrope nor is it in my nature to be, but I would Oh how gladly be
cut off from the world could I but feel and know that I possessed and deserved the portion of his esteem, society and respect, that my too affectionate nature demands. I would in his society, in his instruction, in his
admonitions and in a conginial soul find all the enjoyment that a mind
so organized as mine could desire, that is if it were my blest fate to be
able to [be] to him a sufficient companion. Lost and degraded as I am I
could not wish it in my power to select him as one to make me forget the
past. If so it would not be that I deemed him worse than others that he
should be *my* companion but that he was better, that he was the pinnacle
to which my feelings and hopes would ascend, that he alone was able to
fill the chaos of my mind. Could he look on me as Pygmalion on his own
creation and feel proud or even glad that such was I of his, how great a
charm would hallow the balance of my days. It would be a magic that
would obscure the past and I should count the past a blessing that it had
secured me such a friend. But these are phantasies and only add torture.

Mr C said women create their own sorrows, the greatest the world
knows. Did he know how bouyant my heart once was, did he know that if
sorrow fell on it twas but as a snow flake before the sun, did but see that
I was destined apparently to realize no sorrow, and then see how very
much I have been compelled to sip, did he see the disgrace that looms
over the path I am destined to tread through life, he would think others
had dug the grave in which hope and happiness lie buried and had created for me those sorrows that must end only in the grave that receives
the ill-fated victim. But amidst all there is a debt of gratitude I owe my
God and C. that shall never be paid with repining. I may feel and may
some times express a portion of those feelings but yet, perhaps it were
best there should be even that barrier, for situated as I am, blest with the
privileges I have, enjoying the favour of so noble a soul and then to feel
no blemish on my name as a draw back perhaps I should be too happy
for earth. God being my helper I intend to look forward more and back

less. I will strive to aim at high and noble ends that may be commenced
under all the censure of an ill judging world and under the painful reflections that they are merited and from which I may gain no credit but
which will end in *eternity.* I will strive to merit an increase, or at least retain that sympathy and feeling that snatched [me] from ruin deep and
awful. I will strive at least to be happy if I am deprived of the privilege
of imparting it to others. I will sit me down when others are whirling
in the dance or sporting in the gay crowd, when others are surrounded
with wit and brilliant talents, when others are listening to the cheerful
songs and merry laugh, when there is a thought and a word for all, when
there is an eye that dwells kindly on another in return. Then I will sit
me down and cast mine up to the starry vault and commune with them.
I will search into their mysteries and adore their Creator. I will think
of the day in the future when he who created them will not be ashamed
to call me his child whom the world blushes to see. I'll study upon his
exalted benevolence to me. I will then turn my mind to him who gave
me these glorious opportunities and I will think though no voice falls
on my ear, though no smile beams on me, yet there is a heart that is ever
bound to feel an interest in my happiness for he created it or pity for
my sorrows, for his noble soul would will it otherwise. My days can not
ever be encircled with the halo of purity for that is lost, but I hope they
will be in some degree of tranquility and happiness, for while he is my
friend here and God is above I am determined to make the best of the
free and bounding principle of life that he has implanted on my nature.

"Womans world is home": Mr C. He depicted the charms, the bliss,
the endearments of home, said there all the moral, social and even highly
intellectual virtues had their origin. My home was ever my delight even
when I was dependent on the fate of circumstances of the moment to
send me from one to another, when there were social spirits abroad to
visit, when my gay happy disposition made my company sought after,
when there had come no shade or shadows over the world to me. What
must it be now when I have one of my own, secured to me by the only
one I love on earth, that quadruples the value, when the world frowns
on me and shuns me, when I feel my isolation in the street and fol-

lows me even to the sacred church, when all are at liberty to frown on me, when the tongue of slander is buisy and the finger of scorn pointed how consoling to escape to my own home under whose roof it cannot be heard though the silent monitor within will never let it die. Yet it is a pure consolation to feel that at least on one little spot I can indulge in reflection and study without the comments of the world, and from the doors of which I cannot be turned when detraction fastens on my name and actions. Home is now to me the only temple I dare ever hope to find on earth. Here I can think, reflect, study, and adore, here sentiments, hopes and opinions present themselves that never could have been felt in the public walks of life. Here I can reflect upon that house that I shall one day have beyond those starry orbs I so much love to gaze on. Here I can see not the fashions, and toys of life, but the most beautiful part of Gods creation (the human form not excepted) the flower creation. Here I can, unannoyed by visitors or intruders, read and meditate, and last though far from least, I can think of, and bless the blest donor of all these gifts. When others are around him and the voice of love or friendship salutes his ear, when sycophants flatter, or pleasure fills up his hours, when buisness cares or scenes of amusement employ his time, yet there is a lone heart that will not be lonely for it beats for him the silent notes of untold gratitude. It cherishes his name and enshrines his memory in the deepest and deserted recesses of a well tried heart, and that heart knows no joy to which I cannot ascribe to him. Though mine is not the home of domestic social joy shared by parent, brother or sister yet it is one of happy seclusion and one I would not barter for all the pomp and eclat of fashionable life, were they in my grasp.

In speaking of woman as a Mother he used to me a new idea, that an angel before the throne would covet to become a Mother. He dwelt much on her responsibilities and privileges, such as securing a pure angelic spirit from its Makers hand, entrusted with its destiny that she could direct to Heaven or perdition. He spoke of the grief of a Mother and said truly it was something into which man could not enter into, and he seemed to realize that it was a grief that come[s] not within the bounds of mans conceptions and none but a Mother who has lost a darling child

that bound her to life knows it either. Then how truly and deeply have
I felt that untold sorrow. Four times has it been my lot to see the dear
idols of my heart torn from me by death, and though he did not name
it yet there is one grief that could be greater still. It would be to part
from a dear child on earth to see it no more, to hear and know that it
was training up in shame and infamy without the knowledge that it had
a mother whose heart strings were tearing asunder thinking of it. The
sermon was well calculated to lead the reflecting and prosperous part of
my sex to pause and see what progress these are making in the holy, the
sublime, the beautiful path of life. They should see many of them glorious opportunities passing away unimproved, while the time may come
they will look back and sigh for their loss; but it is to be feared the
greater portion heard it as a pretty sermon and a week hence will not
know two sentences in it. It is to be feared too many of those whose privileges are the greatest, have the least taste for research and study and are
content to while away their time with no book for a companion loftier
than a romance; who are blest with intellectual husbands, fathers, and
brothers whose delight it would be to impart knowledge and train their
thoughts, expand their minds did they but manifest the least disposition
to do so. I often wonder if such had only been my happy lot if I should
have so abused it too. It never was, and now it never can be, but still I
will not dispair for books I have and I will do my best to understand
and profit by them; but I often wonder at others who are blest with all
the acquisitions for improving their minds and who act as though they
were animals living by instinct and felt no wish to rise higher. It is a
mistaken idea in women that if they cannot possess talents and wit brilliant enough to make a great noise in the world that it is not worth while
to attempt to learn any thing more than their school-day studies. They
do not imagine that there is happiness arising in ones own breast. The
more knowledge enters there the greater it is. They cannot understand
by hearing others tell the pure delight if never told, yet felt, in reading
those lofty, sublime and intellectual authors that lie on their shelves un-
opened by them. They do not know how much vacuity of time as well

as mind can be filled up by them. They do not reflect that if they are unable to converse fluently yet they can *feel* in their own heart the force and beauties of such works and which would be worth more to a sound mind than all the empty nonsense and flattery of time. Great are my preveliges above many who would make a better use and greatful am I to him who has made it what it is, and it is my aim to do more to make myself a little deserving of his wishes toward the improvement of my mind, for it is the only way I can show him how much I realize his goodness.

April 28th 1844

Apr. 29. Finished C's vests, wrote a letter to my sister, set out some plants and sewed some seed.

Apr. 30. Made a bet with Dʳ R on the annexation of Texas; hope I'll win.

May 1. Dear C spent the evening with me. Afterwards I took a walk with Mr S and met him [Charley] and ———— [Mrs. Bradbury?] taking a walk.

May 2. An old Miss friend called on me.

Went to the City and learned of a certainty that I am in a certain situation. Divulged it to C; do not believe he likes it much.

Mr S sent me Miss Bremers last work the Sketches of every day life.[34]

May 3. C came to see [me] by sun rise which was to me a treat for two reasons. I am glad he has taken to rise early.

The Mississippian called to day and gave me a dress that he promised me a year ago.

May 4. Finished my work and went down in the City. Saw Dʳ R who will be up tuesday to satisfy my mind upon an important point.

See that Clay has taken sides against the Texas annexation and if his presidential election is lost I think it will be on that score.

C spent the evening with me. After he left I was in bed reading when some one knocked at the gate after 10 oclock and behold it was Henry Josephus. Read the Age and then left. Gave me a dollar pocket money. Very good in him.

Sun. May 5. Feel unusual bad this morning and shall not go to Church but will endeavour to make amends by reading and writing. Wrote three pages in my book of Miscellanies [Writing Book] and then bored to death with company: I wish persons would stay away on Sabbath. Read some in Miss Bremers last work. Took an evening promenad[e] with B. and S[ayre?], got some fruit and ice cream.

May 6. Read Mr Clays views upon the annexation of Texas, and cannot coincide with them, much fear his election that I so much wish, will be lost on the faith of these opinions. Mr C did not come to see me as he promised.

Night. C spent some time with me and brought me Van's letter against the Annexation.[35]

It is exceedingly warm and dry for we are surely going to have a drought.

May 7. Was exceedingly sick last night and all this morning. Oh! how I miss the attention of affection when I am sick. I must go to my sewing although I can hardly hold up my head.

May 8. Was so sick all day yesterday I did not sit up. Dear C came at night and nursed me so kindly, and this morning he was here by sun rise. He is so kind it is worth while to be sick. He sent the D^r to see me, who confirmed my hopes concerning my situation. C came to night and brought me a bottle of strawberries and one of Cologne. How dear he ever is. Mr S called to night and brought me a book. Have eat some of my berries and find them delicious.

May 9. The birth day of my beloved C.[36] He has just left after a mornings embrace from one who dearly loves him. May he live to see sixty more birth days.

Have read the Annexation treaty. The Presidents letter to the Senate, those of Calhoun, Upshur, Everett, Thompson, Henderson, &c &c all included in one paper. See also that Van Buren has taken the same stand that Clay has in the Annexation which will place him in the same or worse position as President than before.

Begin to fear I will loose my bet.

Went down in the City, Gave C a purse I knit for him. re[illegible]ed.

~~C. came to night and brought me a nice bottle of strawberries—~~
~~delicious.~~

The burning of the Ben Sherod in 1837, 175 lives lost.

On Charley's birthday Madaline entered an encomium to him in her Writing Book.[37]

May 9[th] 1844.

The natal day of my beloved C. God grant that he may live to see many, very many more, and may each returning one find him happier wiser and better and if the latter are attained the other will follow and a mind so constituted as his will ever be on the march.

When his next birth day comes the hand that now pens these lines and the heart that now burns with such affection for him may both be laid in the silent tomb. But if a departed one can see and be near a mortal here, he may feel that I am with him, although he will not sit by my side or receive a token of love yet if such should be permitted me, I will hover over him with love and awe. But again we may both see its return together and again be happy. May Heaven ever bless him.

Mad.

May 10. To day I painted a Coon tearing a cock to pieces which I saw heading the Virginia Whig success.[38]

Read a good deal in Miss Bremers Diary and sewed as unwell as I felt.[39] I am resolved to give up as little as possible while I am in my present situation for several reasons.

Night. The musketoes will eat me up so I will get under the bar and read.[40]

May 11. America discovered 1492.

Vegetation as well as animal life seems to flag and mourn during these hot dry days. My poor little garden sinks in the noon day sun but I refresh it at night with the watering pot. I have felt much depressed to day thinking on one thing. How hard it is to submit, where we are compelled to see another so happy by our misery.

I will see my dear C presently.

B and C have just left. The latter looked prettier than I ever saw him. Brought me papers.

Sun. May 12. Finished Miss Bremers last work the Diary &c. and although like it as to style yet think it inferiour as a work to her others. Had company until church time. Met C and Mrs B[radbury] at the Car and rode down and up with them. O if she could have read my heart jealousy would almost have given way to pity for me, but it is ever thus in my life. Heard Mr C preach upon the moral and religious character of Franklin, a beautiful discourse. Laid out an evenings reading but was deprived by company again. I wish to heaven I could be alone on Sabbath. I have had a long cry to night called up by one who meant not to wound me. O my poor heart.

May 13. Rose very unwell after my weeping. I wish I could in a measure quit this fault for it enfeebles both my body and mind and results in no good. Commenced reading Combe on man. Have resolved to read an hour every morning. Have done much sewing and watered my garden. When C came was very glad to see him to forget my tears.

B came and we read the papers and then I went to bed and he to see his Dulcina here.[41]

May 14. C came this morning before sun up we had a long talk. I then rode down in the City to do some business for an old friend. Oh how glad I am to get home to my own cool cottage where there is no noise or dust. Made four bits.

Dear C came to night and gave me his miniature. Oh how I prize it and it will be a source of comfort to me when he is gone as an image of his dear self.

Staid until 9 oclock.

May 15. To day C quits business with the Firm.

Oh I have spent a melancholy day. I cannot shake off this feeling that so haunts me and the nearer the departure of C approaches, the worse it gets.[42] I do not see how I can live under his absence. God knows my feelings and he alone. It is worse than death itself, but little does he realize the depth of my agony. Well he will be happy and I must endure.

S came to night but found me bad company. I refused to walk with him.

May 16. Still unhappy while nature looks so lovely this spring morning. I have just got some work to do for C and will try to shake off my misery in work. Last night I dreamed I saw a lovely infant boy of his and it was his image. I kissed it and loved it, but it was not mine. Saw C and B to night but was too unwell to enjoy their company as usual.

WC was here to day.[43] Is much displeased at my situation. Don't care one farthing for that.

May 17. The moon has changed and yet there is but little appearance of rain. Oh for a shower.

Feel very unwell to day but I will to my work and wear it off.

May 18. I did a hard days work to day but felt the inward joy of meeting C at evening and having much pleasure. But he came and saw S here which gave the conversation a turn that led to an evening of misery for me. I wept until my heart is nearly broken, for it was upon a most tender point and one on which I can bear but little to be said and my situation demands quiet if I could have it. He did not intend to wound me but an unguarded word did it all. Oh God knows what is in the future for me.

A great fire to day which desolated 300 families.[44] Oh how blest are we who did not suffer.

Sun. May 19. Feel wretched this morning after my agony of mind, indeed it preys upon me so that I feel but little able to go to Church to day. 3 oclock. Heard Mr Clapp preach to day upon the duty of man towards woman. He spoke beautifully and feelingly and when he portrayed the character of the seducer and his victim the tears unbidden fell from my eyes and I would have given much to have been alone to give them vent for my heart felt as if it would burst.

A subscription taken up for the sufferers by the fire yesterday.

Edwards reacted to "Man" much differently than she had to "Woman." Sitting across the Strangers' Church from Charles and Mary Ann Bradbury as Clapp preached, she realized that her future was founded on an impossible contradiction: Charley could be true to her only to the degree that he be-

*trayed his wife. If Clapp's sermon were too effective, her lover might throw
her over. Overcome by despair, she burst into tears in the middle of church.*[45]

Man

Heard Mr Clapp preach upon the duties of man towards woman. He
spoke forcibly up [of] the early and pure offering of love from man to
woman and when that love became desecrated that man was no longer
worthy of the name of man. He dwelt on the ruin of young men who
came to this metropolis and for the want of social pleasant families to
pass their evenings with were drawn into the vortex of disapation and
licenciousness and ended in ruin by the illicit connexion with woman.
He then discussed the distrust of the seducer. He said and truly too that
the midnight assassin was far better, that woman was never approached
but by stratagem, that man plighted his love and obtained hers in return
for his duplicity and with it her full unbounded confidence and when
that was gained his mark was carried. She was cast upon the world heart
broken and deserted by all who once knew and loved her. Oh my God
my tears told to more than one close by me that I was such a victim. I
felt as if my heart would burst. A whirl of reflection came crowding on
my mind. I felt as if the finger of the whol[e] world was pointed at me. I
felt that nothing but death could ever wipe out the misery of my life. I
felt that all those holy and exalted affections he spoke of were lost to one
who knew their force so well. I felt as one who is doomed to stand on
a bleak and lonely island surrounded by the Ocean of degradation and
witness at a distance happiness, innocence and purity that I dare not approach, while the natural essence of those qualities were as warm in my
breast as others, but one step has lost all the bliss attendant on them. I
felt if the seducer feels half as much as his victim he is well punished. I
do not believe it was good for me to have heard that sermon for I have
been striving to forget as far as consistent to blot out from my feelings
my degradation for several reasons. It keeps my mind under such sub-
jection that it is unfit for higher duties. I am aware that I am isolated
from that portion of the world with whom I could mingle and exchange
sentiments and social qualities, hence I am dependent on my own mind

to fill up this vacuum, and while I am daily weeping and sighing over the past which darkens the present and will overshadow the grave (but I trus[t] will not enter into which I hope to enter) I am totally unfit for any improvement that is so essential to one so constituted. I am debared the society almost entirely of the only one on earth who does not think his time mispent in trying to improve my mind, from him I could learn, and learn to forget much of my bitter grief. But as his society is denied me I must seek wisdom and improvement from books and Nature hence it befits me to cast aside as much as I can the grief that preys upon my mind that my mental aspirations could soon be destroyed did I do nothing to disapate them. I am convinced I am ruined here and that I must seek a home in another country far from this and there is no surer mode of reaching it than by knowledge. Another reason why I had rather not have heard it is that the one whose happiness is more to me than gold or honours, I fear upbraids him self for the manner in which we stand to each other. I fear from his soul he wishes to place me in another position to him than the one in which I stand, that he thinks I am the cause of all he can reproach himself for as husband or moralist, that he feels I am bound to be a source of self condemnation to him and that he can not be happy under these reflections. I went to church with my mind much harrassed and feelings depressed from a conversation we held last evening and this sermon has sat me almost frantic. I watched his countenance and saw it change. Oh how I prayed for power to read his inmost soul then I could have seen if it was his goodness, his benevolence that prevents his wounding my lacerated feelings more deeply by telling me his wishes and hopes. He knows he is the only tie that binds [me] to life and he fears no doubt if he discovered his will to me that it might plunge me into misfortunes deeper than those from which he rescued me. Therefore he will endure much before he will tell me. God knows I do not wish to cause his grief or remorse and if he will say such is the case I can sacrifice the only hope on earth for his peace, but I must away from this, for live near him I could not. I hope I misjudge his wishes and views, but yet I fear that sermon will place him on a stand with his own mind, and although good and sublime yet it were better for me not to

have heard it, for God placed us here to be happy and if we have thrown
away the chance once, it does not follow that I should sit down and weep
until death take me hence. No, it is more befitting to do all I can to
forget the past myself (for others never will) and strive to be cheerful
and happy as I can and the only earthly incentive to this is the wish of
him who first cast a ray of hope into my desolate heart. I know it is his
desire to see me happy and to improve my mind and it is not from duty
alone I would do this but the pure affection, therefore it were best for a
time that I heard no such desponding discourses at least to those who
merit his remarks. There is no danger of my ever forgetting what I am
nor all my errors, but it is highly essential to dispel the influence [of]
that memory when it destroys all my energies and faculties. He spoke
of mans duties as a husband and it was there I fear C blamed me for
his only deviation from those duties the world calls binding, although
he discharges all duties as husband that relates to a wifes happiness. I
cannot write, tears fall so fast and my mind is almost destroyed and I
feel self condemned because I am not more resigned and govern myself
better for I have so much to be greatful for that [it] is a desecration to Cs
friendship and Gods goodness to weep so much and weaken my mind
that must sustain or fall with me still lower, but yet *feeling* will predomi-
nate over reason. Oh C could you feel for one moment the depth of my
sorrow you would not blame me as much as you do, but yet I would not
have it so for [the] world. I cannot read over this scroll for I have but
one idea the last 36 hours and that is grief, grief. Oh when will this end.
What would I not give now for one soothing word or kind assurance that
my tears and fears are groundless on his part. O my poor torn heart.

19th May 1844

May 20. Have felt gloomy all day but C came to night and partly dis-
apated it. He has brought me the copy of the Act for this property, and
the third No of the Pic Bible.[46] To day we had a refreshing shower which
revives every thing in shape of vegetation. To night the neighbor over
the way watches the corpse of Mr F. I trust his soul is gone to a better
home, but I feel for his poor wife and little orphan.

Columbus died in 1506.

May 21. This morning early C was here and spent some time with me and while here it began to rain and we have been blest with a beautiful shower. I wonder why Josephus dont come to see me? I fear I have made him mad. If so I did not wish it.

With domestic duties, sewing and reading I have ended this day.

Each day brings nearer my loss of Cs company for he will soon leave for the East. Oh God alone sees my misery at the thought.

Sad night C did not come.

Lafayette died in 1834.

May 22. B came this morning before sun rise quite unexpected. Told him a secret and find he is not so well pleased at it. Dear C came early this evening and I have passed one more happy afternoon with him. I am now on bed under the bar to get away from the musketoes. Oh what an annoyance. Some of my cousins came while C was here and I did not speak to them for I did not go to the gate. The starry heavens are so lovely to night I wished to gaze on them long but musketos makes me forget Astronomy or even *Philosophy.*

May 23. Last night I wrote four pages in my journal in bed. To day JC my old cousin that called here yesterday came; he said but little to me.

Read in Combe and finished C pants.

C brought me a pair of black pants to make and I see too many preparations making to go North. It is more than I dare think of.

Had another lovely shower to day. No complaint of dust now.

May 24. I cut down the weeds to make a path for C to come to see me.

I have finished my morning task and now I believe I will go down in the City for a walk for my life is getting too sedentary.

Just got home through the mud. The rain kept me in the City three hours. While down I went to see the destruction of the late fire and is very extensive. Saw the commissioners getting provisions to those who suffered by the fire. May the Lord help them. Oh how sweet it is to get home. Dear C spent the whole afternoon with me, how happy I was.

May 24th 1819. Victoria born.

May 25. I was quite sick last night and never waked in more agony than I have to day but thank God it was no worse. I have laid aside domestic cares and taken to myself this piece of day.

I look for Dear C this evening I hope he will not disappoint me.

Dear C came early and brought me some papers &c spent one more happy afternoon with him, he will soon leave and then farewell pleasure for me.

He gave me his phrenological chart and I find he possesses the highest order of faculties and propensities which he truly merits.

Sun. May 26. Not well but yet I must venture to Church.

I just got home. Rode down with C and his wife. We had a hard rain during service, and the sacrament detained a number who were caught in the last shower. I was in the car and went to Lafayette and back. Got my shoes spoilt but I think the Sermon was worth the shoes. Thought to spend a happy afternoon alone with my books but was sadly disappointed for I had company all evening and now it is night. I wish people would stay away on Sunday.

May 27. Another heavy shower this morning which will prevent C from coming as he promised. I have read a chapter in Combe and now I must make a pair of pants for C.

Dear C came at 11 and staid until 3. I passed those hours very happily indeed. He presented me with a plain gold ring which he put on my finger and I intend it to remain there until my death.

Mr S came in the evening and while here it rained in torrents.

May 28. I looked for C all day but it has rained with but little intermission. I become more and more interested in Combe the farther I advance. Have read a good deal to day and sewed more.

Night. Dear C has just left, and I felt much like weeping to night during our conversation, but for once reason came to my assistance. May God ever bless him.

The President has sent another message into the Senate. It is time we had the news on the annexation question.

May 29. It has rained a perfect flood this morning, but cleared away and my dear C came and staid until 2 oclock with me. I am sure I passed it very happily. I had two visitors this evening who had as well not have taken the trouble to come. I think one of them will not call again.

Oh what a lovely moon light night. How I should enjoy to have C here to admire with me those banks and mountains of beautiful clouds that are now passing over the Goddess of Night.

May 30. I worked my dear flowers this morning after so much rain, then I white washed the out side of my lot and then went to do a days work at sewing, for I hope C will come this evening and I know I will not work while he is here.

Had another at least one who was here yesterday to call again to day. I think he will believe by this time that I possess some firmness.

Pope died in 1744.

C and B came to see me to night. B has the blues. I wish he would shake them off forever.

May 31. Voltaire died in 1778.

The moon fulls this evening, and we have now most lovely weather.

Went down in the City this evening.[47] C was my ladies-maid for he spent the whole morning with me and dressed me for a walk.

The moon eclipses invisible here.

Night. Felt very tired after my preambulation. Had sat me down to reflect upon the exquisite pleasures of home, and my many blessings, with my ingratitude for them, when I saw some one at the gate and it proved to be dear C. He came with a scrap book for me and I will endeavour to make it an object of interest to him in a future day as well as present pleasure to myself.

CHAPTER THREE

A Cup of Sorrow

ike many other middle- and upper-class New Orleanians, Charles Bradbury preferred to leave the city in the summer and early autumn to escape the heat and the deadly yellow fever epidemics. In the summer of 1844 he made a four-month trip north, presumably to visit his family in Ohio and New York State. It was the first separation for the lovers. Bradbury's silence during his long journey was a bitter blow to Edwards, who struggled to retain her faith in his character and good intentions. The withdrawal of his economic support was a painful reminder of her financial dependence.

Saturday, June 1, 1844. Have felt very unwell today indeed and made me some plum pies for I knew my C would be here to eat some.

PM. C came and staid until three. Oh such days passed with him can never be forgotten. Now he is gone I will go to my work with renewed pleasure.

Night 9 oclock. Dear C came again and took a walk with me. It was pleasant to lean on his arm and look at the beautiful full moon, the majestic steam boat and Car. It was solemn to stand by the grave yard with the conviction that we soon parted perhaps to meet no more. Ah he did not read my heart.

Sun. June 2. I have read my usual portion in Combe this morning, and although I feel very unwell will try and attend church for there will be a powerful sermon to day on Mr [Thomas] Paine. Heard Mr C give a most perfect picture of Mr Pains character and reverted to historical facts to shew what he was. He spoke beautiful of Washington whom P so traduced. I have wept and wrote alternately ever since I returned from Church for C is to leave this week and I cannot command my feelings. I have but *one* friend on earth and it is death to loose sight of him. May God protect him.

June 3. Read The Comfiter said to be by Miss Bremer but I do not think so although it is an excellent little work.[1] Dear C spent four hours with me to day and we had some serious talk before he leaves. Oh he little imagines my feelings, but still I feel that he pities me and that is some comfort.

C came to night and it proves I am *excellent* company for he nodded and dreamed he was in England hearing a discourse on slavery. He has gone and I will go to bed.

Finished Combe's moral Philosophy to day.

June 4. I have worked immoderately hard this morning and had just taken a bath and sat down to read some before I went to sewing, when I was aroused by a drayman who had brought me a nice wire safe, a half barrel of flour and three nice hams, a present from Dear C who is the giver of all my joys as well as comforts and luxuries: Oh that I could do something in return for his unbounded goodness. C spent a part of this day with me. Oh how kind he is in trying to mitigate my sorrow at his departure. He brought me some luxuries as well as other things. God ever bless him.

June 5. Dear C spent near half of this day with me and although I was not well yet I enjoy so much to have him near me. We read some and talked more for his conversations are always improving.

Night. I took a walk this evening since the rain in a direction I never was before and came home quite well.

June 6. C came and brought me a letter from my niece, one whom I have ever loved from the moment she came into this world that then presented to me a bright future, but ah! little does she know the sad life

I have led and I hope never will. Dear girl, may her path through life
be as bright as mine has been dark. He also brought me some periodicals—dear attentive one! Mr S came this evening and brought me the
published accounts of the Morton seduction of this place in 1840.[2] He
read the whole afternoon and I will now finish it.

June 7. Last night I finished the seduction document and it has added
another conviction to my mind of mans duplicity and woman's capa-
bility of becoming more than a monster! Poor ill-fated girl might never
have met the doom she did had it not have been for one of the basest of
her sex. I cannot put it out of mind. Hers was a case that called loudly for
sympathy and forgiveness for she was but a child of fifteen, not so mine.
The reading or hearing of such men makes me hug to my heart the name
of the man who is my only friend and see in him a paragon of his sex.

June 8. C spent the best part of to day with me. Brought me some
papers. See that Mr Polk of Tenn is nominated by the Dem° convention
for President: quite a new wonder.

I went down in the City this afternoon and returned in the Car. C
came and just as he was leaving B came but did not stay long.

I feel too tired to read much to night, however will read the days
paper C brought me.

Sun. June 9. Last night I read an attack upon Mr C for his remarks
against Tom Paine. The writer has done himself but little credit either in
composition or sentiments. In the same paper was a reply from Mr B. in
which he did himself credit in defending that great pillar of Religion and
virtue, however all that a host can write against him will fall as a feather
before him. Heard Mr C preach upon the impropriety of attempting to
put down the violation of the Sabbath by civil authority. It was an excellent address and well demonstrated by ancient as well as modern history.

Mr S[ayre] sat an hour or two with me this evening.

June 10. Dear C came this forenoon and staid till three. He was as dull
as could be; laid down and slept. After he left a female friend came and
spent the evening and John H called to see me but I dismissed him in a
trice for I wish no more male or indeed female visitors.

C came to night and staid till nine. Brought me a valuable present, a set of coloured crayons, 12 doz; he gave $10 for them. Oh! how kind and indulgent he is to me. And still before he left one little question caused me intense pain. I do not rightly understand the heart of dear C.

June 11. C came to day and tells me he will leave tomorrow. Oh my God what have I not endured this day. I have wept until my brain is on fire. I could not have lived another hour under such feelings and then the bitter morrow comes. Why do I love so blindly? God will punish me for all this idolatry.

Wrote to Pa.

June 12. C did not get off to day but came to see me. We talked of his departure. After he left I was taken sick and do not feel able to sit up but a few minutes longer.

June 13. Oh! God even now the echo of the boat is sounding in my ears that bears all the earth holds dear to me away. We have parted it may be forever. As sick as I was all day my tears fell in torrents for hours. Little can mortal mind tell my suffering. All is gloom to me and I am quite sick indeed; have sent for D^r R but fear he will not come. C brought me a letter from my poor sister which adds another sorrow to my many to hear of her situation and health.

O my poor heart.

June 14. D^{oct} R came last night, found me so much better in the calm that had succeeded the outburst of feeling that he did not prescribe any thing, but urged me to get a servant to avoid exposure as he was afraid the exertions of domestic concerns might endanger the object I so much desire, but I trust not. I feel mournful as the hours approach and pass of the visits of dear C. but yet nature has wisely ordained a reaction in the mind as well as externals. Yet in this reaction I do not deplore his loss less but trust I will use philosophy to bear it better. God bless him on his journey.

June 15. Mr S came to see me last evening and gave me the most beautiful grand Duke I ever beheld.

I have thought of dear C incessantly, yet I have to day so blended his memory with my books as to make it pleasant instead of painful. Josephus came to see me to night. He begged me not to pine so much after

C but to bear his absence with fortitude. Told me he knew no woman who had more reason, and to use it, but he is sadly mistaken. I have but little where affection is concerned, except for a child.

Departure[3]

What a state of mental agony has my mind been in for many days? I witnessed the preparations and heard the daily notices of the departure of the only being on earth my friend and the only one I love! Yes dear C left yesterday for the West, from there East. To picture the avalanche of intense suffering and tears that gushed from my inmost soul would be useless were it possible. For the sake of his philosophical approbation I would have exhibited less, were it in my nature to do so. But who can tell my feelings or blame them could they realize that he is all the world to me, that I am now at the most poignant term of a critical period in life which so closely connects my every thought and action with him. . . .

There is one hour in which I shall miss him most, it is when my task for the day has ended and I sit down in his rocking chair on the gallery in the same spot he used to sit every night; when I sit down there and cast my eyes up to the bright [moon] about which we so often conversed, when the bright moon sheds her rays on my lovely flowers and imparts her soothing influence to my spirit, Oh! then I will think of him and sigh for the hours that have passed. I feel it a duty I owe my God, my C myself and his unborn to destroy my mental faculties and energies as little as it is possible to do, but my own resolutions are too weak, and ere another page is written I may be giving vent to a violent flood of tears; but I will pray that he who can give strength to the weak and joy to the sad will assist my endeavours. I dare not hope to see him under three months or more and it does appear an eternity to me. May God bless him on his journey

June 15 th 1844.

Sun. June 16. Feel quite unwell, have read my usual portion in Combe. PM. Heard Mr C preach upon the good the belief of a final redemption after death was calculated to do in this life, and the absurdity of the opposite belief. He proved to every mind that was not deeply prejudiced that the former belief was the only one calculated to give any pleasure in this life and leads the mind above the *fear* of death and *Hell* fire.

Mr S spent the afternoon with me.

June 17. Have had a day of excitement with company and work. Mrs C. spent the day with me and my usual reading was neglected. How I dislike to omit it.

Bought half cord of wood to day, gave $2.

See the new moon to night. Looked long at it and Venus and wondered if my beloved C was looking at them as he promised me, and think[ing] of me. Oh how slow time flies now he is gone.

I hear the Treaty for annexation of Texas has been rejected by the Senate.

June 18. Have had a tremendous shower to day. I have worked very hard but there is one face ever present to my mind though far away that lightens toil but not my heart. I have read but little to day but now I am going to enjoy one glorious evening reading.

June 19. There has been another deluge to day. Have had my washing and ironing finished at last, but had to work hard at it myself. I am without any change to get a thing I need and B promised to bring me some for a $5 bill, but he does not come near me. Ah well I feel the loss of C in every respect, I am so unwell I cannot go down in the City myself.

Night. Oh how tired I am and sick too. I must go to bed.

June 20. This day week C left. Oh! it surely is a month. I am in such pain I can scarce hold my pen. No one comes near me.

Felt better this afternoon and rode up in the Lafayette Car to do some shopping for an old negro.

Night. O Venus if you could only tell C how anxiously I gaze on thee ever[y] night hoping he too has not forgotten his promise and tell him my heart aches then he would feel how sad I am when he is gone. Finished Combes moral philosophy.

June 21. Last night as I sat in C's chair rocking I thought how unusual in this climate that it ever rained in the night in this month. About midnight I was awoke by a fine shower. Then I went to sleep and Oh! such a dream I had of dear C. That beautiful river and magnificent brick house we saw and admired together then the after scene, but it ended in a miff on my part at a word he said.

Went to the PO got a letter from Pa with $10 for my sister and a prayer for myself because I am enciente, well so be it. Got home exceedingly tired.

June 22. Have to day made an attempt at a piece of painting I hope will succeed for I wish to give C some pleasure when he comes. I have felt to day like my heart will break. Thinking of C I have stifled my tears until I feel I cannot do it much longer. Oh! none but my God knows how I feel his loss. B does not come to see me atal and I have not a friend in the City. I have strove with my flowers books and painting to forget sorrow to day but I cannot.

I've sat and looked at Venus and thought of C and our promise until my heart is ready to burst.

Sun. June 23. I feel too unwell to attend church but have collected my books, papers and ink and got under my musketoe house with a heart so full that I promise myself but little of the much I wish to execute to day. Wrote two long letters to my Sister and her daughter. MC spent a few hours here to day.

Night. Have just got rid of my last visitors and am heartily glad now I can read as I wish. I do not see through the friendship of B. He does not care one straw for me. Oh! how sadly do I realize that I have but *one* friend on earth. God grant him a quick return to one who loves him more than life. He surely will write to me this day. How anxious I am to see a letter from him.

June 24. Rode down in the City to arrange some things to send to my poor sister. Got home just in time to avoid a hard rain. Have wrote and read some, but feel very, very sad. O Lord how can I live until C returns? A week is now a year. My poor heart aches this day. I have no one to care for me now. I never get a paper, an orange or any thing now dear C is gone and I am afraid to spend my money only for necessities for if I get out there is not one I will call on if I suffer.

June 25. I have been trying my new crayons to day. Painted until

4 oclock then read Combe until night. B came at last to see me, has brought me some papers; he has just left. We talked of my beloved C and I wished I knew where he was. He asked me if I would be jealous if I knew he was kissing some other woman. I told him if I saw it, I should assuredly cry. O how I want to see him it appears that I cannot wait his return

I must read my papers and go to sleep and forget my anxiety in slumber.

Old Dan has gone up to my sisters and took my letters. How I wish I could see them as soon as he will.

June 26. Have began my scrap book C bought me before he left. Have put all the pieces in that I have collected. Have selected all the scraps he gave me and arranged them by themselves.

Night. I feel unusually tired and do not expect to be able to read as much as I hoped to have done.

Nine oclock and half past have written a long piece in my miscellaneous book and now for sleep and dreams of C.

Edwards's writing books contain many sentimental-religious nature essays. "Flowers," a typical example, is a personalized exploration of conventional "feminine" subject matter and gender roles. Edwards assigns characters to many of the plants that grow in her own garden and departs from convention to tell us something, as well, of her girlhood and her introduction to painting.[4]

Flowers.

I have often thought I would dedicate one page in these miscellanies to my little blooming parterre; and now as I sit by the window, inhaling their fragrance heightened by the softly descending shower, now that I am enveloped in my musketoe house with not an intruder near, with their glorious beauties before my eyes whenever I lift them from the pen; now I will try and rescue their memory from the grave to which they are hourly falling. Would that I was competent to pay them a just tribute. Of all the beauties that God ever presented us with there is nothing to compare to the flower creation. To one who is not an observer of their fragile loveliness the idea may seem preposterous and they will tell of the human countenance exceeding all of Gods works. I admit it is often beautiful but sin is not stamped on a single flower that blooms. They tell of purity, they force the beholder to wonder and admire if he does not love; they carry home to the thoughtless heart associations they may never utter, but they are felt. They tell of youth beauty and smiles linked with death and decay. They tell of a garden where there existence will be as eternal as the God who created them, for I am convinced there are flowers in that bright, glorious and eternal dwelling of the Eternal. They speak of the wisdom, skill, goodness, power and condescenscion of their maker. Yes condescend he did when he had created the mighty planets, satillites and comets that fill eternal space, when he had created this globe with its mighty seas and rivers, its majestic mounts and sublime volcanoes, when he had reared the towering oak and thousand rooted Banyan, when he had formed the Whale and Mastadon, when he had called forth the Sun, Moon and stars to shine on them. It is a droll idea but I can't help thinking after he created all these things and formed Adam to rule over them, that he had not given him the flowers, but after he gave Eve unto Adam he saw the man was an emblem of the oak and he then gave Eve her beautiful task of tending the flowers in Eden. I think he condescended for the pleasure of the first Mother to stoop from his mighty works to form the modest violet and the humble snow drop, and in this condescension displayed more skill than in the works of hands before. If Eve could not see perhaps she could smell, but perhaps they were not given her till after the fall that she might gaze on the emblem of the purity she had lost, and that she should feel that loss the more as she turned from that beautiful Eden. Be that as it may there is nothing half so lovely in nature, there is nothing comes nearer baffling the skill of man in his attemp[t]s to copy the works of the Deity, their very fragility constitutes its greatest charm. Look at the colour, the texture, the form, the shades, the variagations, and then inhale their fragrance. Oh there is something so holy, so pure, so *passion destroying* about the odour of some flowers that I have thought it could make his

Satanic Majesty itself weep for the heaven he lost. There is that about others that thrill the nerves as it were with aspirations and hopes that scenes, lectures nor books ever call forth. There are others that sweep over the soul with the mournful associations that must be linked with the notes of the Aolean harp. I have had joys and sorrows that had long been buried in the Ocean tide of memory to gush forth with swelling emotions as a peculiar odour met my olfactories and I have suddenly stopped and wondered if some magic was not afloat. I sometimes sit and look at a garden and in my imagination form a miniature world with its emblems. I call the towering dahlia, sun flower, crown imperial, &c. those bombastic, haughty spirits who look down upon the less elevated as inferiour and contemptible. I call the poppy an egotist, who sees nothing beautiful but in his own red coat. I call the rose the prosperous happy, benevolent and amiable matron who is concious of her worth but not envious and feels assured the multitude will award her all her due. I call the Jasmine and pink the emblem of a pure, benevolent heart who seeks to impart those blessings to others. I call the violet as it is ever called the emblem of modest retiracy. I call the marygold and touch me not the emblem of those who seek to please only by pretty faces or fine clothes. I call the night jassamine and gra[n]d dukes the emblem of him who gave me the pleasure of ever calling any of them. I call them the fit emblem of him who confines not his goodness of heart and benevolent purpose at home but flings them out abroad, that all within their reach may feel their influence and as their fragrance lulls the very soul to quiet so does his kindness win upon the sorrowful heart and soothes it to rest. Oh while life lasts there will be his name associated with these flowers calling up pleasing recollections, and I will ever adore them because he is so fond of them and because they are emblematic of him. They do not choose to cast their sweets upon every passing gale or in every sweeping wind, but wait the calm still hour of twilight to send forth their treasures, feeling they will be better appreciated than in the glare of day, and when gayer colours met the eye so with his acts. They are never intended for applause or show, but in the quiet of soul they are done and blest with the silent tears of gratitude as the dew falls upon his emblem.

I look at the vine clinging and twining around some supporting wall, post or tree and I think of woman as she should be, clinging to the one she loves so devotedly that she can not be severed from him without robbing her heart of half its life that she is not tied and bound by twine or thread of force but clings and grows spontaneously, that she feels he is superiour in strength, courage and power, while her tender tendrils of affection, prudence and devotion are strong enough to bind him fast, while he feels it a joy and not a burden to support the one that clings so fondly to him. I see a moral in every flower, shrub or vine and though in imagination I may have pictured some of them like some people with virtues or vices yet I look on them all as perfect though some are bound to please the eye or smell more than others. Yet in our ignorance of their properties we may err towards them as we do our fellow beings when we judge entirely by externals, for they may possess medicinal virtues that would far counterbalance the fine dress of the tulip or the scent of the rose. There is not one but possesses beauty so absorbing that in closely examining them I become perfectly absorbed and the impious wish has often arisen to become a humming bird that I might live on their sweets, but an insect or any other creature than human cannot possess ideality and hence there would be no pleasure but that arising from appetite. I look at them as they stand and I think the world might read from these speechless monitors an exhortation, to make no vain strivings after higher honours than their sphere in life will permit. As well might the violet or crocus swell, and puff to attain the dahlias height as for some men to become politicians or statesmen. Not but it is laudable to be emulous with proper motives, and we have seen some of the brightest stars, arise out of the deepest obscurity, yet I do not call to mind one great mind on the page of history that arose from the humble lot of the violet upon the same principles that would excite it to become a dahlia, but they have uniformly been men of purer principles, and sounder morals than to seek their sole pleasure in the worlds applause. Oh ye bright-frail but beautiful emblems of mortality, how much could be learned by perusing your divinity-penned lines. I have loved ye from my earliest infancy, I have nursed and treasured you in the days of my girlhood whose frail joys but typefied yourselves. I have planted ye over the tombs of those buds that withered ere the chrysalis of the bloom began to unfold, and have returned to those graves and culled ye as mementoes. While your wafted odours told of hopes and reunions beyond the grave, yet the thorns told of those that had peirced a Mothers heart. But though that heart had scarce tasted of sorrows of which it has since drank so deeply yet it felt, and now doubly feels that those buds withered in the bloom will be presented to me full blown on the other side of Mortality. I have oft gathered ye in my lap, and sat down to recall the joys ye had witnessed, the lisping words ye had heard, the departures ye had witnessed more than once of all so dear that in their loss your own loveliness was no longer felt. I have been tossed upon the billows of misery and shame until I have felt it was a profanation to touch you or inhale your fragrance. I have ever held ye so pure that I deemed a sacrilege to virtue to breathe upon you the breath of shame, and I have turned away and wept for the associations ye called up. I thought of the pure joys ye had witnessed as mine in connexion with yourselves and I felt though you frowned not, or mocked as my fellow worm, yet there was contamination in my very touch. Oh could you tell the scenes ye have been witness to, in this poor heart, it would be more than my pen is able. I have accepted ye as tokens, recd ye with a smile while the worm that curled in your bud concealed, was but an emblem of the canker in my own heart. The first time ye were ever presented to me by the hand of him who has placed it in my power thus to record the fact, I received you as an evidence that he thought of me when out of sight and felt a presentiment that they might please me and therefore gave them. I received ye, and could he have torn away the veil that conceals from human eyes that which God has reserved to himself the right to see, he would have pitied the forced smile that accepted ye. Often after did we caress and admire the beauties and sweets of flowers together, when I longed to unbosom my heart to him that he might see how unworthy I felt to desecrate such purity. But it is surely in thought alone that the whitest snow drop can become tarnished or robbed of its innocence more in one hand than another; but so it was. I could almost have wished not to have beheld another flower in the life I was then leading, and yet they have ever been to me one of the few things on earth that I have loved from first to last. They have ever forcibly spoke to me of brighter worlds, and higher destinies. They have often resigned me to the fate of my early lost children, when I see the beauteous bud in the morning lie scattered at noon on the cold damp earth. I think if beauties such as these must fall, and Holy Writ tells us that God cares for the smallest of them, I think with joy it were better they too should have fallen in the tender bloom of the rose than to have braved the tempest storm of the oak and fallen with sorrows and blight upon their hearts; and I say to my maternal heart, be still! for the death bed of the violet and rose is but the grave of my children and they are now blooming where they will fall no more. If there is any one of Gods works I have [hold] more my Deity than himself it has been flowers. From my first recollections it was so and I feel it innate, not acquired. So great was my anxiety to retain them that when I had procured a selection and placed them in water, returning each hour or moment to look at them, when I perceived decay stealing on I have wept because they would not last, and in my childish heart I thought it perversity in them. When a little school girl so eager was I to imitate them, knowing nothing from even seeing painting that I would select flowers and leaves of different colours, to extract their juice and draw imitations with a pen and paint them the best I could. In more advanced years when my Uncle took me from school in my 14.th year, having given me the rudiments of an english education I could not hush the desire of my soul nor allay the thirst to become a painter. There was a lady then teaching school in the village near the uncles with whom I lived who excelled in water colours. To her I addressed a note begging her to accept my services as an assistant to enable me to take lessons from her in painting. She although a stranger appreciated my ambition and accepted me. In a few lessons I became enraptured and so did she with my proficiency. I took lessons only on Saturdays. After two ses- sions I left with the satisfaction of hearing her say I had acquired more than any pupil she had ever had twice the time. This art then opened up a new source of admiration and pleasure that was not only connected with flowers, but all the beautiful in nature and to that piece of timely perseverance I have been indebted to very many of the hours of pure enjoyment that have occasionally brightened my path in life. Had it not have been for the paint brush I really do not [know] how I could have lived under some weeks I have passed in life. When domestic cares have allowed it books have been one of my blest enjoyments but since the flowers of Maternal love have been laid in the tomb, woes and agonies have arisen that books nor intreaties could allay. I have tried the pen, the needle, the book, the voice of friendship and all but bade my feelings gush the freer. I have taken up the paint brush and inadvertently was drawn away into the dream of the beautiful until I became myself again. There is something so soothing and calm, at times so enrapturing in the little knowledge I possess of the art that I would give worlds to be a true artist. If envy found a place in my heart it was towards the arts, and to my passion for flowers I attribute this source of lasting enjoyment, for unlike too many of my sex when leaving the school room I did not abandon it but have pursued it the more intensely when outward circumstances did not control the current of my ambition. For awhile I did not touch the brush for all my earthly hopes I deemed at an end. I met one who proffered to teach me a new style. The passion I thought dormant was quickly aroused and I soon made myself mistress of his style, but succeeding events would forever have debared my enjoying the advantages if it had not have been for the glorious privilege of meeting the one, the only friend I ever have found. To him I am indebted for an additional advance in the art and for all the privileges of practice and improvement as well as for all I enjoy beneath the sun. To him I owe the rapturous enjoyment of now sitting here quietly with the vines bending to my very window, with the flowers before my eyes with enjoyments on every hand that I do not merit and placing me as he has, has now given me more reliance on the feelings that were never corrupted and I begin again to caress and venerate the beauteous flower creation that has given me so much pleasure in life and been linked with so much pain. I have loved them in life, and in death it will be joyous to be in the open woods where they can waft their odours, and it is pleasant in health to hope when this hand lies palsied in the coffin that there is one hand on earth that will lay the flowers on my tomb, and his heart will ever associate my name with the love of flowers. Not that my innocence or goodness will tell forth the association, but he can enter into my fondness for them.

There is something so sweet, so touching so dilecate and enchanting about the name of *blossom,* that I have ever wished the more practical name of flower was less in vogue. I always think of the dear little bee, humming bird and butterfly when I hear blossom mentioned. I would not be thought to have associated the dear flowers with the passions or follies of men for their purity may call up thoughts not connected with themselves, for all of them from the greatest to the least are exquisite and lovely; and in my heart their loveliness are felt but my pen is not able to pay the merit of that loveliness. I have often wondered how it is that the rude winds can toss these frailest blossoms about with apparent rudeness; how the pelting storm that mortals shun can beat and rage around, how the scorching sun will beam upon, whose rays are too intense for man, and how the birds butterflies and bees can light upon these tender petals and yet all pass away and they remain the same, but our hands may touch them with much less force and we often destroy or tarnish some of its exquisite properties as the touch robs the butterfly of its silky down. Great in benevolence indeed was our Creator when he filled the earth with such care solacing beauties in this life and evidences of a brighter world where they will no more pass away from us. It may be profanity to think God cannot make Heaven as it is with or without flowers but I have ever been led to feel there could not be a place of perfect bliss without them and I have taxed my powers of imagination to think of new wonders in their department when we are ushered into the presence of the Eternal. Would I could write of them as I feel towards them: but will only say of them what Byron said of the stars: "They are the poetry of Earth," and "are a beauty and a mystery."[5]

June 26th 1844

June 27. Well I have began a piece of grecian painting, a scene that C gave me in a ladys book. I painted very closely until 2 oclock then worked and read the remainder of the day. Made a watch guard also for Mr S. B did not come to walk with me as he promised. Thank God I have been enabled to day to fully prove my strenght in one respect. It gives more comfort than could much wealth and proves to one man what he did not believe before. I owe much of this strenght to Combe and all to love and C, the bestower of all the pleasure life holds for me and my hope in the future.

Venus is obscured to night — is it ominous or not. Does C forget me to night. Ah I do not forget him.

June 28. While buisily engaged writing last night D^r R came and a friend of his called on me. They asked for my paintings, looked over scrap books and others for two hours. Appeared very much delighted so I did not get to bed till after ten. Painted and read to day until I am almost dead with pain in my back. How much I need exercise but I hate to go out in the day and at night cannot go alone. I cannot read to night for I feel very bad indeed

This night four weeks ago dear C walked with me to the burial ground, and it was a lovely moonlight night full moon, as at this moment. Oh such hours cannot last for me.

June 29. Finished my pic nic scene — don't like it much. As I sat in C's usual seat this evening reading I cast my eyes up and they met the most gorgeously beautiful Sight I ever saw. It was a perfectly developed rain bow that was [so] expanded that it must have trespassed on some other cardinal point than its own. Its arch was not broken in the least point. While I stood admiring it another or reflection arose just above and though much fainter yet was not broken through the immense arch. I never saw one remain half so long in the sky. Oh it was magnificently beautiful, how I did wish C could see it. How lovely the moon shines, how lonely have I felt thinking of such hours passed with C.

Sun. June 30. Last night it rained and this morning it has the appearance of doing so again. I am very anxious to go to hear Mr C and will if rain does not prevent me. Spent the morning in reading Combe. B came just as I was starting to church. Tried to prevent my going, because it was so warm and behold when I got there Mr W was in the pulpit to read us a printed sermon which I can not endure so I got up and came home to my reading. Mr C preaches his last sermon for the season next Sabbath.[6] Had some company to day. Took a little walk and now to bed. Oh C do you think of me. I passed your lonely house this evening and saw J.[7]

July 1. To day I set my garden to rights as I have felt unusually well. Painted Napoleon's tomb at St Helena, read some and have written none for I am without pens and it rains so I could not get out to purchase any and this writes too bad for any use. To day is the great election. Have not heard how it will terminate but I hope in favour of the Whigs. I feel very lonely for my last companion is about to die. Poor Bob. I feel very sorry for him, poor dog, I wish I could do something for him.

July 2. Could not get out to day again for the rain. I want to go to the PO to see if there is a letter from C. Surely he will not disappoint me much longer. Night. B came up and staid all the afternoon made himself quite social for the first time of late. Before he left Mr S came and he is just gone and it is past my bed time. So no more. Only that he gave me the flying report of the days press over the ought-to-be Election. Hope the Whigs have won.

July 3. Went to the PO early this morning so in hopes to get a letter from C but was sadly disappointed. Called at D^r Rs Office. He gave me some scraps for my book.

Night. Well there has one day passed without rain at last.

B came up two hours before sun set brought me a quire of letter paper, pens, wafers sealing wax, five dollars in dimes to change with me and a whole cargo of Democratic papers and the over sanguine Locos have been completely vanquished and my prayer is granted. Poor Doct can't crow with the Coon on his back. Great is the excitement about this election but they must abide the issue.

July 4. The glorious anniversary is past and I have passed it so differently from what I have done the seven preceeding ones that with every greatful feelings have I all this day thanked my God and my adored friend. O I have this day felt that I was a free woman once more. This day twelve months I was worse than a slave in chains and bondage. No[w] thanks to dear C I am free and independent and not a pang has crossed my breast to day but on account of his absence and that he does not write. I have made all endeavours to let that trouble me as little as I could in order to spend one happy fourth and it would have been perfect had C been here. I walked out this afternoon by his house; how lonely I felt. One year ago I did not know C, now he has made me a happy woman.

July 4^{th 8}

While the guns come booming on this mornings fragrant gales telling that millions of patriotic hearts are now swelling with national pride and commemorating this anniversary so dear to every American heart; while the cannons tones alone reach my ear of all the mighty echoes of freedom's sons, I perhaps feel no less than the warmest heart that beats with gratitude to our forefathers. I am a philanthropist, and I glory in our free born republic, and I venerate the immortal Washington. I hail with rapture all such celebrations that will keep the rising generation in mind of those illustrious names that now [sleep] beneath the free sod their blood and their valour won. I had rather boast of being one of America's humblest daughters than to be an empress or Queen of a Monarchy. In all these things my heart bears a silent part, but the subject that has most engrossed my thoughts this morning while listening to those reverberations are perhaps selfish as they relate to self but as the day calls loudly for greatful as well as joyful emotions I do not think mine are out of place. I have been thinking of the pain, the sorrow, the anguish and tears that by some fatality or other has been my lot to bear for the last seven years on this Anniversary and my mind has wandered over those heart rending scenes; and the events of years have passed in rapid succession before me, and I felt that though I was included among the free-born Americans never had a 4th of July dawned on me as free and independent until this morning and as I sat under the vines that shade my own home with a plate of figs in my hand I thought of the scripture that every man should sit under his own vine and fig tree. I have contrasted this mornings emotions, with those that filled my breast

this day one year ago and if ever I felt reverence to the Deity and gratitude to man I have felt it while drawing the contrast. Yes then I was more
than a slave in bondage, for I was a slave to the worst of misfortunes and
a football for the heartless. Now I am *free* and surely no liberated convict feels the contrast more forcibly. Now on this fourth of 1844 I feel
that the spell of a *demon* that has hung like an incubus over those annual
returns had no longer power over me, and among the many joyful hearts
that beats full of life in this great City perhaps there is not one who has
felt more and exhibited less than I have done in the last hour. . . .

July 4th 1844

July 5. Have passed the day painting reading and writing. This evening took a walk. B came up to night and brought me the last No of the
Pictorial bible. He says I has not got a letter from C, but heard he got
up on the 19th which makes me very unhappy at such long interval with
no letter. Still I console myself that I am not forgotten. I shall give way
to a violent fit of melancholy soon, I feel, unless I do hear from him. Oh
it is death to be thus separated from him.

July 6. This is the Anniversary of the death of my first born. Ah it
calls up to the mind of a Mother many, very many scenes and changes
that I little dreamed of when I pressed those clay cold lips ere they were
consigned to the grave. Blest child thou art safe from all the snares that
would have fallen on a longer life.

It seems I will ever meet well-wishers. Thank God for true ones for to
day Mr Scott whom I have never seen, a friend of my brothers, sent me
a basket of fine peaches, the first I have had, also one of nice figs. They
were a real treat. No letter yet from C. Oh I am almost crazy about it.

Sun. July 7. Heard Mr C preach his closing sermon for the season. It
was relative to the glory of our free government and it was a glorious address to every american breast. He bade us farewell, he said, with greif
but he felt we were all one day to meet again. After church I went to
the PO but ah disappointment again. I came home and went to writing. Mr S came and staid some time. I feel very sorrowful to night. I am
almost frantic about a letter. Dear Charley have you forgotten me? Mr S

brought me the paper giving the details of the tragical affair of love and murder committed on the 5 th on the Shell Road.[9]

July 8. Last night I dreamed twice of seeing my dear Charley. One time I thought he filled my lap with gold, which did not make me half so glad as the sight of him.

Night. Josephus has just brought me a letter which has made me very glad indeed joyous to hear at last from dear C, but still there has been a sad shade stealing over my soul ever since. Why is it?

July 9. Finished my long letter to C but the rain prevented my taking it to the Office but sent it to Mr S to put in tomorrow. Have felt my melancholy ever since I got this. If any thing but he himself could dispel it, the gorgeous sun set clouds would have done it, for it really appears that all the beauty of Heaven itself has been lavished on the clouds of late, to night in particular.

Nine Oclock. Have just finished ironing and am very tired indeed so I shall lay aside my diary for to night. Ah, I can not see Venus to night.

Dear C [will you] think of me to night?

July 10. This morning near day light I heard some one at my door on the out side. I looked out and I saw it was a negro man. I sprang to the door and asked him what he was at. He ran and by the time I got the door opened he was near the gate. I hallooed at him that I knew him and so I do. I wish'I had a pistol I would use it on such occasions for if I am a lone woman I am not easily alarmed. C Columbus born 1447.

Bud came up this evening but brought me no paper. I feel very lonely to night indeed. I have finished my vase of hyacinths in water colours to day.

Oh heaven how much I wish to see Charley.

July 11. Well of all the floods in the form of rain that ever I saw it has been the greatest to day. How lonely I sometimes feel at such a time. It was too dark to paint or read. Oh how I longed for C then to be with me.

The evening sky still continues absorbingly beautiful. It appears as if all Heavens beauties were passing in review before me in different scenes but they are as inexhaustible as their Creator. Painted a view of the ruins of the fort at Ticonderoga on Lake Champlain. Have taken up the plan again of committing piec[e]s to memory in order to strengthen my memory for I find it is in using the faculties they assume activity and I am somewhat indebted to Combe for the fact as well as experience.

July 12. The anniversary of the death of my second child my dear little Mary Jane.

Took a pleasant walk down in the City to order some frames and get some paints for I must paint if I go hungry.

Borrowed a pistol but will not get it before tomorrow then I will dare the negro to come back again.

Painted until I started for a walk but shall do nothing to night for I am so tired. Passed Cs house saw J. He looks as desolate as I do.

This night 7 months ago was the first I spent in my own home.

July 13. I finished my painting and read a good deal to day. I have not got the pistol yet and do not feel so safe as I would.

Venus too has left me, no longer now can I look on her and *hope* at least that dear Charleys [eyes] are there too. No she too has withdrawn herself and I have no other alternative but sit down and think of him. Oh how I wish I was in the country during his absence. But it cannot be and I dare not complain. God bless him to night.

Sun. July 14. Well as I had no church to attend to day, I had arranged domestic affairs, read my usual hour, dressed myself and sat down under my musketoe sanctum to write something or other in my book of miscellanies, had chosen my subject and got interested in it, having written a page when a visitor arrived—wished he was at home. However *after* three hours was again alone, felt provoked at my chain of thought being broken so took my book and began to read when another came, soon after another and then the fourth so I have not had one moment until now nine Oclock. A social hour I sometimes like at an opportune time but this must stop, for I cannot bear it. Read some papers and now for bed.

July 15. I have just got to my books for I am still in so much pain I can scarcely sit up: am very unwell. As I lay in bed so sick this morning the dear little bird that loved to sing for Charley came close to my door and rang out such a peal of joyous feelings, that the tears gushed from my eyes. I thought of hours we had listened to it, now he was far away. I was sick and all alone, the little bird was still happy and unconscious of the associations he was calling up, in his endeavours to cheer me with his notes.

Have thought this long, long day for I am very sick. Have seen no one and am not able to get any thing to eat. I'll go to bed.

Have just finished reading Com[b]e on moral philosophy, and the constitution of man, the second time before I read any other work, and I find much to please instruct and improve. I more clearly understand the relation of moral physical and organic laws now, and it will ever be an additional evidence of the consistency displayed by the Creator in the immutability of his Laws, which to us short sighted mortals oft appears so unreasonable.[10]

July 16. I am striving with books and pens to force myself to believe I am not sick but it will not do. I feel debility, fever and dizziness creeping on so fast I am uneasy. I am alone and no one ever comes if I am sick. I cannot get any nourishment; God knows what I shall do if I get much worse. Oh Charley dearest one how I miss you, how I long to see you. My tears will sustain me perhaps for I never felt more deserted.

Bud came this evening, found me quite sick, scolded because I had no servant.

Having been devoting some time to reading philosophy I now feel the necessity of giving my mind some relaxation and have again commenced Mrs Ellis's works which with Miss Bremers I intend to read through the second time for in them I always find something new to admire and a wish to imitate.

July 17. I have struggled through this day, sick and lonely. I feel as if I shall have the [yellow] fever sure, and I dare not think of it as I am. Oh my poor head aches but my heart still more. Why *did* C have to leave me.

July 18. This morning I awoke with fever and head ache. Did not think I should be up all day but it was off and I excited myself to be well. I painted Napoleon in Russia in the Grecian. I then took a walk to the Lafayette burial ground. Each step told of my night walk there once with C. I spent some time looking at the last abode of poor mortality.

Lafayette Cemetery No. 1, New Orleans. Photo taken by author.

Cypress Grove (Firemen's) Cemetery, New Orleans. Photo taken by author.

I did not feel awful and long faced on the occasion but on the contrary felt there was a home of rest to many a weary stranger and I felt a nearer approach to my own last home. I conversed with the grave digger and thought of Hamlet. The graves were half filled with water and the stench from putrified flesh was very disagreeable. I do not wish to lie there but if I die in Orleans I hope to rest in the firemans, but it little matters so I die in peace yet I would so like to lie in the woods alone under some tall oak with a rude stone to point my grave to one *lone* eye and that eye to drop one tear to hallow the spot.[11] "Alone I live so let me die" and lie alone that I may pollute nothing fair in life or death. I returned home better satisfied with death than I ever felt before.

July 19. Thank God I arose pretty well to day and have enjoyed myself very much writing comments on my grave yard walk yesterday and reading Mrs Ellis's Poetry of life.[12] It is always new to me.

Night. The moon is now up in the sky looking kindly down on [one] who has often enjoyed his smiles more than she now can when he who lent the charm is far away. I wonder if he thinks of me to night. I hope he is happy and well. I hope too he has got my letter before this. There is a glorious breeze to night and so pleasant is it that I hate to go to bed.

How much have I to be greatful for to my God.

Madaline Edwards wrote several essays on cemeteries. In "A Walk" she painted a common picture of the disgusting urban cemetery and contrasted it with an ideal lonely rural burial place. Yet the attraction of a rural grave for Edwards was the opportunity for solitude and personal remembrance: her own and Charley's last resting place, like her cottage at the city's edge, would be a refuge from judgmental eyes. But she also imagined that after a period of rest and reconciliation the rural gravesite would be absorbed into the city and serve as a public monument to her lover. Barring that, she hoped to be buried in the newly opened Firemen's or Cypress Grove Cemetery, New Orleans's version of a rural cemetery. Edwards's essay blurs the simple, invidious opposition between urban life and rural peace, urban burying ground and rural cemetery, that many historians of antebellum America have described.[13] Here and in her later essay on St. Louis Cemetery No. 2, she restored the cemetery to its place as an urban landmark.[14]

A Walk.

Yesterday I took a walk to the lonely Lafayette Cementary. I never was in it before but while slowly tracing my slow steps (for I was sick) I was pondering in mind the walk I had there once before on a lovely moon-lit night with dear Charley. I thought (I trust such thoughts were not unjust nor profaning the spot to which I was going) of the difference in the lives of each at this moment, for conjecture lent her air as far as he was concerned. I thought, while I with step infirm, but heart not desponding was wending my way to the last silent abode of the dead, he was mixing in and among the millions of a crowded metropolis with the mass in the minds of whom death or sepulchres were the last to intrude themselves. While I walked slowly from one humble stone or board to another more indigative of wealth in those who reared them, reading the fond tribute of affection in the elaborate encomium or in the unostentatious name and age, that living friends had placed there as the last test of feelings that death could not arrest, he perhaps was moving in hurry from one massive piece of architecture to another of grandeur and beauty of the living, reared by their own opulence and love of approbation, and told in words too plain to be misunderstood by a mind so philosophical as his, that "we think not of death." While I stood among those weeds and willows that grew over and around those who once lived as we have done and now lie there, many even swept from the page of memory, he perhaps was walking amidst bowers and sweet scented flowers, whilst the name of one who so fondly linked the thoughts of him with every pulsation was swept at that happy hour from the tablet of his heart. While I stood gazing in the new made grave half filled with water talking to the grave digger, he perhaps was gazing into the eyes of some blest fair one as if those eyes were never to be associated with graves or coffin and conversing on themes the most remote from the grave or the monarchs tomb. These on his part were mere suppositions but natural consequences, situated as he is on a tour of pleasure and [it] is justifiable that these should be a few of the results of his travels, but at the same time it was natural for me to draw the contrast: and yet while treading those silent foot paths in that cemetary I thought with delight upon his words that often in his morning walks he had gone there from choice and while beholding them he had felt emotions of peace and pleasure in contemplating the time when he too should throw off the anxieties and the conflicts of mortal life and take a bed with them and find on awaking to immortality the happy exchange he had made. I thought of these words and *I* well knew his walk in life justified them, and that they were not said egotistically, and I felt on that spot the blest hope of a reunion with him in a better world than this and from my inmost soul thanked my God that my mind was almost divested of the terrors of the grave and that Charley, dear Charley in less than one year had wrought this change, with every other, that now gave me hope or joy.

I conversed with the grave digger, upon the number made in a day, the depth, the price, unpleasant occupation as well as stench that arose from the water in the grave arising from the next graves in which lay the decomposed flesh of what had once been the object at least of a Mothers love: and I wondered if his occupation did not of necessity extend to his heart and render him callous to the sympathies of death. I told him it was my desire to be buried elsewhere than in the holes of water he was making, not that it mattered much with me only in the fond associations my mind now bears to all that's rural and lovely in nature, and as I do not expect to have the full extent of my wish as to a grave realized I will make. At least that request is too well known to one who will see it executed if I die in this place. Did I have choice where or how I would be buried and felt interest enough to make a selection it would be in some other land than this. It would be on some elevated slope and beneath my mother earth I would lie that in her breast I might have the embrace that my earthly parent denied me, the caress that the world never gave me, the shield from the scorn and infamy her more favored children have heaped upon me, and that I might rest (at least my bones) where the green grass would grow over the last remains of one who might be thought would contaminate the sacred enclosure of a christian Cemetary, and if the blue sky was my tomb stone, the forest oak my head-board and one dear, dear eye would drop one tear of affection there 'twould hallow the spot and my soul would as it now seems rest in sweeter bliss. Why would I make such a selection? Among other answers that I might give I select the most prominent and forceful one it is that earth now holds one dear very dear object to me, and were it my sad and mournful lot to see his remains consigned to the last earthly home designed for it and it was left to me to choose that spot it would [be] something like this. It should be on some gentle slope with a clear blue stream to murmur at its base, that it might dance on and sing the sweetest requiem to his memory that nature could prompt. There should grow around spontaneously the oak, the magnolia, and my ever loved beech tree should stand by that stream as I now see it around the one that gushed from the spring of my ancestral home. Fruit and vines and flowers should cluster around, that it might not look like a place of solemnity but one of pleasures bowers. There I would have him laid with a neat marble slab commemorating a few of his virtues and *they* are now unknown to the world and these would not have the less bearing on the object of those virtues, if not there transcribed, but that when my heart had ceased to beat its tones of gratitude, and my eyes had ceased to watch beside, and ~~civilization~~ the strides of improvement with another generation had made inroads upon the woods around, would approach that enchanted elisium, that tablet might tell the tale and reveal the potency of the charm. Around this hallowed spot with my hands would I plant a few of his favourite flowers and my tears would facilitate their growth. At his head that had oft been pillowed on the unworthy breast that loved him so truly would I plant the night jassamine that flings its sweets upon the silent night's balmy breath, an emblem of his virtues that are done and enjoyed not to be seen by men. At his feet that had so oft been the missions of joy, and sounded like music upon my thresh-hold would I plant the more classical deity of flowers the rose, for like the odour of that flower his noble traits will live though he is dead, the rose might bloom, fade, and fall at his feet casting its perfume around, and though each leaf was separately borne upon the wind or floating on the stream, the odour would still be its own peculiar charm which will remain though bleached by the midday sun or evening dews.

It would look like selfishness, and perhaps it is. I would so enshrine that sacred spot in my heart that I would not wish another tear to drop over it, or another hand to touch it than the one that knows best how to appreciate the heart that there lay at rest. I do not know that I should ever wish a mortal voice but my own to rise over that tomb while I was living and mine only when I knelt beside it and prayed to his God to make me more like the model beside me in virtue and goodness. Yes existing circumstances lead me to feel there might be *one*, a child and that one his own, that I would take by the hand and lead to that temple of my affections and kneeling there teach it to lisp its first prayer, there to pray that it should inherit the virtues and goodness of its Father, there to ask our God to spare the poor forlorn remaining parent to that dear child to guide it on its course over the stream of life until it was able to pilot for itself, and to ask the help from that strong arm to direct that child in the steps that would have been taught it by that beloved father had he been pleased to have given him the all important task instead of the Mother so little prepared for the momentous and accountable task. Thither would I lead that pure and spotless treasure and pray to my God that he would ever preserve it so and the spirit of the departed would give sanctity to that prayer, and that grave should be so hallowed by affection between my child and myself that its first impressions of death and grave yards should ever after be associated with the cheerful, pleasing and holy. I would not teach it to look upon those scenes with indifference no less than of fear, but it would see from my deportment and my actions while bending the humble knee beside the grave of the Father, that he had left consolations with my heart that would not submit to the desecration of ceaseless tears and endless sighs, and though the silent tear would sometimes reveal to that youthful mind how much of my souls affections lay there it should not breathe of discontent or repining at the will of God, for when these outbursts of feeling so peculiar to myself would force themselves like a torrent over my restraint I would not let that child witness them for fear it might too early be imbued with the spirit of grief and sorrow, before it even had reason to tell the why. And while I taught it to look to life for all that was ennobling and pure in the father, for all that was exalted and beautiful on earth for all the beauties of nature, art, science and ideas, I would teach it to so hold them in reverence that did God desire it that it could live ages with and in them, but that at a moments warning at his bidding they could be laid down with as much pleasure as they were taken up, for it should early see in the tomb that held the father nothing that was melancholy or dispairing but look on it as the door that opened from a beautiful, sublime and lovely world to one that was beyond its conceptions for brightness and glory, for the one of which its father was the inhabitant and it should look upon life or death as equally important, the one to prepare for the other.

Here by this tomb while the Sun shone through the dense foliage above, while the breeze lifted those towering limbs and bade them sing with the stream at their feet natures sweetest requiem for the happy dead, while the little warblers in their boughs spoke of their nests and their young, here then would [with] my child clasped to my breast would I pass the sweetest yet mournful hours of my life. When that child at even had been hushed to its innocent sleep would I sometimes steal away to that loved spot and while the calm silvery moon and twinkling stars looked as sweetly down upon his grave as they had done upon hours that we had passed together watching and talking of them here while the wind was hushed and the bird had ceased to flutter and the bee to hum, here while all was silent but the pushing brook, when no eye saw but the eye of divine love, would I lift my voice in the fullness of an overflowing heart. Here I would pray for wisdom to instruct me to raise that beloved child to reflect all its fathers virtues and to atone for all its Mothers errors, that I might so discipline it that the snares and temptations of life would pass as harmlessly at its feet as that brook that danced in those moonbeams, that it should be all that father could have wished it, could the care been his instead of mine. There I would pray for grace to lead me to the close of that life that had been so badly begun, and for a conciousness that I should be prepared to meet that loved form in another garb of immortality. Then retracing my steps to the unconcious object of so many tears and so much solicitude with the impress of a Mothers love on its cheek, lie down to forget in the balm of sleep, that one so loved and cherished lay sleeping in that silent lonely grove. After all this should have passed to be permitted in my death sleep to be laid by that dear child then grown to manhood, beside that long watched tomb, to know the pure tears unadulterated by the hypocrisy and treachery of the world would sometimes drop a tear over the remains of her who had so cherished him, to feel as he thought of that sainted father he would fain hope the repentant, but ill-fated Mother shared the glory of a better world, and as that son launched out into the Ocean of life, learning now to quit the shores and coasts as he lifts his eyes above, around and looks beneath that he would feel I have a Father in Heaven who will protect the orphan. And as he steers on smoothly or if adverse winds arise, if the passions and follies of men attempt to divert him from the right course, I trust he would give one thought to those far off years and the prayer he so oft had there heard from the Mothers lips while the fathers dead ashes reposed to it and that these thoughts, that spot would act as a talisman to shield him from vice and keep him pure and blameless.

When I started to give a discription of the spot I would choose for the tomb of one I love so dear, I did not think to appropriate but a few lines to what I feel was never (and I am glad of it) to be realized, but looking back just now I am astonished to find I have gone such lengths into the imaginary, and I could now change the subject for what in all probability [will] be real some day. That day may come and very soon when he will lay my last remains in a less romantic spot but perhaps will be as well and if it is the only means of securing to me a look or visit a tear from him I would not exchange for the proudest mausoleum of tyrant kings. He may too have a beloved child of mine, but ah my heart sickens when I feel it cannot be his *pride* as it would be mine. He could not love it for its Mothers virtues as I could do for the Fathers. He could not look on it as the object of his only earthly love and solicitude as I could, for he has others. He is so situated with the world that he might disown his child while I would glory in the acknowledgement. He may then have other children to share its portion of affection while my undivided, unbounded Maternal store would be all its own. He perhaps would never lead it to my tomb or if he did, it *would not,* dare not, be with advice to imitate her who had so blindly erred. He could not make it the object

of such solicitude for he has never had to wade through the *feelings* of
shame and oppression that I have and by that which alone can impart as
it were the very instinct towards those we love, but yet he will be more
capable of directing it than I and will no doubt feel less restraint when
the grave shall have closed over the faults of the Mother, and I trust they
will never reach the child. To God will I commit those circumstances
yet in futurity, but still to one like myself it is natural these conjectures
shall arise in moments like these. Perhaps it is a virtue they should for
they school my mind in time if they should be real, while my pen is thus
employed my heart is free from other follies and at all events can do no
harm. God knows what is best in these cases and all I ask is a due sense
of submission, and a just appreciation of his unlimited blessings that so
cluster around my path in life.

July 19th 1844

July 20. With hard work, reading and writing and drawing I have
filled up the day.

Mr Scott came and spent the night until near ten oclock with me,
brought me some papers and two fine peaches. He appears like a whole
soul, noble heart and says he will transfer the friendship he once possess[ed] for my brother to me.

The nights are now very lovely and makes me think more of dear
Charley.

Sun. July 21. Oh! what would I not give to hear Mr Clapp preach.
It appears like many weeks since I did. Well I have not been so interrupted with company to day but have written and read pretty much all
day until late this afternoon. Mr R came to give me some instructions
in a new sketch which I am anxious to learn.

I feel like I shall be very sick to night. God send dear Charley home
soon for my poor heart is sick at such long absence.

July 22. There has been a shade of gloom stealing over my mind all
this day without knowing any additional cause to Charleys absence. I
could sit down to night and weep outright but if I can subdue the rising
flood I must for it is high time I was learning to bear my sorrows with
more resignation if not less force, for one who is the innocent cause of

my oppression at soul, would condemn such tears and yet I know not why the eyes may not alleviate the burden of the heart for the load is but increased when the tide ebbs not. Mysterious are the workings of my poor heart. Oh dear dear Charley when will you come.

July 23. Last night I dreamed such a singular dream of my dear Charley surely it portends a letter for two others were in part realized before ten oclock. One was my sister sent me a barrel of peaches, chickens and other things of which I am very glad. I will preserve some, have given away a good many. In writing to me condemning my course in morals as well as religion she says "that man will throw you and your child both on a cold world." Ah she is not to blame for she does not *know* the man I now deal with. Would to God her husband was such. She says she is afraid very afraid of death and I should be too if I felt my God to be such as her religion teaches. She says I am in danger; it may be so.

July 24. Have been preserving some peaches to day and feel very tired.

Night. A lovely moon shine night. Was sitting in my chair of contemplation musing upon the world of grandeur and splendour that looked so diminutive to my eyes now, when in walked Bud. Has not been here for nine days before. He was in the dumps and did not stay long, broke my chain of thought and liked to have set me crying.

Dreamed last night again of dear Charley. Oh that it was reality and not a dream. When *will* he come.

July 25. I have sat in the moon light conjuring up all the scenes of my childish home, thinking of the desolation there now in that old castle until my spirit is umbued with the same melancholy and thinking of Charley and my solitary seat I could sit down and weep half the night but it must not be. Oh such nights are too holy to be spent alone. No one to hold communion with upon those silent world[s] that gl[e]am above nor their God who made them. Will it ever be thus?

Dear Charley forget me not. I dreamed again last night I saw him.

July 26. Have finished reading Mrs Ellis's poetry of life the second time. What would I not give to possess the talents the discriptive powers and goodness of that woman. Not for fame but the inward joy and thrilling emotions of soul imparted thereby. I have now commenced Dr Dick again. I wish but few books but I wish to understand and practice those.

Mr S sent me some papers from which I cull some gems for my scrap book. Rain Rain every day this week. I cannot get to walk out for exercise and I feel the want of it very much.

When shall I see my dear dear Charley.

July 27. Oh! what extacy was mine last night as I sat by Charley at his own table and when he spoke low to me and said he would be here at dark. How happy I was. His wife seemed much pleased with me and I did not feel unjust towards her but alas the morning dawn dispelled all this happiness and I awoke to sigh and long for the reality. The first fair day this week and I went down in the City and spent a little money and I bought the first baiby articles to day. God knows if they will ever be needed. Mr S came and brought me Miss Bremers work the Neighbors which I am desirous to read and will lay Dick by awhile.[15] Oh this moon light night is too exquisite to pass unenjoyed with C. It calls up many many things. God bless him.

Sun. July 28. Nearly 8 clock night. Have Mr R here ever since ten this morning teaching me something of drawing. The rain has kept he and S here all evening and at last went off in it. I have read a good deal but wrote none which I was in hopes to have done. Oh how I wish to hear Mr Clapp preach and how I long to have dear C here one such night as last or one like this rainy one. Under my musketoe house all alone with my thoughts and the gentle falling rain I will try and write some.

July 29. Rain again to day but such is the time I best love to read. I have read and painted all day. To night I have been watching the full moon and my heart is full, full. Two full moons have now passed since the night of the one on which I took my last walk with dear C. Now where is he? Ah my sighs tell his image is ever in my heart. He may not think of me but he is not for one hour from my mind: I feel very sad to night. Oh when or shall I ever see him again. I have been looking anxiously for a letter from him but none as yet.

July 30. Well after watching the most lovely setting sun after such a flood this morning. After gazing for an hour on the beautiful moon partly shaded at times by lovely bands of dark sky until (she freed herself and fled on her cours[e],) I plucked a jasmine and now seek my bed with it for my companion for they always speak of Dear Charles. Where can he be? and what is he doing that he will not write to me.

I have painted and read incessantly to day but the gun fires and I will fly to rest.[16]

I have to day finished the Neighbors. Am well pleased, but not enraptured.

July 31. Here it is the last day of July and I have no letter yet. B came this evening only a few minutes and said I had not got one on yesterday. Surely dear C is coming back or has forgotten me one. How I long for a letter but more to see him.

I have been reading Pope today and find more truly than I knew before how little he thought of my sex.

Have resumed Dicks works again. Have finished a very pretty piece of pencilling to day.

Aug. 1. Wrote a piece this morning of four pages on the old home scenes of childhood. This evening I have been pencilling the same home. Took a little walk this afternoon came by C's house. Did not see J. The house seems to say what my heart did that it wished for his return. Alas I fear it will be many a long day first. He has been gone 7 weeks to night.

It thunders and lightens and I am sleepy so away to bed.

Aug. 2. I wished to go out to day and as it was so lovely and pleasant, I dressed all in white and just as I got to Poydras [Street] it clouded up and such another flood as we had. I was in M^r M store. Mr Scott sent his boy to see if I was there, came down and sent for a hack. Mr S came also and finally I was caged in a close cab and got home with much difficulty and my clothes muddy. Saw J stand at the window and look at me for ten minutes for we got stuck in the mud close by. Oh how I wished it was C. I have had the bleus ever since I got home and I wanted to get to the PO. but could not. Oh God C do write to me or come home.

Aug. 3. I have been on the point of a miscarriage from the jolting ride I had yesterday and am not sure yet but it will be. I dreamed last night B rode a horse up and handed me a letter from dear C. I tore it open and it was dated three oclock night all asleep. Said he had heard a sermon on taking the sacrement and had resolved to act paltroon no longer but would from this take it. I began to cry for I felt it was to Sever our connexion. He said Mr Clapp preached it for he was there and he had seen nor heard any thing worth a cent there but from him. Then went on with a great deal of history and hard names, said he had laid by many books for me, but did not talk of home. The letter contained two sheets but just as I read one I awoke, sadly disappointed. Oh will he not write to me? I am almost crazy and sick too.

Sun. Aug. 4. I had four visitors to day, among the rest B who came to tell me that J had got a letter from C written on the 23 which has made me more than miserable for he has not got my letter or will not write me or has done so and I have not got it. Oh that he knew my feelings.

I cannot do any thing but sigh since and I feel I must have a flood of tears to night.

I shall enjoy nothing until I hear from him.

Last night I dreamed some one was describing an Adonis to me and said the reflection from his marble white neck rested on his raven whiskers like the silver fringed dark cloud or snow capped mountain.

Aug. 5. Last night I had a hard cry. I could not help it, and now I could take another for Bud came up this evening and read me a letter he had just got from C. saying he had my letter and would answer it soon. So there is two he has written since he got mine and yet he has nothing to write to B either, and knows my distraction to hear from him yet treats me with such neglect. The least I can think of it is that he is very unkind for he often said judge me by actions and not look for words and if this is a sample to judge from I am of little consequence in his mind or thought. I *could* not treat him so, and well he knows it.

Aug. 6. I feel completely weighed down of late. I do nothing with life or joy, all is mechanical. What is the cause? Alas my heart alone can tell! When am I to feel that my sorrow on earth is oe'r. I went to the garden to day to try and forget.[17] I had some beautiful flowers given me but they failed to cheer. I found the gardener sick and no one to give him anything to eat. I came home and made him some chicken soup. I hope it did him good. Mr S brought me the Ladies book and a paper this evening. He found me gloomy and left.

Aug. 7. I have been trying to analyze my state of mind, but can come to no definite conclusion. Sometimes I think it is all owing to the incessant screaming in the next yard. After so much quiet it almost sends me frantic. I cannot read, if I do I cannot understand, and often lay down my book in dispair. I cannot write, and I have no hope for a remedy in this case for I have a permanent house and so have they, but it is the curse I had such a sad presentiment of when I was enjoying years in the few months I was so quiet. I dare not complain to dear C for he cannot avoid it, but I do feel as if I cannot live under it.

No letter yet. Oh! and am I thus forgotten!

Aug. 8. I went down in the City so in hopes to get a letter but alas! did not. I believe I am forgotten by C. Well it could not be thus by me towards him. I bought some little articles for his unborn and if I am so soon forgotten it were better it had never been my lot thus to be. I came home with a violent head ache and am so sick I can hardly now sit up. I rode home. The City looks dull and I felt so.

Oh, I do wish Charley could know not feel what my feelings are. I do think I cannot bear it much longer.

I dreamed last night that my youngest brother [Albert Cage] now 24 years old whom I have never seen came to see me. I thought he was tall and handsome, was dressed in black, had a dark hat with crape on it. He looked at me mildly and asked if I knew him. I felt in a moment he was my brother and called him so. He clasped me in his arms and we both wept for a length of time. I felt his full forgiveness in his kind look and to be thus embraced by one my soul has ever yearned to see was to me a bliss unknown. Alas! that the dawn should dispel its charm. I have ever felt that had I known that brother there would have been sympathy between us for his disposition I have ever heard is one that I should love and admire. But destiny has ordered that we shall never meet until it is at the bar of God. My dream has so preyed on my mind all day that I cannot feel the least joy in any thing I see read or hear.

Aug. 9. Dr R came up to see me this evening. While here B came and asked me to take a walk for the first time. We went to the garden, got some ice cream and mead came back by C['s]. Saw J writing. The subject turned upon C having deceived him and he got very angry, said some hard things of C and sat until near ten railing against him, and I to make the thing better unfortunately made it much worse. But I cannot help it. Oh is it to be my lot ever to separate friends. It were better I suffer alone than cause others to do so. Their friendship can never be the same it has been.

My head and heart both ache. I will try my only comfort sleep.

Aug. 10. Have been very sick to day but yet I strive to amuse myself to forget the grief arising from the slight from one that so engrosses my whole soul. He forgets, or neglects me without a cause and one is as painful as the other. It has led me to look farther in the future than I ever have since I have known him, and I tremble for my own peace of mind. I fear there is a cup of sorrow preparing for my life more bitter than they have ever yet pressed but he shall not know that such are my fears. I wish he were near me now for I feel that nothing in life but his presence can dissipate my gloom.

Sun. Aug. 11. Well the sabbath is ended and I cannot say very profitably to me either. I have read and drawed some, written none nor scarce know what I read for the incessant clatter the next door destroys all my enjoyment in reading or composing. Mr S spent a part of the morning with me. Since I have been all alone. I suppose I will never get a letter from Charley. Oh he does treat me too cruel. I wish he had the sprig of night jassamine I have now by me for he loves them so much and I would dedicate the first fruits of my garden to the giver.

God ever bless him whether he forsakes me or not.

Aug. 12. This day 8 months ago I moved in my own home and I bless God that ever such a blessing was bestowed on me for I trust I am some more worthy of the mans esteem who so generously gave it to me. To day I have been drawing while the sweet rose and jassamine have graced my table and gave such perfume that seemed to call up fresh gratitude to him who gave me the pleasure of rearing them.

I dreamed last night I heard Mr C preach a most glorious sermon. I wish it had been true.

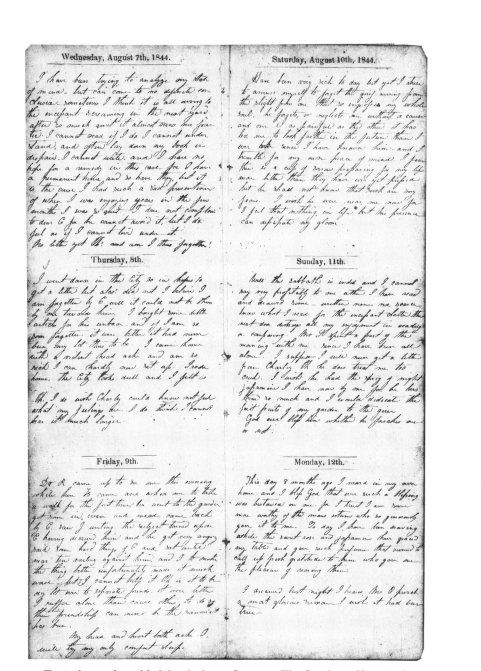

Typical page from Madaline's diary. Courtesy The Southern Historical
Collection, University of North Carolina at Chapel Hill.

Aug. 13. I do not know how to write or what to do with myself. My heart is so full my eyes are filling with tears all the time. Charley has been gone two months to night and I have had but one letter. Oh God it is my destiny to be deceived in those I love but little did I think it in his nature to cause so much pain wilfully. He knows my heart is torn and suspense and anxiety torture my brain but he is happy and he seems to care nothing on earth for one who would sell almost her life before she would give his breast the pang he has inflicted since he has left.

On being reproved for weeping, and asked the cause.[18]

> I weep not for the early dead,
> That once my arms embraced:
> But many tears for them I shed;
> And love is not effaced.
> Those folded buds have gone to bloom
> To fade and fall no more,
> Sinless, I laid them in the tomb.
> And should I now deplore?
>
> I weep not for the early friends,
> Who thronged my youthful path;
> For earthly pleasures have their ends,
> And friendship *surely* hath:
> O'er some of these the grave has closed,
> And some have proved unkind.
> And some in wealth have long reposed
> For this I've not repined.
>
> I weep not that I have no wealth
> To spend in folly's show
> And at its shrine to barter health
> And hopes I yet may know
> But if 'twere mine how joyful I
> would share it with the poor

How oft I'd wipe the tearful eye
And tread at misery's door.

I weep not for false beauties charms
To deck this moral dust
It oft its poor possessor harms
Who solely in it trusts.
It fades at noon like roses sweet
But leaves no sweets behind
No friends stand ready then to greet
The treasures of the mind.

I weep not for the one I choose
To walk this life with me.
He's proved the thorn, and not the rose
My virgin love did see.
He's wrecked my peace too late I saw
T'were best we n'er had met
To violate loves holy laws,
And Gods more holy yet.

I weep that I could not have met
And exchanged a virgin heart
With one who's never brought regret
And death alone could part,
For then no stain was on my brow
My heart was pure as truth
But ah! alas what am I now
And where my spotless youth.

I weep that guilt has stained my brow
Long years cannot efface
And memory's all that's left me now
But sorrow with disgrace.
I feel that love still burns so deep
In this deserted heart of mine

And none can prize. Oh let me weep!
Oer the desolated shrine.

I weep that love so deep and true
Should be deemed pollutions stain
Of all the woes I must endure,
This brings the wildest pain.
For if my love like *hope* was sold
I might live for self alone,
And let my heart with years grow old
And for the past atone.

I weep that one I so much prize
Must deem me guilty vile
I see it in forgiving eyes,
And the melancholy smile
And yet with such assiduous care
From one he would conceal
The pity he has for my dispair
And which he fain would heal.

I weep that guilt is on my brow
And shame is on my cheek
That in God's house I scarce may bow
To none I there may speak.
Shunned, betrayed, condemned.
Oh these are griefs not lightly borne
And stouter hearts would rend.

I weep that like some forest tree
The lightnings flash hath torn
Few pities my sad destiny
And one for me will mourn.
The very birds that nestled there
Have flown to other shades

And few then very few there are
But think my name degrades.

I weep that time will ner efface
This deep and lasting stain
But binds the mark upon my face
Like that of murderous Cain
But even he had one who smiled
And called him still her own
When far from home and friends exiled
His grief, not guilt was borne.

I weep to stand on this waste isle
And cast my eyes oer all the world
With none to share this just exile
From all but memory hurled.
But even this were better far
Than dwell *among*, and still apart.
Then might heal the deep, deep scar
That freshly wounds my heart.

O might I smile the cause would be
That death will end my grief and woe
That God's pure love extends to me
None else my sorrows know.
Its there I hope to be forgiven
For every guilty shame
And in the blest abode of Heaven
Peal loud his glorious name.

Aug 13th 1844.

In reading the above lines it may be thought by the superficial observer that I am ungreatful and exacting, that I do not appreciate the
noble *friend* I have found and indulge in repining, but in this heart

which has I fear never been understood by any but God there exists feelings and emotions that I have never yet been able to find words to express or actions to convey, and it is in feeling that one noble and loved object has given me the assurance that he is my friend and in knowing that I am so degraded and so far below him that with the deepest humility I may dare look up to him and call him such. I see his purity and feel my shame. I realize his unblemished character and feel that I am not worthy of his kind feelings, and I turn within for the cause. And were it not for memory, and the sneers of others I could not realize the truth for I find there a heart as warm, devoted, feeling, sympathizing and as truthful as in earlier days. I find that my spirit is as free from stain as it ever was. I find the burning desire for the pure and perfect that first fired my longing soul ere I knew the cause. I find the same immortal aspirations struggling to mount upward, and the ideal that will not slumber. I feel that though forsaken and deserted by the world I am no misanthrope for this earth is the footstool and my fellow beings the children of my Father who will not spurn the victim of their deception and the object of their desertion. I feel sentiments, hopes and desires is [as] deep and true as those on whom no blemish has fallen. But around all these convictions rivits the icy chains of shame as strong and lasting as life. . . .

Were moral laws so constructed that a fallen female might reinstate herself by any penance that life could endure however severe how gladly would I embrace it. Were it even to terminate my life directly it was accomplished, it would be worth my toil if in my last moments I could be clasped to the breast of my earthly friend as pure and spotless. But this cannot be and so fearfully does the penalty weigh upon my [mind] that I am sometimes tempted to believe it will extend beyond the grave that in eternity I will be looked upon as impure. I am often asked why all my compositions are so melancholy and gloomy. Oh! how am I ever to be any thing else. . . .

My only hope is in death and I wish it were stronger than it is, but I feel that God will at least be more merciful towards me than any but the kind heart that has beat for my sorrows and sought to alleviate them, and even he does not understand them as my heavenly parent. But beyond this vale that has truly been one of tears to me, I hope there will be some joy and hope for me too. I would not; and I do not weep so oft as I did before he changed my life but still I shed many tears of deepest agony, perhaps deeper than those shed before I knew him, for now I feel so lost and despicable beside him that I could often weep when gazing on his face. When I am dead I hope he will realize my emotions in part at least towards him and forgive any unreasonableness that may appear in me or my writings for they are not the effects of the heart.

My heart is sad to bursting of late from other causes and the above combined threatens almost madness. Oh! that I could ever have been loved as I love.

Aug. 22, 1844

Aug. 14. Last night I dreamed Mr Clapp presented me with some of the most beautiful flowers I ever saw. He has indeed given me flowers of hope that will never cease to bloom in Eternity.

To day sure enough I had a most lovely bouquet given me and I have now set it in the night air to breathe all it can before its last decay.

No letter yet. My heart is almost wild with despair. Oh can it be that I am doomed to feel the loss of C['s] interest and esteem. He *cannot* feel for me or he would write.

Aug. 15. I took a pleasant walk this afternoon down to the market. Got my fortune told. Ha well it is all as usual. When I got home Mr H had been up some time, waited at Rs, sat with me an hour with his two little boys. Talked very good and gave good advice for me to go by, is highly pleased that I am to be a Mother. Approves and encourages my love for the father though unknown to him. Oh this is a lovely night. How I have gazed at the stars and thought of C. I have given out getting a letter atal and must make the best of my agony of mind I can. God help me.

Bonaparte born at Azacco 1769.

Aug. 16. I have been litterally crazy to day with tooth and head ache. B came to night and has not yet got me a letter. It does appear that I am fated to be forever deceived for the world could not have made me believe that C would have cared so little for my feelings even if I am not the least dear to him for I thought his goodness of heart would prompt him to prevent all the misery that so easily lay in his power. But it seems not.

Aug. 17. I am totally unfit for any thing. I am suffering so with my teeth that I am almost prostrated, not able to do any thing, and although it is the first time for nine years yet I can not bear it patiently. Oh that there was one in the world to pity me at least. Night. No one can realize the loss I feel of one dear congenial spirit to converse with on such nights as this. To sit all alone with the stars and flowers and not have that loved one by to talk of them, robs them of half their glory. Oh that such is ever to be my destiny on earth I much fear! Father let me submit to thy will.

Sun. Aug. 18. Mr S brought me some papers. Have been reading and culling from them for my [s]crap book. Bud spent the afternoon with me. Appears again in a good humour.

Night. Mr S came and teazed me to death to take a walk after ice cream and to avoid an insult I did so and am so tired I can scarcely hold my pen. It is the last walk I take unless I shall ever have that pleasure with C.

No letter yet.

Aug. 19. Today I have commenced making my baby clothes and I have wept as well as prayed over them. None but God knows my feelings over this unborn child. It is coming into this world that has been one of sorrow to its unfortunate Mother and its illegitimacy may be a stigma forever on its name. I may die early in its infancy and leave it to a kind father but alas he could not be a *Mother* and I dread that another should ever fill my place to it at least in the first few years of its life. These and many other feelings arose while sewing for it. I prayed that if we both lived for wisdom from on high to raise it for Glory and Honour.

Aug. 20. Mr H met me to day very cordially, the first time he has spoken to me of late. Mr S came and brought me the 6th No of the Pic Bible and sat until we almost had a parting quarrel and if ever I am compelled to speak so plainly again it will forever terminate our friendship.

Oh what a lovely moon light night but my feelings are not in accordance for it does seem as if hope had left my heart. May the one who causes it never feel the same.

Aug. 21. Framed a piece that dear C asked me to paint for him before he left. I have tried to day to work, but am not able to do any thing properly, for my mind is in lament. Why am I thus fated! Could Charley feel my situation he would surely pity me unless that too has left his breast. One little letter could save me so much pain. I am always ready to make excuses to my own heart for him but in this I can find no room to do so. What can the cause be? Alas I fear indifference.

Aug. 23. I am scarcely able now to write for B came up last night and told me he had got another letter and there was none for me yet, and that C would be home by the middle of Sept. But this did not allay the rising flood that had been long gathering but gave it vent. I wept until I am almost a maniac to think that I am treated with such slight by the only being on earth I love and [who] has professed so much for me. He too knows my helpless situation and does not seem to care. If he has not written me but once I am certain I never can feel the same confidence in his promises nor his regard, but I still hope such is not the case, and yet there is but little room for hope.

Aug. 24. I have scoured and worked to day until I was almost exhausted, but now I feel quite rested. Bud sent for his clothes and sent me the morning paper and a note saying be of good cheer for I would yet get a letter, but I do not believe it for if C has so far neglected me he will even farther, and if it has been mislaid I will get none. No one knows my feeling upon the subject.

Sun. Aug. 25. The sabbath is ended and a sweet moon light makes me long for the society of one who I fear does not think of me. Mr S has just left. Wished me to take a walk but I have no desire to walk with any one on earth but one.

D^r R called on me to day and offered to bet me three hats that my child will be a boy.

Have read wrote and cooked, and drawed some today.

This day four months ago I felt the first motion of my babe.

Aug. 26. Rose very early and took my bath, read my morning portion, did a good days work and then rode to Lafayette and walked back. Coming up Camp street met Jim and if he does not know or suspect something I am wonderfully mistaken. Passed C's house; the little negro said I looked just like his Mistress.

I feel very tired after my long walk and will go to bed soon although it looks like a real sin to sleep while the moon is walking the azure sky as beautiful as she does to night. Tomorrow night she fulls.

Venus has of late been watched by me in the east. It was [in] the west when C left me promising to look on [it] every night thinking of me.

Aug. 27. I have seen JC who has told me things concerning C self &c that I wish I never could have heard, and which will make C very unhappy if he hears it and I cannot tell whether I should, or should not tell him, but my nature is so candid that I fear to conceal from him any thing. I have been miserable ever since.

I wish I never had met J for I fear he is my evil genius and if he can't force me to do as he wishes to leave here might injure the happiness of C. Oh why was I ever formed to be the cause of sorrow or pain to others?

Aug. 28. Mr S came up last night to go with me to see the moon through a telescope and as I was so anxious to see it I went, but the moon was full and too low to be seen. I saw Saturn with its beautiful ring and its swift motion. Oh! what would I not give to be in a large observatory to gaze my fill upon those sublime wonders. Even that little sight has increased my conception of the Deity. Came home thinking with what rapture I could have enjoyed that walk with dear C.

Aug. 29. Went down in the City and spent half the day. Bought some little lace and it is my last money and the last time I expect to be down soon. I am so tired I can hardly sit or stand for I walked down and up. Saw J as I came by C's. Oh what a lovely night. Would to God C was here. I have given out looking for a letter and do not expect to hear from him until I see him, if ever that is.

Aug. 30. An old acquaintance called to see me to day, a catholic of the old irish school, until now he should not be called one and this arose from my expressing my happy belief of Mr Clapps doctrine some six months since. He then went to studying and read Volney and he says reason has triumphed over all the face of early education and death that

[he] viewed with such terror is now to him a friend and not a Monster.[19] All this arose from dear Charley.

Night. One of the loveliest that nature ever witnessed. Oh Heavens if C were only here.

Aug. 31. Recd a letter last night from C at last and I wish from my soul it had not come for it was as cold as marble and has put me in a state of mind that even his presence could not dissipate. He may not feel indifferent towards me, but I cannot realize it. Did not even say when he will be at home if ever. Night. The last of Summer. The bright moon is just rising to bid it farewell and the flowers look so swe[e]tly. I alone am desolate. I have wept this day until I am not myself. I cannot get over Charleys coldness to me. I do not merit it if love can give me a claim to warmer feelings from him. He may one day feel for my aching heart.

Sun. Sept. 1. Mr S came up this morning with a sad heart having lost a negro man. Brought me some papers sent me by Mr Scott from which I cutt some gems.

Bud came and brought me some dimes which I shall endeavor not to use before C. comes. Bud came this after noon and staid until after night. We spent a very pleasant evening talking, reading, dissecting flowers and combing his hair.

Night. The first of Dear Sept lovely and balmy. Oh for one dear one to enjoy it with me.

To Charley[20]

The little of the mental that did belong to me has of late been intirely paralyzed and you dear C have been the cause, though separated by rivers mountains and leagues. Do not say that I have not striven against such feelings for I have, but it is in vain. I do not expect to be benefited by these lines for I do not know that you will ever see them while my heart beats for you or the unborn that alone (though unconciously) has felt a part of my anguish. But perhaps when I rest from slighted love and blighted hopes, there'll be another who claims all of thy love in which I would now gladly share. Perhaps she may not love so fondly and

I do hope not so madly as I do. If so I would teach you by the bitter tears that I have of late shed and those that now dim my eyes. I would conjure you to imagine the agony of my soul, and learn thereby to spare her the same. When we parted my only hope of joy lay in your letters. This I am convinced I impressed on your mind. Your sacred promise to write often to me I regarded as one you would not violate from pity if affection had not voice in the matter. You know dear C that you left me in the situation of all others demanding the most kindness and sympathy and you are well aware that my feelings at any time are too sensitive to bear much. Still with no buisness on your hands, nothing to do but enjoy yourself, yet to me you were not willing to give one half hour. To ease my throbbing heart and hush the floods of tears not one line could you spare time to dictate until you had been from me near a month. Then I recd one short letter and comparing it with the deep gushing affections of my own soul I thought it cool, but in answer to this I tried again to imprint on your mind my undying love and my torturing anxiety to hear from you often told you to know that you cared for me, thought of me and felt for my solitary situation would reconcile me to any thing. I implored in that letter a direct answer. Judging you not by [my] own readiness to grant every wish of yours, but by your pity and goodness of heart, that would insure me a speedy answer. I watched with all the impatience that my poor heart could feel. Days passed and weeks. Others recd letters but none for me this arose to phrenzy. At last I could not restrain the agonizing tears that laid me up sick. As I got up again I resolved to believe that you had written and it was mislaid. I would not, could not bear to believe that I was not cared for, and had almost become reconciled to await your return to know the reality. When a letter was handed me, I tore the seal and a few cold lines was all that long wished for letter contained, not one kind or consoling word, not even a wish to see me or a word that I might ever see you, but all [that] seem[ed] to fill your mind was the pleasures you were taking and a seeming regret that you should ever again return. Oh how I wept that the thoughts of me had forced themselves upon your mind and broken in upon your joys for the letter was nothing more than a compulsion for forms sake and it would have saved me thousands of tears. I feel convinced that I am to you a thing of burden and not joy. I feel that in your heart you wish I were dead. Then tell me if life is not a curse to a heart like mine. You could not have helped writing to me to save your life. If you loved me it would have been impossible, and it was from this separation that I was to gather hope or misery for all my future life and the latter has filled the measure, for I feel fully assured it is only when by me that I am thought of, and that cannot satisfy the craving of my deathless love. I have strove to be as little afflicted by your slight as possible because I would not imbue the babe I bear you with the sad legacy of melancholy, but it is of no avail I could not, and if it is doomed to live I fear it will be an object of deep seated melancholy and if I am not spared to share and soothe the feelings that none but its poor Mother could enter into its life will be even more miserable, for if the Father cares not for the agonies of the Mother the childs sighs will not be felt. I am totally unfit for any thing but tears. I am miserable for I now feel that nothing on earth loves me and I feel that God cannot for if I were as true and devoted to him as this my heart would find rest from his heavenly spirit, but alas Charley you absorb my whole life. I do not know what to do. I have been revolving in my mind what to do. Commit suicide I do not wish. To live near you and feel that I am an object of no affection to you more than you feel for others is more than I can endure. I should go a maniac and I have at times come to the conclusion that it were better when my child is born, if the poor unfortunate should live to take it and go to some foreign land and there pray for your happiness and that of my darling child till death put an end to my misery. If it dies to go alone. The thought is distraction but I sincerely believe you would be happier by it and I dare not live near you feeling as I do. But yet God may be preparing another home than this which I may soon fill if so I trust he will give me the babe I bear that it may never feel the want of a Mothers love and the neglect of a Father as I have done. Oh the deception would have been a virtue in this instance if you could only have written to me often and kindly and would have added so much to my present and future happiness for now I shall ever doubt your sincerity when I would think and hope you loved me. I could have written and read with so much plea-

sure during the days and nights I have spent in tears, and I should have
felt that there was one heart in the wide world that beat for me. As it is
I *know* there is not one. Charley dear Charley do try and learn the heart
of woman that you may save her so much agony and so easily. When I
am gone for the sake of her who may then repose upon thy breast take
lessons from my grief and spare her such pangs. I feel that I have but
few if any claims on your love but I thought I had some on your pity and
it is this that rends my heart. I have lost all and struggling through my
misery to bring one in the world to share the same with me where I had
so hoped its destiny would have been otherwise. My heart will break. I
must stop. Pity but do not blame me too harshly, for my brain is on fire.

Sept 1st 44

Sept. 2. I never saw a lovelier morning, and I felt so well I was up by
light in the garden.

Had washing done to day and went down to see the cistern maker to
get him to stop my cistern leaking.

Made some dear little shirts for my unborn. Read some and thought
a great deal. Ah that I did not have so much to think of that belongs
to earth.

Sept. 3. Oh how lovely to sit and gaze upon the star gemmed firmament on such a lovely night. I always think of dear C when I think of
the stars and moon. Venus looks lovely as a bride to night.

Bud was here this evening and I really believe he has resolved to
throw the blues to the winds and be cheerful. I am glad of it.

Charley Oh do come home.

Sept. 4. This morning I plucked one of the loveliest sweet roses I
ever saw in my life, it was the first Sept rose for the bush has blown
every month since it began I sat near an hour gazing on it and the spar-
kling dew that wet it, thinking of its Creator with greater admiration
than ever.

My step Mothers neice was here this evening. I walked part of the way
home with her and I fear have lost my dog by it for he has not returned.

I saw dear C's house and J on the banquet[te: sidewalk].

Sept. 5. I slept but little last night for I was up watching and long before day I was dressed to go to look for my dog at day light I started, enjoyed a star light walk but met with no success, but I was repaid to see Venus pale away into the morning cloud. This evening I went down to the dog pound but Bob was not there and I am tired almost to death. Poor dog, I miss his company for it was all I had. I saw Charleys old big Jack dog this morning and dreamed I saw his Master last night. Oh I wish I could.

Sept. 6. Last night I was awakened by a most piteous howl I ever heard from a dog and it was repeated every few moments during the night, and I could not sleep. I could not recognize Bobs voice but this morning lo! it was him and I never in life saw such joy displayed by a brute in my life and I jumped for joy. Bud came this evening and brought me four papers, just finished reading them. He says J will start up tomorrow and C will be down very soon. I hope so but am afraid to suffer myself to hope.

This time last year I was in Mobile at my Fathers where I may never be again.

Sept. 7. I have sat to night with one eye on Venus and the other on Saturn prying into the mysteries of the starry Heavens. Oh how I wish to understand Astronomy. How I thought of Charley and wished he were at my side to talk of them. Now is my favourite Season. The mornings early hour I give to the contemplation of my dear flowers the night hours before bed time to the stars but all are shorn of their purest delight because of not having him with me to love and admire the wisdom and love of their Great Creator. Oh! will the time ever come that I shall be so blest?

Sun. Sept. 8. Went this morning to market with Mr S. He bought me a basket of fruit, and gave me a parcel of papers in which I found that Mr Clapp was to preach to day, but it was too late then to go. Oh how I wished to hear him. If I live I will try to go next Sabbath.

I have been trying to write a tale but my book is full and I have not room to finish it.[21] I wish C would come home and buy me another.

Sept. 9. The stars around the moon were visible to day. The atmosphere was so clear, there is some speculation on the calculation of the

Parisian Astronomer who says that I [a] comet will endanger the earth on the 24.th.

Bud came up this evening and brought me some papers. Says J got off Saturday and that C will await his arrival so I may not look for him until near the last of the month, just as I told him when he left, that I would not see him before Oct.

Wrote to my Sister to day and Bud took the letter to the Office.

Sept. 10. I repotted all my flowers this after noon and have got a severe head ache and lost my comb in the bargain of it. Bought some paper to finish writing a tale I have begun.

I feel very unwell and will go to bed.

Sept. 11. Found my comb hanging in the vines, this morning.

Met with an act of kindness to day which I shall long remember.

Bud came to night and brought me some papers filled with politics of which I am heartily tired. I will rejoice when the election is over. Not much either unless Henry Clay is elected.

Sept. 12. This day I have been in my own house nine months and they have flown rapidly. Nine more and I may be inhabiting my last earthly house.

I had a walk down in the City this evening and got some ice cream, mead & did some shopping and had a most pleasant ride back, but now I have the tooth ache. Oh when will dear C come home. I have finished my book of miscellanies and want another but am not able to buy it. New moon to night, but not yet visible.

Sept. 13. Bud came early this morning from Charley's.

Have been drawing a piece to day for C. Oh when will he come home. I want to see him so much. I cannot realize that he may not yet be here for weeks. He has been gone three months to day.

Sept. 14. Ah I have nothing to write, my mind is so absorbed thinking of C's return that I can do nothing but think of him.

Nature was never more lovely than now and I enjoy the early morning air and the beautiful flowers that alone cheer me, and do not desert me nor bloom less kindly because there are none but myself to admire.

Sun. Sept. 15. I joyfully attended Mr Clapps Church to day to hear him again and though his sermon was far from as interesting as I have heard yet it was good indeed. Mr S came home with me. B had been here and threw the papers in the garden. He came again this evening.

Night. Have taken a walk to market and got some fruit. Cs house was as dark as my mind is gloomy. The 15th is gone and he is not here yet. Ah will he not be by another Sabbath. I trust he will.

CHAPTER FOUR

A Tale of Real Life

*O*ver the course of several days that the diary tells us were rela-
tively cheerful for her, Madaline Edwards wrote the long, autobiographical
"Tale of Real Life" that closes her first Writing Book.[1] *In it, she reflected on*
the mistakes that led to her downfall, but she also reaffirmed her gratitude
to the neglectful Bradbury and her wavering faith in him.

No work illustrates the fusion of Edwards's biography with her imagina-
tive life better than the "Tale of Real Life." As it opens, we find her sitting on
her bed under her "musketoe net sanctum," addressing imagined readers.
The painful experience at the heart of Edwards's tale penetrates the high-
flown language of antebellum popular literature in which she cloaked it.
Through the conventionalized account of her marriage we can readily see
the predicament of a rebellious, intellectually ambitious teenager. Confused
by romantic myths of "the degree of love it took to constitute connubial fe-
licity," harried by older, undesirable suitors, and urged to marry by her
guardians, she wed the least suitable of them all. The "Tale" unfolds from
that first, unfortunate choice.

Well! here I have seated myself in my musketoe net sanctum to try to
do that which I never attempted in my life—to write a tale. "To write a
tale? why I thought says one that was the easiest thing on earth for every
penny magazine, every daily periodical and novel are filled with them

and from that [I] infer the task before you is a very easy one." Now this is one, and a very prominent reason why it is so difficult to write a tale of fiction at least; for every brain from the loftiest intellectual and shining wit, down through the many grades of mediocrity to the old maid and school girl that could connect two ideas has been employed upon the theme of fiction, and consequently the path so often trodden must be stripped of it[s] brightest blossoms, and culled [of] its very foliage, and as one of old said "There is nothing new under the Heavens," it might seem a useless task. But as I am not going to tread upon that path so often chosen by the more imaginative, not even to gather the withered leaves that lay beneath their feet, and weave them into a garland so fit to crown the muse of melancholy, whose influence seems to imbue every subject I touch, I will travel a by path which too has been much trodden and if it had its due would be far more so than the former. I mean a tale founded on facts, for I am fully impressed with the belief that real life contains more soul stirring events, more of the sublime and noble, more subjects for the moralist or sentimentalist more misery and misfortunes, more love, joy, grief and dispair, than the pen of fiction has ever portrayed. True there are not so many broken hearts in every day life as fiction represents, but there are more that are every thing but broken, or as Byron truly says "though broken still live on." There are many to be met with and we dialy see them on whose lips the faint gleam of a mean[ing]less smile may play while the heart has not felt a touch of joy or even hope for years. We may look in vain to read the heart by the words, tears, smiles, or looks when in the crowd. It is to be gifted with almost supernatural power to dive into the depths of the deeply lacerated heart, whose sorrows the world has produced, but holds not in its wide catalogue of remedies, nor possesses the wish to remove. Oh! there are greater and deeper cells within the heart than the pen of fiction ever dreamed of and its griefs are too bitter and blightning ever to be expressed by words, tears looks, or actions much less the lifeless pen. So the deepest sorrows of the heart and the greatest disappointments of the soul are so seldom chronicled from our own life, and *cannot* be by others, but are *felt* and borne in the anguish that words are too poor to express.

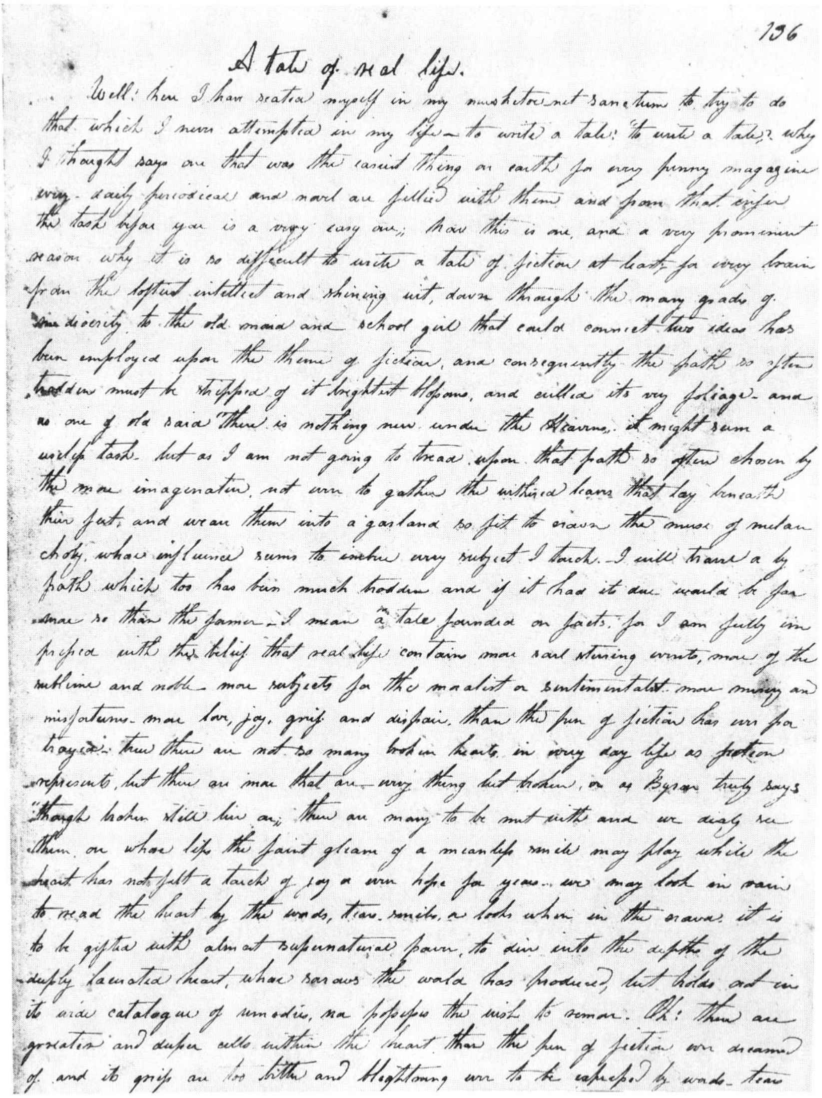

136

A tale of real life.

Well! here I have seated myself in my most retired sanctum to try to do that which I never attempted in my life — to write a tale; to write a tale? why I thought says one that was the easiest thing on earth for every penny magazine every daily periodical and novel are filled with them and from that infer the task before you is a very easy one; now this is one, and a very prominent reason why it is so difficult to write a tale of fiction at least, for every brain from the loftiest intellect and shining wit, down through the many grades of mediocrity to the old maid and school girl that could connect two ideas has been employed upon the theme of fiction, and consequently the path so often trodden must be stripped of its brightest blossoms, and culled its very foliage — and as one of old said 'there is nothing new under the Heavens' it might seem a useless task — but as I am not going to tread upon that path so often chosen by the more imaginative, not even to gather the withered leaves that lay beneath their feet, and weave them into a garland so fit to crown the muse of melancholy, whose influence seems to imbue every subject I touch. — I will travel a by path which too has been much trodden and if it had its due would be far more so than the former — I mean a tale founded on facts, for I am fully impressed with the belief that real life contains more soul stirring events, more of the sublime and noble — more subjects for the moralist or sentimentalist — more misery and misfortune — more love, joy, grief and despair, than the pen of fiction has ever portrayed: true there are not so many broken hearts in every day life as fiction represents, but there are more that are every thing but broken, or as Byron truly says "though broken still live on"; there are many to be met with and we daily see them on whose lips the faint gleam of a meanless smile may play while the heart has not felt a touch of joy or even hope for years... we may look in vain to read the heart by the words, tears, smiles, or looks when in the crowd; it is to be gifted with almost supernatural power, to dive into the depths of the deeply lacerated heart, whose sorrows the world has produced, but holds not in its wide catalogue of remedies, nor possesses the wish to remove. Oh! there are greater and deeper ills within the heart than the pen of fiction ever dreamed of and its griefs are too bitter and blighting ever to be expressed by words — tears

The first page of Madaline's *Tale of Real Life*. Courtesy The Southern Historical Collection, University of North Carolina at Chapel Hill.

The publick thinks there are no such events in real life and, that passionate and ceaseless love, as well as the slow but sure eating canker of grief at the sensitive heart, are things that exist only in the brain of the poet, or the pen of the novelist. But for my own part I have never seen a work of fiction or truth that has expressed in its whole body the feelings that have glowed upon my breast when kindled by love (such as it now feels) or that has agonized under the conflicts that it has often borne.

The only fiction I shall borrow is that the conversation never will take place that I shall here represent, but those parts that shall be called up as having passed between myself and friend in happier days are true. The circumstances are all true and the portion that relates to the present is true with the exception that she is not here to represent herself, but knowing her so well I can do it most faithfully. All (and even more) that relates to herself is true and it is the first attempt in my life to embody a part of mine, or any other persons life into a tale or roman. I expect it will be but a bad affair, however here it is.

"Pardon me!" said Sarah K to her friend, "I would not wilfully intrude upon your sorrows or lonely moments, although I would willingly share them if you think as you once did, that I am worthy [of] your confidence; why is it dear Justine that after years of separation I now meet you so changed? and though I have now been with you but a few days, yet I see that change has been a sad one to you and must be to those that love you, and that miniature you."

"Hold," said Justine, who sat holding in her hand a miniature wet with her falling tears, "this miniature is dearer to me than all in life but the original, speaking of those that *loved* me, has touched a tender chord, of all that loved me when we last parted, not one remains. Not even yourself if you knew all. The miniature you may not see; for the original you never saw. But more of their history anon," (said she as she carefully closed the case and laid it away.)

"Come sit down and we will together call up many past days and scenes, though they stand out now on the page of memory, seared, and bleached with the frosts of sorrow and grief. The time was when the sun-shine of hope gilded the fields and forests through which we have often raced together. Yes Sarah you say truly *I am changed,* in all save the deep feelings of soul over which outward circumstances have no controul, and but a few of those but have met some change. *Hope* for one I thought was gone forever. Friendship is changed for I find but few that wish mine and still fewer ready to give, and worse than this that it is nearly always it is self-love and not pure unselfish emotions of the soul. I am changed in years, in the hopes and joys of life. I am changed in my confidence in mankind, but I still retain my truthfulness of soul my sympathy for others, my ardent desire to help the needy, my joy for the prosperity of others, my burning aspirations after something more ennobling than I have ever found in life, and though my happiness was all lost upon the too oft imaginary sea of love, yet I have in later life found my heart more capable of realizing and feeling the emotions than when you saw me courted by the many who said they loved. In fact Sarah I never loved until now."

"Why Justine! though I have heard your married life has not proved one unruffled by misfortunes yet I thought as there was no compulsion, and less wealth to influence you in that choice that you must have been actuated by love, and yet it was an enigma that I have never yet solved for I saw your hand was sought by two that were men of high standing and wealth besides others who were lower in the scale of wealth but not in merit. I saw you surrounded by many friends and I believe no enemies, and you were ever loved by those of your own sex who envied the power you possessed of rendering yourself agreeable to the hoary headed grand father as well as to the prattling infant and I have often looked around and saw other girls who had nearer relations to aid them in their advancement, who had more beauty and fairer prospects than yourself, but were passed almost unsought whilst you were caressed, and when I sought for the cause I found it in your disposition and retiring manner as well as cheerful and happy life with the wish to make all around you the same. But as the subject has at this period come up of your marriage to be plain with you dear friend I have ever wondered how you placed your choice where you did and with my prophetic eye read for you a sad future, although if my prayers could have averted it, your life should not have been such an one as that of your ill-fated friend who made as bad a choice as you have done. But Justine I often looked at your joyous gambols with my little Mary Jane and the next moment perhaps engaged in deep converse with some man of letters or poring over the page of history or science until I forgot my own ill-suited union in thinking a creature so formed for love must meet a bright future. And you have not forgotten yet the time we took a walk down the shady hill, your intention to find a turkey nest and mine to try and dissuade you from what I was then fearful would end in what it really did your union with Mr E.[2] I depicted to you in the gentlest manner I could the misery arising from a union where no congeniality existed, and the great and mighty risk there was to run in forming that tie that was so often desecrated, but I discovered that your affections that I would have deemed priceless had I been the *man* to possess them, were not likely to be changed by my words, and we both returned to Rose Cottage as you named it with drooping spirits mine because I had not succeeded and yours because you were opposed by one that I well know you loved. And I felt your position for I too had felt it years before and, at that time was rueing that I had not followed the advice of those whose visions were not distorted by the name of love. After that I said but little though I felt much. Not that I had any aversion to Mr E. On the contrary you know I ever liked him as a good and worthy man, but he was not suited for you, there was nothing congenial between you. His reputation was blameless, but his circles of life and yours were different. His education I know but little of yet did not think it was of the depth to make you happy who lived in your books, and I saw that you bid fair to repent with your friend the day you ever met."

These words were uttered without the eyes of the two friends having met, until the last sentence was finished. Sarah looked up and saw that the tears of her friend had ceased, that her pale and care-worn brow showed signs of distress too deep for tears relief, that the tide of memory had rolled back to the days of which she had been speaking, and fearful lest she had broken up the walls of the partly closing Oblivion she paused and waited a reply.

At length she said, "I trust Justine that I have not wounded your feelings in this calling up the past. I had forgotten that your feelings were
ever too sensitive for the slightest touch of unkindness or reproof, and
had thought all could look back, with calm dispair as I had learned to
do, but your look, your heart rending sigh tells me you are still the girl,
in your inability to bear unmoved your own or others miseries."

"Sarah!" replied Justine, "while you have been calling up the scenes
and circumstances that may seem to you as though forgotten by a heart
that has since had so much of greater weight to bear I have listened with
sorrow and deep, deep regret, and as I then *did* not, *could* not analyze
my own feelings let me now do so; the good heart you spoke of my possessing my benevolent disposition has been my ruin. I had other offers
than E. with whom I am convinced I was better pleased; but Mr P. to
whom I should have given my hand, unfortunately sought it at the time
my ideas of the degree of love it took to constitute connubial felicity
were so exagerated from fear of doing as I had seen others before me do
that I felt that I should desecrate the marriage vow to give him my hand
and as I thought without my hand [heart]. Mr K [or R] whom you were
so anxious to claim me as his second bride, was found excluded from a
share of my humblest love from the single fact of his extreme close disposition. His wife and I were very intimate and I could not fail to see
many things which he did not hide from my childish view yet would
fain have obliterated them when he sought my love to fill the place of
one so recently dead. But to either of these, and others there were some
one or all of my friends to consent, and my old Aunt did say she would
compel me to marry M.E. who lived near her and on whom I could not
look with common civility. But when E. paid his addresses to me, none
were exactly [un]willing only from the fact that he was a steady, industrious, and honourable man. Still as I had no Father, Mother or brother
to please in this union I did not conceive that the world had a right to
judge. I felt that he was alone, was not happy and the loss of my love
would make him more so, and in an ill-fated moment construed my
sympathy into love and agreed to become his wife.

"The marriage you know was a hurried one, for my antipathy to what is termed 'a wedding' was so great that I would not let him apprise my Uncle and Aunt until the evening we were united and chose the sabbath that they could not invite any but yourself and Louisa. My old Uncle did not oppose it, but looked tearful as he spoke to me after giving his consent. E then left for the parson and license. From that moment I wept incessantly. I fell down on my bed and wept until my heart was near breaking; Oh! would it not have been better that it had? Dear Sarah you would have pitied me if you had known the conflicts of my soul. I would then, yes when standing on the floor to have escaped. I longed for some one to tell me not to accept him even then. But I felt that I should be laughed at and I yielded. My Aunt sent for you and some others. When you entered my room with cousin M, I felt that I could not see you. I wished to die to escape that which I was imposing on myself. It was near dark before you could face me up to dress and when I was, with my swolen eyes and pale cheeks I was an object for the sacrifice I was making. You have not forgotten how anxiously and long all but myself watched the return of E. It was near nine o clock and how I prayed that some fatality would arrest my doom. At last he was announced, in a rage because he had been opposed in getting license on the Sabbath. Would to God he could have read my heart as he led me in that death-like hall before my friends. As we stood on the floor the tears rolled down my cheeks afresh and when the ceremony was ended I felt a doom that has been more than realized.

"It is a singular coincidence between the marriage of a great man and a poor ignorant girl, that I should have been married on the same day of the month that Byron was, the 2nd of Jan., that I should have felt the same forebodings, and that E addressed me by my maiden name as soon as seated, which was the case with Byron, and it cannot be ascribed to my reading his life before for it was not until after my marriage that I ever read a page in it, for it was not in my Uncles library and I did not possess it.[3]

"From that day sorrow commenced for me, though I scarce yet saw it. Ah Sarah many times have I called up your looks and actions that night as you strove to feel cheerful as if by that act you could infuse into my soul happiness that would gleam along my future path. I remember the

last kiss you gave me as we parted for the night; and the sad look as you
left my bridal bed." And her tears fell fast as she finished these words.

"Dearest friend," replied Sarah, "indeed those days are still fresh in
my memory and time can never obliterate your looks on that fatal night.
Ah too well did I read your doom, as I have heard you pronounce the
vow that would one day be repented. Truly you looked like an offering
for a sacrifice as it was but that is all past, and do not weep thus for it
cannot be recalled. And I trust there are before you yet happy days."

Justine wiped her eyes and looked up as though she strove to master
the deep gushings of her soul in order to reply to her friend.

"Sarah it was the wisdom worthy of God that he so ordained that our
sorrows and disappointments should not come upon us like a mighty
avalanche, but like the little rivulets that collect by degrees to form a
stream, then a sea and at last a mighty Ocean. Thus the heart is learned
by degrees until it dare not believe how much it can endure and still
live, if it may be called life when youth, love, hope, joy, friends, and children are all lost to us forever. When I left you for the South I felt then a
grief that I did not believe human nature could endure, I loved you (Oh
that I had loved E as well) more than it is believed one woman can love
another. I loved many that I was leaving, and I was just launching out
upon a new world to me with all my sad forebodings. No wonder then
that I should have wept all but tears of blood. I came to the South. We
were poor but soon found a home and with our daily toil began to live,
but were not long alone for soon I was the Mother of a dear boy. Then
I first knew love, pure and deep love.[4] Our exertions were redoubled
and we soon lived as comfortable as we could expect. My husband was
kind and devoted to me, but I had felt from the first week that he was
far my inferior in education or natural intellect, and I was sadly disappointed when I appealed to him for information to receive the answer
'dont know' and soon saw that he was compelled to call on me for the
most ordinary assistance in book-keeping or any other subject. This was
a sad blow to my aspiring wishes, but could have been borne could I
have concealed from all but my own heart his deficiency. But the world
saw it and I have blushed in company for an error made or ungram-

matical expression, and as I have ventured to look up and see the half suppressed smile and gaze of astonishment that met my quick eye. I have felt that I could die with shame; and I have looked on men of intellect and talents and felt willing to have been the slave of such an one sooner than the wife of E; and often have I refused invitations and debarred myself from company for no other reason than through fear of being mortified, though I will do him justice to say he possessed sense enough to keep silence upon subjects with which he was not conversant. And being a man of exceeding genteel appearance, made my position less critical than [it] would have been had he possessed the passion that most ignorant men have of appearing exceedingly smart. The truth is he was more to be pitied than condemned for he had no opportunities.

"Years rolled on and I was the Mother of a daughter and in those children I placed my whole earthly happiness.[5] This child I named for your little Mary Jane, and although she was less beautiful still she was dear very dear to me; but these two sickened and died in one week like two buds that grew on one stalk nipped by one frost. The leaves could not screen one, but both fell. Sarah here let me not attempt to profane their blest memory by a recital of my agony for words could not begin to convey to even another Mother what was then my afflictions, but this stroke threatened a termination of earthly sorrows for I was confined to my bed three months, from which I arose to live out the succession of griefs that have so thickly beset my path ever since.

"Soon I had another son but my fears were now alive and if it sighed, my heart was racked with torture; but seven months saw it laid in the cold clay beside the other loved ones.[6] E then moved to N.O. where he began to slacken in his energies and soon refused to do any thing to support his family. I was now the fourth time a Mother and when I looked on my Isabel and thought of her wanting, I have sat up near all night at hard work.[7] I strove late and early to possess the means to support her and if she lived to educate her for that was my greatest ambition. By this time every thing like affection was obliterated in my breast towards him, but I do affirm that I never told him such was the case, or that my feelings were ever hurt by his want of education for I have ever possessed the wish to hurt no ones feelings when nothing was to be gained by so doing at least. At the time my child was eighteen months old he was in no business and had openly avowed that failures had so often befallen him that he had resolved to use no efforts whatever. I told him I thought it a singular conclusion for a man to come to who had a wife and child to support, but he assigned some womanish reasons and I then felt that I had to renew my own [efforts]. I did so but it was little more than a sub-sistence I could earn and do my domestic work. House rent became due and the little that I had purchased with some of my paintings in the way of furniture was seized for rent. Then I told him in a mild but decisive tone that we must part, that the sole care and toil devolved on me and I could better endure it alone. I had often thought of a separation and wished for it, but the fear of the opinion of the world that makes and keeps so many in misery, the opinions that has smiled upon affluent vice and frowned upon poor virtue and must until it has become a law of justice in the world was what I too dreaded and lived my best years with a bad choice doomed to bear the penalty of my sad choice unpitied but not unblamed. He replied that life to him without me was not worth any thing and that he had rather live with me on bread and water than to leave me, but that I was perfectly right in wishing a separation and said that he had ever felt I was destined for some one higher than he was, and knew I could still marry who I pleased. The house was demanded and we had to leave. I sought and obtained a situation as teacher in the female Asylum in New O and I told him I should take charge on such a day: and we must part. He tried to screw up all the courage he could for the task and Oh! how I strove to conceal the tears that often rose to my eyes. At last it was my duty to select and arrange his linen and in doing this the thought of the seven years we had lived together in harmony if not love on my part, the four dear children we had nursed together, of his friendless situation and many things came crowding before me and I bursted into a flood of tears and that before him. At this his feel-ings found vent the same way and it ended in my telling him that if he left the place and shewed that he would change in the course of time I would again live with him. But here let me say the living child was the cause of this for I felt how hard it was to tear him from it when he loved it so dearly and she clasped her little arms around his neck as he wept over her and called him Pa. I thought of my own deathless love for her and wept that he should thus be torn from her, for he vowed he would not force her from me. To this he gladly assented; he went up to M——[Mobile?] and I to the Asylum with feelings better felt than told; before my first month closed my child was taken sick. I finished the month and apprised the board that I must leave for I could not discharge the duty of teacher and Mother to a sick child. They gave their consent with the injunction that I should return as soon as practicable and that my place should not be filled by another. I nursed this child eight weeks and the $20 I had recd for my services was barely enough for the medicine until she no longer needed it. I had recd a letter from E stating he was doing well. As soon as I saw my dear child was doomed to die I wrote him word, he arrived the day before her [death]. Never shall I forget the meeting of the child and father as near death as she had long seemed it then appeared she was well in a moment, but it was only the bright flicker before the dying lamp. She died and her last lisp was 'My Ma.'

"Forgive these tears that are not the first by millions that have fallen to that childs memory. Oh! God that hearts so linked as that of my last darling child's and her desolate Mother should so soon sever. Her little tomb was far from that of her brothers and sister but I knew that their pure blest spirits met beyond the vale of sorrow assigned their Mother and I strove not to lament in hopeless dispair, but it was useless. The more my exertions the more bitter were my sorrows. I felt that the last link that bound me to life was severed, that a sad destiny sported with my every joy or hope and that the last drop that filled my cup had now fallen and I [neither] sought nor wished comfort."

The two friends sat silent, for a length of time, each seemed buried in thoughts of the past, each read in the others life a counterpart of her own, and although Sarah was many years the senior, yet there had in Justines early youth existed a similarity of taste, disposition, and sympathy that drew them together in the closest bonds of friendship. Indeed their love was too deep for that word. After the three first years of

Justines marriage the correspondence by letter had ceased from more
causes than one and the two friends never heard from each other except
on the flying tongue of Rumour which had not been very tender of the
feelings of either one or the other.

"Justine," said Sarah. "I have thought deeply since you have been re-
peating a portion of your griefs through the few years of your hapless
life and I have been some times led to doubt the justice of that God who
holds our destinies in his hands, and the more so now that I find your
path has been through the thorns where your every friend thought you
entitled to tread upon the roses alone."

"Nay dear friend," replied the other, "do not thus speak of the God
whom we once commenced to serve together but if you are still of the
same creed you will find in nothing am I more changed than in this.
But not until recently had I that blessed conviction of the undeviating
justice of [our] Maker, and it has been to me the source of my greatest
happiness to find that we alone are chargeable with very many of the
faults, errors and misfortunes that our ignorant minds have laid to the
charge of the Almighty. It is in learning the laws of nature, the organic
and physical laws that has opened to mind a source of wisdom and a
just appreciation of the mercy and justice of the Holy One that I would
not exchange for all that I ever knew or felt of what is termed religion.
It is now I see that his first framed laws are not violated in order to take
from, or to secure to us the life of a friend or child when those laws have
been transgressed, and since learning these things I have given up the
popular cry of fatality in our every action or privation."[8]

"Our religious views we will discuss at some other time," said Sarah,
"so proceed with your narrative for all that concerns my friend ever has,
and will never fail to interest me; and I have ever thought two happy
hearts could not so entwine themselves as two that have first learned to
love in a bright day of life and had both felt the sorrows and griefs that
draw and cement two such hearts with force stronger than love, for all
can greet us with a smile when we are prosperous and happy and the
continual smile looses much of the charm with which we first welcomed
it, but we find so few to look into our sorrows, to lend even an atten-

tive ear, so few that will stand by us determined if they cannot avert, them that they will at least share them, so few but are filled with their own selfish ends and turn away from us when our hearts are wrung with agony, with the cold unmeaning words 'I am sorry for you, I pity you,' or some such epithet. We find perhaps one through a long life that will say 'Give me your hand and I will walk down the dark vista of life with you sharing alike its joys or sorrows.' But tell me all that has befalled you, since the period of looseing the last loved child that I know you idolized from the many evidences I have of your deep passion for children so often displayed towards my own."

"Sarah! It is a relief to my heart [to] find one of my own sex that possesses a heart to sympathize and to share, for alas! with regret I say it they have ever been my worst enemies and have robbed my heart of more joy than even death has ever done.

"To tell you one half that has since transpired would fill a volume of no ordinary size but I will give you only a few outlines. Suffice it [to say that] after the death of loved Isabel I separated from E. Circumstances, and wants too numerous to relate sometime after again brought me under the necessity of giving my hand to one that I must have loved better than I did the former although had I been left free to choose would not have been my choice. And here again my benevolence caused my misery. He was slandered, as I thought unjustly and he was far from his friends and my pity was aroused; but still this much would never have been acknowledged to my own breast had not my Uncle with whom I was then living, have been indirectly the cause.

"Sarah there seems to be a *fatality* or at least a something I can call no name that has ever attended my life, it is a secret voice that ever speaks of sorrow and not once of joy, it is a prophetic eye. It is the low wail that stirs the forest tops, and ends in the tornado that lays the roots bare. It is not that my natural disposition would cherish or even engender such thoughts, but they have lived in me. This phantom was the same that whispered in my ear when you saw me a tearful bride; and though it departed at times yet it has never failed to make its appearance when danger is nigh. And strange it is, I never have found power to resist its

mournful presages. It seems to possess the charm of the serpent over
me. To this man I was united with fears more ominous than the other.
Oft in the night have I lain by his side with the tears streaming from
my eyes, and I have almost choked in endeavouring to suppress them
for fear he should awake and ask the cause. Twice I remember I stole
softly up and gazed in his face by moon-light and wept 'till my heart
was near bursting. I never had the slightest intimation from any source,
but looks and sighs that spoke of wrong yet towards me. Yet I could not
divest my mind of the fear that he had a wife ere I saw him, and I said
so half jestingly and he laughed so at me I felt ashamed of my suspicion. He was taken sick with the epidemic. Not one dollar had we, no
friends not even an acquaintance to apply to, but my resolution was not
to be at that time shaken. I saw this was the time for action. I went out
among strangers and by the hardest begging, obtained work. For this I
was more greatful than the beggar of alms. To tell of the suffering I endured in a hot little bed room with a sick husband to attend to and to
sew for my very life for the means to keep him alive is more than my
words can convey, but this was not half. So little could I earn that I had
not bread to eat myself, and when I found an hour to crawl to bed I
often went so hungry that I could not sleep, and I have wept from real
hunger, for the sum I was paid for a garment when finished was dolled
out for medicine and nourishments for him and bread and water was all
I had for many days, until I was so weak I could with difficulty ascend
the stairs to our little room that was rented on a credit. I concealed from
him my hunger and as well as I could my tears, but my changed face he
plainly saw and once he wept, as he thought of my situation. Oh a heart
less feeling would have pitied the being that could so devote herself to
one so little deserving as *he knew* himself to be."

"Oh Justine you must at that time have thought of your old Uncle
with his well spread table and the plenty with which his servants were
supplied, and have felt that were the power of foresight given us, you
would still have been there free from want at least."

"Yes Sarah I thought of all these things and many more, I thought
of the home I had left a few weeks before and still did not sigh that I

had done so, for when he was slandered, I said to him in those words of Moores that expresses more true love than any two lines I ever read:

> 'I know not, I ask not if guilt's in that heart
> I but know that I love thee whatever thou art,'[9]

and I now felt it were joy enough to see him restored; this I soon saw. He was industrious and we were soon out of debt. My exertions were now redoubled, not a cent of my rent or house expenses did I suffer him to pay, I did it with my sewing.

"One day he came home excited and proposed a trip up Red river.[10] I then thought he had better leave me until he saw if he could get in buisness first. To this he assented, hurried off to send or come for me in a few weeks. Going to the P.O one day to get news from him, waiting with breathless hope a letter was handed me by his own address. I broke the seal thinking it was from a sister he had spoken of in A—— [Alabama] and the first word that met my eye was "My dear husband." Great God my reason had liked to have forsaken me. I thought I should have fallen in the street, but I walked hurriedly to the little hut that I dwelt in, bolted the door, threw myself on my hard bed read the letter again and again, and could not comprehend it, for her name was signed K and his was E. That night sleep was a stranger and torture that I had never felt was now my doom. In the course of that next day the little I possessed was sacrificed, my rent paid, and I was on board a Steamer destined for the same place. I arrived there, saw him, handled the letter to him and mildly asked if this was the reward for all I had endured. He read it, and asked me to give him time to explain. He saw my careworn cheek and weeping eyes. He saw that in two weeks I was a shade of myself and remorse must have entered his soul. He then went into a minute detail of his deception and the causes, said he had a wife and three children, but for the best of reasons she could no longer look on him as husband; and seeing that my fond confiding nature was imposed on, he said the world was nothing to him if I left him, but if I would live with him and take his children in the course of time he should be supremely happy."

"Heavens! Justine is it thus your love was doomed to be blighted first and last? Is it thus you so clearly divine your doom without knowing why? And as much as I have proved false and erroneous in man this is an act for which I was not prepared, to think he could unite himself to one of such a truthful soul knowing at the time the many sorrows you had seen and at the very moment doing that which he knew would add ten fold to them. How could he have gazed on your devotion from a sick bed and not have divulged all? How could he have felt to see you thus suffer and toil for him feeling guilty as he was? Ah dear friend, the deep gushings of your true heart have been wasted upon the undeserving and deceptive."

"I was then far away from all I knew. He swore love and constancy. About two weeks after, we took a long walk; he spoke sorrowfully and of the past, and womanish nature clung to him now that he was not happy. He spoke of his dear children, and I strove to hide my own broken confidences from my own eyes that I might cheer him, but I felt truthfulness did not exist in his breast and I dreaded what might occur through life if passed with him.

"One morning in Jan. 1840 he was going to take a ride and as he never failed came in my room at the Hotel kissed me and said he would be back at night. I felt unhappy and walked to the window to look after him, he turned on his horse and gave one long look at me, and *that* look was his last."

Here Justine walked the floor with rapid steps and down cast eyes, she seemed to live over again the bitter anguish that must have visited her pillow that night. She seemed to call up in that agonized countenance all the misgiving and suspense that crowded through her mind situated as she was; and yet there was a look of calm dispair which spoke of resignation.

"Sarah, I thought I had known grief before. I had recd the last sigh from the death bed of four dear children, I had suffered the blight of hope, love, joy, and stings of disappointments, I had been deceived by him that I would have died to defend his character when stained but now, to be *deserted* amidst all, without friends, among strangers, discarded by every relative, and without a dollar, this torture, this madness let me not attempt to depict. In a few days I was again on the water determined to beg my way to where I knew he had gone, not to live with him, but to see and know the worst. I could not have lived had I not done so, my mind was at such a stage that the reaction produced by my travelling alone saved my life.

"The painful humility of begging was denied me for the Capt and some of the passengers had learned my position and before I knew how to address the former I was handed a donation from him raised by the passengers and told my passage was gratis. At that moment I was trying to force into my heart the most bitter misanthropy, but when this evidence of pity and feeling was given, the gush of gratitude dispersed all the efforts I was forming and the tears of acknowledgements washed misanthropy forever from my mind. I found that earth must yet contain some pure and lofty spirits, and if it should never be my lot to mingle among them I might be permitted to gaze on them as they soared above, as the humble bird does the eagle in his mighty flight. I felt that there *must* surely be some spot in life that would again welcome my weary feet else why did my Maker permit me thus to live. I had not then learned that which has since taught me better sense and knowledge of his laws. I met with kind friends all along that desolate journey, and not one of them have I ever met since, but wherever they are scattered, and whatever their destinies their memories can never fade from my heart and I trust that God who gives us friends in the time of need will guard them from sorrow or want. Their kindness could not have fallen on one who more deeply felt its weight. Sarah I will not give you the details of that tedious and sorrowful trip. Suffice it I arrived at the house in Ala at which I expected to find him and family. I found he had been there taken her and his children and left for Texas. There I learned he possessed the most abandoned character, had fled from justice when I first met him and did not dare remain in the United States.[11] I learned his whole history, returned to J—— [Jackson] in Miss to sew for wages with a lady I knew. It was now my only alternative for a support. Oh the agony I endured to look back and think on all I had lost for one so lost

and had not only ruined but deserted me. I was hard at work one day
when a letter was handed me. I knew the superscription and cannot say
I tore the seal with indifference. I read it again and saw the same dissimulation. I[t] implored me to say he might again claim me, and he
would leave on the first boat for me. That if he had deemed he should
have lost me by going for his children he would sooner have given them
up for life, but thought to get there, leave the Mother and come back
to me direct but on arriving here learned I had left R[ed]-R[iver] and
writing there had learned where I had gone. He plead undying love and
told of the sleepless nights he had spent since he had clasped me to his
breast. I answered the letter at great length, telling him my confidence
was lost forever, if his character was not, and that the Mother of his children should never be wronged by me knowingly; that he had brought
ruin on me and shame on my family yet I forgave him for the love I
once bore and to try and be worthy of the same from his Creator, that
I could not forget him yet would strive to think of him and his cruelty
no more. This letter was answered in one or two sheets, using all the art
of which he was so capable, to convince me he was innocent and that
her relations were so and so, and the more imploringly urging my return to him. One letter called for another until one from her came. It
was the humblest letter I ever saw acknowledging her fear of my return
to him. I then forbid his correspondence as it was alone productive of
misery to all parties. After this I recd one from him and another from
her. His was bordering on insult and hers the most shameful production
that ever emanated from a females pen. Yes the man for whom I had
lost my all in life could thus treat me because I would not add infamy to
shame, and his wife that he would joyfully have left for me, could now
address me in such words. I gave all up and strove to forget, but in vain.
I worked day and night. I was deserted and now my hands were all I had
on earth. For six months hard work I got only $15, was cheated out of
that and cast upon the same resources among strangers. Thus I toiled
until years have flown over and the inroads those years have made are
ploughed deep in my heart, and time cannot efface them. I cannot hide
them from my own soul but I would hear them from you, and can you

imagine one thousandth part and wonder that you find me no longer the happy girl you saw me the year previous to my marriage."

"No Justine my only wonder is that you are not far more changed, and I think you are only indebted to the happy faculty you have of conforming to all and every circumstance in life as though you were born to it, for the change being as well as it is and you have a source from whence to derive comfort to which he dare not look; for you can feel in your heart that others you never wilfully injured and this is ever a consolation to a good heart. I had not heard from you since 18—— and I did not know till late that you were living, much less of your bitter destiny. But dear Justine I would fain hope the miniature I found bedewed with your falling tears was not that of the man who could thus rob your heart of its best treasures and leave you to mourn over the wreck alone; you could not wish thus to call up his memory. I think it a desecration to tears thus to waste them, and a tribute I would rather see you bestow elsewhere."

Here Justine looked into the face of her friend with feelings so mingled that the combination could not be read by her. For a moment she thought she saw a gleam of joy and hope but it passed away as the lightnings flash and gave place to a look of sorrow too full of meaning not to give forebodings to the heart of her that had just spoken.

"Sarah I have not forgotten to redeem my promise concerning that miniature, but how to begin, puzzles me. It was the likeness of the only being I may say I ever truly loved in the name of man. Yes I am doomed to love once more but I feel its the last and as all my love has been so ill-fated do not wonder that I tremble when I find it taking daily deeper and deeper root in the depths of my soul, when I feel the very tendrils that have so withered by former love, now awakening into newer life and all but *hope* to animate my breast. I have looked upon the stream chained with icy fetters, but I knew the Summer sun would soon loosen those bonds and it would again go dancing on in gladness to the mighty deep to mingle with the thousand that bubble there. I have seen the forest stripped of every leaf and the lovely rose bush shorn of all but its piercing thorns, and I have turned away with the conviction that gentle Spring would soon deck them in beauteous robes and sweeter bloom. I have seen the mountain top bathed in the wintry snow but I knew the first sun beam from mighty Sol would flash upon its dreary summit and send that snow down its sides like the tears from pity's eyes, but I have never yet seen the heart and spirit regain its first confidence, trust, hope, joy and love that it had felt before the blissful Eden had been entered by the fell destroyer. I had felt that all was lost to me in life, even to the pity of mankind. I had lost the joys of youths paradise and had waded through the desert sands of Arabia's desert, had felt all the changes and blasting miseries of life and had taken my stand calmly awaiting the decree of him who had given me being. Sarah I had often loved, for I never met a good, noble and feeling heart but it awoke in my soul the emotions that may be termed love, and singular it is that whenever I have been deeply and truly loved I could bestow the least; but I always felt that my heart had not realized its dreamy bliss in the world of love that had stood out in bold relefe in girlhood that had beckoned me on through and amid years of sorrow, and would not even then desert me, but stood by as a phantom and not a substance. I had loved some for one trait some for another, had realized many things in one, and found as many wanting of those traits and qualities that made the ideal I sought, and I felt that such beings must exist or why were the yearnings of our souls forever going out in search of them, but I felt such an one did not live for me. Sarah the fates that have ever seemed buisy with my destiny sent such an one to my rescue when I stood on the brink of ruined hopes praying for the fabled waters of Lethe to sweep over my memory as the waves of sorrow had rolled over my heart. This being arose from behind those troubled waves and his smile told of joy that I dare not realize. I listened as one in a dreamy trance and called up the past as evidence against the future. His words were few but the[y] were rightly uttered and ere I was aware the heart that had long sought a resting place was given with all its cares to the only man I have ever loved. Yes it has been said our affections can not be so strong as in youth; it is not so at least in my case. I loved them from different motives—the impulse was different. That love was but the ripple of the wave but this is the bed of the stream on which no evanescent bubble rises but moves in the depths of its own feelings. And yet Sarah there are circumstances attending this attachment that must ever remain a secret even from my dear friend. It is said by Mrs Ellis[12] that love is a compound of admiration and pity, but in my case there was none of this towards him, but I am convinced if I possess a portion of his it had its rise in those sympathies and here again I cannot divest my mind of fear, for although I place all the confidence in this object that a heart could do who had never been wronged, yet the demon that whispers my miseries long before I can even point the road that leads me to them will not let me hush the sounds that will echo back to my happy moments. I am far happier than since I first entered the pales of matrimony and could I forget the past would defy all but God to disturb my joy; but Oh! there is one heart rending woe of which we have not spoken. It is more chilling in its nature than desertion itself. It is to love thus to madness and to *feel* and know, however that object might wish to reciprocate that your own unworthiness prevents it. This is my case and the undying love I bear him is to pave my way I greatly fear to deeper misery than I have yet known, and if this last drop is added to my cup it *cannot, must* not contain more. Sarah I have loved him because I have found him a congenial spirit, a forgiving one, a soul in whom there was unison with all the good that existed in my nature and the elevated and good that stood boldly out and soliciting my imitation. He is what I sought long and found last. Oh! God that I could have been the spotless bride of such a man. I love him for all, all that is in his name and nature but yet as often as I have been deluded into the belief that my sympathy was love, I felt that towards him there was no room for this sentiment, I have ever felt that I was no way instrumental in adding to his pleasure but was ever receiving and not giving. I thought he was one on whom the cloud of sorrows and misfortunes had never rested, that his path had been strewn with flowers and that he stood in no need of my efforts to add to his happiness one jot and I have almost been selfish enough to wish him some little mishap that I could remove in order to feel that I was of some service to him. Sarah the freshness of my young confiding soul seems to live afresh towards this man, all but the innocence of former years crowds upon my gushing heart as I think of him, but ah! I wish I could keep down the terrific fear of a cruel [blow] in some shape or other. I trust it is only a phantom of a fearful heart, that may not be realized, and that my separation from him will be for the tomb that will shield me from farther sorrows and disappointments.

Ever since I have known him I have been impressed with the presentiments [of doom] which I have formerly spoken of and I well know with his profound caution he cannot name one instance in which he thinks he has transgressed it but, I have well concealed from his view that I for a moment believed he had concealed any thing from me, for I knew I could give him every action of my life with the deepest trust, but that it was not my place to ask or seek his, that there was an indescribable belief ever in my mind that he would not have me know some things I ever felt, and I have not sought to learn it. He is a man of the greatest caution and will never conceive how or why I conjectured such a thing, but it is what I have often seen that the very means we employ to conceal are those which develop the secrets that we would enshrine so deep within our hearts that we could not call them up ourselves and reading this in the path I have trodden in studying human nature, I saw and felt this with force, and yet I would not have betrayed it to him or others for the world. But circumstances have arisen lately to confirm my conjectures, and I have learned that which convinced me that the placid exteriour often hid the cares of his heart, and I have felt if he was dear to me in his happy hours, how doubly dear was he in distress. I feel that I could live forever with him in joy and happiness yet I could die happier if I knew I could share a sorrow or ease one pang.

I had recently come to this knowledge and I was sitting contemplating each feature of his miniature (for it is many days since I saw him) trying if I could trace a shade of sorrow or care on his fair brow. I thought of the bitter anguish of my own heart and I wept that he too should ever have felt one pang. I would gladly have looked on him and died with the belief that nought but momentary anxiety had ever touched his heart, but it has been ordered otherwise and pains me from another cause. I fear that he will be dissatisfied that I have learned what he so anxiously sought to conceal, not that he will for a moment suspect I was so lost to the better sentiments as to seek this knowledge, for my truthfulness towards him will act as a true talisman to guard his heart from suspicion towards me where I am so innocent. But I now know that his secrets had nothing to do with my own happiness and hence there was no injustice in his concealing them from me, but the buisy world never lets our misfortunes die. It is the last that is forgotten with our faults. We might as soon expect forgiveness as forgetfulness. It is not that I love him less since I heard it, but more, it is not that I fear he will deem me capable of betrayal for that thought cannot exist in his nature. If I thought so I could wring from my soul the last confidence in man and substitute dispair in its stead but yet all that was of a nature to conceal would be locked in my breast forever, not even his most bitter hate could ever cause me to betray his trust."

"Justine it does truly seem that no common destiny has awaited you through life; and your power of divining coming sorrows without the ability to resist is truly astonishing for if you had have taken warning in many instances how much could have been spared you of pain and blightning hopes. But now that you have centred your hearts best treasures of undying love on such an object I trust there is much joy awaiting your future path for I am a proselyte to your faith of later affections being the strongest in the hearts of those who early learned they had made shipwreck of the noble passion of love. . . ."

"Pity my faults Sarah and do not condemn too harshly for it is not in mortals power to see, weigh and understand the causes, temptations and deceptions that have conspired to make your once joyful friend, the changed being that I am."

The tale is finished and will easily be perceived to contain a few of the incidents of my own life. What inducement there was to write it is alone known to myself. Perhaps the eyes of one far away may look over it when I am dead, perhaps the eyes of one dear object whose eyes have never yet beheld the light of life may here read a portion of that which has befallen its Mother and learn to shun the path in which she was led. These considerations have induced me to pen many of the humble lines that these pages contain, at all events they have given employment to my mind and made me feel a deeper debt of gratitude to my God and my dear C.

Sept 12th 1844.

Lest when there is none to vindicate the little good I may possess I will here leave an apology for what may seem very egotistical in the above. Sarah was the real name of a beloved female friend with whom I passed the year previous to my marriage and whose fate since then has run almost in the same stream of mine own; and although she was not gifted with flattery and she possessed such confidence in my being proof against the same, that she often gave vent to her opinions and feelings towards me in words far more extravagant than those in which I have here depicted.

Alas! I have deserved but little commendation in life and yet I would not seem to others an egotist. *If ever* these pages are read when I am laid in the tomb I trust they will not be thought that I left them with the hope of approval or sympathy. Only in the heart of one now living have I ever found it and he will understand my motives. He has strove to increase in me a fondness for writing and I generally take some subject on which I *feel* or I could not do even as well as I do.

Sept 14th [1844], N O.

CHAPTER FIVE

To Controul My Love

*E*dwards resolved that Bradbury's neglect would not destroy *her. Although she gave in to her emotions at odd moments, particularly in the face of his obvious indifference when he returned to New Orleans, she became absorbed in reading, friends, and national politics. Most important of all, she turned to her writing with new energy. With her interest piqued, perhaps, by the "Tale," which was her longest single work, Edwards began to send material to the* Native American *newspaper.*

Monday, September 16, 1844. Rose at day light and watered my garden. Went down in the City on business and have just got home very tired. The moon shines lovely but alas there is not [nought] to trace the beauteous firmament with me. All is alone as far as mortals are concerned but my own thoughts are not still. Will Charley be home before this moon wanes? I trust so.

My hen has got ten pretty chickens so I have something to pet besides the flowers.

Sept. 17. This is the annivirsary of the birth of my first born and of the death of my other little boy. Many, very many have been my sorrows since my first maternal kiss was given to the one and the tears of bereavement to the corpse of the other. But my hope is now stronger of meeting them again. Oh how sweetly the moon beams upon my flowers

181

to night and I have such lovely sweet roses open. I wish C would come home before they are gone. I watered them all to night for there is yet no prospects for rain.

Sept. 18. Pulled at day light a bunch with four full blown sweet roses and sent them to Mr Scott as he is very fond of flowers and dear C is not here to get them.

Sewed pretty constant. Finished reading Volney the second time and still find very much sound sense and sounder doctrine yet cannot coincide with him altogether in his opinions of Deity, and yet he has so mixed his opinions with questions and answers that I am at a loss to know what really are his views of Jehovah.

Mr S[ayre] sat with me awhile to night and has loaned me Miltons works.

Lovely night. Oh dear Charley do come and take one more walk with me.

Sept. 19. My garden looked very lovely this morning and watered it and sat down to my work and this evening did the same.

Bud came up to night and as he started [off] I walked to the corner with him and there saw a beautiful phenomenon in the sky. It was a luminous body which almost blinded us for an instant and as I cast my eyes up it passed off like the tail of a comet.

Sept. 20. I have been far down in the City and after coming home ran a splinter in my thumb which makes me feel very uneasy for fear of the lock jaw.

Mr S came and brought me two papers and to night I have read them and now for bed for I am very tired although this night is too tempting to sleep. Oh that C was here to sit up with me.

Sept. 21. B came up this afternoon and brought me some political papers, because Maine had given a democratic vote. I care not until the final test what the papers or people say.

Worked very hard to day and feel incompetent to enjoy this lovely night. So I will try the bed as a solace.

Sun. Sept. 22. Last night I awoke in great distress from sickness and vomited a great deal. Oh how I felt the loss of dear C at that time. A cold

NE wind this morning which is enough to brace a brick wall let alone our physical frames. Oh how sweet are the Autumn months. I wish to go to church and think I shall. How glad would I be to see Charley grace his pew to day.

Went to church and Mrs R a catholic went with me and was delighted with Mr C and it was really captivating. It has been one of Autumns earliest days. I have read some and drawed some this evening and would write some if I had a book.

Sept. 23. I have felt very melancholy to day for it does appear that Charley will never come home. I am out of all hope. I cannot read or work with any pleasure. Bud came up to night and brought me some papers and I have read them through, but I do not see any thing to make me glad and my only alternative is sleep before I get in a flood of tears.

Sept. 24. Well here it is night again and the time has expired for me to look for Charley. It does appear to me that he never will come home. Oh what is life worth with such loneliness, such torture and suspense. Alas! that I should be so doomed at such a time. I have been and am still reading Miltons Paradise lost as yet I will make no comments.

Oh what a soft moonlight to night and my Jassamines fling their odour in the night air but there is not one here to share it with me that I so long to have.

Sept. 25. I went to market this morning a thing very unusual with me, and I did it more to shake off my miserable feelings than any thing else.

Bud came this evening and brought me papers but all of interest to me in them is but little. I want to see Charley and I cannot think of any thing else. I start at every sound hoping it is him.

I believe we will have no equinoxial gale at last.

Sept. 26. Full moon and still no rain. It is over four weeks since it has rained and I have had no washing done in three for I am without water.

Night. Mr S has just left and I feel in pain. I am going to be sick, I fear. Oh when will Charley ever come home. My heart is almost in torture.

Sept. 27. This was the most lovely morning and I was up long before light to enjoy it and but one thing was a drawback. C was not here to partake with me.

Bud came and brought me some papers and took me on [a] walk and bought me some pickles &c quite good.

To day I finished a pretty little drawing for C.

The odour through my window now from the Jassamine is beyond description. I wish dear C was here for he so loves them.

Sept. 28. What on earth is the matter with the weather. It has been cold enough all day nearly to freeze me, cloudy high winds and such weather as we sometimes have in Dec. I am in misery with cold feet. How I long for a fire. Roses on such a day look out of place in the garden. I fear I shall not be able to get to church tomorrow for I have no warm dress.

Dear Charley have you cast me off and never intend to return. Oh I can hardly exist under my daily disappointment.

Sun. Sept. 29. Well it was cold enough last night and is so this morning to make one believe we had taken a leap into Iciland. I went to church to day and although I had a painful head ache yet I enjoyed Mr Clapps sermon much. It was concerning the trinity and holy spirit, which subject he had been requested to preach on and he relieved my mind upon the same.

I feel very unwell unable to enjoy reading or any thing else. Bud came just as I had closed doors and staid an hour. Strange man he is.

Sept. 30. Here is the last day of Sept and I told C when he left he would not return before Oct and even now there is little hope. Ah my foreboding spirit seldom deceives me.

I suffered almost death last night with cold feet. To night I have made my first fire in the house. I hope I will rest better. It is still very cold.

I wrote a short piece for a paper to day; I know not how it will be recd.

It is now near six weeks since it rained and it is extremely dusty.

Oct. 1. Early this morning while I was in dishabille a female friend called on me. I have watched with painful anxiety for C to day but alas it seems he will never be here again.

The weather is again quite warm but the dust is almost past endurance, and I do not know how I am to get along without water much longer.

I have read but little as I have been buisy sewing to day.

The stars shine lonely and Venus seems to look as though C had forgotten his promise to me of her.

Oct. 2. Bud has just left and has sat here conversing late upon an unpleasant subject to me, censuring Charley and this I do not like to hear and a great deal I wished not to hear. It is now late, my mind distracted and I go to bed not pleased with myself or my not reading to day for work kept me from it in the day and I had calculated on a happy night reading but instead have heard some thing not so pleasant.

Oct. 3. Thank God for the health and blessings he daily bestows on one so ungreatful as I am. I wish I had the gratitude towards him that I feel I should possess. I think of others who are so much better and yet have so much less of this worlds goods than I have and I pray for more gratitude. To day as I sat and eat a piece of dry bread I did not think of the many who was faring sumptuously, but I thought of the thousands who were starving and I blessed God that I had even that.

Oh! that I may never have less.

Oct. 4. DB from Ken[tucky] called to day to see me and appears very glad to see me so well situated.

Bud came to night and sat a long time. No news yet from dear C.

Mr S sent me some papers. I have long wished to have a humming bird to look at closely and this evening a neighbor caught one and I nursed it until it died for it was hurt and I now have it by me. Dear little thing how I wish it was sporting among my flowers. The other one will feel lost like I do.

Oct. 5. To day Mr S sent me the 7 & 8th Copy of the Pictorial Bible for which I am more than greatful, also a No of the Native American with a publication of my own but he nor any one else dreams that I have been so presumptuous as to offer a piece but the Editor offers me free use of his paper and I shall avail myself of his kindness and occasionally drop a line of scribbling in Prose or Poetry.

Sun. Oct. 6. Heard Mr Clapp preach a glorious sermon to day to almost empty pews for it appears the Whig delegation has taken almost all the City away. There was not a gentleman present that belonged to the Orchestra except the pianist. When will all this political nonsense give place to calm reason and self-judgment.

I have written a piece of poetry for the N American I know not if it will be published.

I hear the Ohio is so low it is impossible for boats to get down so God only knows when I shall see dear Charley.

Oct. 7. I feel so melancholy I can scarce refrain from weeping all the while for I have but 25 cents in the world and can get no work and I have not spent a cent to day. All my provisions are gone and beg I cannot. It seems that C will never come and I am sure I do not know what to do. I cannot even buy water to drink much less to wash my clothes with.

I have painted a little to day to try and keep from crying for if I do begin I shall be laid up sick.

Oct. 8. Last night as I sat reading some one knocked at the gate, and it was Mr Scott. He sat with me until after nine, and offered me any assistance on earth I might need in C's absence. I thank God for such friends. I wept from many emotions. I went to bed and dreamed I was dressed in white floating on a wide muddy river and Charley rode on a white horse meeting me on the water and talked with me.

I heard to day that Mr H is dead, my step Mothers neices son-in-law. Both her daughters are now widows on her hands. Poor woman, I pity her. She has truly divined, for he died on the river and was brought home a corpse.

I have just finished reading Paradise lost and think it may well be called a master piece as far as language and conception go. Indeed his imagination was prolific and must have been to Milton a source of pure delight in his hours of darkness thus to dictate but yet it seems so extravagant and out of place to speak or think of God and his angels in the way in which he uses them. And such is my religion at this day that it cannot be atal tolerated, for God never had war and the hurling of mountains trees and stones, and the use of swords in his high courts of Heaven. Had such been the case, could such have arisen without his knowledge, how easily was it in his power to have annihilated Satan and host without all the battling and then when he was in chains to have kept him there. If there was a Hell and Satan how absurd are some passages and how extravagant and preposterous when there is none in my belief. But yet for beauty of thought and chaste language it stands unrivalled, and if Pope had have written it how much more obscene and vindictive he would have been towards Eve at least.

Oct. 9. Agony and torture. I never felt as I now do for I am fully convinced C has got home and I have been out this evening and since my return have looked until I am almost frantic. He will not be here to night and I do feel that I could not live many hours under such feelings. This night twelve months ago he returned from the same place. Oh how happy I was then, my God how am I to take his coldness. I never knew how to pity the suicide so much as I do to night. He may love me but it does not look much like it.

I have heard to day that my beloved friend C Cummings is dead. Oh what a fatality has attended all those Texan Officers and a nobler better man never breathed his last, but I will see him again where friends never part. A tear to his memory and a wish to become as good is a sincere tribute from his poor friend. I rejoice that he knew my situation before his death. I hope he did for I wrote him. I am told Dr Clark committed suicide here a few days ago another of the Ships Officers and mate with Cummings. Very few are left.

Oct. 11. The agony I have endured the last two days and nights is beyond description. C has been home three days before I saw him and then Oh how differently we met to what I expected. He is most cruelly changed towards me but he says not so. I think if I do not cease to love so violently and he continues cold I shall go a maniac. I hope it will not last on his part as he assures me it is other cares and not neglect. I trust it is.

Oct. 12. C promised me he would see me this evening after leaving me in an agony of tears and has not come. I have suffered more than death to night in this disappointment for it tells in tones too strong that he does not care for me as he once did for then he would always come but now he lets any thing prevent when he knows too well what it costs me. The feeling of the last few days is killing me, and unless a change is effected in my life I am bound to die a maniac or suicide soon unless God takes me before. I do not wish it, I strive against it, but Oh God alone knows what I suffer.

Sun. Oct. 13. Last night I prayed that God would cause me to love C less than I do and to draw my mind from resting on him so entirely for I cannot endure life thus and I do hope I have to day felt a portion of what I ask, at least I wish to controul my love in a manner that will not thus ruin me, but unless God assists me it will never be for I love him too intensely for mortal means to effect it.

I heard Mr Clapp preach a glorious sermon to day and I hope it has given me consolation. A lovely shower this afternoon the first for seven weeks. How refreshed every thing is by it.

Oct. 14. Dear C came this evening and appeared more like himself, and has left me in better spirits. Gave me twenty dollars. I do hope and pray he will not again act so cold towards me for it almost runs me deranged.

I sat with Mr R to night until near ten oclock.

Oct. 15. Went to get the surveyor this morning and from there to see Mrs G and her widowed daughter poor woman. I then came home dressed after resting and walked down in the City shopping for my babe. Walked back and now so tired I can hardly write, but think I will take a good rest this night. I fear dear C will think I have spent too much money to day but I could not well do otherwise than get what I did.

Oct. 16. My lot was surveyed to day and I signed the contract for putting up my fence. I have had a part of my six weeks washing done to day, and I have been very buisy.

I did hope dear C would have come to night but he did not and I must try to bear these sad disappointments.

Oct. 17. I expect C went to the large Whig meeting last night and as he has not been here since Monday I did believe he would have come to night but did not, and I do not take it kindly of him for he knows that I expect every day to be confined and am all alone, and no provisions or conveniences ready yet he comes not to know what is my situation and I dare not send to him.

Oct. 18. I am sorry I complained in the last date for dear C came to night and gave me $20 to get coal and groceries, and is very desirous for me to have a servant. I have felt happy since I saw him and have worked very hard to day in the rain and out of it but have got it to do again tomorrow if I live. I trust I will not get down yet for I have much to do.

Oct. 19. Exceedingly cold this morning indeed all day but I went down laid in my coal and hired a servant. Mr S't kindly offered to get and send up the articles I wished and he has just done so and sent me twice as much as I expected for which he paid his own money. He is one of the noblest hearted men that God ever made; may he never need a friend. I went to Dr R. room and he was fearful from my symptoms I should have an abortion [miscarriage]. I had to lie down in his Office for some time. Told me to take a large dose of laudanum which I have just done.

Sun. Oct. 20. The laudanum has partially relieved my pain but kept me awake nearly all night, but as unwell as I feel I will venture to church.

Just got home from church and I was well paid in the sermon. Oh that I had ever believed the doctrine that Mr C preaches. He explained some important points I never heard before. In fact he says tis the first time he ever specified some of them.

Saw dear C, but that was all my comfort just to see him. What a beautiful child his nephew is.

Oct. 21. I got my coal and servant home to day in the rain but the child is so bad I do not [know] how to live with it, but I must do the best I can.

Dear Charley has just gone. He has spent two hours with me pleasantly to me and I hope so to him. I read a Composition of mine which pleased him very much. He read my last publication in the paper and I trust he feels glad that he is the cause of any thing good emanating from me, and proud that I thus use my time. God bless him.

Oct. 22. Last night I dreamed the firmament was all on fire and every thing and person in consternation for the day of judgment had arrived. I was with Charley. We clasped each other and fell on our knees. My first word was "Thank God we are thus blest in dying together" and then both prayed but he could say but little while eloquence was on my tongue and faith in my heart that all would be well. It passed away and Mrs B passed by us in that position but did not seem the least displeased. I may very soon have to die without even beholding his face much less clasped to his heart. One of the hardest showers I ever saw fall this evening.

CHAPTER SIX

Confinement Near at Hand

*I*n the late fall of 1844 Madaline Edwards prepared for childbirth. She also began to publish essays and poems in a local newspaper.

Wednesday, October 23, 1844. I feel very melancholy tonight for I
think my confinement near at hand and I did hope C would have come
to night but he has not and I may die without seeing him and I have
very much to say to him before then. I think he might pleasure me this
far awhile longer. Oh I do wish to see him so much to night.

I trust I may not be so near as I feel.

Oct. 24. I took a walk this afternoon to see my step Mothers relatives and feel very well from the walk and directly dear Charley came
he brought me a lovely rose, a blank book and some apples.[1] He gave
me $45 to pay for my fence. Oh how very kind and dear that man is to
me. My God can I ever reciprocate such goodness. I think of it until I
feel so lost and undeserving, so unable to be or do any thing to shew my
gratitude that I do not know what to do. My God bless him with wealth
forever for he will use it as if only lent to him to bestow.

Oct. 25. This day six months ago I felt the sensation that told me I was
a Mother and I have been down in the City and I feel very well although
the D^r says I will go but little longer.

I bought a grate at $6, and paid $35 on my fence. Saw some old acquaintances and think it will be my last trip down perhaps forever. Mr S came to night and brought me some paper and some apples.

I sat up last night till ten writing in the book dear C gave me.

Oct. 26. To day I expected to have had dear Charley here all the forenoon, but he got as sadly disappointed as I did. I made the best of it I could, and awaited with anxiety for night and he came, has just left and I have passed some happy moments with him. I hope to be able to go to church tomorrow for I cannot much longer enjoy that great blessing.

Sun. Oct. 27. Mr S came up this morning and brought me the Native American with my last piece in it and another complement from the Editor. He and Mr S't think it the best thing they ever read. Went to church but was not so well pleased with the sermon as usual. Saw dear C and Mrs B[radbury]. Got home and found things not pleasant which has made me unhappy all evening. I have now to sit up and write another piece for publication.

Oct. 28. Taken sick this morning in an unusual way for one in my situation, in much pain. Dear Charley came at 11 and staid with me until 3 oclock, and I forgot pain and was happy. He heard me read my last publication, another piece I have written and he was well pleased and that is all the recompense I ask. We talked of what should be done with my child if it should live and I die. I feel he will be all I could ask to it.

I have just finished another piece for this weeks paper. Feel very bad, my grate smokes and I will go to bed.

Oct. 29. Nothing to write for I am not well in body or spirits, and am just going to bed for I cannot amuse or improve myself feeling as I do.

Oct. 30. Slept very cold last night, got up early and went down to see my lawyer and staid until three oclock and did not see him. Came home very dissatisfied, cut out some work and have looked anxiously for C to night but am again disappointed. I wish he had come to night for I feel so low spirited and did wish to see him so much. If he only thought the thousandth part as much of me as I do him he could not stay away this long.

If I live I must go again tomorrow to try to see lawyer H[unt].[2]

Oct. 31. Went down in the car early this morning to see a midwife and paid for being told I was not in the family way, was in torture at the idea. Saw D^r R said he would come up and satisfy me. Did so this afternoon and says all is right and well.

Lawyer Hunt said he would come up tomorrow and attend to my business for me.

Hoped very much C would come but he has not. Mr S just left.

Nov. 1. Great day among the catholics but I did not go out to see any of their parades but sewed all day.[3]

Hunt disappointed me, in coming to attend to my suit.

Night. Dear Charley came and I have been very happy in his company. Oh that it could always last. He is just gone and all will be lonely now until I see him again.

Nov. 2. Went early this morning to see another lawyer but missed him by five minutes. Came home to work.

Night. Mr S came and took me down to see the Whig torch light procession and truly it was a grand affair and I could not have realized that N.O. contained half so many Whigs. The colored transparent lights were beautiful and the Clay steam boat, cabinet shop, black smith do printing Office &c &c presented an imposing spectacle by torch light. All was conducted with order and decorum. Came home at ten, not very tired either.

From the Bee:

WHIG TORCH-LIGHT PROCESSION.

The Whig Torch-Light Procession on Saturday night, was, in point of number, respectability and splendor, by far the most gorgeous pageant ever gotten up in this city. We will not pretend, for it would be impossible, to describe the patriotic Whig mottoes, quaint devices, etc., on the 2,500 transparencies borne in this vast procession. At 7 o'clock, the procession took its line of march through Chartres street headed by the Clay Dragoons, Frelinghuysen Rangers and Mill Boys, numbering between six and seven hundred, all of them mounted on horseback and each, with very few exceptions, carrying a transparency. Next followed a band of Music seated in a car, followed by a miniature STEAMBOAT thirty feet in length, with steam up, all hands on board and the name of the beautiful craft, HENRY CLAY, shining in large transparent letters through the wheel-house. . . .

The Clay Minstrels, seated in a car decorated with numerous transparencies, with their beautiful banner waving aloft, made the air ring with their patriotic Whig rondelays. . . .

The BLACKSMITH'S FORGE with several members of the craft busily engaged at their vocation, attracted universal attention. . . .

Next came a car containing a PRINTING PRESS, worked by Printers, who issued during the procession some thousands of sheets, containing whig songs and an extract from Mr. Clay's speech to Mr. Mendenhall. . . .

The side walks of the streets through which the procession passed were one dense mass of living beings, and the balconies, windows and even the house tops were seized upon and secured by thousands upon thousands who wished to obtain a view of the brilliant cortege.[4]

Madaline Edwards's essay "Domestic Happiness" expresses common sentiments about the subordinate role of wives.[5] In the context of her guerrilla war against Mary Ann Bradbury, the essay can be read as an argument for the superiority of mistresses to wives. Does this essay incorporate Charles Bradbury's marital complaints to Edwards? Some passages do address specific wifely faults.

One would almost be induced to believe that there were no bad wives from the popular cry "Oh such a woman has such a bad husband," and it may seem strange that one of my sex should take sides against these oppressed wives, but honour, truth and close investigation compels me to do so if I take any grounds, and as it is a bleak rainy day without and a good coal fire and not even a chick to disturb me I feel like availing myself of this charming opportunity to write some thing, and as I feel a predilection for this subject I will run the risk of all the animadversion that may arise therefrom. It is much oftener the blame on womans side than mans that there is so little real happiness in the married life, and if I cannot demonstrate it to others, nevertheless my opinion is still unchanged. To enter into all the minutia that constitutes or promotes happiness or the reverse in the domestic circle would fill a volume, so I will avail myself of a few prominent ones. As a general rule females are affectionate and confiding in their natures and they are so unreasonable as to think the same should be reciprocated in after years as much so as in the days of the honey-moon and in a degree they should, and more certainly would if they used the proper means to ensure it. The honey-moon itself is not always free from it[s] anxious cares on the part of the husband much less years later. How then can he so often render those assiduous attentions the wife so thoughtlessly exacts, when at the very time his heart is the seat of care, and sorrow, and to conceal the same from her may be straining every nerve with mocked composure. Woman in any station has her cares too but as a wife they are increased ten-fold as mistress, it is still greater, but as Mother it is untold still they are those of every-day occurrence and confined to a spot over which her one glance may reach and consequently she can become more habituated to them than the husband can his, and although this field of action and ro[u]tine of discipline may seem (to those who have never tried it) a life of dull monotony yet no two days finds it the same. It is or should be, so varied and yet so systematical as to make it a pleasant duty instead of a task. Not so with the husband. He often has cares, anxieties and perplexities that arise so unforeseen as to unman him, so overwhelming in their nature that for the life of him he could not smile even in her presence, whose slightest look once had such power over him; but must she take this as an evidence that his heart is estranged, and upbraid him with such accusations when at that very moment his hearts chords are wrung to torture, on account of her and his children. Men however prosperous cannot always return from their employments with brow unclouded and in the inability to do this they are more to be commiserated than blamed, for they have not by nature the gift of concealing behind a smile their deep feelings that woman has, and we are too often taught this from sorrow but yet oftener our desire to please. If our own heart is burdened with grief we do not like to carry the influence in [the] crowd with which we must mingle, therefore we dash back the tear, and the lips quiver with a smile that tells to the deeply versed in human nature the agony it cost to produce it. It cannot be so with man. He is made of sterner materials. The greater portion of his life has been passed among those whom to win with smiles or please by condescension, would have been a libel upon his honour, his independence and unflinching integrity, and his heart has been but little schooled to these finer emotions of the womans soul, yet he may possess a heart keenly alive to all our wants, sorrows, and cares, and while he would [spend] thousands to redress them, and spend sleepless nights to prevent them, yet could not give a tear or word or condolement, and yet woman places a higher estimate upon the latter. It is the want of a proper discrimination between the times and places, to smile, to sympathize, to sigh or rejoice that often causes much unhappiness between man and wife: for it soon requires but little discernment on her part to see as soon as he enters the door in what mood he is in. She can see if it is a proper time to use silence or words, to meet him with a smile or sympathizing look and silent pressure of the hand that tells him his troubles are understood. She soon learns if she will to humour these events for they do not occur every day, and although their dispositions may be as numerous as their features yet the wife should so understand them as to indulge or banish as the case may justify. Some men always prefer to be left alone when in a gloomy state of mind, and to find its own reaction. To such nothing is more annoying than to be bored with ceasless and trifling questions as soon as he seeks his home to ponder undisturbed upon important matters. Instead of leaving him alone on such occasions or taking her seat quietly waiting an opportunity to administer the comfort that the watchful but unnoticed eye is longing for, instead of reading his thoughts as if by magic, instead of seeing it costs him a pang thus to appear before her, the wife not unfrequently makes an effort by her volubility to draw him into conversation and finding herself only answered in monosylables, looses her patience, flies in a pet, makes some unjust remarks, flirts out of the room or takes a seat in the corner as silent as the tongs determined not even to answer in monosyllables if he should address her. . . .

~~Women are too proud and overbearing in their nature~~

Women are too apt to place too great a stress upon the word *independence,* and think it humiliating to yield their point to a husband even when they are convinced they err, and many think they are elevating themselves in his eyes by such a course whereas they are sinking in his esteem. Even when it is necessary for woman to maintain her opinion against that of her husband it can be done in that manner that will make him feel it is sometimes better to be wrong than always right.

Again husbands cannot always so arrange their buisness or unexpected calls or some passing occurrence may at times prevent their punctual return at meal times or at night, and wives too often make this failure, the theme of ceaseless surmises and reproof which so annoys him that he determines to avenge himself by not undeceiving her; which course is again misconstrued and ends in distrust on one side and displeasure on the other. In fact it seldom ends atal, for the wife so imprudent at first ever after seeks for causes to complain afresh, which nine times out of ten makes the husband regret the hour of return to the home that should and would, be the temple of his affections if the wife would continue the divinity she was in other days.

Again some wives wish to appear such excellent managers to their husbands that as soon as he enters his dwelling he hears nothing but scolding or blows inflicted upon children or servants, a finding fault with every thing to shew him her taste, a railing at what is really her own negligence to convince him of her economy, a hurry and flurry about every thing that makes him feel more like he was in bedlam, than by his domestic fireside. Still all is done from the purest motives as far as it concerns him. Is it to be wondered at that he should the next day look at his watch and give himself just time enough to reach home at the dinner hour, to leave as little time as possible to this din and confusion? But even here he is again disappointed for with such wives as these there is but little uniformity in any department and he may have to wait an hour for his meal, to the neglect of his buisness; and still she looks for him always to be cheerful, bland and attentive. For my part I wonder men keep their temper as well as they do under such circumstances as I could cite. . . .

In the middle and higher circles of life there exists a fault too little acknowledged, (for in the lowest it is not taken into consideration), and yet one which alienates more husbands affections and so imperceptible too than any single fault of which wives stand chargeable. I mean neatness and taste in dress and propriety of words, and I have often wondered how it is that women are so blinded in this respect, for they are aware that they would not have dared make their appearance before their husbands during courtship in the garb they now seem pleased to present themselves in at all times to him. Does the wife think his taste has changed since marriage or does she think wedded love never cools whether attired with neat precision or in slovenly neglect? If so she is wonderfully mistaken for if the husband is negligent in dress, he cannot bear to see his house in disorder and his wife in dishabille. For a man there are many allowances for a woman few and often none. The husband too often seems not to notice this falling away of neatness in dress for he fears to wound the feelings yet they never escape his look, and when he witnesses the preparation to receive visitors or go abroad he writes down on the tablet of his heart close to his affections *deception* in his wife, and is bound to love her less who takes more pains to please the gaping crowd than she is [does] his fancy, that was so late her ambition. He does not expect or even wish to see her always dressed in curls and laces but he has a right to believe she will [keep] her dress neat and free from holes, that her shoes will not be slip shod nor rents in her hose, that her hair will be combed and not always in papers to please some one else, and that her conversation to him will ensure his respect for when a man ceases to respect his wife, the foundation of love has fallen and it soon follows. A woman who really loves and admires her husband and respects his taste will take as much pains to make her morning wrapper appear genteel and becoming as she will her silk walking dress, and it is not half so hard a task as is often urged to keep house children and self in neatness and order. It only requires a rule to go by and no deviation from that rule in the onset will soon bring all to follow as a matter of course, no matter what the trouble, what the pains what the cost. They are surely nothing to be put in competition with the love and approbation of a husband. I would rather spend an hour to dress myself to please my husband and then sit down with him by my side than to parade the street admired by an hundred. . . . Let wives keep their children and domestics under proper discipline, their houses neat and comfortable, plain but genteel in their own dress, kind, gentle, cheerful lively or silent, submissive or persuasive as the time or case may justify and few ill be the contentions between her husband and self. I am here alluding to reasonable men for some are very unreasonable as well as women, but as a general rule I say wives are more to blame for the neglect they and their home receives from the husband than he is. She has it in her power by a thousand nameless attentions, of winning him to all her wishes. Her province is to win and not command, to soothe not irritate, to smile not frown, to forgive not resent, to cherish not neglect, and to yield instead of contending, and by so doing will seldom be heard complaining of disagreeable husbands. At the same time I would not have her do this from servile fear as if he was her master. Not so: she is his companion and equal, and this should not be done with a spirit of humiliation but from a sense of duty made pleasant by the purest affection making herself doubly happy in seeing him so. It is the easiest thing on earth to lead a happy married life or a miserable one, so much so that it is painful to witness the little conjugal felicity that exists around us, and alas it is but little and perhaps it is well that so few know how scarce it is. It is wanting in the higher and middle stations of life far more than the lower. . . .

Oh if women only knew the way to preserve the[ir] husbands hearts as well as to gain them how much more happiness there would be among them and yet few will ever learn but by experience then it is too late. Men as husbands are unjustly called fickle. They are not so much so as woman and it is her fault that he becomes so as often as he does. But all my preaching will be of no avail, and I feel no charge could ever be laid against me as a wife and as I shall *never* be another it is not worthwhile to say more upon the subject.

Nov 2ᵈ 1844.

Sun. Nov. 3. Heard Mr Clapp preach a most excellent sermon to day and felt some consolation in his arguments. Saw dear C there. Bought some ink and came home. Sat down to write a piece but up came B and as I was combing his hair in walked GW. and TB. but they remained a short time. B and Mrs R conversed until dusk and I have done not a thing this day in way of improvement. I feel very dissatisfied at it too. My mind is upset and I do not feel fit for any thing atal but I must strive to get up a piece for the Native.

Nov. 4. Went up to Lafayette to see the register [of deeds] and did not get the chance as the polls were open. Walked home which proved a very long walk. Feel dispirited indeed.

Night. C came but could not stay long. After he left I took a good cry for I felt bad and have not a cent to spend and he did not offer me any and I could not ask. I would not mind it so much only I owe $3 and will be dunned for it, and have a servant that is not used to doing without something to eat as I am.

Nov. 5. The Whigs have a majority of four hundred in the City.

Paid Mr Scott for hire of servant. He sent me some books and came up himself. I am unsettled in mind and cannot write any thing.

Nov. 6. Early this morning word was sent me to move my house off of D^r [John Leonard] R[iddell']s line.[6] This is trouble for me and I cannot tell how to act until I see C. Went and examined the records and see that I can sue for my fence. Sent my servant home and have enjoyed myself more writing since that squalling child left than for two weeks. Wrote a piece for the paper in case I get down, [for] then I cannot do so. Hear the guns for the return votes; wonder if it is the Whigs. Hope so.

Nov. 7. Oh how sorry I am it has rained this evening for it has prevented dear C from coming. I have tried to do the best I can.

I have lost my watch key and have looked the whole house over and cannot find it.

Nov. 8. Dear Charley came and spent a happy evening with me but yet he is very much dissatisfied about my house having to be moved. He tells me to go down and see the D^r tomorrow and try what he will do.

I am almost crazy with the head ache.

Nov. 9. Rose at day light dressed myself, and left at 7. Saw Dr Reddell and I think he will not act rashly with me about my house. Shewed me a part of his collection of plants, also the different apartments of the mint which is quite a curiosity to me. Got home at 12 and am near dead with my head. Got a letter from my sister.

Oh we have had two of the loveliest spring days I ever saw.

Sun. Nov. 10. I was so unwell last night with head ache and fever that I cannot attempt to go to church, and I much regret it.

Afternoon. I have read and written a good deal. Mr S brought me the papers and my last piece was published. A little rain but has cleared away. A most lovely day and so calm and holy it should fill my soul with love to my God and gratitude to my best and only loved friend for the ability to enjoy them as I ever do.

Nov. 11. To day I have painted a vase of hyacinths for Mr Scott. Perhaps it is the last I may ever paint.

Dear Charley was to have been here to night but has rained all the afternoon and even now in torrents so he cannot come. Oh I am frightened for I have felt for several hours as if I am commencing my labour pains and I am all alone, dark night and raining floods. God grant me assistance for I do not know what on earth to do.

Nov. 12. Rained all night and nearly all day in floods. I got some work to day and went at it with good will but I am not well able to sew for bending hurts me.

Dear Charley came to night and found me in tears but his presence soon banished them and I was happy in combing his hair and reading him some of my compositions. Just gone.

Thank God for his many blessings and dear Charley for his goodness and attention. God ever bless him.

Nov. 13. Bitter Cold but went very early to Lafayette to see about my suit. Sat in the cold two hours. Bought me a pair of winter shoes thanks to dear C.

Worked at a coat. Mr^s S came to night. Oh I wish dearest C could be here this cold night all night with me.

Nov. 14. Dearest C has just left and I always feel happy after his visit,

but Oh how cheerful does every thing seem when he is here and I cannot say it is gloomy when he is not for his memory, his goodness and
even his very smiles and kind words cast a ray over my heart and home.
God ever bless him.

Nov. 15. Mr S stopped at sun rise and left me a paper. Directly Bud
came; for a rarity staid as long as he could which was not long.

I made a pair of pants and then went down to look up my witness for
tomorrow and have just got home somewhat tired.

House looks lonely, my mind ill at ease, wish I had some thing light
to read.

Nov. 16. Went up to the Court and got judgment, came home and did
a very hard days labour, and to night have had the pleasure of C['s] company. He is just gone, but he is almost overpowered with the supposed
defeat of H Clay as it is almost certain that such is the case. If so few are
more sorry than I am, but yet all may be for the best God alone knows.

Sun. Nov. 17. To day my time is out if I am in the family way and I
did not dare to venture to church and Oh how I miss not hearing Mr C.
I fear it will be a long time before, if ever I do.

Dr Riddell came to see me to day about my lot, but makes no
definit[e] conclusion yet. Got the paper with an apoligy for my peice not
appearing as it got in too late, but will be in the next.

Nov. 18. Cold, dark, gloomy rainy day. Feel bad but have made a pair
of pants and now the remainder of the day is mine.

Mr S called, brought me some apples. Have read some and written
a piece.

Night. Dear C could not come such a night as this God bless him.

I have now got a dear sweet rose on my table. It looks out of season
with the bright coal fire.

Well I suppose the Democrats have beaten the Whigs. Hang it!

Nov. 19. I have written all day until my hand is cramped. D^r R called
on me this evening says I will have a son in a week. I hope he will not be
mistaken. Oh how sadly I am disappointed in not seeing dear C to night
the more so because I think he is sick for he was unwell when here last.
I am very unhappy about him. God grant he may not be, for Oh what

could I want to live for if he were dead, and yet it is not selfishness for I could freely die that he could live. God bless him I pray.

Nov. 20. A pleasant day and I have passed it very pleasantly reading and writing, only I was uneasy about dear Charley. However he came to night and was not well yet he brought me a book and some fruit, gave me some money and I have been very happy in his company, for he is so kind and good. God only knows how I love that man, but yet I feel unhappy on one account. He seems in some difficulty concerning money matters. Oh how I wish he could never feel a want or wish ungratified but one of such goodness of heart must often feel it. I will now read his gift.

Nov. 21. Another rainy sloppy day. Have written and read it through. Mr S brought me some papers and I got on very well. Could not get out as I desired.

Sat an hour with Mrs R and will go to bed for fear I may be up again before day.

Nov. 22. Cleared off to day most beautifully but I have been very unwell all day.

Night. My dearest Charley came and brought me brandy, cologne, apples, oranges, paper and pens. Oh he is the best man being so kind and attentive. How much gratitude I owe him. Alas my heart is too small to contain it. He is just gone. Heaven bless him.

Nov. 23. I feel pretty well and will now go to hard work. I have just finished and have also been down in the car, bought me a pair of blankets. Just got home. Now for writing for I feel a presentiment C will not be here to night.

10 oclock. Was quietly writing when in walked Bud. Made me comb his hair and chatted for an hour so I have had to work late since he left.

Oh I hope I will not always be in such suspense.

Sun. Nov. 24. A beautiful glorious morning, the sweet rose buds are laughing in the sun. The church bells are Chiming and there is a pleasing stillness around. Oh I wish I could hear Mr C to day but I am afraid to go out until I know my destiny. May God bless those who can go. Have written some and read more. Mr S brought me the paper with my last piece and many compliments.

The moon is now in eclipse, but is passing off. She both fulled and eclipsed to night and it is now only half past seven.

Oh how sick I am.

Nov. 25. This has been one of the most miserable days I ever spent. Slandered and abused by one too low to notice and yet it makes me miserable. I wish no visitors would ever darken my doors.

WC came to see me to day.[7]

Night. Dear Ch has just gone and he brought me the most beautiful bouquet I ever beheld and some fruit. Oh how good he is, dear One, he is all that makes life joyful to me.

Nov. 26. Up at 4 walked down in the City before the milk men were out, to send my piece to the Office. Rode home. Sewed awhile then went up to Lafayette to see about my suit again. Got a pair of sho[e]s, came home almost crazy with the head ache. D^r R came just now, says I may go near a month longer. Oh how unhappy I am in such suspense. God help me.

Had just sat down to work when I heard some one at the door and who should it be but dear C. Oh how glad I was. He staid near two hours.

Nov. 27. Worked a good deal in my little garden to day and feel quite sick from it. Sewed and read the balance of the day; rained to day and spoiled the streets again, just as they were getting good. I wish to write some to night but do not feel much like it, however here goes for an attempt in my miscellanies.

Nov. 28. O God such nights of agonizing tears as this would soon place me where my prayers have been for this night. Am I wrong? or not. None but God can tell.

Nov. 29. Sick sick after last night. Oh I have worked this day in pain more at heart than body though. I have this evening taken a walk to try and dispel a portion.

God have mercy on me. Oh that it was his will to take me away it would be better for the only being I love on earth and his happiness is dearer than mine.

In "A Visit to St. Louis Cemetery No. 2," Edwards's fictional walkers travel to the major Roman Catholic cemetery of New Orleans.[8] Their comments about burial customs in Creole New Orleans are sympathetic, but they also reveal that for Edwards, as for many other English-speaking New Orleanians, the French-speaking city was exotic and unfamiliar. More important, this sketch, which was probably written for the Native American, *extends the alternate interpretation of the nineteenth-century cemetery first advanced in July in "A Walk." For Irene and Caroline, the cemetery is an integral part of the urban community, its extension in time.*

"Come Caroline lets take a walk this lovely sabbath morning for we have of late been forced to lead a very sedentary life from the necessity of these flood like rains," said Irene to a young friend of hers who was on her first visit to the south.

"With all my heart," she replied, "though it sounds oddly to my ears to talk of walks of pleasure at this season of the year. Yet if I could forget that Autumn was breathing her last sighs I could fancy it a May morning, for I see your monthly rose bush below is full of bursting buds, and the geraniums are gemed with dew drops, but now I am equipped. Which way shall we wind our steps?"

"To the grave yard of course," replied Irene, who loved that field of the dead, even better than walks among the living.

"Mercy on me what a choice you have made, or rather what a necessity you impose on me."

"Not so I trust, for as I seek your pleasure first, then my own I would not willingly inflict a penance on you, though you rightly deserve one for that look of horror and amazement at my proposal," said she smiling. "But I wish you to take one walk there at least and as I know of no time or day more appropriate than the present I wish your consent."

"Oh certainly I will accompany you in any walk you may like, but it strike[s] me as a singular selection for one of your age and one who has lived so much among the dying, but I presume here you have very many grave fields to contain all the millions of dead who breathe their last in this dismal emporium of yellow fever."

"Yes there are several but the one towards which we are walking is the Catholic Cemetary. Not that I belong to that denomination or any particular sect, yet I wish to show you how devoted these creoles are to

SKETCHES IN LOUISIANA.

THE FRENCH CEMETERY, NEW ORLEANS, LA.

St. Louis Cemetery No. 2, New Orleans. Courtesy The Historic New Orleans Collection.

their dead, how sacred they hold the dust of the friends and kindred; how neat and even beautiful their dead City. And though some condemn such parades and show over departed spirits, yet I think it beneficial to themselves and to many strangers who visit this place from curiosity for this eagerness to *see* extends even to the Cemetary by strangers visiting this place and I do think it a beautiful and expressive form they have of strewing their tombs with flowers. But here we are, now see for yourself. And as I am not of that superstitious mass who think it a desecration to speak above a whisper, or an unpardonable sin to smile over a tomb, we will converse freely as we walk, not with levity or in idle words as others do, but relative to what we see and believe respecting these sleepers and the customs of their surviving friends. See here is a tomb, I wish I could read french! However I can understand that it is a mothers heart that has been wrung over this tablet, that her hand has placed these flowers here, already withering to fall like the flower of her heart."

"Stop here," said Caroline. "I am glad this is in english; let's read," said she looking up to that just tribute to true benevolence. "Well Irene I am glad to see that your City so famed abroad for immorality has some redeeming spirits among the dead if not the living, for this monument tells of the efforts of one to moralize and make happy that class that too often compose the dregs of society, the unfortunate and abandoned orphan, and this tomb is more to be envied than Napoleons in France, not for its gilt or marble but for the thanks, the tears, and untold gratitude of the orphan boys who surely often visit it. Oh! Irene how much happiness have the rich the power of bestowing."

"Tread softly Caroline for though I fear not to speak among the dead yet I would not intrude upon the sorrows of the living, and yonder is one whose attitude bespeaks the mourner."

The two friends ceased speaking as they passed one who sat leaning against the tomb on which her eyes were intensely riveted. In her small hand was clasped a pocket bible whose crimson binding was in bitter contrast with the marble whiteness of that hand. The friends lingered not around the consecrated spot for fear it might interrupt the devotions of this young being who had chosen this early hour to escape observation, and to mix her tears with the dew on the flowers her hand had here planted, but a passing glance told it was an orphan daughter in the bloom of youth mourning over the tomb of a fond Mother. . . .

"What is this Irene—Casadous! Ah yes I see now the Masons. Here I suppo[s]e the bones of that mysterious fraternity rest from their labours, and truly the works of some at least do follow them. Do you know I love that class of beings whom of all others I know the least, that is of their worship &c. but of their acts I do know something. The very mystery that shrouds them to me constitutes one of their greatest charms, and this much is not often acknowledged by our sex, and per- haps it is because we are accused of never keeping secrets that makes me love those who can. Of my numerous connexion I do not know that I have one who is a mason and yet I feel a reverence for them because I once knew an unfortunate lady far from her friends, and without means, relieved by a stranger to her as I was afterwards told a mason, and that one of their most binding laws was to do this; and I have heard of many noble disinterested acts of that body, so little understood, as a band of brothers here let them rest in quiet. Their religion as far as I am per- mitted to see is free from ostentation and vain-glory and this Monument though neat is in accordance."

"See here is not this a most touching farewell to the wife and chil- dren of him who lies here, and how sacred this spot seems to be from the care that is taken of it. The beautiful carving of this marble tells of affluence as well as taste, the design is rich and these shrubs and blooms tell of care and attention."

"Let's take a turn round this way and you will see where thousands rest in more humble tenements, for the City of the dead is a counter- part of that of the living, for some have gay and costly edifices whilst others are scarce sheltered from the snow or rain but as humble as these ovens look after viewing the others, they are palaces compared to the thousands that fill the Potters field and other Cemetaries I have seen.[9] And yet it is only to we living friends that it matters, for one reposes as sweetly as the other, and after the breath leaves our bodies it is of no consequence to us. Yet in my opinion if death and tombs were always associated with flowers, vines, trees, gravel walks, and marble monuments there would not be such a dread and horror attending the very thought of a grave yard. I have always been astonished at the reluctance manifested by persons in general to visiting such places and attribute it as much or more than any thing else [to] the superstition taught us in our early years of ghosts, and spectres, being so often seen among the tombs and years nor education ever erases this dread which few are willing to admit and yet their actions prove it, for what is there to fear from the breathless form of our most bitter enemy! But we call up these suppositions and feel it insupportable to remain by a corpse and walk alone at night among the tombs, and yet there is something beneficial in these visits for callous must be the heart that could walk through this Cemetary and leave it with the same angry revengeful feelings with which it may have entered. And yet how 'strange an animal is man' for we see him in the field of [battle] slaying his scores. We see him surrounded by the dead and he hears the moans of the dying. We see him go out with one who has once been his bosom friend, measure the steps between him and his coffin, count the pulses that are yet to beat for him and in the face of his God take that mans life and all this can he witness and perform without betraying one symptom of cowardice. His cheek will not blanche nor his nerves tremble, but ask him to walk to the midnight tomb or even midday of that individual or to lay his hand on the clay cold corpse his hand has just made and his ablest efforts to conceal his emotions will be fruitless."

"Well Irene I confess I am one who must plead guilty in those superstitious fears, and think it a great folly in teaching children such dread of death, for certainly we banish those things from our mind, as much as we can that give us pain or produce terror. But I am truly glad I have taken this walk with you for already I feel less repugnance to such scenes and I certainly feel much admiration for the Creoles who thus bring home to the minds of the thoughtless and superstitious that there is nothing to dread in approaching the sepulchral marble: and this I assure you will not be my last visit while I remain in this City, but shall expect you to take me with you to the American Cemetary also before I leave."

"Yes Caroline I will do so but you will find a great contrast and one of which I am often ashamed, not that I believe it commendable by any means to herald the virtues in lettered marble that perhaps never existed in the being while living, nor that it is requisite to tell even all they really were, but a neat tomb, a few flowers, grave trees, warming Oleander, shelled walks, creeping vines &c are of little expence and require but little time and they are so calculated to divest the mind of much of that dark gloom that so often pervades it while treading among the dead. Ah here we are at home and it will soon be church hour you will now have the opportunity of hearing Mr C. and you will also before you hear him often understand why it is that I have learned to seek the Cemetary as a place I delight to contemplate in. Not that I am a christian, I wish I was, but I will say no more and leave you to hear for yourself. So we will prepare to be there in time."

M.

Nov 29th 1844.

Nov. 30. After I managed all my domestic concerns I felt like I had better take a walk to raice my spirits so I went down in the City, borrowed some books bought some plants and bu[l]bs, staid all the afternoon and after I got home dear C came, brought me a present of a writing set he had got at auction for me. Staid till after 8. He is ever kind and forgiving for all my follies and injustice.

Sun. Dec. 1. Rained last night so I could not get to Church to day, wish I could have gone. Have read and wrote all day. It has been a cheerless day, and I feel badly. Winter seems already to have entered my soul.

I put my hyacinths in the glasses to day so I will see how long it takes them to blow.

Dec. 2. Cloudy but pleasant. Worked in my garden all the morning, then read some and did some sewing.

PM. Mrs W brought me a dress to make for her. I am glad to have got some work to enable me to earn a little money. Had my chimney swept to day.

Night. Sewed late for dear C did not come. Now I have some writing to do.

Dec. 3. Sewed all day and am now looking for dear C.

8 oclock. C has just left. He brought me oysters, oranges, apples and papers. Oh how kind and attentive. I wish to heaven I could repay his goodness in some way but I trust God will recompense him here and above also I know he will.

Dec. 4. I have sewed very constant to day and felt bad enough and just a few minutes ago I got badly frightened and I feel uneasy about the consequences. I shall now read awhile in the book dear C gave me last night.

Dec. 5. This morning I was up before light and went to see Mr R[iddell] about this fence business, went to market and got home tired and dispirited. Mr A[dams] brought me some trees and set them out for me. He is very kind indeed.

Night. C has just left and I could not help weeping. Oh I sometimes feel like I could break my heart, I feel so lost in seeing him so seldom and so short a time. Oh heavens will my lot ever be thus. Yet I know it will and perhaps for others it were better I were dead.

Dec. 6. I took up some running roses and set them out in more suitable places, arranged my pots of flowers and then read my daily chapter in the testament and went to my sewing.

Finished the novel dear Charley wished me to read. It was beautifully written and the language unusually chaste for such scenes but Oh! it were best for my happiness I looked no more into these things for it calls up that which I have no power to undo and I find myself shedding tears of bitter agony at the thought that even in the future I cannot be pure. Oh God alone sees my agony and I feel it.

Dec. 7. Cold and windy. Worked hard, read some and played some too.

Night. My dear C has just been here. He brought me a pair of gloves and a knife; he is so kind. We have spent a pleasant afternoon talking over a great many things. He says my last production is published and he admires it wonderfully. I trust I may get to go to church tomorrow.

Sun. Dec. 8. Our first frost, still it is a lovely day and I shall endeavour to go to church.

PM. Heard Mr C preach a beautiful sermon. Oh what a man that one is how great and *how* good. Saw dear C there, but Ah another more dear was by his side and all my joy was to see and lament.

Night. B has been here all the evening and I have not got the chance to read as I wish. I got a good number of papers to day among them my own composition.

Dec. 9. A white frost and thin ice. Up at dawn and did a good days walking and sewing. Have felt well after my long walk.

The sun was in eclipse to day and the moon changed.

Night. Dear C has been here near three hours. We had some unusual conversation and although I felt very unhappy at some of his confessions yet I stifled my emotions for once and did not let him see my pain. He brought me fruit and gave me some money. How dear and kind he is. Oh God ever bless him.

Dec. 10. Bitter cold to day. Had my washing done. Could not get down in the City. Had my garden hoed up, gave $1.50.

Made a dress for Mr⁵ R.

Dec. 11. Frost and ice. Up early at work. Went over to Mr⁵ Ws and wrote a letter for her poor woman. Then went down in town, eat dinner at Mr J's, went to see E.S, bought some candy to send my sisters children. I did some little buisness and came home directly after dear C came and soon after Bud. I feel very unwell to night. God grant I may soon have my fears dissipated and my hopes confirmed.

Dec. 12. This day twelve months ago I took possession of my Cottage home. Oh how swiftly has this year flown and how thankful I would be to him who has caused it to pass with so few regrets, and so much happiness and to my God how truly greatful would I feel for his unbounded goodness to me in health and many very many temporal blessings. This night one year I slept on the floor in the shavings cold and lonely, but now I will go to a good bed, and quit not.

Dec. 13. My dear C has been here to night and our conversation took a new turn. Oh how I grieve that he was not more warmly cherished when young for it is so calculated to make one happy and to impart it to others. Yet he is one of the best of Gods creations. To have been his wife and worthy to be such would have been to me the acme of happiness. God ever bless him is my prayer.

Dec. 14. Went down to get the phrenologist to examine my head but was disappointed in seeing him. Went to the garden and came home.

Night. C has spent another evening with me. Oh his visits are truly all that sustains me in life. They are the only sunny spots in the landscape of my existence and he the sun that gilds all the present and the twelve months past. Oh that the world was full of such noble spirits. God do bless him with prosperity and happiness.

Sun. Dec. 15. Mr S called early and left me some papers. Soon after Mr S't came and gave me another also was so good as to give me some change to get some nick nacks for my sisters children. He is a true friend. Then came B so I did not get to dress until this afternoon nor read much either. Mrs R and myself took a pleasant walk and came back, found B here again; has just left. I saw dear C's house but Ah no glimpse of him.

I am not happy to night atal. Why, Oh why will it ever be thus.

Dec. 16. Was drest this morning at day light to go out to work for a lady and as bitter cold as it was I went, staid all day, came home made a fire and got warm just as my beloved came. He was kind and more affectionate than usual to me and although our conversation was upon a serious subject yet in one word he gave me consolation for many sorrows. Oh how dear he is to me and how doubly so does he sometimes become by a little word. God ever bless him for he possesses the noblest heart alive. Oh how cold it is to be alone.

Dec. 17. Up very early after a poor nights rest, went down and bought some raisins, figs, oranges &c for my sisters children. Got in the omnibus and went to Lafayette to get a dress to make, cut it out and got home at three. Oh it is bitter cold. Now I am once more happy to find myself alone by a cheerful fire with no noise, children and confusion. It is bliss to be at home. I wish I never was compelled to go out when I could hear so much of distraction and news. Bless my quiet home.

Dec. 18. I have worked so constant to day and to night I am in pain, for I have now five dresses to make before New Year and three more promised. I am so anxious to be enabled to get some little things I need without taxing dear C that I know I am doing my health injustice. Oh how I was disappointed in not seeing C to night. I hope there is a cause for I did wish so much to see him. I am very tired. Ten at night. Now for bed and an early start in the morning, if God enables me.

Dec. 19. Rained so that I was very uneasy for fear dear C could not come but he did although he could not stay but an hour for there was sickness at home. Brought me a book and I am so tired sewing I will quit and read some. Poor Mrs O died to day, a near neighbor and I did not know she was sick. Oh I fear she needed attention. I feel unhappy about it. I trust she is better off than those she left here.

Dec. 20. Last night I stole time from my sewing to read Blackwoods Free thinker that dear C brought me and I was delighted with the character of the Baron and Sebastian. Oh that there were many such real characters. It is pleasant to think or read even if fiction of such ennobled spirits in this selfish world of ours. C is personified in both. Would to God he had the Barons wealth, he would do as much. I have worked hard to get time again to night for reading and I hope it will be profitably spent. A lovely moon light night.

Dec. 21. Finished some sewing and took it home. Came back, cut out a dress and almost half made it. While busy dear C came stealing in he was very cheerful and pleasant brought me two bibles, two oranges and two ladies Books and now he is gone and I have just two hours more to sew, so here goes.

Sun. Dec. 22. The sun shone brightly and the thunders rolled heavily just now which has ended in a shower, and the sun is again shining. Just got to my reading when up came B. Did not let me read any until after two, then Mrs R came which gave me not a moment to myself until night. Oh how I hate intrusion on Sabbath for I cannot go to church and I do so love to be alone, with my books. Brought me papers but hang them.

Dec. 23. Well I have sewed until I am almost dead with pain. D^r R called here this evening, Mr S stopped to give me the paper. Dear C did not come to night as I expected and hoped but he has a good reason I know and I will try to feel as little disappointed as I can but his visits are all the bright stars in my darkened world, and I do so watch for them. God bless him I pray.

Dec. 24. Night. Moon shining bright and is just full, troubled mind for the usual hour had passed and C had not come. I had some egg-nogg waiting for him. My eyes filled with tears and I snatched a book and began a tale when in he came, how glad I was. He could not stay but a few minutes for he had stolen away from a crowd. Brought me a pair of side combs and oranges, dear friend. He is gone and I am sick. Christmas eve. Oh how good is my Creator that he spares me to see yet another while so many have gone to sleep forever.

Dec. 25. Christmas is passed and I have passed it more happily than for many years, and I was so in hopes that my loved C would have come to night and completed that happiness he has given, but he has not and although I know he has a good reason yet it casts a gloom over my hopeful feelings. Mr[s] R and I have just taken a glass of nogg all alone for even B disappointed me in coming and it was made for him. Will I live and in this house when another Christmas comes? God alone can tell if so will I be as happy as to day. I trust even more so.

Dec. 26. I have been unusually depressed in spirits to day from some remarks made to me by S[ayre] about C. I wish people would let the little happiness that can be mine alone and not say ought against him to me. I could have wept Oceans but I strove against it and he came but I was not so happy as I affected for my heart was full. He brought me a Christmas gift, a head dress, beautiful. Bless him. He gave me the coat of arms of his family to paint for him, an old relic just loaned to him and I have been drawing it since he left. I will do it if I can. Rained a few minutes ago and now the moon is bright as ever.

Dec. 27. Cold, cold to day. Partly painted C's piece, succeeded very well. Sewed fast until dark then he came and I passed an idle hour but have made it up since he left.

Clear but Oh how cold to sleep alone but I am too tired to sit up any longer. C brought me the Presidents Message on Mexican affairs but I shall not more than glance over it this night.

Dec. 28. To day is my birth day and instead of being joyous to me is sad, not that I fear age but I weep at the time so misspent. Dear C came to night and we had a glass of egg-nogg in celebration of my birth day. He gave me two more pictorial bibles. We spent a happy afternoon but he is gone and I have promised to go over to sit with Adel.[10]

Sun. Dec. 29. I have as usual passed an unprofitable day. Did not go to church but painted C's piece, read the papers, had company and now to night is my leisure for myself. Oh how I wish for more time to read and write but I have of late been so pressed with sewing that I have had but little pleasure that way but I must expect to deny myself those pleasures at times in order to help from being too great a burden to my only beloved friend. I hope yet time will be more at my command. I have now a little writing to do and then prepare for an early rise tomorrow if I live.

Dec. 30. Rose an hour before day and sewed by candle light. Did a good days work and then went out to fit a dress. I was very glad to get to walk a little for I have lived too sedentary of late. Mr S sent his boys up to learn their books today. C does not like for me to undertake it and I am sorry for I did it in order to make a little.

I felt as if I was to be disappointed in seeing dear C, but at 7 he came. Oh how glad I was he staid till after 8. I hope he will come on New Year. I will go to bed for I am very sleepy. Adieu

Dec. 31. Have sewed very constant to day in order to have some holiday tomorrow. Gave the Children their lessons, had manure put on my lot in order to have a garden. Night. B came up and sat until after 8. Gave A[delle] a beautiful New Year gift or gave it to me to give to her, gave me six dollars to get me a bonnet. He has been very kind to me and at the close of this year I have many very many blessings to be greatful for and among them some kind friends. Oh God has ever been mindful of one for in no instance have I been so destitute of friends as many others, and one year has proven I may yet retain true ones.

Last day of the year has been warm as a Summer day. It is finished and the last night is passing away. God only knows if I ever may end another but if not I trust this little humble book may sometimes call my memory up to his eyes who has bestowed on me the boon of happiness that has filled my cup [at] the last. I wish he could realize how truly greatful I now feel towards him and how much I owe my God. Eternity will alone unfold to him what he has done for me words nor imagination never can. Oh that every year of his life may end with more happiness than falls to mortals lot in general and if another New Year finds this heart cold in the grave that others more deserving will beat for him and that he will not cast me from the tablet of his memory forever. Bless him my Redeemer, Oh! bless his every step in life make him all my fond heart would have him be.

Heavenly Father, the present will soon be the past and the last night of this year will soon end another year that hurries us into the future. Grant to give me more gratitude and humility to begin the next. Let me feel how forbearing thou art. Let me feel that thou alone can bestow the gifts that will make me happy. Teach me to feel and place it in my power to alleviate the sufferings of others. Thou hast given me a priceless friend to assuage my miseries. Let me return it to another in an humble manner. Teach me to love my fellow beings with all their imperfections for I am not their judge. May the next year find my heart better and my actions in accordance. Give me wisdom to understand that Holy Writ and knowledge that will enable me to investigate and enjoy thy creation above and around. Bless the suffering portion of the human family and open the hearts and hands of th[os]e able to alleviate their distresses. Bless all it is our duty to pray for enemies first and friends next. But dear Father if there is one prayer thou wilt grant let it be in behalf of dear C. Oh my God thou alone wilt ever know what he is to me and what he has done for me. Give earths and Heavens choicest blessings and if it is thy holy will let me see him happy this night one year.

Thy will be done. Amen

CHAPTER SEVEN

Wishes and Desires

adaline Edwards was understandably ambivalent about the possibility of having an illegitimate child. She had no doubt that its life would be hard and her own harder. But she was gradually convinced, in the face of daily evidence to the contrary, that the baby would cement her bond with Charles Bradbury. This is evident in the two very different testaments she wrote as she confronted the possibility of death in childbirth. One, entered in her second Writing Book and dated November 10, 1844, about the time she expected her child to be born, was a long essay that reflected on her own fate and gave directions for the child's upbringing. Edwards distinguished between appropriate male and female education (although she wanted a girl to receive instruction in subjects traditionally reserved for boys), but most of all she stressed qualities of character that she hoped Bradbury would instill in either a boy or a girl.[1]

My best beloved, and adored Charley. The time is close at hand that brings to me a period of suffering and it may be death also, and feeling that if such should be the case that you will not be near me to hear or I able to give the parting injunction towards the object for whose being my life may pay the forfeit, I here leave a few of those wishes and desires towards it, the better that you may sometimes look on these lines feeling they were wrung from my soul at the thought they have awakened. That they are not merely dictated for form sake or to "be a shew," you will believe, but that they are penned by the hand that may soon be laid to the last rest this earth can yield and dictated by the mind that has but little of eloquence to adorn these pages, and that the heart that beats so warmly for you and swells with the deepest thrilling emotions as I see thy destiny so closely connected with the tie that must still link us together though one lies sleeping in the tomb and the other moves and glories in the joys of life. The eye that weeps over the sad thoughts that fill my soul may soon close forever upon all that earth holds dear and upon the earth itself, but that time with care destroying power may not obliterate me from your memory I ask you some times to look in this book that you have kindly presented to me this night.

Dearest, should I die in giving birth to the dear pledge of our love and it should survive me, my wishes first as respects my burial I feel will be attended to by you. All I ask respecting this is that you will visit my grave sometimes. Yes, I would wish *often* and that a future day would behold you standing by that grave with our childs hand clasped in yours and say to it "here lies your *Mother*." But should it die soon or late lay it on one side of me and I do implore you in purchasing my burial spot to locate yours by its side. As to adorning my grave it will need nothing but your periodical visits to make it all I could ask. Let it be very humble as best befits me.

My Child. Oh what a crowd of reflections and agonizing emotions swell my soul to bursting as I call that name with the thought of death taking me from it, to trust it to anothers hands anothers love. It is not that death so terrifies me. Oh no, it is not that I fear you will not be all my fondest hopes could desire towards it, as far as your charge lay but more conflicting emotions throb my breast. I have never known a Mothers *love* and parental care and Oh! what have I not lost? What have I not endured by it how often have I sat down and wept till my childish heart would almost hurt when I saw other children caressed and made happy, while I had never known such caresses. Since then I have learned a *Mothers* love and if any thing this side [of] Gods love, can be compared to it, I have never learned what it could be. I have seen four beloved children sicken and die and felt that life nor death again could give such greif; but now to die and leave the babe that I have so yearned to caress, and to train for heaven and you, the babe that was to me thy second self, the tie that could bind my heart to many joys and loose it from many griefs, now to sink down and leave it in its infancy to anothers love, which could be no more like mine than the rivulet like the Ocean to feel that it must believe, and live under the belief that another is its parent, is maddening in the extreme for as unworthy as I am yet I would not have my memory concealed from that hearts treasure, though the grave had torn me from it, for nothing in life could do it. These are very serious reflections more particularly if it shall be a girl. You may think dearest one that those on whom fortune has smiled, one who had passed through life serenely blest, one on whom blight had never fastened and no one had ever censured was better calculated to take charge of schooling a young heart to the joys and thorns of life, but sad experience has taught me better. Such an one has been taught to grasp the roses without knowing the thorn was below or the worm concealed within. Such an one has been taught to look on life as the Ocean in a calm, with her bark floating smoothly had never thought of storms, breakers or shoals, such an one too often thinks caution is not necessary to ensure a correct deportment at times believing it either innate or not to be taught. Oh! dearest Charley this nor ten other volumes could contain all I know, all I *feel* and all I have *realized* and which I could train my daughter to imitate or shun. I have plucked so many thorns that I know too well where to look for them, have pressed the cankering worm so oft to my heart that I know how they coil and conceal, have so oft watched the calm unruffled Sea of life gather into raging billows and dash its victims upon the sand-banks of life. That I too early and yet too late have learned to watch the gathering sky and tell its effects. I have so long stood aloof from the social world that could not rob me of the power to comment and the privilege of beholding the virtues, vices, follies, foibles, dissimulations with all that is amiable in human nature, so long been an object on which a kind act fell with such force that impressions were made too indellible to be erased, and have analyzed so much of human nature that I say it not boastingly, but sorrowfully, that my once pure heart should have learned so much. But I believe those who have endured the most are not always the most competent to shun the most themselves, but they have more than their own being wrapt up in the destiny of a daughter, at least one of my nature, and I do believe few women on earth would be more capable of raising a child than I am, for so well have I been schooled by experience and observation that if God blesses me with a child and spares my life to direct its youthful steps I trust I will be able to atone for a portion of my errors in guiding it clear of the same. Still the barrier to my efforts and hopes I know is great and glaring. I would have that child to know that I was its Mother and yet if the world will conceal from it my errors never let its happy youth be embittered by the sad knowledge of the same, but if it should be forced to learn the same let it sooner hear it from your own lips for they will do me more than justice and soften the pang it will be doomed to feel.

I cannot write any thing that could possibly induce you to feel or realize my anxiety towards my offspring nor any thing that could convey to your mind how keen and quick my perception would [be] in every thing that related to its immortal happiness, for I wish it never taught any of the humbuggery of religion and yet I would raise it to *live* and *act* religion from its early infancy. I wish it taught the beauty and perfection of The Deity in every shrub it may meet, and would never imbue its mind with any thing relating to melancholy for circumstances in later life might arise to teach it this as it did its Mother. Teach it innocent joy and cheerfulness, teach it benevolence towards the smallest insect or brute, teach it to guard against evil speaking. Tell it it was my dying words that it should never utter a word of detraction against the poorest African and where it was compelled to do so or remain silent, to always choose the latter. Learn it to love every thing but vice, and its concomitants, for there is nothing so likely to make one happy itself and others around as to feel an interest and solicitude for all our fellow beings and it is sure to prevent pride and arrogance from springing up in the childish breast. At all events I trust these feelings and dispositions will be innate for it will be all its Fathers own child, and it cannot fail to be good, unless early separated from your care and ruined by other associates.

Dearest Charles, I trust be the sex what it may of my darling unborn, that you will be compensated for all your care with it in a future day by seeing it all my fond heart could wish it, and all your ambition could desire. I have been more explicit in the foregoing lines in case it is a girl than if a boy, not that my love or anxious thoughts towards it are less but that I know you are far more capable of attending to the first impressions as well as education [of a boy] than you could be of a daughter and indeed if I were to write or talk to you until one century had rolled by, I could not lay down any rules to guide you. It only requires the maternal eye and heart keenly alive to all the minutia that few are so well versed in as I believe I am. A father can often see the defects in his child and yet has not the tact to correct them. He does not understand the thousand little avanues to its heart nor the many traits of its disposition and the best way to win upon them. As to the lettered education of either I say nothing, for if God still prospers you in life I know it will receive all my debting heart could ask, but it is the education that begins in the cradle, and is read in looks and acts more forcibly than words, it is the education that it first lisps and sees around in every object. It is that which is wrapt in a ~~Mothe~~ parents approving smile or conveyed in the mild but decisive reproval, it is the education it learns to shun or imitate in all it meets with in live [life]. It is such as the parent may teach when it takes its little hand and walks away from the schoolroom into even the woods and shew[s] and explain[s] to it the unfolding of the bud and expanding leaf, in pointing to it the birds love for its young, telling it how beautiful all these things are and yet a destiny awaits it where beauties untold presented to it, to walk through the buisy street and point to it the aged cripple teaching it sympathy and thanks to God that you or it are more blest teaching it to give a mite sometimes, to impress on its mind the true definition of liberality, to teach it the little ragged children it meets is just as good but no better than itself except by conduct. Oh do this that it may never be selfish, teach it gentleness and forbearance but if a boy to act with becoming spirit when and where it is honourably demanded. These form a portion of the catalogue of studies in the education I would give my child and they are but seldom attended to by those who instruct it a b c, and none can feel their importance like a Mother. Oh! I could never tire in leading the darling child in the path my tried [tired] feet have proved to be right and learning it all of the very little I feel to be holy and just towards my God and fellow beings. It could almost make me amends for the years of anguish I have endured to be permitted to train my child as I hope I could do. But if that lot is assigned to you, I thank God that it devolves on one of those few men who are competent to do so with credit to yourself and happiness to it. But dearest I know not what awaits you, perhaps a second marriage and other children, and forgive the tears that dim my eyes when I say you may love those better, perhaps you will look on the little orphan and contrast the Mothers and their destinies and feel a coldness that you could not conceal from its penetrating eye if it inherits my too vivid perception in slight or contempt. Perhaps you will wish it was not thus closely connected to those more honourably yours, and will feel less love and solicitude for the babe that I could so idolize. Oh Charley, if ever the day dawns on its hapless head in which your pity awards it what your love denies, I pray that God who gave it will take it to his blest abode as a favour to you and a blessing to it. Do not, Oh do not love it less on account of its Mothers destiny. Think not these words have lost their potency by years, for if I could ascend from the grave in 1854 I would repeat the same. Then do not cast these lines among things that are forgotten as you learn to love another, but think of my deep devotion and unearthly love for you and my maternal love for the object I may leave to you.

You may wed another and give to her and her first born all that love and ten fold more than you have ever bestowed on others or myself but remember, and Heaven can witness the truth, she *cannot* love you as I do. Her child may be more interesting than mine but it cannot so claim your tender sympathy. Then never let it feel the death chilling conviction that my Mother who would have adored me lies in the grave and my Father loves me but little. It sends the most paralyzing emotions to the heart of all things on earth, for I never knew a Mothers love though living, and but little of a Fathers only by letter and too well I know the pangs I would spare my poor child.

In its education if a girl there are a few studies I would ask it should

be very perfect in. I do not make the request for fear you will omit them,
but that you will feel them impressed on your mind as my wish and that
you will tell her they were my earnest desire and she will feel a renewed
interest in prosecuting them as being the wish of her departed Mother:
Astronomy, Botany, Chemistry and Minerology. I would sooner have
her to know and feel the beauties of these studies than all that relates
to kings, heroes, the rise and fall of empires. Not that I object to her
being perfect in history, far from it, but these will convey to her mind
the greatness, goodness wisdom, love and benevolence of the Deity and
the other the ambitious passions and vices of mankind. I would sooner
she knew how to analyze and [appreciate?] the beautiful flower creation
than to understand the history of the famed Cleopatra. I would sooner
she knew the revolution and magnitude of one bright orb than to know
all the deeds of a hero or Alexander. I would sooner she knew how to
arrange and class the fossils, shells and minerals that beautify the sea
shore and lie embedded in the bowels of the earth than to be able to
recount all the butcheries of a Robespierre, Antiochus Lathryus and
others. I would sooner she understood the properties of fluids, solids,
gases and substances than to be the admired beauty of an empire unless
that beauty was composed of something more than personal features. I
trust she will possess capacity enough to induce you to try her upon all
these. Do not think I would have her remain ignorant of the study of
history, but she will ever see enough of the follies, passions, and ambi-
tions of human nature to understand their bearings but of the other she
may admire and love without *understanding* which will be as the moon
beams compared to the sun, for she will feel tenfold interest and pleasure in the rose and a more elevated conception of The Deity than if she
merely admired it for its colour and odour. These will elevate her mind
to higher and nobler aims than vain admirations. Teach her gentleness
of soul towards all of Gods creation, keep her mind free from selfishness and envy, be kind and forbearing to her for my sake but Oh do not
spoil her. I have said thus much of a daughter and yet perhaps it may be
a son and if I am to be called away from it I trust for your sake and its
own that such may be the case but even then there is much of the fore-

going that will apply to it. If a son I trust it will be like his father, but yet teach it warmer feelings at least to shew them more, where it may be so much needed, a better heart it can never possess nor nobler soul, then make it all you could ask for it must surely possess capacity. If my child lives and Mr C does too let it see and hear as much of him as possible for God alone knows how I venerate and bless that man. If a son there is but one study usually omited in a classical education that I should like it to be master of and let its profession or occupation in life be what it may. I should like him to understand that one: it is Anatomy. In the first place it will teach him the veneration for God that he could not possess by merely knowing his blood circulated through his heart, or played upon his lungs. It will fill his soul with admiration for the wisdom that had constructed such a piece of mechanism and, in the next place it will so familiarize him with his own constructions as well as constitution that he will have it in his power to enjoy life two fold by knowing how to avoid many very many of the diseases and pains that ignorance of this beautiful study entails upon us. I say beautiful and even sublime, not that I have any knowledge of it from the dissecting room and must say that portion must be the off-set to its pleasures, but from the little I have acquired from good sources concerning the wonderful and mysterious organization of the human frame, the exactness it requires that all the different parts of the curious machine shall move in order that all shall harmonize and the promptness that one thus versed can detect the cause, must seem to me to be a most interesting and all important study. It is a key to ones own health and consequently happiness for where can it dwell apart from health and will often give us the unspeakable pleasure in being able to assist suffering humanity independent of a medical education. I may be wrong but I should like much to be conversant with the science myself if it could be thoroughly acquired without the aid of dissection. Then if it meets his approbation when old enough to decide give him this one branch and nothing else I feel will be omitted that your affection or pride can bestow on him in education.

My own beloved Charley I could say volumes concerning the beloved and cherished object that causes me so much solicitude for my more than soul seems centred in it but I feel it could not make you do more for it than you will do. All it will lack will be a Mother, and as ill fated as I am yet none to it can fill my place, but I feel that Mary will be kind to it while she lives but I fear it will again fall to anothers care, too soon for its years, but to God first and you next I trust all that is in the future. It may be my blest lot to raise it and see it an ornament and pillar in the world from which I am excluded. God only knows; but I will endeavour to rely on his promise to those who trust him.

A word then beloved and dearly loved Charley. Perhaps your eye will only rest here when mine is beaming on the scenes of the future we too often dread, but ere I go let me tell you that no words power, or art can ever convey to you how intensely I have ever loved you. That love has not been based on ordinary taste or circumstances. You understand a part and God the whole. It has been well for me and all that relates to me that I love you as I do for it has been a talisman to sheild me from vice and degradation since I knew you and although I love you too intensely to insure my happiness situated as you are towards me, yet it was better to feel the torture of love than that of shame. When I live in the grave Oh! do some times think of me, not as I have been but such as I would have been could I have met you sooner. I know that I deserve to be forgotten by the world but yet in one heart would I still live though shame was linked with my memory. Oh! love my child with my tenderness. Cast it not from you as my blighted name arises to your mind. It is innocent then love and cherish it. But I do not fear any mistreatment from you for your noble heart would never use it towards any much less one in whose veins your own blood ran.

Dearest Charley I cannot say much but Oh God what do I not feel as I think of this separation for life yet believe me my confidence in the God you have taught me to trust aright is unwavering and to him I commit all. Farewell my adored One.

Nov. 10 th 1844

Edwards's second testament was shorter and written more as a will. It was undated and appeared in the back of the 1844 diary.

Beloved Charles, if I die in my confinement and my babe lives and is a girl I wish you to retain the little jewelry I wear some of my pencillings and paintings and a few very few of my clothes merely that it may see what once belonged to me than for profit. The remainder of my wardrobe I wish you to send to my Sister and Neice directed to Jackson Miss Mrs Eliza D Coleman, also a few mementoes of drawing, but before doing so give my wash woman two or three of my wrappers one petticoat and linen also one Common piece of painting. The vase of hyacinths to Mr Scott and any little memorial Sayres may wish give him for they have been to me real freinds, also Bud if he likes any thing. If my child is a boy and lives give it the ring I now wear and pin with hair in it, my books and some of my drawings and I charge you to preserve your miniature for either. I would like for all that could well be sent to my sister to be done for she is needy. Mr Scott or S will attend to the forwarding if you direct. In the first place select any thing you would keep, for I trust you would honour my poor memory this far.

If we both die do accordingly. As to my [house] lot I feel that it is justly yours but if you could wish to render me a still farther service it would be to give my poor sister and children the rent of it at least a year or so and then your own heart will tell you what to do. I trust you will keep my book of miscellanies and Diary and if my babe should live to proper age to shew them to it. Burn all that you think best.

If my babe dies with me send its clothes to my Sister. If she never needs them tell her it is my wish to give them to her daughters first.

Give my tubs basket hens and chickens to Aunt Sarah.

Sit my white rose at my grave. It grows nearest the gallery on the left.

Keep my scrap books and card case for my child and if it dies for yourself and my gold pencil I trust you will keep as a special token yourself.

Among my things you will find one small piece of gold which I have reserved for a special purpose and for fear a suspicion might tarnish my memory, I got it from Mr S which was to be paid in paintings.

I have Now painted the other piece for Mr. Scott which I hope he will get if I do not live.[2]

CHAPTER EIGHT

Disappointments

*T*he New Year arrived, but no child did. Still, Madaline Edwards *clung to her belief that she was pregnant, for her hopes for the future of her relationship with Charley now depended on a baby.*

Wednesday, January 1, 1845. The New Year has set in with one of the most lovely, balmy, calm summer days I ever beheld. It is hard to conceive it is winter. God grant if I live to see another I may be better thereby being better able to appreciate the many blessings that are so filling up my last days. Dear C has given me this new diary. May he live to see very, very many happy years.

Night. Mr S. Miss D. her sister and myself have had a good egg nog to day and I send a glass for dear C. who has just drank it.[1] Henry Josephus gave me a new hat for a New Years gift of which I am more than glad and C gave me a pretty Comb. Bless them.

Jan. 2. Went out to see about some sewing I had to do and from thence down with the lady shopping. Came home very tired for Miss D. Mr S and myself had taken a walk last night to the lower Market and I have not got over it yet.[2] Came home and went to work for I cannot allow myself any more holiday.

Alas, this night will ever stand out on the page of memory as the most prominent one I would blot out from it, my ill-fated marriage. Tell me not there is nothing in presentiments for I know there is, but I trust they too have passed.

Jan. 3. Another beautiful bright morning and I get up so early I see how beautiful Venus looks before it is light. Oh how my heart yearns to feel the deep sense of gratitude to my God for such blessings as health to enjoy these prospects and hopes of happy days. Yes one year has flown by with rapidity for I am almost happy. Great God give me to feel my dependence and a full sense of my duty towards thee for the gifts daily given to me.

Took a long walk and now I must read some and then go to bed.

Jan. 4. A thick heavy fog this morning which threatens an end to our May weather. I have worked very constant to day but with the hope before me of seeing my only dear friend to night. He came and brought me some presents and the Native American in which my last little piece appears with some compliments. I have settled up my weeks work and I do hope I will be able to go to church if I live tomorrow. Has cleared off and the stars are bright and it is very late so adieu my pen.

Sun. Jan. 5. This morning it was with difficulty I could decide whether to go to church or not on account of the weather but I at last resolved to go. I did so and I am truly glad I did. When the Organ first struck up its deep toned notes I felt for a moment like my soul was floating away on those notes, and then Mr C delivered one of the most eloquent and appropriate sermons on the New Year I ever heard. He told us that the past year was not dead but would live with us in eternity and witness for or against us. I do believe I came home a better woman. Night. I have just finished a piece for the press. Late at night. Must yet read some. Mr C proved what I have long advocated that Nature taught us religion.

Jan. 6. I am very unwell this morning but compulsion drove me to work, which brought on deep melancholy thinking of my situation when the d^r as if realizing my suspense came in. He says all is as it should be, but it is so unusual for a woman to go in pregnancy over ten months that I am alarmed. Dear C came in, did not appear as lively as usual but began some jesting words which I feared was half in earnest, which with my gloomy feelings ended in tears. I am sorry I am so sensitive and sorry that he cannot foresee what weight such things have upon me, but it will ever be thus. My candle is almost out.

Jan. 7. Went out with some work this morning early. C passed by me without even looking at much less speaking to me which hurt me very much. Came home with a violent head ache and have been down sick all evening. Did not get any money, paid all my cash for washing. Oh I feel like I shall be very sick to night and if so I trust God wil not forsake me for I have no other help now. I am low spirited withal and fit for nothing.

Jan. 8. The glorious 8 th has been duly announced this morning by the artillery and I hope will pass off with good feeling and decorum among the joyful multitudes.[3]

Noon. B came up and staid a short time. Mr S came and had an egg nogg. We made and divided it with our friends. Night. Dear Charley has just left here. He was himself again and I was happy, but I feel my head-ache coming on. I must go to rest. May I live to record this day another year.

Jan. 9. I must confess I have shewed a great want of patience in my temper to day of which I am ashamed. It was towards a little child learning to spell.[4] I hope I will have more hereafter.

Dear C came in to night quite unexpected and found me darning stockings. How glad I was to see him, but he is gone and I must submit, God bless him. I have not read much of late but hope the time will come when I may. Oh that my mind was at ease on one point and God alone can give it.

Jan. 10. Have had such a crowd of visitors to day that I have had no real enjoyment only the little time I had with my flowers. Some dashing ladies. I presume they did not think the same of me and little do they judge me if they think I would exchange with them for all N.O. could give. I have no heart to bestow on glitter or ease, 'tis all centred on him who placed me in this Cottage as humble as it may seem to others I am content. Thank God and dear C.

Night. B came with a host of papers. I will sketch them through now as I have laid by the needle.

Jan. 11. I jumped out of bed with a head ache but went to white-washing and scouring until I made it worse, for I looked for dear C. Sat down to my sewing with half a wish that he would not come for I felt so unwell I feared he would wish himself away, but he came and with one kiss and dear smile I forgot all pain. He brought me the Native with my last publication and Brother Jonathan full of plates.[5] Oh I have been happy with him to day for it has been a long time since he staid so long with me. God bless him to the end of Eternity.

Sun. Jan. 12. Well it is night and although I have had much intrusion yet I have accomplished a good deal of writing and some reading my hand is cramped. Oh! how I wished to hear Mr C to day but was afraid to go. Mr and Mrs W called on me this afternoon and Mr M to day with some strangers but I did not admit them for I wish no more male acquaintances and it is time the old ones knew I did not even want them. I must go to bed for I am tired and sleepy.

Jan. 13. Went down in the car and saw D[r] D who told me he had a case in which the lady was pregnant 13 months, and that I need not be the least uneasy. I got me an axe and brought it all the way home. Went to see the famed Camelias at the flower garden.[6] They are the most magnificent things in they way of flowers I ever saw.

B made me a present of a drum of splendid Smyrna figs. They are a great treat.

Night. Dear C came and staid as long as he could and presented me with a dress for which I am very greatful.

Jan. 14. Feel very unwell but I must work for Mr S will leave tomorrow and I must finish his work.

Night. Made one dollar to day besides being sick. Oh dear C had just came in and took me a very long walk and I feel very bad indeed since and it may be the last I shall ever take. God grant it may not though for I trust my babe will live and that I will to enjoy it. Oh how I hated to see him go home and leave me all alone dreading what I do.

Father give me assistance I pray thee.

To C.[7]

My Own Beloved, This may be the last walk your poor Mad will ever take with you and it is more in consideration of this, than pain that I have wept myself sick to night. The future is darkness to me and yet there is but one thing on this vast globe that makes my soul linger. I can say it from the depths of my soul, not one human being now living could call up in my soul a wish to remain here but thy own dear self. I love my little home for thou hast given it to me, but if my Father calls me he will give me another. I love my books, for thou hast made them valuable in my eyes; but he can give me knowledge. I dearly love my flowers but Oh! I *feel* that I shall there behold such as never yet took root in earthly soil. I love the beautiful clouds that float over our heads but may I not one day flee above them. I love Earth with all its beauties for they are the workmanship of my Heavenly Parent, but yet I grasp at none of its treasures, nor wish they were mine. I look around and find not one but will rejoice that my place is left vacant, unless it should be felt by thee, and to leave thee even for *Heaven* Oh! impious thought is hard to me. *You will not you cannot* ever be loved again as I love you and yet one so unworthy to love you should not dare to avow it, but if ever time should bring to your breast deep and hopeless love think of mine and believe your own is but a shadow. But yet I know all earthly love must sever and I would submit. If my babe lives Oh! my God how I pray that I may live at least a few years for its sake, and if I am to die grant it may pillow its little head in my cold bosom in the tomb. You asked me to night Love where I wished to be buried if I died; I thought you long ago knew that I wished to lie in the Firemans burying ground, for many reasons and one is that few who have ever known me will there point the finger of shame at my cold ashes. Another is I hope you will sometimes come and sit on my tomb and that you will be buried by my side, and this last is my most urgent request and it has once been promised me and if you break it, and I shall be permitted to know it, I cannot but feel that even beyond the stars I should feel the pain of that broken promise. Life divides us; Ah promise me, that death shall not! Think of me, for it seems it would be madness in Paradise to know I was forgotten by the only being on earth in whose breast I wish my memory to live. I am not I believe even afraid to die and yet I am not fit—how is it?

Charley My Beloved. Farewell.

Tuesday Night [Jan.] 14, 1845

Jan. 15. Rose with the determination to try and endure things better. Sat down to my work and partly forgot my pain. Gave the children three lessons and read some. Night. Dear C came and during his stay we talked of our very early years and their recollections and both were filled with pleasant and yet mournful associations. Oh how those days will come up, and it is well they do. I have again commenced Combe the third time and I asked him to begin it likewise and tell me his views as he proceeds. It will benefit us both, by so doing.

Jan. 16. Got up and read near an hour before it was light. Did a good days work, spent two hours with dear C and have now written nearly two more. I wonder that people misspend so much time when they feel so much happier after passing one day itself profitably. If we are always profitably employed I believe we would be very happy. I hope I shall be enabled to pursue a desired course in my reading and writing I have laid down but unless wisdom and perseverance is given me from above it will not profit me much, which I hope to attain.

Jan. 17. Dr Franklin born 1706.

Oh what a delightful day I have had in reading and writing for it has rained in torrents all day. I wrote a good deal and though I had no idea of seeing dear C in such a night yet he came and brought me some oysters and also a piece of his *machine* poetry as he calls it which was only written for fun but is surely a laughable production. I wish he would write more. I think he would be able to write well with some desire to do so. He left in the rain and I did hate it so much. He has been very attentive this week, God bless him.

11 months to day [since conception].

Jan. 18. Rainy and cold. Well I must finish this piece of sewing and then go to hard work rain or shine.

4 oclock. Oh! my back is almost broken for I fear I have been rather imprudent in lifting so many heavy things and getting my feet wet so much.

Night. Oh! it has rained so much and is yet at it that dear C cannot get here to night how sorry I am for it for I do so want to see him.

Sun. Jan. 19. Cold and bleak. I feel more like a confinement to day than Church, but as much as I should be pleased at the former yet I wish I could hear Mr C to day, but I dare not venture. I feel sorry for my plants they look so cold and dreary. I read some time and then pasted all my last gleanings in my scrap book for I thought no one would come, but B. came then M^{rs} H, M^{rs} R and D^r R and to night dear C came a few moments. I got the Native with my last piece. I feel bad but the D^r thinks I am not so near my confinement as I think but I hope he is mistaken.

Finished the New Testament.

Jan. 20. Began the N Testament again. I read one chapter a day and on Sunday two. I hope I will understand it better this time and each succeeding one.

I went down to the City, did some little shopping and got my fortune told. How foolish! Bought me some dishes and got home in time to have a good fire before dear C came. Has just left and I feel very tired so I will to bed. My mind is ill at ease about my babe since I heard what I have. Oh that I knew my doom.

Jan. 21. Finished my new dress C gave me and have had the pleasure of seeing him in it. He brought me some paper and fruit. I had a severe fright this evening.

Have taken a fine dress to make for a wedding, and I must get up early so I must go to bed.

C brought me another specimen of his poetry. It is better than the other.

Jan. 22. I have been very tightly engaged this day.

Dear C sent me a nice clock to day and I am sure I am proud of it. He came to night but could not stay only a few minutes for he was going to the Theatre. He gave me a pair of silk hose, and I wrote a piece of nonsense.

Jan. 23. Oh what a hard rain last night but now it is clear moon light. The moon fulled this morning. Mrs W called on me this evening. Dear C came to night.

I am so busy I have scarce time to eat.

Jan. 24. Clear and cold but Oh what a pretty moon light night. I am almost melancholy for I am more than uneasy about my situation but all I can do is to submit to Gods will be it mine or not. Dear C was here to night and his visits alone keep my spirits from sinking.

A poor beggar woman called to day. Oh that it was in my power to assist the needy.

Jan. 25. Finished a tedious piece of work to day and took it home and in missing the car I had to walk home. C came but was going to the theatre. I felt bad and began to cry but yet I did not wish to detain him from any pleasure, for there is but little allotted me only in his company yet I love him too well to wish any diminution in his. Heard that my youngest sister passed through on her way to my Fathers yesterday. I hope she will be satisfied there but I doubt it.

This day is nine months since I felt the motion of my child.

From Luther Tower's diary:

Heard Rev^d. M^r. Clapp preach on the Trinity. He argued that Unitarians was the true doctrine and that Trinitarianism was not ent[ert]ained by the early Christians for several centuries after Christ. Believes Christ was a divine person and that he derived all his powers to work Miracles, heal the sick Calm the tempest &c. from God but that he was not equal. That the Holy Spirit instead of being a distinct attribute of Deity was only his influence over man.[8]

Sun. Jan. 26. A white frost. I feel inclined for church to day so I will dress and start.

PM. Heard a most beautiful and explanatory sermon on the Trinity and I must say was happy to find my own humble views on that subject are correct if those of our learned Mr Cs are and I feel safe that such is the case. The audience was immense. Saw dear C. Came home cooked my dinner and walked about looking at the workmen putting up my fence sabbath as it is. B came and had the pleasure of seeing A[delle] here.

Oh I feel very unhappy to night.

Jan. 27. I spent a happy morning in my little flower garden. It has been enlarged a foot and a new fence which gives me more room for my flowers. To day my sister sent me two bushel of potatoes, four dozen eggs some fresh butter some nuts and some plants. I was glad to hear from her yet sorry for she writes to me to do a thing which mortal power will never effect, to leave C. No! he is the only *friend* I have on earth and if he were no longer mine I would be his as long as life lasts.

Jan. 28. Rainy and cold this morning, but cleared off but is quite chilly. I went out to see M^{rs} W and spent a few hours. C came to night and gave me two more pictorial bibles. I bought the most lovely flower to day I ever saw and I gave it to C to take to Mrs ———— [Bradbury] as she is very sick and I felt it would please her.

God knows how uneasy I am about my situation. I cannot sleep half the night.

I have before me a flower full blown that opened at my sisters.

Jan. 29. Oh how cold it was this morning. Mrs W came to get me to go shopping with her and I was compelled to do so and while out I met C. Got home and adjusted things when he came and spent two hours with me.

Jan. 30. White frost but I covered up my roses last night. I hired a boy to day and had my front garden well filled up and my trees set out to please me. Mr A[dams] came up and helped to fix the beds. He has always been very kind to me. I trust to have much pleasure in my garden, for I so delight in one.

Dear C came to night and has left me quite melancholy by the chance turn of our conversation, but I strove to hide it from him.

Jan. 31. Made some more improvements in my garden. Did some sewing and prepared myself for an hour in dear C's company. He came and we agreed to adopt another mode to improve our minds. I made a grammatical error and he reproved me for it. I felt ashamed for it was not ignorance that caused it.

C says he will try to get me Swedenborg to read.[9]

Feb. 1. Worked very hard to day and then sat down in my arm chair by the window to read Dick. I soon felt some of my last Summer emotions while perusing that excellent work. I always feel better after reading it.

C came and gave me the Native with my last publication. He was pleased at it and that was recompense for me. Also gave me a sweet rose bud. God bless him.

The population of Cincinatti is 10,000.[10]

Sun. Feb. 2. I am now ready for church and I trust I may hear something that will make me feel more greatful towards him who bestows so many blessings on my unworthy head. Mr C preached upon what was meant by the Church and in so doing went into deep investigations and quoted from the most ancient Fathers, and clearly demonstrated that, no form of church government was essential, although highly necessary and that one pure heart composed a church. Was accosted by a stranger on my return who mortified my feelings much in offering me the language though chaste he did.

Feb. 3. Have had my garden well spaded up and began to white wash the fence, but I am afraid the rain to night will injure it. I have felt very gloomy all day and one word from C to night set me a crying, which has almost choked me up. I can not do any thing my heart is so full.

Feb. 4. Last night I thought the house would fall there was such a tremendous wind and rain.

Have been much vexed at the little work I have got out of the gardener and have sent him off.

Night. Dear C has not come and I am afraid he is vexed at me. I am so gloomy I cannot sit up.

Feb. 5. Oh it was bitter cold last night and is so yet. I have had my washing done.

C came to night and gave me some more No of the Pic Bibles and says he was at a lecture was the reason he did not come last night. He was kind and good.

I am lonely and will wind up matters and go to my cold bed.

Feb. 6. Went out to get some paint and tin ware. Bought me another beautiful passion-flower.

Mr B of Tenn called on me to day and has made me a bet of a fine dress. I hope for two reasons I shall win it, if I do I am to inform him by letter. Told me Mr SH was dead. He was a noble man and I trust is far happier than earth could make him.

Night. Dear C came and as usuall brought me some things and for one a song book to take to church.

Feb. 7. I have been white washing although I am sick and while I was in the most awful plight in came Dr R. He took a hearty laugh over me, but I did not care. He says I will not be confined under Six weeks. It will be thirteen months then. He begged my pretty flower from me.

Night. C came but could not stay as he had to go to a concert with the family. Gave me some apples and a kiss and left. I have a hard days work ahead tomorrow if I am able so I will rest to night for it.

Feb. 8. I have worked harder to day than I thought it possible to do but feel very well indeed.

Dear C came and eat some of my pies and praised them very much. I saw the new moon and trust we shall have some lovely weather. I am so tired I will go to bed and read the Native C gave me.

Sun. Feb. 9. The sun has risen in that soft splendour that fills the mind with delight and the soul with love. I am determined to try and spend the Sabbath more profitably than of late God help me. I intend to go to church.

I attended church and was amply paid if I only bear in mind one sentence that I heard. On my way home saw an uncle and five cousins who are not my friends. They did not see me. God knows I wish them no ill yet they deem me pollution.

Mr S got back from Miss, was delighted to find me well. B was here when I got home so did not get to write any 'till night. Just finished my piece for the Native.

Feb. 10. I set out some roses this morning and then wrote a note to Mr S, read some papers and sewed the rest of the day, but I felt all day that if C came he would go away early and as soon as he entered the door I asked him. He said yes and I really feel low spirited. I did wish to go out tomorrow but I believe I will not for a very particular reason.

Feb. 11. Oh me how much pain I have suffered this day and am still very unwell. Dear C came to night and was very unwell which made me feel very bad indeed. I hope he will be better before morning.

Feb. 12. Had a fever and head ache all night but went to work in the garden very early. I have got my walks made and the yard will soon look very pretty. This night 14 months ago was my first in this house. Thank God and bless my dear C for the difference in my feelings now and then.

Some unknown sent a boy to me to day to ascertain if he could call to see me, and my answer I trust he will remember.

Oh, here is B. Staid till ten oclock.

Feb. 13. Went down in the City to get some garden and flower seed. Mr A[dams] gave me a great many and some plants. He is very kind. Met B Cage. I think he knew me, hope so at least.

C came to night but I do not feel happy since he left atal. Indeed I am not well or in a state of mind to enjoy much.

Sun. Feb. 16. Have been too unwell to attend to diary or any thing else, for the rheumatism has laid me up and I was sadly disappointed in not attending church to day, and as much so in not getting to read or write any for company. Oh that I was so situated that my Sabbaths at least would never be molested. I wish to heavens dear C was able to sell this and place me elsewhere that all my time could be spent as I could wish it but even here I am so much happier than I merit I do not complain. Dear C came.

Feb. 17. Thank God I am nearly well again and to one who has so much to be greatful for there is not a moment but I should feel it. I have done a good deal of work and have had some ladies to see me.

This day makes the 12 th month that I have been inciente and I trust I will not go over another.

Night. C came and in good spirits. He gave me six dollars to get some things. I shall go over and sit with Adelle awhile.

Feb. 18. I found a poor woman sick and no one to get her any thing to eat and how I wished to be able to do more than the little I did. Oh how greatful *I* should be when so many are worse off.

C did not come to night and as I have my matrass emptied and will have to sleep on the shavings I will go to bed for I am very tired.

Feb. 19. To day I bought two brooms, the first I have had since I moved here and as I then had but two and it is now 15 months I think I am not extravagant, nor have I let my house go often unclean. Also had my matrass newly made and now I think I shall sleep finely.

I do not, and can not feel happy when I read so little but I must work all I can to help to live for I would not tax C's generosity as much as I do. He was here to night and I did hope B would have come according to promise with the grapes.

Feb. 21. Went to see the animals and birds at the menagirie yesterday afternoon and from there to the circus at least Amphiatre and was much pleased indeed, and felt even there how much we have to thank God for in this life.[11] Did not get home until near 1 oclock and for me it was very late and I did not get up until 7 then I went to work in my garden and planted all my flower seed. This evening I white washed my fence and piled my lumber and before I got my Clothes on Mrs M and L called. C sent me some nice hams and sugar to day God bless him.

From Luther Tower's diary:

The Military made a grand appearance as they left the City on their way to the battle ground which they have already reached. The Mimic warfare began. The deep thundering of Cannon & Sharper report of Musketry is distinctly heard.

In the City every thing seems to go on as though it were any other than the birth day of the father of his Country. How different would be the sensations produced on the Multitude by the sound of cannon & musketts of contending armies if it were a matter of life and death. If the gay troops which passed through our streets this morning had gone to meet a foe to preserve our city from devastation & pillage. Thoughts for safety of wives and children would take the place of business. Men would not be found in their Counting houses d[illegible] & Ch[illegible] for profit but girding on the armor of battle to defend if worst should come their firesides. These narrow minded pernicious Merchants who will not permit a clerk to belong to a Military Company methinks in time of danger would be very glad to have them go to the port of danger.

The Schools of 2 Municipality Assembled at Mr Clapps Church to hear an Oration from Mr Benjamin. I stepped in a moment and heard them sing Hail Columbia. The military festivities close[d] with a grand ball at the Washington Armory hall.[12]

Feb. 22. The birth day of our immortal Washington has been celebrated with a sham battle in hearing of me. I have toiled through this day but yet I was not too wearied to set out some plants given me since the rain.

Night. Dear C brought me a pair of gloves and has just been gone long enough to get home before the rain that is now falling so sweetly.

My last production is out and my friends are delighted.

Oh I fear I can not get to church to morrow if I live.

Sun. Feb. 23. Heard Mr C preach a most excellent sermon on mercy. Oh! God that other ministers were as fearless and as honest in their opinions this world would not be so filled with so much misinterpretation and contention as it is. I gloried in the emphasis he placed on "I *will not* be cheated out of my opinion" and his call on all to use their common sense in spite of theologians; God is merciful and I truly should know it; as little gratitude as I exhibit.

My sisters birth day.

Feb. 24. I worked the ground and planted my lettuce, radish, parsley, ocher and flower beans. It has been a lovely day and I have done much work. I have felt melancholy all day, so I told dear C to night not to make me cry for a trifle would have done it. I am not over superstitious but I do not like his dreams. One was about my child and the other the loss of all his teeth. I hope it bodes him no ill.

Here comes B. Has made me a present of a bottle of cologne.

Feb. 25. To day I set out some cabbage and lettuce plants Mrs L gave me and watered all my garden. Dear C came but could not stay but a few minutes as he was engaged out. Brought me a no of Blackwoods Magazine.[13]

Mr S sent me two papers. I wish very much to go down to see Wests painting of Death on the pale horse.[14]

Feb. 26. Dear C came this evening at 5 oclock and staid till 7, and has gone to the concert.

I have not done much in finishing my piece of composition to night as there are a courting couple here [Bud and Adelle]. I have almost done all my sewing but am expecting more. How beautiful my little garden looks! Oh how I love to look at the seed springing up and to see the buds peeping out. I have not watered my cabbage to night for it was too late after Q left.

Feb. 27. I have an engagement to go to an equestrian performance to night, and I must water my flowers and be dressed early.

Feb. 28. Came home late as well as tired, and was very well pleased. Rose early and watered my garden, and at 1 oclock I went down to visit Wests painting of death on the pale horse likewise the public gallery of paintings. I was delighted with the one and awed by the other. There are some pieces, St Peters church Rome, and Naples that I could never tire looking at. The Church and Naples are exquisite in perspective they cannot be conceived, the wreck of the Medusa is surely as great a design as execution. I have been too much enraptured with those works of art to have my feelings much disturbed by other things after but thus it will be. I have had a kind of an offer to day for my lot, and C was here just now and says he will see what he can get one over on the rail road for and I would so like to have one far away. Dear C is all the dear dear object earth holds for me and any place is happiness if he is there, but I wish I was more retired.

Mar. 1. It is raining and bids fair to do so all day so I am going to write and read very happily for I cannot account for my fondness of a rainy day.

Night. I wrote a good deal and thank heaven it did not rain enough to keep dear C away, for he eat supper with me and I was so happy to have him by me thus, but he is gone and I am sleepy.

Bought a pair of Muscovy ducks to day. Gave ten bits.

Sun. Mar. 2. I did not go to church to day for it was very unfavourable this forenoon and I had much writing to do. I have written a len[g]thy article for the Native. Have been buisily engaged all day. Dʳ called to see me and wishes to hire me a negro girl and if dear C was able I would like much to have her. I have not read much to day but will read some now before I go to bed.

I was so in hopes C would have called to night.

I borrowed two dollars from Bud. I am sorry to have been compelled to do so but I have not a dollar and must have washing done.

Mar. 3. A hard shower early this morning but my washwoman came and got my clothes ready to dry. Had my garden finished and I shall now get all my seed in before I get sick.

Dear C came to night and tells me to take the girl that Dr R wishes me to hire, and if I like her he may yet buy her for me. God bless him for his goodness to me already.

I feel melancholy to night and I hardly know why.

Mar. 4. Well Old Tyler is now ex president to night, and the democrats are making great exultation with guns &c.

Dear C came to night and gave me some money, and a pair of snuffers. He was not altogether well.

Dr Richey sent the girl Maria up to night. I like her appearance and I hope some day will own her if she suits but that is to wait patiently for dear C has done much for me and I can expect no more.

Mar. 5. A beautiful day had my washing done.

RP an old friend called to day to see me whom I have not seen for near two years. He waited on me once when I was sick. Poor fellow he is not long for this life for he has the consumption.

Dear C was here and as he left met B at the gate.

A[delle] and B have just left.

Hopes of the Annexation.

Mar. 6. Hear the annexation bill is defeated by one vote. Hang it.

Went to see a sick child, poor Mother.

C came late to night and as soon as he left Adelle her sister and B came. Just gone—am sleepy.

Mar. 7. Well Texas is annexed at last and I hope it will be much benefit to dear C some day as he owns property that will be of great value.

C came to night and as happy as we were together a circumstance oc-cured before he left that set me to crying and I am foolish but cannot stop and B came and caught me thus asked if C had been unkind to me. I told him that was what he was never to me. My head aches badly I will try to sleep.

Mar. 8. Oh I do feel horrid. I am in pain and suspense. I cannot under-stand my situation. I shall go crazy unless I am satisfied soon.

Mr T and Miss D have urged me to death to go to the french theatre to night but I am too unwell.[15]

Dear C came and brought me some nuts, apples and the Native. Oh I fear he has gone home with a heavy heart on account of what has been said about ———. I wish I had not told him. God ever bless him.

Sun. Mar. 9. I have been very bad off to day so that I could not go to church.

D^r R came up and made me take 50 drops of laudanum and says I must be careful or I will have an abortion [miscarriage].

I have written and read some to day and if I had been well would have made good use of this one Sabbath free from intruders.

The D^r says I may have the girl at 4 dollars per month and furnish her clothes.

Mar. 10. Last night I was alarmed by a fire for I thought my house was on fire. I was very unwell and have been all day, I took 75 drops of lau-danum and it has almost prostrated me. I was so in hopes dear C would come to night but the rain I expect kept him away. I do wish to see him so much. I hope I shall be able to work tomorrow for I cannot bear to be so idle although unwell.

It is cold and dreary to night and so warm last night.

RP has bet me a fine dress to be paid this day twelve months I think I shall win it. He has the following figures to repeat from memory.

3 7 3 5 17 9 9 2 9 7 0 4 8 2 2 7 2 8 7 7 7 2 8
7 1 7 2 4 1 2 7 4 9 00 5 9 5 7 2 7 2 7 3 7 3 5 1 7
9 9 1 9 9 2 2 8 2 8 2 2 2 0 1 7 2 9 2 7 2 2 9 8 9
2 7 5 29 0 7 2 6 8 8 9 8 2 2 7 3 2 7 2 5 5 2 7

8 1 8 7 2 2 1 5 5 2 2 6 7 2 7 5 5 7 3 9 7 2 0 8 6
9 9 2 8 7 2 6 9 9 2 8 9 3 5 2 6 9 5 0 7 2 3 5 2
8 7 2 8 5 5 0 5 5 2 3 9 9 6 9 2 8 2 7 8 9 1 4 0
0 2 8.

Mar. 11. Raining and cold as Dec. and has rained all day long so that I know I need not look for dear C to night and it is a bitter lash for me to do so long without seeing him. I feel like it is too much to submit to but yet I have it to do.

I have got some sewing to day which will keep my mind somewhat employed till I can see him.

Mar. 12. Rained all day. B was up here this evening and C cannot get here. Oh my father I cannot bear it much longer for it is now four days since I saw him. I am almost crazy about it.

My ducks are gone and I am afraid I shall not get them again.

Have written a good deal to night.

Mar. 13. My ducks were hid making a nest so I had two eggs this morning instead of minus ducks.

Rained all day and not more profusely than my tears for I have wept until I am almost distracted. Why does not C come to see me. I shall go mad. He could if he wished, unless he is sick and conjecture will kill me. He might pity me at the present state of things, if he killed me after my confinement. What can I do. If I knew he was not displeased at me I would endure it better but Oh God forgive me.

Mar. 15. I could not write last night for I wept until I thought I must go into spasms. I took an ague and could not sit up. B came and took a note to C, came back and said all were out on pleasure while I was suffering death on his account. I rose early so weak I could hardly walk and tried for an hour and a half to intercept him on his way down, but did not see him and came home broken down with the firm hope and belief he would be here to night. His time is past and I am still in ignorance. My God if this is mans love grant another may never feel even sympathy for me. I cannot live under this, I could not deem him so cruel.

Sun. Mar. 16. I did not get up until after 9 this morning for I felt as if I could never rise. My God have mercy on me. I then dressed and took the girl out with me to walk and came home exhausted. My head seems crazy, my eyes almost out and fever high. B came and told me he gave C my note, but did not get a word from him. I do not know how to act. I cannot bear it.

RP came and spent the evening with me and as my mind is too out of order to read I did not regret it. Now I am so unhappy fearing I may not see C for a long time yet.

Mar. 18. Last night I suffered more mental agony than I ever did in my life. I never prayed so earnestly to die and if it is my Gods will I do not care how soon for I am undone. C has laid his first charge against me and murder would have been light compared to it. I feel like an iceberg was on my heart that even the burning of my brain nor scalding tears can remove. Oh I pray that he may never have me to make him endure half no nothing of what he has me by this one thought. I have told S to visit me no more, and I wish I was on an island.

Mar. 19. Oh! how cold it is to day, it is almost hailing. I went out and got one barrel of coal. RP. came and spent most of the day with me. To night dear C came and staid pretty late and seems almost again himself but as happy as I hope I may yet be still I do not yet feel so well as I should wish. Alas that I should ever be happy like I was. Yet I will do all to reconcile my feelings that I can. He seems anxious to sell my lot and get me another and build me another house.

Mar. 20. Went down in the City this evening and got me a market basket and some handkerchiefs, rode home very tired. R had been here twice while I was gone. C came only a few minutes as he had company. B came after he left.

Mar. 21. R[P] came this morning before he had his breakfast. He staid until 11 oclock and returned at 4. He has said serious things to me. I wish I could make him feel his position. He is too good to have such a destiny. I wish he were happier. I expect he will go up Red River tomorrow but says he will come to see me before he goes.

Dear C staid tonight until near nine. I told him what R[P] had said and he actually persuaded me to accept his offer, but Oh I love him too much.

B and Adele are here.

Mar. 22. Went out early this morning to see an old gentleman about purchasing a lot as dear C requested but it was in vain for he will not sell. Besides I have done a great deal of work and had company too.

Night. Dear C came and brought the Native with the conclusion of my last piece and says no one believes a female writes my pieces, which is surely very strange when such abler pens are daily used by females too. But so it is.

Sun. Mar. 23. I was much in hopes to have heard Mr C preach to day but it is raining and I cannot go. I have some papers to read but here comes R and I shall be interrupted.

Well it is now 3 oclock and I have not done any thing towards improving my mind. How I regret it too. Oh! God will I ever be what I wish. Teach me to rule myself if I cannot circumstances. I would be better and suffer others to intrude less. I feel unworthy of C for I make so little progress in the mental.

Night. I've written a long piece and I do not feel well.

Mar. 24. Last night Adelle had a fine girl. I was awake a good deal, rained very hard. Oh I am almost crazy about my situation I wish I did know what is my fate. B came to night to see A and brought me some papers.

I fondly hoped to see dear C to night but was sadly disappointed. I am so full I can scarce keep from shedding tears again.

Mar. 25. I have been in some pain to day but nothing indicates any approach of my confinement. I am literally crazy. I do not know what to think.

Night. C came and I wept myself sick. B came and I have had to sit up over at Adells with him until 11 oclock.

This day is 11 months since I felt the motion within me.

Mar. 26. We are creatures of circumstances, the most trivial often affecting the tenor of our whole lives, and unfitting us for even social intercourse where we once anticipated much real happiness. I was sadly disappointed to day in a principle I hoped a friend professed and it will not end in a trifle. I went down in the City saw the D^r and came home

saw C who had been to see a French D[r] on my account who says I am
not in the way I have so long hoped.

Got a letter I little expected.

Mar. 27. I worked hard the forenoon on my banquet[te] and then at
my sewing and paid a short visit. I am too low-spirited to do much of
any thing.

Dear C was here to night and is gloomy as well as myself. B is here
now with some papers.

Mar. 28. I have waked in pain from my head, proceeding I fear from
my mind. I can read nothing nor study as I should. I feel so impious in
the sight of Heaven I dare not pray. Oh how ungreatful I am. God have
mercy on me I pray. I cannot overcome my feeling mental while in my
uncertain situation. Dear C has just left he is again more like himself.
Still I wish he had never thought as he has. Alas for human nature.

Mar. 29. My mind was never less at ease than to day, and I cannot
shake it off. The causes are partly developed and fear of coming evils
distress me. I try in vain to read. I cannot understand.

Night. Dear C has gone to the theatre and will not be here to cheer
me any; but B will be up soon to see A[delle] and I will have to go over
with him.

I have sat rocking in the old arm chair thinking of happier days, when
at that time I was looking forward for still happier.

Sun. Mar. 30. It looks quite cloudy but yet I hope I shall be able to get
to church for really I feel like it will be of service to me to hear Mr C.

½ past 2. Just returned from church but did not hear such a sermon
as I hoped. There were not half so many as at other times, taken off by
the foot race I suppose. I saw dear C but that was all. Very warm indeed
to day. I saw two persons who I wish to see no more until Eternity. I do
not feel happy atal and I fear I will not be so soon.

R called this evening.

Mar. 31. My mind is full of torture, and as I sat pondering I saw C and
his wife come by my door and look in my garden. Oh how I wished it
was I at his side.

Night. I have just got back from the City and have been told it is positive I am not in pregnancy but some thing more dangerous. C and I have talked it over and he is much distressed. I have wept over my disappointment as much as the pain I shall endure. God give me submission for I am so wretched.

Apr. 1. To day has been of adventures to me. Mrs ——— [Bradbury] called at my gate to make some trivial enquiries in order to see me. Went home and told C that she knew he was acquainted with me. He came to night much distressed for fear of the future. I hope she will not learn any thing more. I have sewed all day to drown excitement.

April fool has not been made of me to day.

C gave me $5.

Apr. 2. R[P] came and spent the after noon with me and brought me a novel to read. Do not know that I shall for I have scarce mind or taste left for any thing now. I looked my poor eyes almost out to night for C but he did not come. B is here full of trouble for there is much difficulty between R[P] and A[delle].

I got my rocking chair to day. Glad of it.

Apr. 3. A commission to B that I little expected to ever bear and he bore it better than I thought.

Dear C was here to night and has just gone.

Apr. 4. Rained last night and I did not sleep much. I was alarmed at nothing however. I have not done much in my garden for I have so much sewing.

Dear C came and gave me a paper of pins. God ever bless that man the more I know him the more exalted he stands.

Apr. 5. Have read some to day. Feel bad indeed.

C brought me the Native with my last production. He is gone home and I am very sleepy.

Bud just came in with a budget of papers and wishes to hear how A[delle] takes their separation.

Sun. Apr. 6. Walked down to church but learning M^r C was sick and that there was no preaching there I then went to the Methodist and heard Mr Nicholson and I do not think I was prejudiced but it will be for the future almost mockery of religion for me to hear that denomination.[16] To hear him (a luminary too) after M^r C is like drinking slops after the richest wines. Just got home as it began to rain and now there is a fine shower falling and I feel too unwell to enjoy the first quiet Sabbath afternoon I have had for a long while.

Apr. 7. I have been surely more miserable than tongue can tell. I am now convinced that I am not in the family way and this disappointment has almost maddened me. Then I have been most outrageously abused to day by those whom I have done so much to befriend. Oh God how ungreatful this world is. I must try to bear it the best I can.

Apr. 8. Sick as I was I went down to day to try to see D^r R but did not. I came home tired and soon after dear C came. He tells me to try and make the best I can of such tales and abuse that all will yet come right. Oh I am not myself. God help me.

B just gone. Has had a pill to swallow from our neighbors as well as to hear me abused. Says he deeply regrets my feelings having been so wounded for my best motives.

Apr. 9. D^r R came up and finally acknowledged that I am not in the family way but that he has been grossly deceived. I feel that I am doomed to be eternally a creature of disappointments and sorrows. I fear that I shall never again be an object of as great interest to C as I have been, indeed I can already perceive it. Oh I am so miserable on the account of it. I have now to undergo a course of medicine. C did not come to night and he knows how I expected him.

Apr. 10. What a world of wonders is this! To day an old friend whom I have not seen for 14 years sent me word she and family were here and I must come to see her. Before my heart had learned the cares of life half my existence was wrapt up in that woman and her children.[17] I went we both shed tears and still we were glad and melancholy. Oh the little girl I had so loved was there a Mother. How proud they were to see me.

Apr. 11. To day I have painted my house, that is I had some help. But Oh how tired I am.

Night. All my friends came to see me this evening and It made me feel like other days, but yet I told M^{rs} W my position and if she did not wish my visits say so but she says on the contrary I am still her dear friend. I have no delight in company and do not feel happy in being compelled to visit or receive others.

Apr. 12. Finished the painting and worked almost to death but all is now nice and clean and I had dear C here to night and if I did not have to take medicine I should feel a little happy to night.

Sun. Apr. 13. As sick as I was I went to hear Mr C to day. His text was "man was created upright" and he gave us a most edifying sermon and I hope I shall profit in feeling at least by it. Night. This has been an afternoon of anxiety and disappointment. Nothing but company and no time to read or write. I wonder if things will ever alter that I can be as much alone as I wish.

I saw dear C pass by my gate while I was talking to JC. Oh my heart is heavy and I have no one to unburden it to.

Apr. 15. I have been and am yet so sick I cannot write or do much else, and my mind is less at ease than my body. My God I wonder if I shall ever again be myself. I feel like a blank in life.

Went down and sewed all day for Louisa got home near dark and found R here.

Apr. 16. PM just returned from a visit to Mrs W. Took tea there and got home in time to prepare a surprise for dear C. I had a nice cucumber and some ham and eggs for he is so fond of them. His wife is very sick indeed so that he could not stay but a few minutes.

Oh how sweet my honey suckles smell.

Apr. 18. To day has been one of more excitement than I am used to for I have had a crowd to dine and spend the day with me, my old Time friends. I am quite alone now and Oh so much happier.

C has not nor will he come to night and the musketoes will not let me have any rest atal.

Sun. Apr. 20. RP walked nearly to church with me to day for the Car had just left the stand. M^r C preached a sermon concerning seamen and a collection was raised to assist in giving them a home and place of worship in this place. It was a great eulogy and I believe in the main a true one that the sailor had never two faces like those on shore who would bow and smile while your enemy at heart. I will now try to write a piece

if no intruders come for my mind has been so long in torture and is yet
that I do nothing towards improvement.

Apr. 21. Wept myself almost in spasms last night and rose this morning with a hurting head and heavy heart. Went down very early to sew
all day for L. C came to night and is gone I am so tired.

Apr. 23. My God what will come next to fill my cup of disappointments and sorrows. C is almost crazy for fear his wife is on the point of
discovering our amour and wishes to move me up to Carolton. I wish
to procure his peace of mind before all other things in life and will go
far away from this if he will only say go, for life with the knowledge of
having caused his misery will be a curse and not a blessing. We have but
little pleasure of late; all the fates or people are against us.

Apr. 25. Last night I again took a bitter spell of weeping. Oh it is ruin-
ing my health mind and every thing else. I never so sincerely longed for
the sleep of the silent tomb for there I might rest, at least my poor body
and the world seems not to think I have a soul.

From Luther Tower's diary:

Heard Mr Clapp Preach this morning, one of his usual original without head or tail discourses. They have decidedly the best singing in
town.[18]

Sun. Apr. 27. Dear C did not come last night as he promised to bring
me a paper and I feel very afraid some fresh news has reached her ears
for he would not have so disappointed me. My life is one of torturing
suspense.

Went to church and heard Mr C preach a most edifying sermon on
concience and of what little use it was without the aid of reason. I felt
informed if I am not bettered by it. Saw dear C.

B is here now and I have done very little towards reading to day indeed I am near an idiot of late. God help me I pray.

Apr. 28. Well little can we trust in one another, and I find more and more that C is the only man I ever have or shall find who is any ways near perfect. Oh what am I not now suffering.

Apr. 30. For a moment I felt glad of late for I saw my little humming bird had come back again this evening. Strange he knew I was friendless, and has come to cheer me, but even its efforts only prompted a few melancholy verses from my pen.

May 2. Trouble of mind has so filled every hour this week that I find no heart to write or read.

I am sick and feel deserted although dear C says he is still the same in feeling.

May 3. C came and gave me $5 to pay Maria's hire. She hates to leave me and I do so much regret to have any thing attached to me for it is ever thus.

Sun. May 4. My spirits are so deeply depressed, my health bad and weather gloomy that I shall not go to church.

Night. My Father came to see me and when I saw the old man weep I did wish more than ever that the grave had long closed over my head. He staid all the afternoon and wept over my productions which I read him. He said nothing to me about my situation or prospects; but told me my youngest brother was over here not long since and tried to find me. Oh I wish he had for I never yet saw him. Oh I am so desolate for Maria too has gone home and I am alone.

May 5. Rose at 4 oclock and was down in the City at half past six. I got the work I wished and was returning home, when who should accost me but FG, the young man who brought me to my ruin when he was assuming the garb of friend in Vicksburg. He looked guilty and well he may. I mad[e] a very cold recognition and he soon took his leave. God forgive him for all he has made *me* endure for tongue will never tell it, but we can never be again any thing but strangers to each other.

Night cold, dark and dreary. C will not come and I feel very desolate.

May 6. C came to night and I had another cry. I do not feel like I ever can be happy any more. Oh if God only saw fit to take me out of this life I would not grieve to go. I wish I had what I call religion. It would make me resigned at least.

May 7. My father called this morning before he left for my sisters and will be back in a few days. Had nothing to send the children.

PM violent head ache have been to the druggist after pills.

May 8. I have been almost crazy all day with my head. C came to night which partly cured it.

May 9. Dear C came to night and brought me some delicacies. He was on a visit out and could not stay a moment.

May 10. Rose at 5 and went out to the St Marys Market to see M^rs L before she left the City.[19] Brought the younger sisters home with me and cleaned up my house and did my cooking. Planted seed, read some and am now sadly disappointed in C's not coming with The Native for me. I wish he had for I wanted to give him some black-berry tart and to get a kiss too. Well the musticks [mosquitoes] will not let me read or write in peace.

Sun. May 11. A quiet lovely morn. I have found much time to read and write this morning and though my mind is far from its former tone yet I shall still hope. I will now dress for church and I hope to hear a sermon that will make me better.

Heard an excellent sermon which was a repetition of his last Sabbaths discourse as he was called on by some of the members to modify some expressions that he then made. He stated and proved arguments fearlessly and freely. I did not hear the other but could find nothing in todays to cavil at. I feel very unhappy indeed to night. Oh am I ever to be thus.

May 12. My God what a day this has been to me. May I never see such another.

May 14. Started down to see the gallery of paintings and was stopped by a shower.[20] Came home and sat all alone. Melancholy enough.

May 16. Visited the paintings and have an invitation to go again next week before they close, which I shall do for there are some pieces there always new to me.

Got my half-barrel of flour which I fear will not prove good.

May 17. JR wrote me a note which has upset my equilibrium more than I believed it could do. I gave him an equal reply.

JC called to see me to day. My relations meet with cold receptions.

Dear C came and brought me Mrs Ellis's last work and I am very glad.[21]

Sun. May 18. One of the loveliest sabbath[s] my eyes ever beheld and I have been kept at home by a sore face and I much wished to have gone to church, however I have enjoyed myself in writing and in perusing Mrs Ellis's last work with which I am delighted. Have had not a visitor until just now Mr S and his two children called on me.

R came and sat with me until ten oclock.

The opening of the grandly named National Gallery of Paintings in purpose-built rooms at 13 St. Charles Street gave Madaline Edwards an opportunity to try her hand as an art critic. The gallery contained a miscellaneous collection of works by the proprietor, George Cooke, works on loan from local collectors, and copies of European paintings. The views of Rome and the Forum mentioned by Edwards were made by Cooke. The portrait of Davy Crockett was by John Gadsby Chapman (1808–89), Cooke's student.[22]

Edwards's art criticism, which was written for the Native American, *was her most public attempt to claim a place in the world of intellect and to distance herself from the intellectual shallowness of the "company of females." In reviews of large dramatic paintings such as Benjamin West's* Death on the Pale Horse *and* Christ Healing the Sick, *or Francesco Anelli's* The End of the World, *she looked for a kind of plot or story but appropriately devoted most of her attention to artistry of characterization and to the ways the painters individualized the figures in their paintings and depicted the inner qualities of individual actors through their appearance. At the same time she wanted to find in the paintings a catalog of distinct emotions appropriate to the theme of each piece. Thus she combined principles that were similar to those widely used in discussing mid-nineteenth-century literature with critical precepts of nineteenth-century art and architectural theory that stressed association—the ways particular characters, places, and visual forms could convey distinctive ideas or moods. These strategies (which resembled those of other newspaper critics of painting), as well as her commentary on purely formal values, reveal a woman who was initiated to intellectual life primarily through the printed word.[23]*

The National Gallery of paintings[24]

Mr Editor. Although my visits to this place have not been so frequent as I could have desired, yet they afforded me much pleasure, and
I must say no little chagrin at seeing so little patronage given where
much should have been bestowed upon the exertions of those who see
and lament the lack of taste and a just appreciation of the beauties of
art in this mighty City. I do not profess much taste but I have an indescribable fondness for a fine painting and I can enter into the feelings
of the projectors of this school of refinement. They are not, they cannot
be as too many think of a lucrative nature entirely, but original from a
higher source, from nobler and loftier emotions, akin to the patriots love
of Country: the painter loves the piece of his creation not less than the
Native scene from which he has copied the same. His very soul seems
floating on the etherial cloud his pencil has called up. The very smile
that plays upon his lip when success crowns his toil seems impa[r]ted
to the lifelike foliage and climbing vine, and the very stillness of his
greatful heart as he has finished a much desired piece and sits contemplating it with gratitude to the Author of all the beautiful in Nature and
glorious in art seems but a counterpart of the calm blue lake in the fore-
ground. No wonder then nothing but stern necessity often compels the
artist to part with that which is a portion of himself. It is like selling
one of his children, and yet an artist is not a mizer with his productions. He would love them not less but more that others should look on
them too and appreciate the skill and patience that could so embody
the beauties of earth sea and sky, and this does not arise from vanity
and a desire for flattery, but by an impulse that seems to emenate from
the Creator alone. There are others who can love, admire, and glory in
the beautiful productions, but their love is no more the same than they
could love anothers offsprings as their own. Feelings like these have determined Mr C[ooke] to make a strenious effort to kindle in the breasts
of these money loving Southerners to admire something besides cotton
bales and sugar hogsheads, and if he succeeds to win their affections in
part to something more refining and pleasing he will have received to his
own breast an additional pleasure to that of being an eminent artist and

have made others [realize] their time has been profitably spent. I have merely alluded to the beautiful in this art, but when those who visit this gallery and gaze upon the Roman forum upon St Peters church, Rome Naples and other noted scenes, they will at once call to mind all the history they have ever read of these antiquities and they will find that these miniature worlds of knowledge have the power of awaking feelings unknown while poring over the pages of lettered history.

I paid a visit to this gallery and the first thing [that] attracted me was a company of females that were fleeing about from one piece to another in such rapid succession that one could compare them to the humming bird lighting upon every flower in a moment scarcely realizing that one was less sweet than another, but I am afraid upon retiring they had not even the humming birds store as an evidence of having been there. And I thought this is it and if the artists who contributed to compose that or any other gallery could only witness the little soul thrilling emotions that actuated them, while thus engaged bestowed upon their toil by the superficial observers (no lookers on) they would feel their works desecrated; and if their breasts afforded no higher recompense, might abandon this profession with disgust. I was then attracted to that thrilling scene the wreck of the Medusa, and though bold in its design and execution yet it possessed too much of the terrible, distressing and awful to claim my attention long when sympathy was useless. I passed a few moments before the excentric Crockett and sighed for the unhappy fate of one so brave. Then came the glorious Washington, and all his untarnished and undying fame rose up in mind as only fit to deck the brow of that unpretending calm, yet dignified sage. I then took a look, a long look at that beautiful scene the Roman Forum and as I looked at the desolation of greatness I felt that mans works are of short duration, that all his greatest skill, art wisdom and wealth were here reduced to a common Cow pasture, gazing upon those broken half buried colums I thought of Byrons dream and wondered if this very spot did not give rise to "couched among fallen colums" for many doubtless have fall[en] where so few stand. Then that one desolate column that commemorates Romes last emperor told my heart of those less renowned and more modern I have seen standing alone in life unhonoured from other causes than a fallen empire. The very darkey that patiently toils up the ascent with his panniers, the cows that cross the grass where gold had once litterally paved these streets, the figures reclining on the turf, the old cartman, and sheep seemed to lead the mind away from its former glory until the eye rose again to the steeples, and domes in the distance that brought back the conviction that "all is vanity beneath the sun." I then [had] a view of the scene of Rome as a whole, and to describe the pleasure I derived would be useless as well as impossible then, last, of the most prominent I gazed with wonder and admiration upon the far famed St Peters Church, which to pass casually by would not rivet the attention so much, but when viewed as a perspective is superb in the extreme and one cannot realize but he can walk right in the church up the aisle and behold all its wonders. I could gaze at it for weeks. Then I took a cursory look at all the minor productions, the portraits of some great and good men, of others who would make themselves so by being hung up there. There was innocence and female beauty, and many other things better seen than described, but finally I stopped before a picture of my conceptions of rural felicity, a cottage surrounded by shady trees fruit and flowers, the dark green oak waving over the lovely blue stream on whose bosom the geese and ducks were gliding, while I thought I could almost see the fish at the bottom, My thoughts turned away from all the lofty, noble and magnificent on which I had been pondering and all I asked of the worlds stores of wealth was such a cottage by such a stream far away from the noise and bustle of human life. Oh I could then forget much of the past and not look with dread upon the future. I learned while there the gallery would close this week and I intend to go and take one farewell look at my favorite scenes, and although I do not know Mr C[ooke] or any one connected with the apartment yet I trust they will return again in Dec and persever until they shall have created a taste for the fine arts here which seems less appreciated here than in any other City in the Union, and I trust those ladies who can so well enjoy four or five evenings a week in seeing comedies and tragedies will at least give one a month here, and if they will only look with half the interest upon those laborious productions that they can upon the dancing girl, They will soon have their taste more refined and their knowledge improved. I wish my solicitous appeals to the publick on this score was worth something. I would use it, but time and perseverance will prove all things and all I can say is God speed the cause.

May 18th 1845.

May 19. This is my fathers birth day and he was here having just got back from my sisters. He is 62 years old. He staid some time but leaves for home tomorrow doubtless I may never see him again. My sister and myself will correspond no more thus all have forsaken me but those on whom I have no claim. God bless them all, but particularly the few friends I have on earth.

I looked anxiously for C to night but he has not come and I do feel so melancholy.

May 20. A hard shower this afternoon which did not prevent dear C from coming to see me. I am glad he did, but yet I am not happy yet.

I have nearly finished The Bennets abroad and like it exceedingly. Oh what a lovely moon light night.

May 21. I had some very unwelcome visitors this afternoon and one of them took the pains to tell me as my character was lost and I could make it no worse by doing as he would persuade me, but I trust my language and conduct will not be soon forgotten by him. Alas what do I not have to hear as well as suffer. And that very mans wife was in a great measure the cause of my ruin.

May 22. Another shower to day and I fear I will not be able to get down tomorrow to see the painting[s] again before they close. Oh I was in hopes dear C would come to night but he has not. It surely does not enter his mind how lonely he would be situated as I am but I dare not complain and I wish I could not feel so much, but my nature is still the same on the score of feeling.

May 23. I again visited the national gallery and staid over three hours, then left without being half satisfied; in fact I came home so much an enthusiast upon the subject of the works of art that I am half mad. I have looked at Rome and Naples until I feel I could not die without beholding them as well as their galleries of painting and statuary. This gallery closes tomorrow. I am much indebted to Mr Lennard who was so struck with fondness and desire to understand that he made but one charge for three visits. I wish them much success on their return.

May 24. Worked very hard to day and then finished the Bennets abroad and as is the case with all of Mrs Ellis's works I am delighted reading her visit to Rome. It has added an additional pang to my breast to know that one so humble as I can never behold them. How I long to stand where thousands have who if they know more have felt less than I should there feel. Her delineation of moral as well as natural beauty is happy and well attested by a few at least. I intended giving it another direct perusal.

Have got the loan of Josephus.[25]

Sun. May 25. I feel unusually unwell yet I intend to go to church for the morning is too lovely to stay at home, as dear as it is to me. PM. Mr C preac[h]ed from "work out your salvation" and in speaking of every one possessing a besetting sin I for one felt that I have so many for the soul of me I do not know the most prominent one. He said truly we were all placed here to work literally and mentally and we could not gain heaven without the latter at all events. I wish I could realize all of his assertions and yet I feel in one I am happier in my own way of thinking.

May 26. Went to market very early this morning and have had a young lady here all day. Mr H died this morning. Poor widow was this time last year a bride.

Night. It is raining in floods and dear C could not come. It is now three days since I saw him.

May 27. C came and brought me the Native, and promised me to come to night but he has not done so, and I never felt more melancholy. One cause is I have not a dime and no marketing and my work will not procure me any for several days.

May 28. I am sick and low spirited but still do not give up hard and constant work.

May 29. Dear C brought me a pamphlet containing comparisons between the ancients and moderns, which I shall read with much interest. He also gave me $1 and if I do not get some sewing soon I know not what to do.

May 30. Have read that pamphlet and find some very good things in it but others quite light.

Ha! There is Henry Josephus, the most unexpected visitor I could have thought of. He gave his reasons for not coming sooner and got his presents that were returned [by Adelle] and has gone.

May 31. After a hard and constant days labor I have had one happy hour with C. He brought me the Native with my last production and thinks it very good indeed. These momentary visits from him are looked for with anxiety. They constitute all the happiness I derive from earthly sources but were they more frequent I feel that I should enjoy life far more but yet I will not complain for I feel that he would like to be with me oftener if he could.

Sun. June 1. Went to church but was sadly disappointed in not hearing Mr C for he had some one there to fill his place who read us a written sermon and these things I cannot endure. The sacrament was taken to day.

Had some female company this afternoon and took a walk with them. Feel too bad to write or read.

June 2. Had my washing partly done and C has not come to give me any money and I told him how I was situated for I cannot get my two dollars I worked so hard for and I now have no sewing. My health is getting worse and my spirits bad.

June 3. C came to night and I had a good cry at least a bad one for I fear I was unjust in it.

He gave me five dollars.

June 4. C sent me a keg of lard and three hams and I am very glad of it for I have been out some time.

C came to night and I gave him a piece of my plum pie.

Dr Richey was here this morning and prescribed for me.

June 5. Went down and left a note for D^r S to call. Got some ice cream and when I got home felt literally dead.

Had M^{rs} W and daughters here to dinner to day.

June 6. D^r S called this morning and prescribed for me, but still I do not think he understands my case. However he says it will not result in any thing serious.

Took a short walk and was so in hopes C would have come to night but he has not.

June 7. Planted some corn this morning and then went down in the City to get my prescription made out and to choose M a bonnet. Have trimed the bonnet, and will now claim the remainder of the afternoon to read.

C came to night and brought me some candy. He staid his usual time, an hour, and it does seem so hard to have so little of his company.

Sun. June 8. Awoke in the night and heard it raining, and felt certain I should have no sermon to day and indeed there have been alternate and hard showers all day. I have been reading Josephus all the time I have not been asleep for I never felt so debilitated and drowsy in my life and I think it must be the medicine more than the weather. Oh! how I wish C was here this evening to talk to me.

(Genl Jackson died)[26]

June 10. General Jackson died, and the news reached here on the 16th. The papers have gone in mourning and the City are requested to do the same. The Father of our City is gone at last and I trust to a better and more greatful world than the one he left.[27]

June 12. Dear C came to night and brought me a blank book in which I purpose keeping a historical vocabulary and other references.[28] Also a lot of pins and some nice bannana's. Oh I wish that he could be more with me for I do feel so loth to see him go.

My dog is gone and I feel afraid to night.

June 13. This day twelve months C started to the East. Oh heavens I hope never to spend such another one of bitter agony. This Summer he will be near me at least.

June 14. Dear C was here to night but could not stay long as he had an engagement. I have read a good deal in Josephus to day.

C wishes me to write a piece of poetry on the banner presentation as

I have a publick invitation to the same. I wish I could go. I'll try and fill his request.

Sun. June 15. Went to church and heard an excellent sermon on "we must be born again." Very warm indeed. Have been composing my piece. Do not know how it will do.

I do not feel satisfied with myself. Oh God I feel ungreatful and I do know I am too unmindful of thy kindness to me and I fear C thinks I am not greatful to him. I wish I was better I feel that I should be born again. Oh for understanding and wisdom, my Father give it me.

June 16. Wrote my piece and a note to the Editor. Expect it will be rejected.

This afternoon had some buisness near C's house and I saw him and his wife mounting their horses for a ride. I wish I had not seen it. Although I could not feel envy towards her yet a flash of bitter feeling comes over me on such occasion[s] that makes me perfectly miserable for days. I feel that all enjoyments in life are cut off to me and yet the one I so much love can partake of all while I am doomed to solitude and sorrow. I strive against it yet I am human.

June 17. The banner presentation was pos[t]poned on account of a riot which called off the company.[29]

From the Daily Picayune:

THE N.A. ARTILLERY FLAG. — We yesterday were gratified with a sight of the flag to be presented this evening to Capt. Forno's company of "Native American Artillery." The flag is the handiwork of two young Creole ladies in this city, and is indeed a superior specimen of skill in needle-work — surpassing anything of the kind which we have ever seen. The ground of the flag is a rich yellow, trimmed with silver fringe, tassels, &c. The device is a cannon, surmounted by a spread eagle holding in its beak a scroll, on which is the inscription of "LIBERTY"; a drum, a pile of cannon balls; and the whole ornamented with flags in graceful folds, is on a beautiful bank of green. Every particle of the work is of embroidery, and such is the exquisite touch and finish of the shading, that without a close inspection we really thought it a painting, and no mean effort of the artist's brush at that. Each side of the flag is alike beautiful, and reflects the highest credit on the fair hands which wrought it.

The presentation takes place this evening at the Armory Hall of the Washington Battalion, at 8 o'clock, by a lady, and it is to be hoped that all who take an interest in such matters will be present.[30]

June 20. Went down and bought me a parasol a pair of shoes and netting for my musketoe house, which I have just had finished, and I hope I shall enjoy the benefits of my money, for it will be a treat to read unmolested by the musketos.

The banner presentation came off to day and, the description of the affair will be given next week.

June 21. Dear C came to night and our conversation was upon a subject that was calculated to run me almost frantic. I wept until I am almost frantic. I hope to God I may not be too severely punished even in this life for my more than human affection for him.

C gave me money to pay my carpenters bill also brought me the paper with a compliment to M and a notice of my piece which will appear in the next.

From Luther Tower's diary:

Revd Doct Clapp preached a funeral discourse on the death of Genl Jackson to a Crowded house.[31]

Sun. June 22. We have exceeding hot weather but I hope to attend church for Mr C will deliver a sermon upon the death of Genl Jackson.

Have heard the sermon alluded to and felt proud to have heard it and if the young men felt the glow of patriotism for themselves as I did for them it will not be so easy to yield this country as foreigners think. It was eloquent and [I] hope a just tribute, and I trust the good old Hero is now enjoying the reward of his goodness on earth.

June 25. C came to night in a little better humour than of late, but after he left I had quite a farce with one who saw him come out of here. I wish persons who accidently become acquainted with me would let me act as I please.

June 26. I witnessed the grand and solemn procession to day that commemorated the demise of the beloved Hero of N.O. For thirty four years there have been annual rejoicing[s] here for his victory and this is the first of mourning. Party feeling seemed forgotten to day and all classes and nations of the metropolis joined to swell the train that paid this last tribute to his memory. Came home very tired and will now go to my rest.

From the Daily Picayune:

The Funeral Ceremonies.

The funeral procession in memory of Gen. Jackson took place on Thursday afternoon, according to the published programme. The cortège was imposing in the highest degree. The military and civil authorities, the fire companies, benevolent and other societies, and our citizens generally, joined in rendering this last sad tribute of respect to the deceased warrior and patriot as impressive as the occasion was solemn and affecting. The muffled drum, the shrouded banner, the deep black hearse, and the war horse dressed in the trappings of the field, and yet no soldier in the saddle, were symbols of woe that had their prototype in the breast of every one who took part in or witnessed the ceremonies of the day.

Immediately following the hearse we noticed a line of carriages containing the survivors of those who fought the battle of the 8th of January, '15 — a sturdy and venerable remnant of a brave and victorious army. Sorrow sat upon the countenance of each veteran; the fire of other days was quenched with years and grief; but there was not one of them who did not appear as though a blast from the war bugle would find him ready to do battle again whenever his country might need a soldier.

The spectacle at the *Place d'Armes,* at night, was truly sublime. The immense platform, covered with black cloth, upon which were wrought the devices of mourning, surmounted with an obelisk that penetrated high into the air, which in turn was crowned with the American Eagle holding a scroll in its beak, was of itself grand and imposing: but when covered with people — a large portion of whom were ladies in befitting attire — when the flags of the numerous military companies, the banners of the various societies were collected upon it, as the gorgeous lights that studded the area threw their rays upon the brave men and fair women gathered there upon a solemn and melancholy duty, the entire scene deepened into awfulness. Amid this throng of spectators, surrounded by the beauty and the chivalry of the land, encompassed by whatever there could be in sable trappings shrouded escutcheon, mourning device or symbol of woe; to add depth to the solemning of such an occasion, the orators of the day arose and pronounced impressive and eloquent eulogies upon the character and services of the deceased. Thus closed the ceremonies of the day — thus ended the obsequies of one whose prowess and courage had caused rejoicing throughout the land as heartfelt and universal as the grief that is now poured forth over his honored grave.[32]

In her Writing Book, Madaline Edwards described the tribute to Andrew Jackson.[33]

Yesterday I witnessed the mournful procession that celebrated the death of our beloved Hero of N.O. There was a large concourse of citizens and it was truly an impressive scene to witness how party feeling could be laid aside to mourn over one so long distinguished as has been Andrew Jackson. As warm as the weather was, all the military and firemen turned out, and the hearse that moved in the procession, the war horse that was covered with black, the old veterans who fought here with him, the muffled drums and, the publick school boys who seemed to say *he* was our preserver. All conspired to cast a mournful yet pleasing feeling on those who witnessed this just tribute to merit and valor. Then the publick square was beautifully decorated and in the centre stood a beautiful temporary monument hung with mourning drapery and there were addresses given but a small portion of such a concourse could hear a word. I felt that the honours paid to his memory would fire the hearts of many young men and boys who saw it to emulate his greatness. May they succeed. He died June the 8th and this ceremony took place here on the 26th 1845. M.

June 28. Dear C came and brought me the Native in which my poetry on the banner presentation was published. He was much pleased with it, and says the Editor was delighted.

Sun. June 29. I went down and got Lutitia to go to church with me and when we got there behold Mr W was up in the pulpit which made me regret having gone for I do detest hearing a sermon read, which he always does. He however read us a pretty good sermon on self sacrifice.

The weather is so excessively warm that my system as well as mind is completely prostrated. I saw dear C to day with his wife.

July 2. Had my washing done this week.

Dear C was here to night.

July 3. This evening Miss L myself and my wash woman took a ride up to Carolton, which was very pleasant indeed. We strolled through the garden and brought home some lovely flowers.

July 4. The glorious 4th is upon us again with all its claims to our notice, and veneration, and yet there seems but little attention paid in the celebration to what is usual.

Sun. July 6. I took L and three little girls to church with me and we heard a good but short sermon which will be Mr Clapps last for the Summer. I then came to R and took dinner and eat some delicious water melon and when I got home I found a fine plate of figs a present from Dr D.

Now here I am with an insolent bore who forces himself where he has no buisness and he must feel it for I keep on writing before him.

RP. called on me this afternoon.

July 7. We have had quite a shower this forenoon which has been so long needed. I feel very uneasy in mind for I predict something not pleasant will occur soon for I have now two visitors who assume more to themselves in my favour than I like and I foresee the consequences.

July 12. Dear C was here to night and brought me the Native papers and some others. He is now in buisness and appears cheerful. I went with him as far as S street on my way to visit my friends who have just moved up here. The D^r came home with me, and now it is time I was asleep.

Sun. July 13. Since there is no church open now I shall read and write to day although I feel very unwell. I have four papers beside me to peruse and then to my writing &c.

July 16. I have been and am still so busy sewing that I do not spare time to read or write.

July 17. I went to the Recorders to try and stop the slander of Mrs R. He put her under a bond of $500 to keep the peace. Such things are very unpleasant but her tongue is far worse.

July 19. Dear C was here just now. He brought me the Improvisatore to read and some peaches.[34]

I will not begin this book to night as I will have all the day tomorrow for reading as I have no church to go to.

Sun. July 20. I thought to have a glorious days reading but I have been very sick all day. I sent for the D^r. I feel some better now.

July 22. I went to the Recorders and he told me he had put the Madam under a bond of $500 to keep the peace and so I had no more to do but I had heard such language of hers before I went that I had taken a good cry.

This has been a day of trouble to me and ended in a night that was even more so. I trust it is the last of the kind for me.

July 23. Such a fracas as I and the D^r have had I never was partaker in. He was on the point of leaving his place and the City but now thinks otherwise. He told me he had this day ruined his constitution and in two days I would see it and he regrets having done something.

July 25. Last night the D^r sent for me in a hurry, said he would not live. I went immediately. He was in agony and almost all the time crazy, but he gave me his key and told me all he left was mine. I did all in my power sent for a physician and a cupper. He surely suffered a thousand deaths with inflamation in his stomach. He was a little easy but I must now go to see him.

July 26. The D^r is extremely low but we have moved him to a friend of mine where he will have every attention. He says he is certain that he will die but seems not the least afraid.

Night. C was here and I went a part of the way with him on my way to see the D^r.

Sun. July 27. This morning I found the D^r much worse. Indeed his two D^{rs} said he was compelled to die, no means could save him. His pulse sank very fast in one half hour. I informed him of their opinion and he made every preparation and was perfectedly composed. I did not leave his bed side until four oclock when he had so far changed that he was out of danger. I returned after an hours absence and he was able to insult me and I threw him his key and left the house.

July 29. I have finished reading the Improvisatore and admire the style and feeling very much only there is too much of the ideal and spiritual to make us feel it is a novel we are perusing.

July 30. Dear C came to night and I passed a pleasant hour in his company.

D^r D is better but badly salivated. I do not go near him although I would do any thing to assist him in sickness, but I have now another lesson from his deep deception that has tended much to disgust me with the world.

$1.

July 31. Just had my washing done and I am entirely without money and all my debtors seem not to pity me in the least for I can not get a dime.

CHAPTER NINE

Feelings, Purposes, and Hopes

adaline Edwards's and Charles Bradbury's liaison was in trouble from the time Mary Ann Bradbury began to suspect a connection between them in the spring of 1845, and the tone and frequency of contact between the lovers altered noticeably after the memorable April 1 confrontation between Madaline and Mary Ann. Madaline managed to maintain her composure, but Charley was terrified. Edwards's exhausting illusory pregnancy and her decision to back off in the face of Bradbury's coolness further estranged the lovers. After the spring of 1845 Edwards's journal keeping, centered as it had been on life with Bradbury, petered out. She was completely silent while convalescing from an arm broken in a carriage accident and the painful, bungled treatment she received from her physicians. Edwards's imaginative life picked up the slack in her relationship, and the second Writing Book was increasingly devoted to work intended for publication, rather than the more personal essays and poems that had occupied her in the preceding year.

Tuesday, August 12, 1845. I have been confined with the intermittent fever [malaria] but am now nearly well with a heart full of troubles and difficulties.

Paid $6 to day for taxes which makes $12 C has given me since I was taken sick.

Aug. 13. Went down in the City and purchased a bolt of linen for which I paid $11.

Aug. 14. Paid my State tax $1–5 cts.

Aug. 15. It is now two weeks on this day that I took a ride to the Lake and on our return the gentleman who accompanied me overturned the vehicle and broke his left arm and mine likewise. Oh God what have I not endured since then. D ^{r} R set his that night and mine next day. Even now I cannot use my arm a particle and [it] pains me all the time. It has been a dear pleasure trip to me. I am almost crazy for fear I never will use it to any advantage.

This essay appeared in the only surviving issue of the Native American. *It is a revision of the undated "Life," written more than a year earlier and included in the first Writing Book.*[1]

What is life? Is it merely to breathe, eat, and sleep? is it to fill our places on this stage of action, as father, child, or friend? is it to fill some important office in Church or State? to be a leader in art or science? is it to strive for preeminence in wealth or fame? to rack the brain and toil for the necessaries of life? to visit the church and possess the externals of piety? is it thus to pass through the years allotted us, with the gloomy fear of the grave that is before, and in which we soon lie down, that we call life and its termination? No! this is not the blessing, the enjoyment of life. It is just that we should act the part of citizen, parent, child or friend: it is laudable to seek the noble offices of [line worn away] gifts— it is praiseworthy to toil for wealth or fame; to clime the ascent of the latter as high as mortal faculties can ascend—it is right to encourage morality and religion by voice, but more by example—but may not all these be accomplished without feeling the quintessence of Life? For I conceive that it is action and feeling alone that define that vital principle, and when it rises no higher in the thermometer of existence that fills the veins of the joyless self, it can scarce be called by that name. I look around and see the beasts of the forest and field in their natural state happy, and it is only when man brings them into servitude and makes them feel the torture of the lash, and pinching of hunger, that we see them flag and mourn as it were over their slavery. I look above, and hear the birds sing for joy; they never sit moping or repining, as man does; or here again the exception takes place from captivity, I never see a bird caged but I pity the possessor, and the bird more. I envy not the pleasure derived from the song the little captive gives while darting its wild eye around for the means of escape to the green tree and sunny vales, that it cannot forget, and when I hear its song I feel that it comes more from the force of habit than the thrill of bounding life, that once animated its every hour. A man in prison and a bird in a cage are alike to me, with the exception, the former may be guilty, the latter innocent; in suffering, one day in the wild green trees is worth more to the caged bird than years in prison and exile. I look into the stream and see the fish leaping and sporting with the principles of life. The pool, tree, shrub, the flowers, the earth, and all nature swarm with insects and reptiles, enjoying their ephemeral existence. Many of them so repulsive in form that we shudder to behold them, yet they possess the faculty of being happy, and we look on with discont[ent]ment. I see the forest oak wave, while the vine and flower respond to its motion. I hear the morning breeze play among the beauteous flowers, and I think all nature animate and inanimate realizes what life is, and what it should be, but man. Did God create us so much above the reptile in point of intelligence and deprive us of the pleasure he gave them?

Life consists in glowing gratitude to the all wise Creator, who not only gave us the principle, but who has hung the heavens with wonders and sublimities; who has bestowed upon us the treasures and beauties of earth and sea; and given to us health, home and friends; it consists mainly in a just appreciation of his wisdom, goodness and impartiality, (however hard the latter may be to force upon our doubting minds,) it consists in a thrill of joyful animation, in the desire to rise daily in knowledge and goodness, and in the assurance that God has set no limits to either; it consists in paliating the faults and alleviating the sufferings of our fellow beings; and though we have no home, friend, or health, it even then consists in the full assurance that though we lie down in the dark tomb, yet we are destined to live as long as God himself, and that we will rise higher and higher in the immortal divinity that here makes the weakest of us yearn for a future life, however veiled from us. Life consists more in investigation than we imagine, for if we would but peep into the wonderful properties and the microscopic myriads that revolve beneath the opening rose, we should find so much to admire, so much to exalt our views of our Creator that we should be constrained to go farther, and find hourly some evidences of what he is, and what we are which would so fill up the chaos that indolence and ignorance [illegible: worn], that we could not avoid partaking of the impulse that actuates the sportive animalcule, and acknowledge that life should not go stalking about with iron clogs. Life is joy, animation, reverence, gratitude, reliance and dependence, and these are summed up in the just appreciation of God and his works.

M.

Aug. 30. I have leached my arm to day until I could hardly sit up. I have no soul to do any thing for me and this spell has taught me who are friends.

I fondly looked for C to night but even he treats me more indifferently than I believed it in his nature to do, but I must endure it all the best I can.

Sun. Aug. 31. A lonely dismal rainy day. Cannot read for pain. Have leached my arm again this forenoon. No soul comes anear me and my head I cannot comb. I have only bread to eat, and I feel how unfeeling the being is whose negligence placed me in this situation for he is now well while I am not only suffering but deprived of the power to earn my living.

Sept. 17. The birth day of my first born.

Sept. 26. On this day D^r [Albert] Stone Dr Richey and two others to assist broke my arm over. My God what can we endure before death ever comes to our relief. Were it Gods will I had much rather have died. But they were so exhausted that the setting was postponed and I had to go to the Hospital when all exertions on Stones part was fruitless.

Oct. 1. It was on this day that I submitted to the last operation on my arm at Dʳ Stones Infirmary.[2] Oh God the pain no tongue can ever utter and yet it was all for nothing. But I shall ever cherish the warmest gratitude to him for his exertions, and if I had only gone to him first I should now have been well.

Oct. 3. Came home from the Maison de Santé and I may say truly that I am literally deranged, for now all hope is done. Dʳ Stone cannot put my arm in place and I must submit to bear with it for life in this condition. After three of the most painful operations that any mortal ever endured, all is given up. My God if ever I needed thy help it is now to keep me from Sinking.

Sun. Oct. 5. To day Mr C preached his first sermon since July and Oh how I longed to be there but I fear it will be a long time first.

Oct. 7. The children returned to school but in my state of mind I do not know what I can do.

Sun. Oct. 26. Half past 7. What is the matter with the clock, it has stopped all of a sudden. I hope it forebodes me no ill luck for I have enough already.

Oct. 27. Bought half cord of wood to day and paid $2.50.

Sun. Nov. 2. Heard Mr C preach for the first time since last Summer but he did not preach so well as usual.

B called on me this afternoon and afterwards J.A.B.

Lines to Mary.[3]

I feel all thy kindness dear lady indeed
But thou knowest how vain is the task
To raise one of your sex who has fallen
Then leave me to grief let me ask.

Was the world full of spirits like thine
The erring might oft be reclaimed
Instead of being crushed in their fall
And oft for appearances blamed.

But too well do I know from the past
That the future is nothing but sadness
If a moment I indulge thy fond hope
I awake to a sense of my madness

But pray do not think I am reckless
For I'd suffer all life could endure
If by torture and suffering I knew
Forgiveness from the world I'd secure

And through the dark future vista of life
I'll think of thy wishes with pleasure
And feel though my cup's full of sorrow
There's a sparkle of joy on the measure.

But God will reward all thy love
To one who will cherish the same
And I'll rejoice as I ever shall think
Thou gavest more pity than blame.

M. Nov 17th 1845.

Nov. 25. My Diary presents nothing but blank, the facsimile of my heart unless perplexities will constitute a whole.

There is a benevolent lady who has learned that I am M and has taken it into her head she can elevate me to the standing her kind wishes alone dictate and I am in torture about the unpleasant feelings it may create on her husbands part. I know it can never be but God will reward her intentions and may he ever bless her.

Nov. 26. JB was here this evening and I do not wonder if he will make his visits fewer for he so often leaves me in tears.[4] It must be unpleasant to him as well as bitter to me.

Nov. 27. Oh! what would I not give to be as happy as I was a year ago then I saw C much oftener and felt he cared for me. Now I scarce ever see him and feel the maddening fear that he wishes to get rid of me. Did he but realize half I feel he would pity me at least. But may he never know the depth of my misery and he alone can dissipate it.

Nov. 29. Mrs B[reedlove] and judge C called on me to day. If I should live to see this day twelve months I wonder if they will be my friends. God only knows my destiny.

Sun. Nov. 30. Cold and rainy cannot get to church but will try and write all day.

PM. JB prevented my writing as much as I should, however I wrote a good deal.

As a writer who believed that her actions were misunderstood and her conduct harshly judged by hypocrites, Madaline Edwards identified strongly with Lord Byron. The essay "Byron" makes her case for the poet's redemption and, by implication, for her own.[5]

As egotistical as it may seem in on[e] so humble and incompetent to attempt a vindication of what she deems the wrongs of this master spirit yet the spell is upon me and I must indulge it. That he had his faults his most enthusiastic admirers have ever admitted but that he should deserve the bitter reproach, the deep enathemas that I have heard hurled against him I cannot realize. Who that would take the pains to note down all his misanthropic views, all his seeming impiety, his murmerings at fate, his exposure of human frailties and even every unchaste thought, and compare them with Shakespear, Pope, Sterne and others will not find a part or all these faults more glaringly developed in the works of the latter, and yet they escape the bitter invectives that are heaped on Byron. And on the other hand [who] would collect the brilliant conceptions, the glowing thoughts the burning aspirations, the tones of deep feeling, the gushing of the immortal mind, the faithful delineations of the human character, the evidences of his boundless imagination, his love for the beautiful, his admiration for the sublime, his pathetic strains and priceless gems but will find the scale so weighed down by the latter as to induce their overlooking [or] at least palliating his errors. Were the bed of the Ocean raked for gems and pearls rubbish and sediment would be found surrounding the brightest. No one can appreciate the immortal Shakespear more than I do and as the annals of history furnishes no instance in which a man rose from such obscurity as well as adversity to such an enviable elevation, nor one who understood the human mind as he did, he will ever be looked up to with reverence amounting almost to veneration, but the disparity in the positions of the two in their outset for fame, or perhaps the one for a livelihood, so far from detracting the merits of Byron in my mind only enhances them; for it seems to be an indisputable fact that the majority if not all of our wealthy men have started pennyless that our most energetic, lofty minded and intellectual men have seldom been born and reared to the indulgences of nobility. Such was the case with him, and thousands would have given themselves up to all the sensual gratifications that this independence would have secured them. Many with his too sensitive feelings would have flown to the inebriating cup for relief for natures defects. He appears not to have written so much for fame as he cared so little for mankind in general, but from the fact that the electric spark that burned in his soul was forced to have vent, and I can not think as some, that it shone and burst as a metior to be forgotten. And though I have the most unbounded reverence for the opinions of our dear Minister yet in none do I dissent from him more than in one I heard him advance not long since that "in a half century Byron would cease to be thought of." If such is the case I cannot now realize that the coming generation will be more famed for taste than we or that another so mighty will arise as to eclipse his splendour.

It is urged he was fickle, not more so than many of his accusers but perhaps less dissimulation or more independence which prevented his concealing what they can. It has been said with his lofty intellect and pecuniary advantages he was the more reprehensible for permitting a slight personal defect to prey so upon his mind as to embitter him so with life. Such blamers should remember that the more expanded the mind is the finer are the feelings, and though in a manner we may rise superior to the feelings such misfortunes would naturally produce upon our minds yet the curious gaze, the unfeeling glance and brutal remark will oft set those finer feelings of our nature to work until our very souls seem crushed beneath their weight.

I may worship at the shrine of his muse more enthusiastically perhaps than the free and happy for there is so much congeniality between his melancholy and my own that I never tire poring over some of his productions; but I often think the old caution "tread lightly on the ashes of the dead" is as little heeded toward this hapless bard as any who repose beneath the green sod that envelopes him as kindly as the sainted pilgrim. I may err but I think there are gems of Byron's that will live as long as earth itself and that if human productions are permitted to cross the line of immortality and live in our memories his will be among the number. But that there are other portions that cast a dim shade before his priceless effusions I too admit but let us reflect that

> The eagle which soars to the sun
> Will not only descend to the mountain
> But is oft known not to slake
> Its thirst at the free running fountain

M. Nov 30th

Dec. 1. Much ice this morning and bitter cold. I saw C in the street and begged him to come to see me but not till tomorrow night he says. Oh he little knows my fears and sorrows and I now fear he little cares.

Judge C called on me this evening.

Dec. 5. Mr C sent me word I can see him next week and I shall go.

Dec. 6. Dear C was here to night and for the first time in a long, long time he appeared like his former self. Oh I felt more happy than I had dared hope again to be. He gave me a pair of gloves.

Sun. Dec. 7. Heard Mr C preach a most glorious sermon to day and I trust I shall be the better for it.

Got wet coming home and am quite unwell.

Dec. 9. I went to see Mr C to day and though our conversation was short and my feelings so overcam[e] me yet I found him the same kind and dear being that he is in the pulpit. I told him many of my errors but he said all was not lost to one who wished to return.

Dec. 12. This night two years ago I moved in this house my own home. Oh how time has flown for though many things have transpired to make me unhappy yet these two years have passed so differently from many past ones that I may say I have been almost happy and may God eternally bless the one who has caused this change.

Dec. 13. Was at a wedding.

Sun. Dec. 14. Dear C spent three hours with me to day and in his company I forget all sorrows.

Dec. 20. ~~Saw a couple married by Mr Nicholson~~

Sun. Dec. 21. ~~Dear C came this morning as it was raining all day and staid three hours with me, which has made me very happy. Oh I do so love to see him and be in his company. He brought me the Stranger to read which has made me shed tears.[6] Also the Presidents message which I shall read.~~

Did not get to Church to day.

Dec. 25. Almost dead with a cold but yet I sewed all day.

Sun. Dec. 28. My birth day.

Dec. 30. Dear C came this afternoon but our conversation was only calculated to make both unhappy.

Dec. 31. Mrs B[reedlove] has got me a seat in Mr C's church for which I shall feel eternally grateful to her.

Did not get to church to day.

In the two playful poems that follow, Madaline Edwards addressed the pseudonymous Coelebs, whose essays and poems in New Orleans newspapers lampooned women, courtship, and marriage from a bachelor's point of view.[7] As in many of her newspaper writings, Edwards, writing as "M.," played a game of hide-and-seek, hinting at her "true" character and daring Coelebs and her readers to find her out. Privately, though, she worried that she would be exposed and ridiculed. None of Coelebs's poems addressed to M. survive, but the two Edwards responses that follow give a good idea of their tone and content.

(An answer to an advertisement for a wife who must be perfect)[8]

A bachelor of course thou art
But sure not *hard* to please
Such wives as you in verse depict
You'll find with every ease

The ladies I will have you know
Are linguists from the cradle
And very often they enforce
Their lingo with the ladle

And such a fate you may expect
In tying hymens noose
How dare you even think about
"Bustles and big shoes"

Are you so perfect let me ask
To seek a wife like this
For dove and owl have never yet
Mated with much bliss.

But tell the truth you would'nt care
If she even had no shoes
Nor if she could but barely talk
About the church and pews

Her hair might be the deepest red
Her eyes as gray as ganders
Her tongue be very eloquent
In gossiping and slanders

Her waist and hands both very large
Her temper none the sweetest
Her dress might be the so, so, so,
And house none of the neatest

Provided she has got the gold
'Twill turn her eyes jet black
What virtue with some millions
Could she to Celebs lack.

The tabernacle gold will be
And gold will be the graces
But Oh! how you will hate the gold
When she shows you her grimaces

Your choice displays the best of taste
Of common sense no atom
For such perfection dwells aloft
Where you cannot come at 'em

But should you ever come across
A wife like you have painted
Then take her in a single trice
For wives are seldom sainted

M. Jan 1ˢᵗ 1846

Answer to Celeb's reply.[9]

If Father Native will extend
To me almost a column:
Our paper quarrel now shall end;
I'm growing very solemn.

My opinion now of course I change,
And call you henpecked husband;
No single man's so ungallant;
If 'tis in freedom's land.

Old maid Oh! how I wish I was;
Such I would live and die;
Ah no! that *rueful* wedding,
Betwixt yourself and I

One truth more glaring than the rest;
From out your lines doth gleam;
You *do* possess no common share,
Of priceless self esteem.

Now ever since old Eve did eat,
The apple so forbidden:
The errors of her daughters frail
The *men* have seldom hidden.

For Father Adam shewed them how,
To throw the blame on woman;
So if the son but seems in fault,
He pursues the fathers plan.

How else could you so comprehend,[10]
the unspeakable dominion.
Which I admit is very wrong
In the picked ones opinion.

That man is often *ruled* 'tis true
I see it cross the street
But all the ruling used by me
Are words but kind and sweet.

I've often sworn I never would,
Another time be married,
When men have talked to me of love;
I've all their reasons parried.

But now that I an offer have,
From one so famed as Celebs,
I mean to take it at the flood
No time allow for ebbs.

The offer I of course accept;
And I bet you what you please

Before one year you will admit
My like's *not* found with ease.

So if you ever feel inclined,
To withdraw the offer given,
Remember 'tis in black and white
If not coaxed you shall be driven.

So you perhaps will like to know,
Something of your intended.
Before the knot is doubly tied
Which cannot then be mended.

Perhaps you will not like my size
I'm just five feet seven
And well proportioned so I'm told
To vanity not given.

A forehead high and well defined
A large and full green eye,
Which if it saw you in distress
Would seldom be seen dry.

My *age* you think I will not tell
If it is *more* than twenty
Come judge yourself if I'm too old
And this is saying plenty

I sometimes paint but not my face
I neither sing nor dance
Of flowers I am very fond
And have innate romance.

But dearest me, now heres the rub
The gold you want is lacking
And while I'm owning this sad truth
I see you off are pa[c]king.

I have a little cottage and
A garden, dog and cat
Now what more can I to you say?
True *Native* am I that.

So if you will but come and live
With me in peace and quiet,
Why get the parson, and I think
We surely can but try it.

Your whiskers I will curl so neat
(Not pull them like a scold)
In all things I will be so kind
T'will make amends for gold

I'll lavish on you so much love,
And shew you such devotion,
For very shame you will admit
Erroneous was your notion.

That if I should become your wife
You knew you would repent
For you shall soon begin to think
I am an angel sent

A hapless one as you declare
There's no admittance given,
To such poor wretches as myself
In that male allotted heaven.

I know that you will now confess
That I am no old maid,
For long ere this her bitter spleen
To you would be betrayed.

This picture C is drawn with truth
With hope I do present it

That you will close our bargain now
As seemeth meet and fit.

So heres my heart and also hand
But then I'm *not* perfection
Yet one thing I will promise you
Enough of pure affection

M Jan 24.th/46

The following poems, addressed to Charles Bradbury, are in striking con-
trast both to the carefree tone of the newspaper poems and to Edwards's
previous characterizations of Bradbury.

The past is dimmed with care and grief,[11]
The present is all gloomy sadness
The future I hope though bitter is brief,
So death will bring with it gladness.

M

To C.[12]

And have I lived to see the day,
That thou canst too despise:
And will not hear a word I say,
To acquit me in thine eyes.

Two years ago, I did not deem
The bliss you had created
Should pass away, a bitter dream
And leave all hope prostrated.

And yet I trembled at the joy
That made my heart so blest
Why thus create? but to destroy,
And leave me, more distrest;

Have I deserved this cruel change
From one I've idolized
It is less true, than passing strange
How I could have surmised.

But this crushed heart too truly tells,
My doom is sealed forever:
Not in this life, for *me* hope dwells
I'll trust again, *no never.*

I would not call you back to me,
To see the tears I shed:
Oh! God I trust you do not see,
The coming fate I dread.

No, go loved one, where peace is thine,
To know the blest is all,
Of life that's worth a care of mine
None heeds my coming fall.

The books by thee, made daily dear,
And flowers with thee admired,
Have lost their charms and drink the tears
Thy absence has inspired.

Long have I felt there was *one* heart
That felt for me some sorrow,
And now from thee I'm doomed to part,
There is no source to borrow.

I'd leave the world to follow thee
Through want, and degredation:
If I could only hope through me,
Your heart had consolation.

Then why so grieve, to give thee up,
Thy lot is bettered by it,

It pours the wormwood in my cup
But now I must abide it.

Oh! God smile on the one I love
Dispel his annxious care,
And may I meet him far above
This world of grief and prayer.

M. March 25 th.

This is a teasing, hide-and-seek poem. W.A.P. was Coelebs.[13]

Answer to W.A.P.

The truth I boast will not allow;
That you should undeceived be
You have not seen M I avow
Some one has April-fooled thee.

I cannot claim anothers praise;
It seems to me like treason:
I am not *vain,* nor yet always
Guided by my reason.

But yet I tell you, when you see,
Old Natives true-souled daughter;
You will aver most candidly
She's unlike you had thought her.

Yes! in my heart devotion burns,
For truth and justice too;
Then from the praise it inly turns
To list, it will not do.

The truths from out my grey eyes gleam,
Whether ruled by joy or sadness

There is *some* good in me it seems
But yet I fear more badness.

M. April 17th 1846.

Edwards's poem in support of her favorite political cause implies that women expected to influence men's votes.[14]

For the Native American

To the Native ladies, on Father Natives offering for justice of the peace.

Come Native ladies hear my call,
Be up electioneering;
Old Native runs, don't let him *fall*
No odds or numbers fearing.

Say to your father, and your brothers
Do vote for Father Native
Secure you these, then turn to others
Whose votes will surely give.

Rouse up your husbands and your friends;
To come to Natives rescue,
For all your pains he'll make amends
Believe, he'll not forget you.

The Crescent[15] lingers in our course
I am ashamed to own it
Come! now's the time dont let us pause
For we can surely change it

M. May 3rd 1846.

As the lines about family advice and broken vows show, Madaline Edwards addressed this poem to her second husband, Mr. Edwards.[16]

To one who heeds not the woe he has caused

'Tis not with love, I think of thee,
And yet it can't be hate;
Comes gushing up from memory,
The wrongs thou didst create?
For one who left the joys of youth
And clung to thee in matchless truth?

Call back the time I gave my hand,
To thee, in spite of others;
When I heeded not the stern command
O[f] Uncle or of brother.
Who told me I this step would rue
But still, I madly clung to you.

Say! do the thought of broken vows,
E're check thy guilty smile?
Thinkest thou of her who sadly bows
To the woes caused by thy guile
With few to pity, none to bless
And feel the cause of her distress.

If in this heart could hatred dwell
A heart once wholy thine
Long since on thee, it must have fell
For sorrows such as mine
But no! contempt is all I feel
Receive it on thy heart of steel.

June 6, 1846.   M.

The very height of meanness is to see a man cut down his fruit tree, thereby depriving himself of the fruit that falls inside of his enclosure, sooner than give the little urchins that which falls in the street.[17]

In this passage Edwards writes of slander.[18]

    Oh! how crushing it is to hear those traduced we love, and it appears it is ever to be my case. I did not know until to day that I could hear, to appearances unmoved, ——— —— name coupled with infamy. Oh! could my informer have read my heart when he was so needlessly torturing it, he would never have revealed what he has. I have been miserable all day, not from a belief of his guilt for I am convinced to the contrary, but I would not have a mere suspicion of shame attached to him. I feel that he is so wronged. I would to God people could *know* such things before they give them utterance. The day will come when goodness will have its reward and I know his day approac[h]es to be more rightly judged, for there is an end to all things but truth and justice. Dear ——— ——— ——— pity my feelings when you read this.

Aug. 23 [1846]   M

CHAPTER TEN

The School of Experience

*O*ith Charles Bradbury's help, Madaline Edwards found a job *as a public-school teacher. The events that followed from this, vividly recounted in the letters and documents included in this chapter, led to the collapse of their relationship. In the final exchange of letters, we hear Bradbury's own voice for the first time.*

From the minutes of the Orleans Parish School Board, fall 1846:

The state of the schools requiring the appointment of Teachers, the Committee [on Teachers] have examined Mrs Edwards . . . .[1]

These ladies have been appointed not only subject to the approval of or rejection by the Board, but are liable to be removed at any time, if their services be not needed and they have accepted the appointments with a full knowledge of this fact on their part.[2]

Madaline to Charley

Nov 15 th [1846] Sunday

Dearest C

Long ere your eyes were unclosed this morning I was seated on the door step contemplating the remnant of the *tell-tale* Moon, now verging on to her days, *no nights* of secrecy. I could compare her crescent to nothing else than the hull of some noble bark while the dim circle seemed as the well filled canvass bearing her over the calm blue expanse of heaven, wafting her onward through the never ending *eternity* that is also ahead of you and I, so calm, so placid, and so etherial seemed she and her Ocean that I wondered if she could be freighted with *ill-fated* beings like our two selves. The stars gazed upon her like the eyes of angels, watching well pleased, her endless course. I thought to myself Oh! why is it that I have not the power to transport myself to C or him to me, that I might commune with him upon all I feel and enjoy. Why is it that I am doomed to live not half of my days (though they should be fourscore) in living allways apart from all intellectual enjoyment. "Do I ever think of you when reading any thing sublime." Oh! I wish you could realize all I think. I never feel a thrilling sensation in contemplating the beautiful and sublime, I never feel an emotion of rapture in beholding a beautiful painting or the lovely flowers of earths eden, I never read a beautiful passage but my thoughts fly out to you and so allied are you with the stars that I never look on them but you are the next thought, for the first happy hour I past for years was with you and our lovely star before I emerged from my degradation. Yes Charley hard as my fate is, still it is far better to commune in spirit with one dear object than not atal. Distance cannot separate minds or souls. Before the reading of this you will have been sadly disappointed if you went to your Church, for as I learned from M rs C that W 1 would preach I resolved to stay at home. I have been very melancholy since yesterday afternoon for M r C[lapp] is firmly impressed with the belief he will die, and he is almost entirely prostrated. She says she thinks he is hippoed but from his moaning and his presentiments I fear all is not well.[3] Let him go when he will, earth cannot replace him as a *man*, and God knows it cannot as *my* friend.

Since writing the above I have been annoyed with company and have wept since I was never more out of a happy frame of mind. Old B[reedlove] seems determined by his visits to carry out the worlds suspicion though I remain innocent, and I will no longer keep you ignorant that he is pressing a certain point. I told him today that I would rather he would dismiss me from the School than to hold me under obligations I could not fulfil. That touched him he said *no* nothing on earth would induce him to desert me as a firm friend, that he did not wish me to do any thing against my concience &c. I do wish from my soul no one on earth would ever do me a favour with selfish views for my disposition cannot bear it like many. I am miserable under it. Oh! how preferable would be an Ocean home on some lone island with none to dread or despise. I cannot talk when affected, but will hand him a letter tomorrow which I hope to God will induce him to act and expect differently for the future, but I am very wretched.

Now dear as to Jack Hays, in less than two hours after he arrived Sayre asked him to come to see me.[4] He sent me word I might rely on a visit the next day at 3 and told S to meet him for that purpose, but great Lordy he was worse beset than any monkey show on earth or even in the Moon. Besides that day he was closeted nearly all day with the big men on war business, and could not possibly do so. I told him I had once lived with a married man but that I was now in the School and had quit him, that I had written to him once to know if he would sanction my coming to him in Texas (which letter he did not get). Jack made no comments but said "By the Gods, if she wishes to go there or any thing else I can do for her I will do it." The last word he said as the boat was leaving was to tell me he would call on me as soon as he got back. He has an office in San Antonio with 4 young men employed to transact his Land buisness. Said he thought the war would close in 6 months. As soon as ended, he would settle and make a fortune and then if I wished to go there I should and when that day arrives I am *Oph* for I feel that *your* interest will yet be identified with that country too. Jack will meet Gen Houston here on [torn] 28th when I shall surely see him. I did not find the pac[kage (torn)] until I went to wipe up the gallery, it lay close behind the [torn]. Many thanks for the nice gloves, and the poetry, but it is singular many times that the Oct. piece has been preserved by you and me. Last year I saved one and you cut the other out which is now in my scrapbook, and now here is another. Oh! but it is beautiful I intend you shall have this one and when I am mouldering in the tomb this piece will then seem truer if you care for me atal. I have read but little to day in fact none and my head is almost crazy. I am taking tea to try and relieve my coming sickness which is now oppressing my head so much. Come up early some night when you like but then you must not stay late. I cannot say much more. I am sick low spirited and every thing else. I hope some day I will be from under all restraint of other people for with you I have ever felt free even though under more obligations than all the world beside. Dear, dear Charley, think of me. I am getting fat. Yesterday I weighed 146, 2 pound more than I ever did before. I do not know if I can get to hand you this in the morning, if not I will put it in the Office. truly truly M. [Outside of fold:]

Opened again

Who do you think introduced himself just now? why *young Native* ahem. Well we have spent *two* hours in chatting and he is gone.

Sunday Night.

From the minutes of the Orleans Parish School Board, January 18, 1847:

A Letter was read from Mess.rs Picton, Quarles & Hill calling the extra meeting & Mr. Quarles explained the object of the meeting being to investigate certain charges against one of the Female Teachers.

On the Motion of Mr. Maybin the following resolution was adopted:

Resolved that a Committee of four be appointed to investigate the rumors in relations to Mrs Edwards, a Teacher in the Marshall School & report at the next stated meeting of the Board of Directors, or at a special meeting if they deem proper to call one; as well as to her conduct as a lady; as to her treatment of the Scholars.[5]

Reply to W.A.P.[6]

Alas! the're none *my* wrongs to feel
Though noble ones there are.
Who grieve for those far less severe
And lesson others care.

I do not ask the world to weep
For woes it cannot heal
But might I dare, I'd truly ask
To make it this appeal

To add no more unto the weight
That's crushing day by day.
This heart which none have understood
On earth they never may.

Yes! true my lot has adverse been
Loved ones betrayed my trust
And others dearer still than these
Have mouldered into dust.

To love was stamped upon my soul
By wisdom undefined
Oh! would it not been best for me
Had adamant enshrined.

But yet the fields and birds and flowers
And skies of peerless blue
Are objects I too still may love
For they alone are true.

Fain would I pour out all the love
That wells up in my heart

Upon my books and Natures charms
To me they bliss impart.

But this cold cruel world of ours
Wills not such peace to me
It robbed me of lifes brightest flowers
And seared Hopes blooming tree

Yet not content it seeks to wring
And torture, for pastime
This heart which far too feeling still
Must silently repine.

And yet there are a few who feel
My heart is not at rest
And how consoling 'tis to know
They'd joy to see me blest.

None seek to draw the veil that hides
Sorrows to none revealed
Proud is the spirit that has half
Behind her smiles concealed.

When there are none beside to see
No ears to catch the sigh
This *then* the truth is mirrored in
The overflowing eye.

To pour ones life blood out for me
Are words which do to write
An emergency far less than this
Would put my friends to flight.

But many thanks to thee dear P.
Believe I'll n'er forget
The kindness in your verse displayed
Although we n'er have met.

> The only hopes that's let to me
> In your lines is truly given
> Prepared, it is that I may be,
> No outcast from high Heaven.

Jan. 24th/47.   M.

From the minutes of the Orleans Parish School Board, January 30, 1847:

Mr. Quarles offered the following resolution:

Resolved that it is inexpedient for the Board to confirm the appointment of Mrs Edwards as Teacher in the public schools and the Secretary be requested to notify her to that effect.

On Motion of Mr Maybin the following resolution was adopted.

Resolved that Mrs Edwards whose nomination has not yet been confirmed receive a months pay.[7]

Madaline to Charley

Sunday Feby 28th 1847.

Dear Charley, for such you will ever be to *me*, think of me as you may. One month has passed away since we last met, bringing the conviction that you too have forsaken me in my darkest hour of trouble; be it so. I did not *dismiss* you, hence I cannot recall you. If in my agonizing moments of conflicting emotions I used words that made you fear for my conduct for the future, you should have pitied the grief that could wring from me such declarations, and you should have known these ill-timed words executed before you forever abandoned me to shape my cause with a tenfold incentive to error in having lost your friendship. You knew me too well to believe that I could abandon myself to mankind in general and if I had felt disposed to choose *one* I could long since have done so in justice if there was nothing to look to but *mercenary*

views. I make no protestations to you of *innocence*. I make no avowals
of guilt nor do I say believe or doubt me, for I feel what I am to you.
I do not wish to implicate any, but I fear a third person has a hand in
this change on your part. Had you have believed me in earnest in saying
what I did, would it not have been worth your time and efforts to have
dissuaded me from such a step, knowing you had more influence over
me than all others? Has your heart become so callous that you do not
commiserate the sufferings of mind of one whose smallest woes could
once interest you, and one whose soul was ever at variance with the step
in question. No Charley if the truth must come from my pen, as it has
been forced on my heart, it is this, you saw me again thrown upon my
own hard exirtions for a subsistence, and fearing that I might wish to lay
claims to your assistance, you thought it the best time to sever the tie of
a *friendship*, if so it must be called. Oh! if you wished to leave me as you
have, why did you not seek the time when I was less miserable, when
I was temporarily sustained by the proud conciousness that I should
no longer be compelled to ask from cold charity the work that would
procure my bread, but hoped I had the power to live above want; and
the fallacious hope of placing myself one step higher than I then stood,
there was the time to have taken your leave of me, and not wait for the
moment when all other sources of comfort failed me to throw the beam
which only needed your desertion to keep it down forever. Can *you* even
wonder that I have not gone farther astray than threats or appearances
may indicate. I strive in taking some little amusements, in my constant
toil, in trying to read, to forget some gone by days, but memory will have
her sway, and the full conviction comes over me even when others see
me smile, that real friends, will never cross my path. I am one doomed
to misery as long as life endures and you have done well to separate your
destiny from mine as soon as you have, for I entail sorrow on all I ever
loved; but do not I beg you ever think that I intended to cast myself a
burden on you because I said I would not work again, and if I did not
prefer work to other offers I need not now do it. I may not hold out all
I could wish, yet I feel these steps to which I cannot go, lower in hope

I cannot go. The world is against me, friends have all fled me, and it is only at grasping at the hope of death that destroys the object.

Charley I could say volumes to you but it would only be an indication that I sought your return which I dare not do or wish for your wish is my law and I have long felt you deemed me unworthy of you and now the worlds desertion renders it justifiable that *you* too should shun the doomed. I no longer see or speak to you but this *does not,* cannot prevent my thoughts my prayers, my tears, and gratitude. Your happiness is far dearer to me than my own, and I wish that you could realize that I would cut this hand off if it could pen a line that would be construed into a wish to obtain favour relative to a certain point. No on my honour I would not care if you turned me out of doors tomorrow, without a home to shelter me. The more crushing the load the sooner it would kill. This would not influence me to lift a pen to you, but mind *this* when we meet in another world *then* and not till then will you ever understand me.

I dare not trust myself to say more or I might betray all I wish to conceal.

Farewell

Here are Charles Bradbury's first surviving words to Madaline Edwards.[8]

Thursday
March 5/47

Mad

Your note of last Sunday I rec^d on tuesday. The charges, therein expressed & preferred against me, and the motives by which I was actuated in my apparent withdrawal, are most unkind, unjust and all together uncalled for. Still as the world goes, I will not deny you the right of passing judgement on me as you would on any other individual. I used in times gone by to think that I was a little better than the meanest characters, but it must have been a delusion for you have placed me in their company and there I suppose I must remain, at least in your estimation. Well be it so, although I must Confess I was amazed, and altogether unprepared for such accusations. I am sorry, very Sorry that you have written what you have. There are parts of your note which are so misty that I Cannot Comprehend them. I could wish they were explained. More much more could I say but I presume it would be useless, therefore I refrain. What is passed is passed. May the future, as I pray to Heaven it may, bring you better friends, health and happiness.

C.

Charley to Madaline

Tuesday Evening 9th March 1847

Madam

Your letter without date was handed to me this morning, and was read with much interest, and no little surprise.

You say "that you have made up your mind and that you must say & you hope for the last time, that you cannot reconcile the thing to your mind in any way, and that you prefer your present poverty and its increasing difficulties to an act so revolting to your feelings." And you go on to say "that you hope the friendly grave will come to your rescue before you are compelled to seek assistance in that way." Had you expressed such sentiments to me in our first few conversations held immediately after you left the schools, you would never had occasion to express the determination you have done in your letters, for you cannot have forgotten your frequent expressions to me, that the turning you out of the schools, left you no hope but that of abandoning your self to a life that you detested, and you cannot have forgotten how earnestly I implored you not to think of such a thing. And you must recollect, also, that you never gave me to understand that those feelings had been abandoned, under an impression that you still entertained them, and fearing that you would fall into the sway of some man who would forever ruin you beyond hope of redemption and then desert you, I determined to propose to you to muster your little means together, and with the aid of one or two friends, commence a small retail establishment by which I then believed, and do still believe, that you could make a support, and perhaps realise a handsome little living for old age. But this scheme did not seem to meet favor in your mind. I was then prompted to make the other proposition, which you have now rejected, and connected with it a charge, which, had I been guilty of, I should have been too base even to be called a man. I mean the charge, made, as you say, by two different persons, that I had you put out of the schools in order to make you feel your dependance, so as to place you in my power. Such a sentiment could only have eminated from a deamon, for heaven knows how I labored and exerted every influence in my power to sustain you, and your own mortification was little, if any, deeper than mine. And I tell you now, that whoever these two different persons may be, do you be ware of their lying tongues. You ask me to take care of the little box left in my charge—it shall be done. You also say that Mr C. advises an effort to get into the 3rd. Mupty. Schools.[9] You add, you have no friends of influence & that you have no further energy. I am on intimate terms with the chief manager of the 3rd Mu-pty schools, and will most cheerfully make an effort to get you a place there, if you make up your mind you would like to move down there. But of this you must be the judge. I obtained Mr Merrills letter in your behalf for the express purpose of being used in your behalf when ever occasion might call for it, and for that purpose I now send it with the other papers which you placed in my charge.[10]

You do me injustice by insinuating that I have been activated from selfish motives in all my movements towards you. I acknowledge myself a human being, and profess to be a christian, yet I do hope that I have never attempted to injure the feelings, the character or prospects of any living being, but have endeavored throughout my eventfull life to aid and assist, all of my fellow beings that I believed deserved it, and I sincerely pray to god, that I may cling to these feelings as long as life may last.

I freely confess to you, that it was the *Animal* that first prompted me to seek an interview with you, for then I was as ignorant, as the child unborn, of your identity. But when I found out who you were, & your desolate situation, I determined to use all my efforts of place, and influence to raise you up in the scale of human happiness as far as possible, if you could but know the strong appeals I made to [school board member Joseph A.] Maybin to place you in the schools, how I urged it on the score of the happiness the event would afford your relations, & how much more happy they would feel, when they knew that I had been the instrument in bringing about such a happy result. My entreaties had the desired effect, and words cannot express the joy I felt, when you were placed in the Marshall School, where I believed you would remain, and by your usefulness bring yourself into respectable society, all of which would have been accomplished had it not been for the viliany of one *individual*.

You requested in your letter, that I should not visit you again. As my presence at your House would be disagreeable to you, your request shall be strictly complied with. That you may find some more disinterested friend than I have been, shall be my constant *prayer*. When you have read this epistle, burn it, as I have burned yours.

I will here repeat what I have often said to you. When ever you find yourself in want, send to me & your wants shall be supplied, as far as my limited means will enable me.[11]

Farewell

Madaline to Charley, March 13, 1847

Dear Charley,

Why was it that I could not help feeling at dark last night as though you would be here? And could I have stifled the conviction that I was deserted I should have watched the fulfilment of the presentiment. As it was I had just laid my head to rest in order more to forget the cares of life, than that I needed sleep, when I thought I heard something fall on the floor again. I thought it seemed as though you were near, but as before I felt my doom and soon fell asleep, little dreaming the cruel message that awaited me as soon as I opened the door. I lit the candle, sat down and read it through twice. Need I say I have not drawn one whole breath since I seem to have passed into another existence. Charley did I ever insinuate in word or line that you were like other bad characters? Have I not ever said as I believe that you were more clear of faults and

errors than any man I ever met? There was but one thing in my last that
you could have taken any exception to, and it was the impression left on
my mind that you had forsaken me, for fear I might again be a burden
to you. Now I ask in the name of *Heaven* if I could predicate this belief on any other ground, or why did you not leave me before I lost the
situation that induced you as well as myself to feel that I could live independent of any ones means? And if in this I was mistaken would it not
have been better in your once kind language to have said such is not the
case, but these were my motives, and have given them to me. You may
have misconstrued my meaning relative to turning me out of doors. I
only alluded to that atal in order to shew you I would not try to *buy* your
good opinion at the cost of *fear*. I did not intimate that such a thought
(nor do I believe it) ever crossed your mind, but I said if you would or
I almost wished you would if it could hurry me to my grave. I said you
deserted me in my darkest hour of sorrow, and did I say any thing but
truth. No Charley you[r] own concience has long since told you it was
not the time to have taken your leave of one who had so long clung to
you alone, and more than this that I could never have forsaken you wilfully only at the gate of happiness closing on you, while I remained as
something no longer essential to your peace. In happy days I have clung
to you but Oh! how much more closely would I do so in *your* hour of
trouble, and should the time yet arrive that you should be in distress
that I could mitigate one iota I would lay aside all fear of your displeasure and seek you as far as I dare go. It would only require the evidence
of prison walls or galling chains to shew what I would do for you, and
before God I would do this though you could turn me a beggar on the
world tomorrow, for I never looked for one moment what you *would* do
for me nor *did* I, nor can I ever forget what we have been to each other.
Oh! Charley that you could say I had placed you among the lowest class.
You know better, you *feel* in your own soul that I now place you above
all other men I ever met in point of moral goodness, elevation of soul
and benevolent feeling, though I must say and you have more than once
said the same, that the latter was undergoing a change, and in this I do
not say you are to blame, neither have I ever said you were in no longer

assisting me. You have too many relying on your exertions. Charley remember your promise to me, and also remember it was not an idle one,
but almost in the form of an oath, and ask yourself how you have fulfilled
it. You vowed never to leave me without telling me to my face that such
was your intention and giving your reasons. I ask *this* of you at least.

If I have long since seemed to moderate in my feelings towards you,
it was only because yours towards me induced me to feel mine were re-
pugnant to you, but the heart you never read. Long since I saw that you
could not give me what you once had done, warmer feelings than mere
friendship, and you have only seen a small portion of the agony this conviction cost me. But as I knew this was beyond your controul I strove to
feel less and *hide* more of my own emotions. Oh! God what would I not
give to know [show] you all you have been to me, and feel I was the same
I once was to you. I have ever told you when we ceased to be any thing
to each other I was undone though only the half of that is as yet accomplished, for you will never cease to be *much very much* to me. Thank God
we cannot snatch our memory, image nor very presence from the minds
of others, or I might thus be forced to give you up. Do not make my
last any excuse for your desertion. No Charley act *nobly* and feelingly
towards me once more, for it had commenced before, and wherefore I
am in utter ignorance. I will at least be generous. If I have done you
wrong in word or line I would on my knees ask all the forgiveness, your
heart would once have granted me, and which one so unhappy could
need. I am not allowed to come to you, or long since I should have sought
from your lips (though *you* deserted) the cause of your conduct towards
me. You dare not say that you were not as ever the most welcome visitor
here. Then why have you acted thus. You were here when the message
came that shewed you how more than ever in my life I should need
the voice of friendship to sustain me now.[12] You witnessed my agonizing tears, had heard words from my lips doubtless which made you feel
bad, but of these I plead guilty at least their execution. You then coldly
and it does seem heartlessly left me [to stru]ggle without one consoling
thought or word of pity to meet my ear. I must [be less] than mortal not
to feel this. And now you tantalize me with your prayer for *better friends*

for me. *Never will* I *trust* another, if *you* can cast me off as no portion of your creating, if you can now feel that I am less to you than the dog that was once, and still is at least patted by you, if *you* can feel that greif like mine deserves no solace, if *you* can gild my path for three years with sunshine and then hurl me into midnight gloom, if *you* can say let the past be as though it had not been, then Oh! what could I ever hope from another. I may as is human listen to momentary friendship but I will place no reliance farther than I can see. Oh! it seems all have forsaken me but those whom I wish to do so. I am forced to seem cheerful before the few I meet in order to hide what I feel. I go out to dispel misery, and I catch a glimpse of you but to awaken a keener sense of the past. *I* do not know what portion of my letter to explain; I charge you by the God who *knows* our motives and feelings not to rob me of that miniature. It is mine *do* not ask it back. The shortness of yours seems purposely intended to warn me if I dared reply to imitate its length, but such could not be the case, as much as I have suffered while penning it I would extend it to another sheet if I did not fear to aggravate you. Oh! Charley if I am in error forgive me I pray, more I cannot say. I *did* not, *I* could not mean what you represent, *far far* from it. I would acknowledge an error when convinced of it to any one, but to you alone would I sue with penitence for what you even supposed a *wrong* from me. Oh! God has our happiness come to this. God ever bless you is my fervent prayer
M

Charley to Madaline [13]

March 25 th 1847.

Mad

Your note which was written in reply to mine of the 5 th inst. Came duly to hand and the contents perused carefully & dispationately, with a View if Possible to dispel a hellish conflict that has been going on in my mind for some time past and one which I have not yet entirely mastered & put down. Your note Mad appears to be Stamped on its face with truth, candour & sincerity, but the world has Come to such a pass, (or I should have said the people that are in it,) that it is hard to judge aright. It is a very difficult matter for me to make up my mind that you are *not* what I once believed, truly and sincerely believed you were, namely, an exemplary woman at least in *heart,* if not always so in action. If you could only be let alone, I am quite sure your heart is in the right place, but then it would be very uncharitable in me to expect you to act different from other women under similar Circumstances. You have, I freely admit Mad, had a great deal to Contend with, probably more than you can well bear, still with the assistance of a proper exercise of our mental faculties, (usually called good common sense,) we overcome immense obstacles. Your suspitions, that a third person has influenced me with regard to you, are totally unfounded and I would only add that I never allow third persons to have the slightest influence with me in such matters. I beg your pardon, if in my last note, I used any harsh words or was to[o] abrupt.

C

Madaline to Charley, April 9, 1847

Dear Charley,

I sit down with the resolution not to shed a tear (if I can help it) while I answer your last, for I feel that a few more will send me a maniac. I do not know why I ventured to church to day for I had almost fainted while there. Charley do no lingerings of former times ever rise up in your breast as you approach this once happy cottage? It seems to me there must be and that there is a kind of magnitism between us at the time, for I think you must pass there at some few times beside those in which you throw your *icicles* on my heart, for there are times when I feel so sensible that you are near, and always so when you have left traces of the fact. Has it come to this from you! And yet I commiserate the circumstance in your life which has so changed your confiding, and unsuspecting nature. I did hope you would have answered my inquiries more explicit and not in such a vague, cold manner. Charley it must be that you have fears of Breedlove. If so, what can I think. I curse the day that he ever spoke to me. I curse from my soul the hour I ever entered that school. And if *he* is the cause of our separation, I curse ten fold the circumstances that led him to damn instead of befriending me. Did I not tell you all our talks, and shew you our letters upon that subject. But since I got out of the school he proposed to buy me a negro and give me all I could wish if I would say he might visit me occasionally. I *detest* as I do perdition the bare writing or thinking of this act. I wrote him upon the subject such a letter I wish you had seen it. The answer I have reserved with the hope of shewing it to you. That *hope* is past. I here enclose it; destroy it as soon as read. Charley can you say from your heart that I am mercenary. If so why did I not act it out before I was getting a salary. If on the other hand, am I passionate. Do you think Oh! these thoughts are too revolting? My God tell me what you do think, and let me know. Oh! Charley [if] these are your reasons for acting so differently towards me long before I got out of school, under the pretence that you had too much respect for that time to ask favours, then you too can dissemble. Is it that you suspect me with others because your generous, noble, and trusting disposition allowed me the privilege of keeping their company, all of which I ever told you. As yet I keep none but what Jim knows of and all my actions. I have been to a few public places since we last met and were it not for the little company I see and the little I go out I might become what you would hate to charge your cruel conduct with, a maniac. Yesterday a gentleman of Jims acquaintance, called on me to know if I would go to the theatre when he found me bathed in tears. His efforts at consolation only increased them. He of course was ignorant of the immediate cause but could in part enter into my emotions concerning my situation. Why can my heart not break in some of these outbursts of feeling God alone can tell. I have often thought of suicide at a distance but never reflected so seriously on it as of late. I do not lack resolution to put it in force but if I am to loose a portion of the peace beyond the grave that will fall to my lot I can better bear the few years that await me here than loose so much in a purer world. Charley I have ever noticed one thing. If men neglect their wives, that is extend to them no pecuniary assistance, or, if men do not treat their mistresses as they had once been able to do, they

at once think they loose their love and then their fidelity, and this is too
often the case, but had I searched the world over for an exception to this
rule it would have been in you, and yet I cannot see why your surmises
have gone out as it seems unless that you no longer extended to me the
means of living. But of this have I ever complained, on the contrary I regret that you did not sooner let me into the knowledge of your situation
and the many dependent on you. I at one time was even more able, and
fully as willing as I have been since to do with less from you, but since
my arm has been broken could I have done more than I have done in
order to live deserving of your respect and clear of your bounty? Have I
called on you for means? Have I ever grumbled. No, often have I wanted
a dime so much that I would resolve to ask you, but my heart or pride
would fail me, and I would eat stale bread and sometimes none until I
could get a trifle for my sewing. Many have been the dimes Sayre would
give me, for he would pry into my situation and pity and blame me at the
same time, and has ever said if there was a feeling of my heart to admire
it was that which prompted me to be faithful to one who cared no more
for me. This I would repel with a proud conciousness that I *was* cared
for, that one kind assurance from you, one fond embrace, one token of
trust was worth more to me than wealth. But all these day dreams are
past. You speak of a right use of common sense, taking me through. In
no way will it apply to my case but in hard work and I know not how
much more I can use in that way than I am doing. If ever I am lost lay it
to your own [obliterated by sealing wax]. I will not deny in your desertion I have tried to love well enough to gi[ve my] hand in marriage but
cannot. I daily prove to my own heart that I can love not again. Unless
you will give me your reasons for your belief, or will say positively you
do not wish me to annoy you I shall take it for granted you do not wish
to hear from me again, indeed I feel that I am trespassing this on you.
Oh! God Charley remember years back my sad foreboding. I can say
more, your confidence in me is lost, and you are the first [obliterated by
sealing wax] ever had any claims on me who has made that charge and
I al[ways] felt that if such had been my case in a married life and I was
innocent one hour would not retain me with my accuser. In our case you

have been judge and jury and if you deem me guilty you have a right to leave me but not in justice, as you did without my knowing wherfore. A thought has this moment flashed over my mind. Your philosophy induced you to say to me a short time before you left me that all our misfortunes were the result of our errors. Now you jumped at the conclusion that if I was innocent I would not have lost my place in school. I have looked on you as something so far above other men that I cannot reconcile inconsistencies with you. No Charley I will not buy your opinion. You have pronounced me guilty. My uncle did so once and ruined me upon a charge of which I was as clear as my angel babe before Gods throne. As to your charges they must rest with your own heart. You who so often told me you must see with your own eyes before you would condemn me. Have you done this? Answer the question. Do not think I have kept my resolution at the head of this. How could I. I sit down in the door at night and look out upon what has made me so happy, and I rush to bed to forget my misery. I wish *but no* may I hear from you. Say I am *base* and you *hate me*. This will suffice. Better this than all this suspense. Oh curse the day I ever entered that school or saw B. May you be happy happy. I regret no pain of my mind that brings you this.

Farewell

Madaline to Charley

April 25ᵗʰ/47.

Dear C.

When I last wrote to you I stipulated a sign by which I should know that it was your desire that I should no more intrude my letters upon you, and as you have convinced me by that sign such is the case, I regret that I am compelled to violate your wish, for I do not wish to do ought to displease or pain you.

I would not again trouble you to tell of what is on my mind, but that I have another motive in so doing. Charley I always told you when we parted I could not willingly live near you, and before this I should have fled this place had it not have been that I awaited my cousin's promises.

Jack told me when last here that he had bespoken me a situation in the
Academy now building in San Antonio, that if I would go he would give
me land and do a brothers part by me. The past, he said he forgave,
the future was all he asked of me. He wrote me the morning he left, as
he could not call again, saying he would be over in two months and expected it might be necessary for me to go over then.

I rely upon nothing again not even while it is transpiring, but will
hope my wishes in this will be realized not that I expect to be happy,
far from it, but our separation leaves me no wish to remain here, and I
write this to ask you kindly to give me an order by which I can get the
things you took charge of for me. The mortgage note you hold on this lot
of course you will not deny me. The letters and miniature I implore you
to give me. I do not ask for the right, in order to part from this lot. No
Charley by the honour you once rilied on I vow to keep it as a memorial
over departed happiness and present anguish. I wish to lease it out but
not to part with it. My MS.S books I wrote with the sole hope and belief
that they would be yours. This fond hope is now crushed for it would be
an outrage upon your feelings to offer them, and yet how I wish them
to be in your possession for many reasons. Little did I think when penning the most of those pages, a day was so close at hand when you would
spurn them and me. Your name occurs so oft in them that I cannot well
leave them to another. I pray you will not rob me of the miniature, unless you could tear from my memory that which is stamped too deep for
life to erase.

I am certain I have at last arrived at the right conclusion as to your
desertion of me, but I will make no comments as your happiness not
mine is involved in the same. *This* I say when it is too late to benefit me.
You will see how you have wronged one who will ever love you. I am
content to bear the black stigma, the contempt and hatred you feel for
me under your impressions sooner than undermine one pillar on which
your hope leans.

The promises made by you, and treasured by me relative to my tomb,
the last hope that could cheer me, they too are gone like all my day
dreams, and some distant land must receive my crushed heart, beneath

its friendly soil where I trust no tear will moist the sod over which the briar alone will grow.

Let me not intrude farther upon one who has so plainly forbid my writing. Say to me by some means or other how I am to get those things. Do not deny me, nor trifle with my feelings too long or I shall trouble you again which I fear much annoys you.

Farewell. As ever. M.

Madaline to Charley

May 16th [1847]

Dear C,

As meanly as you try to think of me, yet I cannot realize that you could believe under any circumstances I could be induced to make you a *threat,* not that you would fear such a thing, but because it is entirely beneath me. Thus I trust the following will not be misconstrued. I wrote to you at length upon the subject of this lot, and *begged* an answer but you refuse me any satisfaction in your silence and I am again compelled to the same request, and if I receive no answer by a certain time I must very reluctantly seek a verbal one. Is it just or even honourable to tantalize and torture one merely because we have them in our power? Such is my case and changing as you have so suddenly done, how may you not change yet towards me. At all events I must know my fate concerning this property, as I am resolved to leave this place, and the last word almost M^r C said to me was *not* to sell my house. I assured him it was far from my thoughts. If it is mine why not give me the evidence of it. If such is not the case the sooner I know it the better for me and surely none the worse for you.

Charley you must *know* I feel humbled, and crushed in so often forcing my letters on you so against your will, but what can I do. I once had you to go to for advice in an emergency. Now you know it would take much to induce me to ask advice in this affair from any one. I have promised old C——n the refusal of the house when I leave it upon good security. I am awaiting Jacks action in the affair of my leaving for Texas and he did not induce me to believe it would be earlier than fall. And in case of his death or non action in my favour, I leave forthwith for California upon the *determination,* I have lately formed. But why trouble you about that which doubtless irritates you — *myself* or my affairs. But distance nor time, no not even death will make me *forget.*

Will you be so good as to let me know my doom in this and not keep me in ignorance as you have done the other even more important point. If you refuse me you *cannot* surely get angry at my adopting the only alternative. Every line I always feel increases your hate towards me, hence I will stop.

As ever M.

Charley to Madaline

New Orleans May 20th. 1847.

Mad.

Your note under date of the 16th instant was duly recd. as also two previous ones, which you will never forgive me I know for not answering. In the last you exultingly accuse me of tantalizing you because, as you Say, I have you in my power. Now I should be very sorry to have any one Consider themselves in my power, and I do not think there is such a person in the world.

You wish to know about the Lot. My original intentions were for you to have it during your lifetime, provided New Orleans was your place of residence. I hope you will excuse this short epistle, for under existing circumstances you cannot expect me to write much.

C.

Madaline Edwards spent the summer of 1847 in Mobile with her father, while Charles Bradbury rented a house at Bay St. Louis, Mississippi, a popular summering spot for New Orleanians eager to escape the city. In the fall she resumed her campaign to obtain title to her house.

Sept 12/47

I leave this place blank which I might once be allowed to fill with the purest emotions of my heart, but now I am forbidden even to think of you were it possible to hinder me. I have been sick, I *am* sick, in fact I *never* expect to be well again and against all orders to be up yet am I resolved to write you again though the tears that are now welling up should cost my life. I took up your letters a few days ago and read them all over. Some which I got about and after this time last year made me weep until I took a relapse. I then collected them all and your little poetical attempts enveloped, sealed, and directed so that *you* will secretly get them if I die. I feel that I dare not trust myself to read them often for then I must have been dear to you, or you could not have written as you did. Now Oh God what am I to you?

I have asked, I have begged, I have prayed to you and all has been met with silent contempt. If you imagane a cause it is as if you have one. I am no longer judge for myself and never was for you. I could say volumes to you but I feel I am despised, and trust a day is not far distant for me, when my heart will be done with beating towards you as it does, and that when you meet me you will *understand* them.

Going to Mobile I thought all the way over oh! how different are now my emotions from this day 4 years ago when all at once a certain spot called up to my mind so forcibly what I said to myself while gazing at it. I thought of you with feelings full, full of devotion, and trembling for so much happiness, I prayed to God that he would only grant that I might be to you what I felt I then was, only *three* years and then I would be willing to die. Here it struck me as if by magic and I looked back to see and sure enough *three* years we had been together when you cast me again upon the turbid waters of *fate*, but oh! death has as yet denied its rescue.

I am *nothing* to you only an object of hate. Then why keep in your possession any thing that is mine. I have prayed for that miniature that I have so often kissed, but it seems you think a tear from my eyes on it would almost contaminate the original. How much I wish for it God only knows, but I fear my eyes have beheld it the last time. Oh! C is this fair.

Ever since I have been sick I have desired to make a will and cannot do so as you will give me no assurance that this property is mine. Why keep me in this wretched state of mind as even concerns a home? Do I deserve all this too? I ask it for the last time: will you satisfy me upon this point. Are you trying my patience in order that I may expose the thing by asking advise from any one. Oh! then you little know my honour. If you think me not entitled to or worthy of it, why not say so and at least divide and give me my part of the money whether I die or live, move away or stay. I am dissatisfied and unhappy as things stand. I implore you to give me an answer to this. Give me my box you had for me. Oh! Charley you surely have robbed me of happiness enough without taking this my only hope. But restore the former and this will be nothing.

Any way you wish to give me either the box or answer you can do so. I would if I dared ask to see you one time more no matter where or how, but I know you will hate me even for the desire. Oh! God can you ever know my feelings. If this is unanswered I am hence a doomed woman I feel, I know it. I cannot but harbour a dread that words or an insinuation has caused much of the feelings you entertain for me. If so God forgive a foe in disguise.

You never gave me liberty to write to you so I feel like one treading on fire coals every line that I pen for fear each one produces fresh hatred.

If you wish—oh! I can not write. God ever bless you.

Charley to Madaline [14]

Sept 16 th. 1847

Mad.

Your note written last Sunday, was received to day; and as you seem desirous of seeing me I have thought it best to have a personal interview, as in justice to you, I feel that I ought. When I see you I will make the necessary explanations and apologies for my not answering Your letters. As the proposed meeting will in all probability be the last one, of course my determination with reference to our affairs will be divulged freely and candidly, however painful it may be to me. After receiving your note to day, I had thought of writing you my views, but upon reflection, to see you personally, seemed to me the proper course.

C.

~~I will call to morrow night between 7 & 8 o'clock and if the gate is open I will enter and if it is locked I will pass.~~

Any night which you choose to designate, by a note to me through the Post Office, I will come.

Madaline to Charley

Sept 25 th/47.

C.

Strange it is that yours has not reached me until this moment, though I have sent twice since it was written. I shall put this in to day Saturday, but as it is not likely you will get it now I will name an interview Sunday night. If you cannot come then say Monday. When J returns he will call on me and then may sit until near 10. If he is not here you will find me awaiting you at the back gate say at 9 o clock in order that the children may be asleep.[15] Should any thing occur to prevent you either of these nights the gate will still be open each night after until I see you. Yes! C I hope you will say all you wish openly and freely. God only knows my sensations since getting yours. Do not fail for death is preferable to my state of mind, not in relation to the lot but to hear from your lips your condemnation and its nature.

I have deciphered the crossed line of yours in which you say between 7 and 8 oclock if that alone will suit you come then. I shall await with painful anxiety.

Again. Perhaps you had rather come in the front gate. I thought as the moon was so bright, otherwise, but if any one is here I will be on the front gallery. If not the gate open. I can watch both as I have done under happier circumstances.

This is the last surviving letter, from Charley to Madaline.

N.O. Tuesday Sept 28th. 1847.

Mad.

Your note dated last Saturday was recd. on Monday, and in Conformity with your own wishes I Called at 9 o'Clock last night both at the front & back gates, but to my great surprise I found them both locked, and apparently not a soul about the House. I can hardly think you are humbugging me in saying you wish to see me, but if you are, I Certainly Cannot see the advantage to be gained by it, probably my excessive stupidity prevents my seeing the object in view. When I am assured, if ever, of the night you Can Positively be found at home I will probably call.

C.

Fortune's Hill

With the last angry exchange of letters, Madaline Edwards's and Charles Bradbury's voices fell silent. To learn of the former lovers' fortunes after 1847, we must turn to the kind of public documents on which historians have always relied: the newspapers, court records, and directories in which names and numbers substitute for lives. In them we discover that the lovers' disentanglement was painfully drawn out.

In her determination to gain title to her house, Edwards overlooked a compelling reason why Bradbury could not give it to her, were he inclined to do so. Charley's "gift" was legally a sale: Madaline had signed a mortgage due on December 30, 1844. Her lover reserved the "privilege . . . to excuse the payment of said note," but by law Mary Ann Bradbury would have had to sign away her dower rights to the property.[1] At the end of the affair, however, Bradbury's ownership of the house was still secret. Edwards's threat to expose him was pointless, for forgiving the mortgage would betray him anyway. Thus Charley chose to foreclose rather than to confirm the affair that his wife had long suspected, and even as he foreclosed he tried to disguise the connection to Madaline. He had legal papers drawn up that referred to her as "Mrs. Selima Madaline Cage, widow of the Late Dempsey Elliott," a name that few people besides Charley and his friends would recognize.[2]

Bradbury won a judgment in 1849 and sold the house to Albert Q.

Cary three years later.[3] Edwards decided to fight, and she won a kind of victory, for the foreclosure was declared invalid on technical grounds. Both Bradbury and Cary were ordered to pay rent from the date of the repossession until the date of judgment, but Edwards was held liable for the note, and the property was ordered resold to Bradbury. Both James Waller Breedlove and Charles Bradbury's own brother testified against him on her behalf. Breedlove swore that Edwards had not left town to avoid the debt, as Bradbury implied, but had openly declared her intentions to leave for some time before June 1849. James Bradbury refuted his brother's claim that Edwards's default on the note had left Charley in debt to him. He explained that "the note . . . was a note used by witness brother, C. W. Bradbury, for his, C. W. Bradbury's own interest" and thus acknowledged the subterfuge Charley used to buy Madaline's house. For whatever reasons, Breedlove and Jim Bradbury took Madaline's side over Charley's.

Anger as much as money must have driven Edwards to fight the repossession, for she had to travel to New Orleans from San Francisco to initiate the suit in the winter of 1853. Unemployment and lack of prospects had left her at loose ends after Charley broke off the affair. In June 1849 she let her house and immigrated to California.

The easiest passage from New Orleans entailed sailing to Chagres on the Atlantic Coast of Panama. From there, it took two to three days of arduous travel by flatboat and on foot to cover the sixty miles across the isthmus to Panama City, where another vessel carried the immigrant to San Francisco. If one took steamships rather than sailing vessels and had no trouble finding a berth in Panama City, the entire trip could be made in two weeks. Was Madaline, then, the "Mrs. Edwards" who arrived in San Francisco on the bark *Madonna* on June 30, 1849? Possibly; at any rate she would have been a conspicuous arrival. A total of 39,888 new immigrants reached the city in the last eight months of 1849, but only 1,421 were women. She did not remain in San Francisco long, for the next June a United States Census enumerator found her living in Sacramento.[4]

In July 1849 her cousin John Coffee Hays, who had suggested that she join him in Texas, started overland to California from San Antonio. The cousins reunited in San Francisco the next summer. Hays, a celebrated founder of the Texas Rangers and a surveyor by training, had arrived in San Francisco in January 1850 to great public fanfare. For a couple of years the two were close. Jack lived in a boardinghouse that Madaline kept behind the Marine Hospital on Stockton Street, in what was then a "thickly peopled and fashionable part of town."[5]

Eventually their paths diverged once more. Hays traded on his fame as an Indian fighter to win election as an independent candidate as San Francisco's first sheriff. Then he was the United States surveyor-general, a post he held until 1860. By 1852 Hays's wife had immigrated to California, and they were living at 325 Powell Street. Later in the 1850s, Hays participated in the founding of Oakland, sold land to the University of California, and lived out his life near Mountain View Cemetery in Oakland, where he was buried after his death on April 22, 1883.[6]

Edwards's path took her in other directions. After the trip to Louisiana to try to win back her cherished house, she returned to San Francisco, where she lived on the south side of Union Street near Kearny. In contrast to her boardinghouse in a bustling part of the city, Edwards's new home stood on then-sparsely settled Telegraph Hill, a poor, marginal neighborhood on a steep rise above San Francisco Bay. She was unmarried, a widow with no stated occupation, perhaps living off the proceeds of her lawsuit against Charles Bradbury.

In August 1854 the following item appeared in the *Wide West:*

> [Died] In San Francisco Aug. 20 at her residence on Union Street, Mrs. Madeline Edwards formerly of New Orleans and cousin to Col. Jack Hays of San Francisco, well known as the Madeline of the New Orleans *Delta* and *Picayune.* Interred in Yerba Buena Cemetery, San Francisco, Aug. 21.[7]

A cryptic notice in the *Daily Alta California* attributed Edwards's death to "congestion of the liver" and reported the death of a three-month-old infant, Marion Ascension Edwards, of croup. No parent's name was listed. Was Marion a fifth child of Madaline's? If so, mother and child may have died of cholera. Other cases were known in the city at about that time, but physicians and publishers were notoriously reluctant to report the disease, since epidemics were bad for business.[8]

Edwards's family connection to the powerful Hays did nothing for her or her (presumed) child. Both were buried in coroner's graves in the potter's field of Yerba Buena Cemetery, "one of the most dreary and melancholy spots that surround the city," an "unenclosed waste . . . in a hollow among miserable looking sand-hills, which are scantily covered with stunted trees, worthless shrubs, and tufted weeds," according to contemporaries.[9]

Even death brought no end to Madaline Edwards's wanderings. San Francisco's Yerba Buena Cemetery was abandoned in 1860, and the bodies were removed between 1865 and 1870 to Laurel Hill (Lone Mountain), the city's new rural cemetery. Laurel Hill was in turn dismantled between 1939 and 1941, and the remains were reinterred at Cypress Lawn Cemetery in suburban Colma after World War II.[10]

Charles Bradbury lived out his life at 356 Baronne Street, in the house he had bought in 1841. His death certificate read as follows:

> Charles W. Bradbury. (White.) a native of New York aged Sixty five years. Departed this life yesterday (22 June 1880) at #356 Baronne Street, in this city.
>
> Cause of Death Fatty Degeneration of Heart.[11]

Inventory of Madaline S. Edwards's Surviving Works

Items not included in this volume are marked with an asterisk (*). Those excerpted are marked with a cross (+).

FOUR LETTERS TO CHARLES W. BRADBURY, AUTUMN 1843.

SEVEN POEMS, 1844–47.
Loose sheets, various sizes. None of these poems are included in any of the bound manuscripts.
* To C. N.d.
* To C.W.B. N.d.
* To one I truly love. N.d.
* To C. Feb. 1, 1844.
* You asked me if I wished to go back in the City to live. Apr. 12, 1844.
* To Dear Charley. Jan. 1, 1845.
* New Year. Jan. 1, 1847.

WRITING BOOK 1, 1843–44.
Writing Book 1, a composition book that has lost its cover, is about seven and a half by ten inches and contains 147 pages. On the first righthand page, Edwards wrote, "Madaline S Edwards 1844. / New Orleans Dec 4th 1843." On the reverse of this page, she wrote, "Moved Dec 12th 1843."
Contents (starting page number in brackets):
   [1] Miscellaneous subjects. Dec. 14, 1843. Essay.
   [3] Saturday night. Dec. 23, 1843. Essay.

    [5] Sabbath. Dec. 24, 1843. Essay.

*   [7] Untitled. Dec. 24, 1843. Essay on Edwards's preference for autumn over spring.

*   [11] Untitled. Dec. 28, 1843. Critical essay on Benjamin West's painting *Christ Healing the Sick,* then on exhibit in New Orleans.

*   [13] My childhood's home. Jan. 7, 1844. Essay.

*   [18] Untitled. Jan. 12, 1844. Essay on astronomy as a path to understanding God.

*   [20] Untitled. Jan. 21, 1844. Meditation on salvation, Charles Bradbury, and Theodore Clapp, occasioned by reading Thomas Dick's works on astronomy.

*   [23] The grave yard. Feb. 4, 1844. Essay.

*   [24] Untitled. Mar. 3, 1844. Essay on the knowledge that men have a higher destiny than this world.

    [27] Untitled. Mar. 17, 1844. Essay on loneliness.

*   [30] Untitled. Mar. 22, 1844. Essay on aspiration.

*   [32] Life. N.d. Later published in the *Native American.*

    [35] Untitled. Apr. 1, 1844. Essay on parting with Charles Bradbury.

*   [35] Untitled. Apr. 7, 1844. Poem on nature as evidence of God's goodness.

*   [36] Untitled. Apr. 14, 1844. Essay on a Clapp sermon on eternal life.

    [41] Woman. Apr. 28, 1844. Essay.

*   [46] Dr. Dick. Apr. 30, 1844. Essay.

    [49] Untitled. May 9, 1844. Comment on Charles Bradbury's birthday.

*   [49] The birth day of C. May 9, 1844. Poem.

    [50] Man. May 19, 1844. Essay.

*   [53] Happiness. May 21, 1844. Essay.

+   [57] Departure. June 15, 1844. Essay.

*   [59] Untitled. June 16, 1844. Essay on Clapp sermon from the text "Perfect love casteth out fear."

    [62] Flowers. June 26, 1844. Essay.

*   [69] Clouds. June 30, 1844. Essay.

+   [73] July 4th. July 4, 1844. Essay.

*   [75] The country. July 12, 1844. Essay.

*   [84] C gave me these lines. July 16, 1844. Poem.

    [85] A walk. July 19, 1844. Essay.

*   [91] Clouds poetical. July 21, 1844. Essay.

* [97] Nature is religion. July 26, 1844. Essay.

* [107] Moon light. July 27, 1844. Essay.

* [109] Thunder clouds. July 28, 1844. Essay.

* [112] Desolation. Aug. 1, 1844. Essay.

* [117] Imitation. Aug. 6, 1844. Poem about missing Bradbury.

* [117] The humming bird. Sept. 23, 1844. Poem.

* [118] To C. who has been gone two months and only wrote me once. Aug. 8, 1844. Poem.

* [119] The bee and the frog. Aug. 9, 1844.

[122] On being reproved for weeping, and asked the cause. Aug. 13, 1844. Poem.

+ [122] Untitled. Aug. 22, 1844. Comment on the preceding poem.

* [128] Old papers. Aug. 25, 1844.

* [130] The last day of summer. N.d.

* [132] The last eve of summer. Aug. 31, 1844. Poem.

[133] To Charley. Sept. 1, 1844. On his neglect.

+ [136] A tale of real life. Sept. 12, 1844.

[162] Untitled. Sept. 14, 1844. Comment on the tale.

*[N.p.] Untitled. N.d. Notes on astronomy from Dick.

DIARY, 1844.

The 1844 diary is a tall, narrow book with a black, burgundy, and brown marbled cover, four by twelve inches. It has room for a short paragraph under each date. The title page reads, "Diary, / for / 1844: / or / Daily Register, / for the use of / Private Families / and / Persons of Business: / Containing / A Blank for Every Day in the Year, for the Record / of Interesting Daily Occurrences / and Future Engagements." The page also notes that the diary was published annually by Hymen L. Lipman and by Thomas, Cowperthwaite and Company, both in Philadelphia. On the second righthand page, Edwards wrote, "Presented by C. ——— / 1844."

WRITING BOOK 2, 1844–47.

Writing Book 2 is eight and a half by twelve inches, contains 147 pages, and has a burgundy, blue, and gray marbled cover. On the first righthand page, Edwards wrote, "M. S. Edwards / N.O. October 24/44."

Contents:

      [1] Untitled. Nov. 10, 1844. Will.

*   [8] Untitled. Nov. 15, 1844. Essay on the blessings of natural surroundings.

\+ [10] Domestic happiness. Nov. 2, 1844. Essay.

* [17] To Dear C. who alone can understand it. Dec. 24, 1844. Poem on death and parting.

* [18] Lines. Nov. 21, 1844. Allegory on true and false value.

* [19] Lines to Charley. Nov. 22, 1844. Poem on nature.

\+ [20] Untitled. Nov. 29, 1844. Sketch of a visit to St. Louis Cemetery No. 2.

* [24] A copy, written by request. Jan. 12, 1845. Extract on male-female courting.

    [26] To C. [Jan.] 14, 1845. Essay.

* [27] An evening in childhood. Jan. 17, 1845. Nostalgic essay on the sound of a cowbell.

* [31] Untitled. Jan. 17, 1845. Note on how the foregoing came to be written.

* [31] Untitled. Jan. 17, 1845. Poem on the same subject.

* [32] Untitled. Mar. 2, 1845. Reminiscence of a childhood friend.

* [39] The liberated convict. Mar. 9, 1845. Poem.

* [41] The Indian chief. Feb. 23, 1844. Poem on the eviction of the Indian from his traditional home.

* [42] To C who said I might yet hate him and call him mean. Feb. 23, 1844. Poem.

* [43] Ingratitude. Mar. 14, 1845. Probably for the *Native American.*

* [46] Lines. May 4, 1845. Poem about rejection.

* [46] Extract. N.d. Quote from Napoleon about religion.

* [47] To the humming bird that returned on the last day of April, and who lost its mate last fall by accident and I have preserved it. May 1, 1845. Poem.

* [48] The human heart. May 11, 1845. Essay.

    [49] The National Gallery of paintings. May 18, 1845. Essay.

* [52] Desire to travel. May 25, 1845. Essay.

* [55] Untitled. May 26, 1845. Essay on the same subject.

* [60] Lines dedicated to Charley because my thoughts have been so much with him this dull lonely sabbath. June 8, 1845. Poem.

* [61] Lines by request, on the presentation of a banner to The Native American Artillery company by the ladies of N.O. June 15, 1845. Poem.

[62] Untitled. [June 27, 1845.] Note on the procession in memory of Andrew Jackson.

* [63] Life. July 31, 1845. Poem.

* [63] Death. July 5, 1845. Poem.

* [64] By the dying wife of a sporting inebriate. Sept. 15, 1845. Poem.

* [65] The husband of Ellen. Nov. 8, 1845. Poem continuing the story of the previous poem.

* [67] To J.A.B. Oct. 25, 1845. Allegorical story on morality.

* [68] To J.A.B. Oct. 26, 1845. Essay on Edwards's belief in heaven.

* [71] To a lady who sent me an exquisitely delicate and sweet Bouquet though unknown. Oct. 28, 1845. Poem.

* [72] Life and death. Nov. 9, 1845. Essay.

* [73] The eclipse of Nov 13th 1845. Nov. 16, 1845. Essay.

* [75] To J.A.B. who related to me the scene described. Nov. 26, 1845. Poem about a childhood scene.

[76] Lines to Mary. Nov. 17, 1845. Poem.

* [76] To the same. Nov. 20, 1845. Poem.

* [77] The Indian summer. Nov. 26, 1845. Poem.

* [77] On the presentation of a boquet. Jan. 18, 1846. Poem.

* [78] The rainbow. Nov. 27, 1845. Poem.

[79] Byron. Nov. 30, 1845. Essay.

* [81] The suicide. Dec. 7, 1845. Essay on the injustice of denying Christian burial to suicides.

* [82] The suicide. Dec. 12, 1845. Poem.

* [83] To my brother whom I have never seen and who has attained to manhood. Dec. 21, 1845. Poem.

* [84] To a lady on her birth day. Dec. 31, 1845. Poem.

[85] An answer to an advertisement for a wife who must be perfect. Jan. 1, 1846. Poem.

* [86] Music. N.d. Essay.

* [89] To J.A.B. Jan. 5, 1846. Poem.

* [90] To a lady, on an absent daughter. Jan. 11, 1846. Poem.

[91] Answer to Celeb's reply. Jan. 24, 1846. Poem.

* [94] Mr. Clapp. Feb. 1, 1846. Poem.

[94] Untitled. N.d. Poem: "The past is dimmed with care and grief. . . ."

* [95] To Miss D——. Feb. 4, 1846. Poem.

* [95] To the same who is an adopted child. Feb. 6, 1846. Poem.

* [96] Thoughts on Mr —— telling me the first time he conversed with me, he thought I was cold and misanthropic. Feb. 22, 1846. Essay.

* [98] Mother. Feb. 23, 1846. Essay.

* [101] To D.B. Mar. 1, 1846. Poem.

* [102] A dream. Mar. 15, 1846. Poem.

* [102] To the unknown. May 31, 1846. Poem.

[103] To C. Mar. 25, 1846. Poem on Charley's cruelty to Madaline.

* [104] Untitled. Apr. 5, 1846. Essay on true and false love.

* [106] The astronomical lectures. Apr. 4, 1846. Essay.

[108] Answer to W.A.P. Apr. 17, 1846. Poem.

[109] For the Native American. May 3, 1846. Poem on elections.

* [109] Answer to W.A.P. May 3, 1846. Poem.

* [110] Savages Cannibalism &c &c. May 12, 1846. Essay.

* [115] To the N.O. volunteers who have resolved to aid Texas in claiming her rights from Mexico. May 16, 1846. Poem.

* [116] Reply to W.A.P. May 25, 1846. Poem.

[117] To one who heeds not the woe he has caused. June 6, 1846. Poem.

[117] Untitled. N.d. Brief comment on stinginess.

* [118] To my warrior cousin. June 6, 1846. Poem.

* [119] To Antoinette. June 21, 1846. Poem.

* [120] On some lines written by one unknown. June 28, 1846. Poem.

* [121] On being presented with the night blooming Ceres. June 24, 1846. Poem.

* [121] On an exquisite boquet from the same. June 26, 1846. Poem.

* [122] Lines on dreaming that I was again at my Uncles in Tenn with whom I lived many years and at whose house I was married. July 5, 1846. Poem.

* [123] Our flag. July 19, 1846. Poem.

* [124] The charity hospital. Aug. 20, 1846. Sentimental story.

[128] Untitled. Aug. 23, 1846. Comment on slander.

* [128] To Mrs Clapps babe, on his birth day. Aug. 20, 1846. Poem.

* [129] To ——. Sept. 12, 1846. Poem imagining her own wake.

* [130] Lines on the return of Celebs after marriage. Nov. 8, 1846. Poem.

* [131] A farewell to Jack Hays, upon his joining his regiment. Dec. 8, 1846. Poem.

* [132] An answer to the unknown. Dec. 13, 1846. Poem.

* [133] Answer to WLF. N.d. Poem.
* [134] The end of the world. Jan. 17, 1847. Newspaper commentary on Francisco Anelli's painting *The Opening of the Seventh Seal; or, The End of the World,* then being shown in New Orleans.
  [137] Reply to W.A.P. Jan. 24, 1847. Poem.
* [138] For J.A.B. to Mary. Jan. 31, 1847. Poem.
* [140] Lines on the beautiful group of a poor widow and two children in Anelli's great painting *The End of the World.* Jan. 26, 1847. Poem.
* [141] Suggested by seeing a bird fluttering in its cage. Feb. 7, 1847. Poem.
* [142] On seeing the beautiful painting from Anelli of Gulnare releasing Conrad from prison. Mar. 21, 1847. Poem.
* [144] Untitled. Apr. 4, 1847. Poem on a rose bud.
* [145] Reply to Celebs. June 26, 1847. Poem.
* [145] A story. N.d. On meeting a man while horseback riding.
* [148] Financial accounts.

DIARY, 1845.

The 1845 diary is the same size, format, and color as the 1844 diary. The title page reads, "Stewart's / Diary, / for / 1845: / or / Daily Register, / for the use of / Private Families / and / Persons of Business: / containing / a Blank for Every Day in the Year, for the Record / of Interesting Daily Occurrences / and Future Engagements." It was published by Samuel M. Stewart of New Orleans and Hymen L. Lipman of Philadelphia. Edwards emended the title page with her own inscription: "Cant [be] Stewart's 'tis Mads."

["LIFE"], *NATIVE AMERICAN,* AUG. 20, 1845, p. 1.

The only surviving published Edwards essay. It is a slightly modified version of the undated essay "Life," on pages 32–34 of Writing Book 1.

EIGHT LETTERS TO CHARLES W. BRADBURY, 1846–47.

Notes

Abbreviations

AC	*Daily Alta California*
BL	Bancroft Library, University of California, Berkeley
BP	Charles W. Bradbury Papers, University of North Carolina at Chapel Hill
CWB	Charles W. Bradbury
D44	MSE Diary, 1844, in BP
D45	MSE Diary, 1845, in BP
DLB	Conrad, ed., *Dictionary of Louisiana Biography*
DP	*Daily Picayune*
HNOC	Historic New Orleans Collection
LSM/CF	Louisiana State Museum, Cemetery Inscription File
MDAH	Mississippi Division of Archives and History
MSE	Madaline Selima Edwards
NOCB	Conveyance Books, Orleans Parish, New Orleans City Hall
NONA	New Orleans Notarial Archives, New Orleans City Hall
NOPL	New Orleans Public Library
OPDC	Orleans Parish, First District Court records, 1846–54, in NOPL
OPSB	Orleans Parish, School Board, Second Municipality, Minutes, June 3, 1843–Sept. 4, 1847, University of New Orleans Library
Riddell	John Leonard Riddell Diaries, vols. 17–18, in TUL
SFHR	San Francisco History Room, San Francisco Public Library
Tower	Luther F. Tower Diaries, 1845–46, Louisiana State University
TUL	Tulane University, Howard-Tilton Memorial Library
WB1	MSE Writing Book 1, 1843–44, in BP
WB2	MSE Writing Book 2, 1844–47, in BP

Preface

1. MSE to CWB, Apr. 25, 1847.

2. When CWB died, his bank safe-deposit box contained only an insurance policy and "an old newspaper," and he left "no surviving wife" or other heirs. Orleans Parish, Louisiana, Second District Court, Succession Records, 1846–80, no. 42088, microfilm, NOPL.

3. All Edwards's and Bradbury's extant writings are contained in BP. Except for D44, D45, WB1, and WB2, all the writings are unbound documents stored in chronological order.

Introduction

1. WB1: 30, 53*; WB2: 87*. (References to MSE's writings not included in this volume are marked with an asterisk.)

2. Nina Baym, *Novels, Readers, and Reviewers: Responses to Fiction in Antebellum America* (Ithaca, N.Y.: Cornell University Press, 1984), 72–76, 80–81.

3. Marshall Sahlins, *Historical Myths and Mythical Realities: Structure in the Early History of the Sandwich Islands Kingdom* (Ann Arbor: University of Michigan Press, 1981), 67–72; idem, *Islands of History* (Chicago: University of Chicago Press, 1985), 136–56. Social scientists sometimes use the terms *structure* and *agency* to denote the dichotomy of context and human action, and refer to the entire reciprocal process of structure guiding agency and agency reshaping structure as *structuration.* See Anthony Giddens, "Time, Space and Regionalisation," in *Social Relations and Spatial Structures,* ed. Derek Gregory and John Urry (London: Macmillan, 1985), 265–95; and idem, *A Contemporary Critique of Historical Materialism,* vol. 1 (Berkeley: University of California Press, 1981), 26–29. For an archaeologist's view of agency, see Ian Hodder, *Reading the Past: Current Approaches to Interpretation in Archaeology,* 2d ed. (Cambridge: Cambridge University Press, 1991), 156–66.

4. On the expansion of historians' social vision, see Lawrence W. Levine, "Clio, Canons, and Culture," *Journal of American History* 80, no. 3 (Dec. 1993): 849–67.

5. WB2: 92. On her weight, see MSE to CWB, Nov. 15, 1846.

6. Biographical details of MSE's life before 1843 were pieced together from her own writings, as well as from Jeannette Tillotson Acklen, comp., *Tennes-*

see Records: Tombstone Inscriptions and Manuscripts Historical and Biographical (Nashville: Cullom and Ghertner, 1933), 98, 137–38, 428; Jay Guy Cisco, *Historic Sumner County, Tennessee, with Genealogies of the Bledsoe, Cage, and Douglass Families, and Genealogical Notes of Other Sumner County Families* (1909; Nashville: Charles Elder, 1971), 191–95; Silas Emmett Lucas Jr., ed., *Marriages from Early Tennessee Newspapers, 1794–1851* (Easley, S.C.: Southern Historical Publications, 1978), 69; Silas Emmett Lucas Jr. and Ella Lee Sheffield, eds., *35,000 Tennessee Marriage Records and Bonds, 1783–1870*, 3 vols. (Easley, S.C.: Southern Historical Publications, 1981), 1:275, 413; Joyce Martin Murray, *Sumner County, Tennessee, Deed Abstracts, 1793–1805* (Wolfe City, Tex.: Henington Publishing Co., 1988); and Edythe Rucker Whitley, comp., *Marriages of Sumner County, Tennessee, 1787–1838* (Baltimore: Genealogical Publishing Co., 1981), 10. MSE's older brother is not included in Cisco's sketchy Cage genealogy, but MSE wrote explicitly that in her fourteenth year "I was called to the death bed of a brother who had just attained the age of manhood" (Cisco, *Historic Sumner County* 195; "Music," WB2: 86*). MSE was known as Selima at least until she was married, and she changed her surname several times. For clarity, she will be referred to as Madaline Edwards throughout the Introduction.

7. In addition to the sources cited in the previous note, see Walter T. Durham, *The Great Leap Westward: A History of Sumner County, Tennessee, from Its Beginnings to 1805* (Gallatin, Tenn.: Sumner County Public Library, 1969), 38, 75, 80; and idem, *Old Sumner: A History of Sumner County, Tennessee, from 1805 to 1861* (Gallatin, Tenn.: Sumner County Public Library, 1972), 37–38, 94, 108, 111.

8. WB1: 96*; WB2: 32*; WB1: 9*; "Music," WB2: 86*.

9. D44: Aug. 8; WB2: 1; D44: Mar. 13.

10. WB1: 67; MSE to CWB, Apr. 9, 1847; D45: Feb. 9.

11. D44: Jan. 2; WB1: 141; United States Census, Mobile County, Alabama, 1840, microfilm, p. 143, MDAH.

12. WB1: 137. Mississippi kept no vital records until the twentieth century, so there is no way to establish exact birth or death dates for any of the children.

13. All quotations in this and the following paragraphs derive from "A Tale of Real Life." (See chapter 4.)

14. On divorce, see Jane Turner Censer, " 'Smiling Through Her Tears': Ante-Bellum Southern Women and Divorce," *American Journal of Legal His-*

tory 25, no. 1 (Jan. 1981): 24–47; Suzanne Lebsock, *The Free Women of Peters-burg: Status and Culture in a Southern Town, 1784–1860* (New York: Norton, 1984), 68–72; and Victoria E. Bynum, *Unruly Women: The Politics of Social and Sexual Control in the Old South* (Chapel Hill: University of North Carolina Press, 1992), 63–76.

15. Recall that Dempsey Elliott had lived next door in 1840. MSE never mentioned this, or him, in connection with her visits to Mobile.

16. D45: May 5; CWB to MSE, Mar. 9, 1847. See also WB1: 3.

17. WB1: 126.

18. Cathy N. Davidson, *Revolution and the Word: The Rise of the Novel in America* (New York: Oxford University Press, 1986), 117–22; Bynum, *Unruly Women* 44; Jane H. Pease and William H. Pease, *Ladies, Women, and Wenches: Choice and Constraint in Antebellum Charleston and Boston* (Chapel Hill: University of North Carolina Press, 1990), 10–11; Michael Grossberg, *Governing the Hearth: Law and the Family in Nineteenth-Century America* (Chapel Hill: University of North Carolina Press, 1985), 300–301; Mary Kelley, *Private Woman, Public Stage: Literary Domesticity in Nineteenth-Century America* (New York: Oxford University Press, 1984), 34, 145; Lebsock, *Free Women of Petersburg* 112; Elizabeth Fox-Genovese, *Within the Plantation Household: Black and White Women of the Old South* (Chapel Hill: University of North Carolina Press, 1988), 256.

19. This was the argument of "Walker on Women," a book that MSE read: Alexander Walker, *Woman Physiologically Considered, as to Mind, Morals, Marriage, Matrimonial Slavery, Infidelity and Divorce* (New York, 1843), 25–26.

20. Lebsock, *Free Women of Petersburg* 97–98; Christine Stansell, *City of Women: Sex and Class in New York, 1789–1860* (Urbana: University of Illinois Press, 1987), 11–18. The school district's rule 2 of 1843 "stated that teachers were to hold their stations at the pleasure of the Board of Directors; and superior qualifications in reference to moral character, literary attainments, industry, and practical skills were required for their appointment and continuance in office" (Alma Hobbs Peterson, "The Administration of Public Schools in New Orleans, 1841–1861," Ph.D. diss., Louisiana State University, 1964, pp. 54, 62).

21. Lebsock, *Free Women of Petersburg* 22–27; Stansell, *City of Women* 11–18, 71–73, 111–12; D45: July 31.

22. Accounts of income and expenses in the back of D45; Peterson, "Administration of Public Schools" 70.

23. OPDC, case 8573.

24. MSE to CWB, Oct. 9, 1843; D44: Nov. 4.

25. CWB to MSE, Mar. 9, 1847. The "other proposition" was never specified.

26. MSE to CWB, Apr. 9, 1847.

27. Ibid.

28. D44: June 10; D45: Mar. 18, Jan. 6; D44: May 18; CWB to MSE, Mar. 9, 1847.

29. D44: Nov. 25; D45: Feb. 2; D44: Aug. 18, May 30.

30. United States Census for New Orleans, 1840, p. 129, MDAH; United States Census for New Orleans, 1850, p. 268, NOPL; *DP,* Feb. 9, 1876, 4:5; LSM/CF, Girod Street Cemetery; NONA; NOCB 34:53, 35:124, 427; city directories.

31. BP; NOCB 29:659; *New Orleans Commercial Bulletin,* Nov. 13, 1871, 1:1.

32. Karlem Riess, *John Leonard Riddell, Scientist-Inventor; Melter and Refiner of the New Orleans Mint, 1839–1848; Postmaster of New Orleans, 1859–1862* (New Orleans: Louisiana Heritage Press, 1977); *DLB* 659; Tower, Jan. 16, 1845; NOCB, vols. 31–42; Early Assessment Records of New Orleans, 1836–47: Second Municipality Roll, 1843, microfilm, NOPL; Riddell, vol. 18, Jun. 18, 1846; city directories.

33. CWB's obituary suggested that he was born in 1815, but a letter from his brother, discussed below, implied that he was born no earlier than 1816. I have assembled CWB's biography from the following sources: BP; Andrew B. Booth, comp., *Records of Louisiana Confederate Soldiers and Louisiana Confederate Commands,* 3 vols. 1902; Spartanburg, S.C.: Reprint Co., 1984), 2:80; Harvey Hall, *The Cincinnati Directory for 1825* (Cincinnati: Samuel J. Browne, 1825); C. S. Williams, *Williams' Cincinnati Directory, City Guide and Business Mirror; or, Cincinnati in 1856* (Cincinnati: C. W. Williams, 1856); New Orleans city directories; United States Census for New Orleans, 1860, NOPL (Bradbury's only appearance in the United States Census, although he lived in the same house for thirty-nine years).

34. Cornelius S. Bradbury, Cincinnati, to CWB, New Orleans, Feb. 24, 1836; James W. Breedlove to CWB, June 6, 1838, and Nov. 9, 1838, all in BP. All the Bradbury family letters cited are in BP.

35. NOCB, vols. 28–45; BP; city directories; Orleans Parish, Louisiana, Second District Court, Succession Records, 1846–80, no. 42088, microfilm, NOPL. Sources reporting to the credit agency R. G. Dun and Company wrote in 1854 that "it is not known that he has any means" and dismissed the pro-

spective partners of his second cottonseed-oil factory as men of even less consequence. Louisiana 11:269, R. G. Dun and Company Collection, Baker Library,
Graduate School of Business Administration, Harvard University.

36. CWB, New Orleans, to Mrs. Sarah Bradbury, Cincinnati, Nov. 7, 1835.

37. Marcus J. C. Bradbury, Madison, Ind., to CWB, New Orleans, Feb. 15,
1836.

38. Cornelius S. Bradbury, Cincinnati, to CWB, New Orleans, May 15, 1836.
See also First Congregational Church, New Orleans, Marriage Records, 1834–
47, microfilm LN60, 1:77, NOPL. Mary Ann Bradbury had two children, but
they are not mentioned in CWB's or MSE's surviving writings. There is some
evidence that CWB expected his wife to die young and to leave him her money.
A letter from Mary Ann to CWB implies that she was a chronic invalid, and
MSE raised the possibility of her early death several times. Mary Ann was
still alive when the 1860 census was taken, although she disappeared from the
records after that. There is no New Orleans death certificate for her, and when
CWB died on June 22, 1880, he left no surviving wife. Death Certificates,
Orleans Parish, 76:1061 (June 22, 1880), NOPL.

39. Cornelius S. Bradbury, Cincinnati, to CWB, New Orleans, May 15, 1836.

40. D44: June 25, Oct. 2, Dec. 26, Dec. 9.

41. Henry J. Leovy, *The Laws and General Ordinances of the City of New
Orleans,* rev. ed. (New Orleans: E. C. Wharton, 1857), 376; Mary P. Ryan,
Women in Public: Between Banners and Ballots, 1825–1880 (Baltimore: Johns
Hopkins University Press, 1990), 107–8; Judith K. Schafer, " 'Open and Notorious Concubinage': The Emancipation of Slave Mistresses by Will and the
Supreme Court in Antebellum Louisiana," *Louisiana History* 28, no. 2 (Fall
1987): 165–82. Although the term *Creole* has acquired racial connotations in
twentieth-century Louisiana, in nineteenth-century Louisiana usage it meant
only "a native of," as in "creole de Saint-Domingue" or "creole de la Louisi-
anne," but it implied a French speaker. Similarly, "American" strictly meant
someone from the United States north and east of Louisiana, but it implied an
English speaker.

42. Boze, "Nouvelles Diverses," Sept. 26, 1839, Mar. 25, 1831, Apr. 27, 1832,
May 31, 1832; "Suite au Bulletin," Mar. 28, 1836, all in Henri de Ste. Gême
Papers, HNOC; Schafer, " 'Open and Notorious Concubinage.' " According
to Boze, Macarty "n'a pas meme lainé un picaillon a Ces Enfans naturels du
premier lit" ("Nouvelles Diverses," May 31, 1832).

43. Petition to Mayor Nicholas Girod, Mar. 17, 1817, John Minor and Bonnie Matthews Wisdom Collection, TUL; *Ordinances Ordained and Established by the Mayor & City Council of the City of New Orleans* (New Orleans: J. C. de St. Romes, 1817), 6; *Journal de la Première Municipalité* (New Orleans, n.d.), 1, Favrot Collection, TUL; Leovy, *Laws and General Ordinances* 142; Ryan, *Women in Public* 107–9.

44. Craig and Stanley to Budington, Nov. 2, 1843, NOCB B12:394; Budington to J. A. Bradbury, Dec. 27, 1843, BP; OPDC, case 8573; D44: Dec. 28; D45: Mar. 6, Mar. 21, Mar. 24 (the birth), Mar. 29, Apr. 2, Apr. 3, Apr. 5.

45. Riess, *John Leonard Riddell* 29, 39, 51; *DLB* 659; Riddell, vol. 17 (Dec. 2, 1844, May 26, 1845), vol. 18 (June 18, 1846 [quote], May 17, 1847); LSM/CF, Girod Street Cemetery.

46. D45: May 21.

47. Albert E. Fossier, *New Orleans, the Glamor Period, 1800–1840: A History of the Conflicts of Nationalities, Languages, Religions, Morals, Cultures, Laws, Politics, and Economics During the Formative Period of New Orleans* (New Orleans: Pelican, 1957), 391; LSM/CF, Girod Street Cemetery; *DLB* 108; Dun and Company Collection, Louisiana 9:90.

48. *DLB* 108; WB2: 76; D45: Nov. 25. M was MSE's newspaper pen name. Also: "Mrs B[reedlove] and judge C called on me today. If I should live to see this day twelve months I wonder if they will be my friends" (D45: Nov. 29).

49. D45: Nov. 26; MSE to CWB, Nov. 15, 1846.

50. OPSB 235; MSE to CWB, Nov. 15, 1846. The Second Municipality included that part of the city upriver from Canal Street. New Orleans's free public school system had been established in 1841. The Marshall School, a boys' grammar school, was on St. Mary Street between Girod and Julia streets. *Cohen's New Orleans Directory . . . for 1853* (New Orleans: Daily Delta, 1852), 315.

51. OPSB 256–57; MSE to CWB, Apr. 9, 1847.

52. CWB to MSE, Mar. 9, 1847; MSE to CWB, Apr. 9, 1847; OPSB 256–57.

53. MSE to CWB, Apr. 9, 1847.

54. D44: July 8, May 27; D45: Mar. 21.

55. MSE to CWB, ca. Sept. 1843.

56. Ibid., MSE to CWB, Oct. 12, 1843. A reference to one gift of flowers can be found in D45: Jan. 28.

57. D44: July 27, Oct. 22, Aug. 3.

58. D45: Mar. 31, June 16; "Domestic Happiness," WB2: 10–17.

59. D44: Apr. 17; Walker, *Woman Physiologically Considered* 3–11. Walker's point was also made by Sarah Stickney Ellis, whose *Poetry of Life* was a favorite book of MSE's. "From the peculiar nature and tendency of woman's character, love and grief may be said to constitute the chief elements of her existence." But Ellis believed that "she is preserved from the overwhelming influence of grief, so frequently recurring, by the reaction of her own buoyant and vivacious spirit, by the fertility of her imagination in multiplying means of happiness, and by her facility in adapting her self to place and time. . . . , happily for woman, her internal resources are such as to raise her at least to a level with man in the scale of happiness." Sarah Stickney [Ellis], *The Poetry of Life* (Philadelphia: Carey, Lea and Blanchard, 1835), 2:46–47.

60. "Departure," WB1: 57*; D45: Jan. 31.

61. This paragraph benefited from an observation of Zeynep Kezer's.

62. MSE to CWB, ca. Sept. 1843; D45: Jan. 10, July 17, July 22, June 25.

63. D45: Apr. 11; D44: Aug. 15; MSE to CWB, Apr. 25, 1847; D44: Aug. 8.

64. "Woman," WB1: 41–45.

65. "Man," WB1: 50–52.

66. WB1: 3, 2, 41; WB2: 6.

67. My account of Clapp's career is based on Theodore Clapp, *Autobiographical Sketches and Recollections, During a Thirty-five Years' Residence in New Orleans* (Boston: Phillips, Sampson and Co., 1857); *Cohen's New Orleans Directory . . . for 1854* (New Orleans: Daily Delta, 1853), vii–viii; J. R. Hutchinson, *Reminiscences, Sketches, and Addresses Selected from My Papers During a Ministry of Forty-five Years in Mississippi, Louisiana, and Texas* (Houston: E. H. Cushing, 1874), 169; Eliza Ripley, *Social Life in Old New Orleans: Being Recollections of My Girlhood* (New York: Appleton, 1912), 120–24; John Duffy, ed., *Parson Clapp of the Strangers' Church in New Orleans* (Baton Rouge: Louisiana State University Press, 1957); Timothy F. Reilly, "Parson Clapp of New Orleans: Antebellum Social Critic, Religious Radical, and Member of the Establishment," *Louisiana History* 16, no. 2 (Spring 1975): 167–91; idem, "Religious Leaders and Social Criticism in New Orleans," Ph.D. diss., University of Missouri, 1972, pp. 106–39; John F. C. Waldo, *Historical Sketch of the First Unitarian Church of New Orleans, La.* ([New Orleans: First Unitarian Church], 1907); and Samuel Wilson Jr., *The First Presbyterian Church of New Orleans: Its Buildings and Its Ministers* (New Orleans: Louisiana Landmarks Society, 1988), 13–17. The church building where MSE worshiped stood on St. Charles Avenue near Gravier Street. It was built in 1819 and burned in 1851.

68. Clapp, *Autobiographical Sketches* 251; Ripley, *Social Life* 120–21; Tower, Apr. 27, 1845, May 4, 1845; D45: Apr. 6. Tower's first comment referred to a sermon that MSE thought was "most edifying."

69. Reilly, "Religious Leaders" 108, 124–32; idem, "Parson Clapp" 170, 183–86.

70. Waldo, *Historical Sketch* 8; Ripley, *Social Life* 124; D45: Dec. 9.

71. Clapp, *Autobiographical Sketches* 168–73; Theodore Clapp, *Theological Views, Comprising the Substance of Teachings During a Ministry of Thirty-five Years, in New Orleans* (Boston: Abel Tompkins, 1859), 205. My summary of Clapp's theology is based on these passages and on *Autobiographical Sketches* 268–69, 290, 412, 415; and *Theological Views* 176–77, 187, 192, 195–96, 202–5, 210–11, 272, 286–87, 296–303.

72. D45: Feb. 23.

73. Constantin-François Volney, *The Law of Nature; or, Principles of Morality, Deduced from the Physical Constitution of Mankind and the Universe* (Pittsfield, Mass.: Seymour and Smith, 1807); D44: Aug. 30, Sept. 18; "Dr. Dick," WB1: 47*; Thomas Dick, *The Christian Philosopher* (1824), quoted in *Encyclopedia Britannica*, 20th century ed. (1902), s.v. "Dick, Thomas"; D44: Aug. 28; "Nature Is Religion," WB1: 106*. Clapp also described astronomy as a testimony of divine purposes (*Theological Views* 185).

74. George Combe, *The Constitution of Man Considered in Relation to External Objects* (New York: William H. Colyer, 1844), x, 307.

75. Ibid., 7; WB1: 5; "To J.A.B.," WB2: 70*; WB1: 24–25*.

76. Lebsock, *Free Women of Petersburg* 112–45; D45: Mar. 7; D44: Apr. 30, Mar. 26.

77. D44: May 6; [Robert J. Walker], *Letter of Mr. Walker, of Mississippi, Relative to the Annexation of Texas: In Reply to the Call of the People of Carroll County, Kentucky, to Communicate His Views on That Subject* (Washington, D.C.: Globe, 1844); Frederick Merk and Lois Bannister Merk, *Fruits of Propaganda in the Tyler Administration* (Cambridge, Mass.: Harvard University Press, 1971), 23–27, 98–101, 123–28.

78. D44: June 3; Combe, *Constitution of Man* 237–38.

79. Lebsock, *Free Women of Petersburg* 101–3, 141; WB2: 3; D44: June 3. An obvious exception to MSE's kindly view of African Americans is an incident of 1844: she found a black man trying to get into her yard, frightened him off, then tried to obtain a pistol in case he should return (D44: July 10, 12, 13).

80. "July 4th," WB1: 73–74.

81. Kelley, *Private Woman, Public Stage* 40–43, 57.

82. D45: Mar. 22.

83. MSE to CWB, Nov. 10, 1843.

84. "Byron," WB2: 79–80; "Tale of Real Life," WB1: 141–42.

85. MSE to CWB, Nov. 10, 1843.

86. WB1: 29.

87. D44: Oct. 5. On women writers and the authoritative male point of view, see Mary Jean Corbett, *Representing Femininity: Middle-Class Subjectivity in Victorian and Edwardian Women's Autobiographies* (New York: Oxford University Press, 1992), 90–91.

88. On the avoidance of self-exposure in nineteenth-century women's autobiography, see Corbett, *Representing Femininity* 92–98.

89. Kelley, *Private Woman, Public Stage* 125–28 (quote on 127).

90. In an 1846 list of letters at the New Orleans Post Office, there is one for a woman named M. S. Eliott (*DP*, Jan. 2, 1846, 1:4).

91. Obituary, *Wide West*, Aug. 27, 1854.

92. "Answer to W.A.P.," WB2: 108.

93. Nina Baym, *Woman's Fiction: A Guide to Novels by and about Women in America, 1820–1870*, 2d ed. (Urbana: University of Illinois Press, 1993), 33–34.

94. WB1: 137, 161.

95. Baym, *Novels, Readers* 65; Felicity A. Nussbaum, "Eighteenth-Century Women's Autobiographical Commonplaces," in *The Private Self: Theory and Practice of Women's Autobiographical Writings*, ed. Shari Benstock (Chapel Hill: University of North Carolina Press, 1988), 150; Beth Maclay Doriani, "Black Womanhood in Nineteenth-Century America: Subversion and Self-Construction in Two Women's Autobiographies," *American Quarterly* 43, no. 2 (June 1991): 204; Baym, *Woman's Fiction* 35–36.

96. Doriani, "Black Womanhood" 204–5.

97. WB1: 149; D45: July 17.

98. Nussbaum, "Commonplaces" 149.

Chapter Two: My Own Cottage Home

1. Sale by the Sheriff of the Parish of Orleans, to Charles William Bradbury of Real Estate, Sept. 6, 1853, BP.

2. WB1: 1–2. This essay is headed "Miscellaneous Subjects," and the title is evidently intended as a general one for the volume.

3. Theodore Clapp of the First Congregational Church in the City and Parish of New Orleans, popularly known as the Strangers' Church. Clapp's unitarian and universalist doctrine made a deep impression on MSE, who mentioned the pastor often and who sometimes wrote summaries of or reactions to his sermons.

4. WB1: 3–4.

5. Except as noted, MSE used "C" to refer to Bradbury and "Mr. C" to refer to Clapp throughout her writings.

6. WB1: 5–6. Clapp was expelled from the Presbyterian church for denying the doctrine of the Trinity, and it was a favorite sermon topic.

7. January 8, 1844, was the twenty-ninth anniversary of the battle of New Orleans. The "old Hero" was Andrew Jackson, who lived at the Hermitage, near Nashville, Tennessee.

8. Thomas Dick (1774–1857) was a Scots astronomer and theologian. In December 1843 New Orleans bookseller J. B. Steel advertised for sale at his Camp Street store an eight-volume edition of Dick's complete works, which included such titles as *The Christian Philosopher; or, The Connection of Science and Philosophy with Religion* (1824). *DP,* Dec. 17, 1843, 2:5.

9. This day's entry was written sideways. It is one of several in which MSE records scientific details that she learned from Dick's astronomical treatises.

10. Entered after the fact, probably when MSE felt the first movements of her child on April 25.

11. Henry Joseph Budington, a close friend of CWB and his brother James. Budington played a central role in facilitating CWB's affair with MSE, who called him, variously, Bud, B., Henry Josephus, Henry, and Josephus.

12. *DP,* Mar. 10, 1844, 2:1. Judge Benjamin C. Elliott was dismissed from office by the legislature for selling citizenship to (mostly) Irish and German immigrants. Allegedly he sold thousands of naturalizations, including 387 in one day alone. The proceedings in the state legislature were widely reported in the New Orleans papers. Despite Elliott's surname, MSE apparently had no connection to him. She was interested in the fortunes of the Whig Party, which she supported ardently. *DP,* Mar. 10, 1844, 2:1; *Bee,* Mar. 11, 1844, 1:5–7, and Mar. 14, 1844, 2:2–4. See also the entry for April 6, 1844, below.

13. The New Orleans and Carrollton Railroad, built in 1835, operated along St. Charles Avenue. It was the predecessor of the present St. Charles Avenue streetcar. Joan B. Garvey and Mary Lou Widmer, *Beautiful Crescent: A History of New Orleans* (New Orleans: Garmer Press, 1982), 86.

14. *DP,* Mar. 17, 1844, 2:5.

15. WB1: 27–29.

16. Probably Mr. A. is John B. Adams, a horticulturist whose business was located on Clio Street between Apollo and Bacchus streets, near CWB's house.

17. "Gen'l Hamilton's Letter" to the Muscogee Clay Club renounced partisanship and praised Henry Clay and Martin Van Buren while expressing Hamilton's personal preference for John C. Calhoun as president of the United States. *Bee,* Mar. 20, 1844, 1:2–3.

18. [Walker], *Letter of Mr. Walker.*

19. *The Pictorial Bible; Being the Old and New Testaments According to the Authorized Version; Illustrated with More Than One Thousand Engravings, Representing the Historical Events, After Celebrated Pictures; the Landscape Scenes, from Original Drawings, or from Authentic Engravings; and the Subjects of Natural History, Costume, and Antiquities, from the Best Sources,* 2 vols. (New York: J. S. Redfield, 1843–44). Like many such works, the *Pictorial Bible* was sold in individual fascicles before it was published in bound volumes.

20. Astronomer Wilhelm Olbers (1758–1840) discovered the asteroids Pallas and Vesta. *Encyclopedia Britannica,* 15th ed., *Micropaedia,* s.v. "Olbers, (Heinrich) Wilhelm (Matthäus)."

21. Dr. James Ritchie was MSE's principal physician.

22. WB1: 35.

23. MSE's scrapbook, begun at the same time as her diaries and writing books, has not survived.

24. Old Style date; April 13 by the current calendar.

25. Sayre, whose first name and occupation I have not been able to discover, became one of MSE's most persistent suitors.

26. See "The Impeachment—the Result," *Bee,* Apr. 8, 1844, 1:2.

27. This might be any of several Cage relatives.

28. Walker, *Women Physiologically Considered.*

29. Gormley's Canal terminated in a basin on the north side of MSE's block.

30. The Jewish Cemetery was at Jackson Avenue and Saratoga Street, a few blocks from MSE's house.

31. George Combe's *Constitution of Man Considered in Relation to External Objects* was a work of phrenology based in Enlightenment theology and Scottish moral philosophy.

32. MSE's first notation of her apparent pregnancy.

33. WB1: 41–45.

34. Frederika Bremer, *New Sketches of Every-Day Life: A Diary Together with Strife and Peace*, trans. Mary Howitt (New York: Harper, 1844).

35. Martin Van Buren, *Letter of Mr. Van Buren: Texas* (Columbus, Ohio, 1844).

36. CWB was twenty-eight or twenty-nine years old.

37. WB1: 49.

38. The raccoon was a symbol of the Whig Party, and particularly of Henry Clay, called "The Old Coon" or "The Same Old Coon," references to his unswerving Whig principles. The cock was a derogatory emblem of the Loco Foco wing of the Democratic Party. Images of raccoons attacking roosters were popular during the 1844 presidential campaign. See Roger A. Fisher, *Tippecanoe and Trinkets Too: The Material Culture of American Presidential Campaigns, 1828–1984* (Urbana: University of Illinois Press, 1988), 55; Edmund B. Sullivan, *Collecting Political Americana* (Hanover, Mass.: Christopher Publishing House, 1991), 129–31; and Robert Gray Gunderson, *The Log Cabin Campaign* (Lexington: University Press of Kentucky, 1957), 130.

39. Bremer, *Sketches of Every-Day Life*.

40. A bar was a mosquito net suspended around a bed.

41. The last word is unclear. Dulcinea del Taboso was Don Quixote's beloved.

42. CWB was preparing for a lengthy trip to the North.

43. An unidentified Cage.

44. The fire began in a carpenter's shop at the corner of Franklin and Jackson streets near the present location of Charity Hospital and burned nearly everything in a ten-square-block area. "Disastrous Conflagration," *DP*, May 19, 1844, 2:3–4.

45. WB1: 50–52.

46. MSE refers to the notarial act, the document recording the property's description and title under New Orleans's French-based land-transfer system.

47. MSE uses this in the southern sense, to mean afternoon.

Chapter Three: A Cup of Sorrow

1. Frederika Bremer, *The Comforter* (Boston: Reading and Co., 1844).

2. I have been unable to locate any such publication.

3. WB1: 57–58.

4. WB1: 62–69.

5. Slightly misquoted: "Ye stars! which are the poetry of Heaven! . . . , ye are / A beauty and a mystery" (*Childe Harold,* canto 3, st. 88).

6. Like many of his parishioners, Clapp left town during the summer. Church services were suspended.

7. CWB's brother James Anson Bradbury.

8. WB1: 73–74.

9. A married man named Bond enticed Catherine O'Brien, a young woman with whom he was in love but who was engaged to another man, to accompany him on a carriage ride along the New Shell Road toward Lake Pontchartrain. During the ride he shot O'Brien dead. Bond escaped but was found in the woods near the scene of the murder, dead by his own hand. "Most Shocking Tragedy," *DP,* July 6, 1844, 2:3; "Suicide Added to Murder," *DP,* July 7, 1844, 2:2.

10. To Combe, moral, physical, and organic laws operate in entirely different spheres. Where evil results from the operation of physical or organic laws, he argues, it is always outweighed by the good they do. We would not want them not to exist. For example, a roofer who broke an arm falling off a roof would realize on reflection that he would be even worse off without the gravity that caused him to fall. Combe's argument also implies that accident or illness cannot be thought of as divine punishment for moral transgression.

11. The Firemen's Cemetery, also known as Cypress Grove, was established in 1840 beyond the northern edge of the city. It was New Orleans's first rural cemetery.

12. [Ellis], *Poetry of Life.*

13. See Thomas Bender, "The 'Rural' Cemetery Movement: Urban Travail and the Appeal of Nature," in *Material Life in America, 1600–1860,* ed. Robert B. St. George (Boston: Northeastern University Press, 1988), 505–18; David Schuyler, "The Evolution of the Anglo-American Rural Cemetery: Landscape Architecture as Social and Cultural History," *Journal of Garden History* 4, no. 3 (Sept. 1984): 303: David Charles Sloane, *The Last Great Necessity: Cemeteries in American History* (Baltimore: Johns Hopkins University Press, 1991), 76.

14. WB1: 85–90.

15. Frederika Bremer, *The Neighbours: A Story of Every-Day Life,* 2 vols. (New York: Harper and Bros., 1843).

16. A cannon was fired on the Place d'Armes each summer evening at 9:15 to mark the slaves' curfew.

17. Probably John Adams's horticultural garden, near CWB's house.

18. WB1: 122–27.

19. Constantin-François Volney (1757–1820) was a French philosophe who immigrated to Philadelphia in the late eighteenth century. His principal work was *The Law of Nature; or, Principles of Morality, Deduced from the Physical Constitution of Mankind and the Universe* (1807).

20. WB1: 133–35.

21. This is "A Tale of Real Life," which was dated September 12 when it was completed. See chapter 4.

Chapter Four: A Tale of Real Life

1. WB1: 136–62.

2. Dempsey Elliott, MSE's first husband.

3. MSE married Elliott in Sumner County, Tennessee, on January 2, 1831.

4. MSE provided no name for this child anywhere in her writings, and although she recorded her children's birth and death dates, she did not give the years of their births. This son was born in Clinton, Mississippi, on September 17, in 1831 or 1832. He died there on July 6, three years later.

5. Mary Jane Elliott was born in Clinton on March 5, 1833 or 1834, and died on July 12, 1834 or 1835.

6. William Elliott was born in Clinton on March 1, 1836, and died there on September 17 of the same year.

7. Isabella (or Isabel) Elliott was born in New Orleans on April 8, 1837, and died there in the winter of 1838–39.

8. This is a reference to George Combe's *Constitution of Man*, which MSE had just read.

9. Correctly quoted from Thomas Moore's poem "Come, Rest in This Bosom."

10. A river in central Louisiana. "Red River" in this story probably refers to the area around Alexandria, Louisiana.

11. In 1840 Texas was an independent republic.

12. Sarah Stickney Ellis, a popular English novelist and essayist. MSE had just read her *Poetry of Life.*

Chapter Six: Confinement Near at Hand

1. The blank book was WB2.

2. Attorneys Randall and T. G. Hunt practiced at 12 Exchange Place.

3. All Saints' Day was and still is a major Roman Catholic feast day in New Orleans. In Edwards's era, processions moved to the Catholic cemeteries, where crowds of strollers and onlookers joined them to maintain and decorate graves and to hear religious services.

4. *Bee,* Nov. 4, 1844, 1:4. See also "Grand Whig Torch Light Procession. For Saturday Evening, November 2, 1844," *Bee,* Nov. 2, 1844, 1:6.

5. WB2: 10–17.

6. John Leonard Riddell (1807–65), a chemist and official of the United States Mint, owned property in many parts of New Orleans. In 1844 he lived in the Mint. (See entry for November 9, 1844, below.)

7. An unidentified Cage relative.

8. WB2: 20–23.

9. The "humble tenements" were *fours,* or oven tombs, coffin-sized niches built into the walls of New Orleans cemeteries in ranks four or five rows high and rented for a modest fee to those who could not afford to build tombs.

10. Adelle was Henry J. Budington's lover. On March 24, 1845, she bore his child at MSE's house.

Chapter Seven: Wishes and Desires

1. WB2: 1–8.

2. This sentence appears to have been written later, since the ink is conspicuously darker and the line weight heavier than in the remainder of the testament.

Chapter Eight: Disappointments

1. New Year's Day visiting was a custom in many antebellum American cities. In mid-nineteenth-century New Orleans, men usually visited while women remained at home to receive visits.

2. The lower market, on the levee in the Vieux Carré, included the structure now known as the French Market. It was New Orleans's first and principal public market.

3. January 8, 1845, was the thirtieth anniversary of the battle of New Orleans.

4. MSE kept a school at her house from time to time.

5. Probably *Brother Jonathan,* a semiannual pictorial sheet published in New York at Christmas/New Year and the Fourth of July (1839–60).

6. Le Jardin du Rocher du Ste. Hélène was the city's largest and most popular flower garden in the mid-1840s. It was located at the junction of Miro and Galvez streets and the Carondelet Canal, behind the French Quarter. Roulhac Toledano and Mary Louise Christovich, *New Orleans Architecture,* vol. 6, *Faubourg Tremé and the Bayou Road* (Gretna, La.: Pelican, 1980), 46.

7. WB2: 26.

8. Tower, Jan. 26, 1845.

9. Emanuel Swedenborg (1688–1772) was a Swedish scientist, philosopher, and theologian whose followers organized the Church of the New Jerusalem after his death. Swedenborg's interests in astronomy, rational religion, and the correspondence between the natural, moral, and spiritual worlds, as well as his antitrinitarianism and his advocacy of a kind of universalist theory of sin and redemption would all have attracted MSE.

10. CWB's family lived in Cincinnati.

11. The circus was in the former Carrollton Railroad depot at Poydras and Baronne (Bacchus) streets. Benjamin Moore Norman, *Norman's New Orleans and Environs: Containing a Brief Historical Sketch of the Territory and State of Louisiana, and the City of New Orleans, from the Earliest Period to the Present Time . . . .* (New Orleans: B. M. Norman, 1845), 180.

12. Tower, Feb. 22, 1845.

13. A popular literary magazine, early on associated with Romantic writers, published in Edinburgh beginning in 1817.

14. Benjamin West's *Death on the Pale Horse* (1817) was sent on a two-year tour of America in 1829–31 by the artist's son, and another in 1835–37 after it was purchased by the Pennsylvania Academy of Fine Arts in Philadelphia (where it remains on display). MSE apparently saw it on another, unrecorded fund-raising tour on behalf of the Pennsylvania Academy. See Helmut von Erffa and Allen Staley, *The Paintings of Benjamin West* (New Haven, Conn.: Yale University Press, 1986), 150–52, 388–92. "West's great painting" was displayed in New Orleans in the Poydras Street Methodist Church, beginning on February 20, 1845, where it could be seen for an admission fee of twenty-five cents (*DP,* Feb. 20, 1845, 2:5, and Feb. 21, 1845, 2:6). Itinerant paintings

were commonly exhibited in churches, where they were considered part of the institutions' moral instruction.

15. The French Theater was the popular name for the Théâtre d'Orléans, built on Orleans Street between Royale and Bourbon in 1817. Performances were given in French. Another part of the complex, the Salle d'Orléans, which still stands, was the site of the most famous of the city's quadroon balls.

16. Cage's Bend, Tennessee, where MSE grew up, was a "hot bed of western Methodism," and she was probably raised a Methodist. Durham, *Great Leap Westward* 157.

17. This woman was probably the model for Sarah K. of "A Tale of Real Life."

18. Tower, Apr. 27, 1845.

19. St. Mary's Market, between New Levee and Tchoupitoulas streets in the Faubourg St. Mary, was the public market nearest to MSE's house.

20. MSE often visited the National Gallery of Paintings.

21. Sarah Stickney Ellis, *Look to the End; or, The Bennets Abroad* (New York: Harper, 1845). See the entries for May 20 and 24, 1845, below.

22. Norman, *Norman's New Orleans* 169–72.

23. Baym, *Novels, Readers* 82–89; Peter Collins, *Changing Ideals in Modern Architecture, 1750–1950* (London: Faber, 1965).

24. WB2: 49–51. Written for the *Native American.*

25. Flavius Josephus, the ancient Jewish historian.

26. This line was added later by MSE.

27. An *X* was marked through this paragraph, along with the notation "a mistake."

28. This blank book has not survived.

29. On June 16, 1845, some residents of St. Bernard Parish (adjacent to New Orleans on the downriver side) "who had made a living by hauling sugar to the city in ox-carts" rioted in opposition to the construction of the Mexican Gulf Railroad, which crossed their property and would have deprived them of their hauling business. The Native American Artillery was dispatched to St. Bernard along with other militia units to quell the uprising. "Almost an Emeute," *DP,* June 18, 1845, 2:1 (quote); "Disturbance on the Mexican Gulf Rail Road," *Bee,* June 18, 1845, 1:4.

30. *DP,* June 20, 1845, 2:2. The banner was presented on behalf of "the ladies of New Orleans" by Mrs. T. B. Winston. "Presentation of the Flag," *DP,* June 22, 1845, 2:6.

31. Tower, June 22, 1845.

32. *DP*, June 28, 1845, 2:3. It was common to commemorate the death of a national hero with a funeral procession complete with an empty hearse. Another such memorial ceremony was held in New Orleans in 1850 to honor Henry Clay, John C. Calhoun, and Daniel Webster.

33. WB2: 62.

34. Hans Christian Andersen, *The Improvisatore; or, Life in Italy*, trans. Mary Howitt (London, 1845).

Chapter Nine: Feelings, Purposes, and Hopes

1. *Native American*, Aug. 20, 1845, p. 1.

2. Stone's Infirmary was the Maison de Santé, a private hospital built on upper Canal Street in 1839.

3. WB2: 76. "Mary" was Maria Breedlove.

4. JB was James Waller Breedlove, whose attentions precipitated CWB's final break with MSE.

5. WB2: 79–80.

6. Possibly *Stranger of the Valley; or, Louisa and Adelaide, an American Tale, by a Lady* (New York, 1825).

7. See, for example, "Babyphobia," *DP*, June 18, 1845, 1:6–2:1.

8. WB2: 85–86. Probably for the *Native American*.

9. WB2: 91–93. Probably for the *Native American*.

10. Marginal note: "this should be 2nd" [after the next stanza?].

11. WB2: 94.

12. WB2: 103–4.

13. WB2: 108. Probably for the *Native American*.

14. WB2: 109.

15. The Crescent City; that is, New Orleans.

16. WB2: 117.

17. Ibid.

18. WB2: 128.

Chapter Ten: The School of Experience

1. OPSB 227 (Sept. 5, 1846).

2. OPSB 236–37 (Oct. 5, 1846).

3. *Hippoed* means given to overblown self-delusion; its connotation was similar to the current *hype*. Clapp recounts this illness in his autobiography: "During this time I was unable to close my eyes, and had abandoned even the hope of recovery. One night I said to Mrs. Clapp, 'I am dying.' She thought so too" (*Autobiographical Sketches* 284).

4. John Coffee Hays (1817–83), MSE's first cousin, was a Texas Ranger, a U.S. government surveyor, and later sheriff of San Francisco.

5. OPSB 256.

6. WB2: 137–38. Probably for the *Native American*.

7. OPSB 257.

8. Draft letter.

9. Between 1837 and 1852 New Orleans was divided into three municipalities, or quasiautonomous subdivisions. The Third Municipality was downriver, at the far end of the city from Edwards's house and from the Second Municipality, where she had taught. The implication, therefore, was that she might find a job where her story was not known.

10. Merrill was principal of the Marshall School, where MSE taught.

11. Bradbury added this paragraph, which he wrote in a smaller hand, before he sent the letter.

12. The message told MSE that she had been fired from the Marshall School.

13. A draft letter exists as well.

14. A draft letter exists, as well as a partial draft that says, "I had hoped that you would not again urge on me the necessity of replying to your questions with regard to the House and lot."

15. MSE was keeping a boarding school at her house.

Afterword: Fortune's Hill

1. Sale by the Sheriff of the Parish of Orleans to Charles W. Bradbury of Real Estate, Sept. 6, 1853, BP; OPDC, case 4219, Nov. 12, 1849; Sale by the Sheriff of the Parish of Jefferson to Charles W. Bradbury of New Orleans, Aug. 18, 1852, NOCB, bk. D, fol. 8, copy in BP.

2. The foreclosure and Edwards's countersuit are documented in OPDC, cases 4219 and 8573; Sale by the Sheriff of the Parish of Jefferson to Charles W. Bradbury of New Orleans, Aug. 18, 1852, NOCB, bk. D, fol. 8, copy in BP;

and Sale by the Sheriff of the Parish of Orleans to Charles W. Bradbury of Real Estate, Sept. 6, 1853, BP.

3. At the time of the foreclosure Edwards's house was occupied by her tenant, Henry Judson, a partner in Judson and Witter, commission merchants and dealers in western produce. *Cohen's New Orleans and Lafayette Directory . . . , for 1851* (New Orleans: Daily Delta, 1851); OPDC, case 8573.

4. J. S. Holliday, *The World Rushed In: The California Gold Rush Experience* (New York: Simon and Schuster, 1981), 51, 414, 416–18; Charles Warren Haskins, *The Argonauts of California, Being the Reminiscences of Scenes and Incidents that Occurred in California in Early Mining Days* (New York: Fords, Howard, and Hulbert, 1890), 478; *The San Francisco Directory, for the Year 1852–53; Embracing a General Directory of Citizens; a Street Directory; a New and Complete Map of the City; and an Appendix of General Information, an Almanac, etc.* (San Francisco: James M. Parker, 1852), 14; United States Census for Sacramento County, California, 1850, p. 171, California State Library. MSE's life in California is documented in these sources and in Charles P. Kimball, *The San Francisco City Directory, Sept. 1, 1850* (San Francisco: Journal of Commerce Press, 1850); and Josiah J. LeCount, *LeCount and Strong's San Francisco City Directory, for the Year 1854* (San Francisco: San Francisco Herald, 1854).

5. Frank Soulé, John H. Gihon, and James Nisbet, *The Annals of San Francisco* (New York: Appleton, 1855), 452. The information on Hays is drawn from the sources in the previous note, as well as *AC*, Jan. 24, 1850, 2:4, Feb. 1, 1850, 2:2, May 18, 1913; Soulé, Gihon, and Nisbet, *Annals of San Francisco* 269–72; "Sketch of John C. Hayes, the Texas Rangers, Incidents in Texas and Mexico, etc., from Materials Furnished by Col. Hayes and Major John Caperton," n.d., MS BL; John Coffee Hays Correspondence and Papers, 1850–54, BL; *National Cyclopedia of American Biography* (New York: James T. White and Co., 1899), 2:241.

6. San Francisco *Call*, Apr. 23, 1883, 3:4.

7. *Wide West*, Aug. 27, 1854.

8. Ibid., "Interments in Yerba Buena Cemetery, from July 31, to August 31, 1854," *AC*, Sept. 1, 1854, 2:5; Charles E. Rosenberg, *The Cholera Years: The United States in 1832, 1849, and 1866* (Chicago: University of Chicago Press, 1987), 19–20.

9. Soulé, Gihon, and Nisbet, *Annals of San Francisco* 594. See the card index, California Mortuary Records, 1849–1900, California State Library.

10. William A. Proctor, "Location, Regulations, and Removal of the Cemeteries in the City and County of San Francisco," San Francisco Planning Department, 1950, mimeo, pp. 1, 7, 15, SFHR; Edward A. Morphy, " 'San Francisco's Thoroughfares,' Published in the San Francisco *Chronicle* from January 1919 to July 1920," 5 vols., n.d., typescript, 4:396, SFHR.

11. Death Certificates, Orleans Parish, 76:1061 (June 22, 1880), NOPL.

Bibliography

Primary Sources

MANUSCRIPT COLLECTIONS

California State Library, Sacramento, California
    California Mortuary Records, 1849–1900
    United States Census for Sacramento County, 1850
Harvard University, Graduate School of Business Administration,
Baker Library, Cambridge, Massachusetts
    R. G. Dun and Company Collection
Historic New Orleans Collection, New Orleans, Louisiana
    Henri de Ste. Gême Papers
Louisiana State Museum, New Orleans, Louisiana
    Cemetery Inscription File
Louisiana State University, Louisiana and Lower Mississippi Valley
Collection, Baton Rouge, Louisiana
    Luther F. Tower Diaries, 1845–46, 2 vols.
Mississippi Division of Archives and History, Jackson, Mississippi
    United States Census for Alabama, Mississippi, and Louisiana, 1840
New Orleans City Hall, New Orleans, Louisiana
    Conveyance Books, Orleans Parish
    New Orleans Notarial Archives
New Orleans Public Library, New Orleans, Louisiana
    Death Certificates, Orleans Parish
    Early Assessment Records of New Orleans, 1836–47: Second Municipality
        Roll, 1843
    First Congregational Church, New Orleans, Marriage Records, 1834–47
    First District Court, Docket, 1846–54, Orleans Parish
    St. Louis Cemetery No. 2, Interment Book, 1877–80
    Second District Court, Succession Records, 1846–80, Orleans Parish

United States Census for Louisiana, 1850
United States Census for Louisiana, 1860
Tulane University, Howard-Tilton Memorial Library, Manuscripts and Rare
Book Division, New Orleans, Louisiana
   Favrot Collection
   John Leonard Riddell Diaries, vols. 17–18, Jan. 22, 1843–May 22, 1849,
      Riddell Collection 599
   John Minor and Bonnie Matthews Wisdom Collection
University of California, Berkeley, Bancroft Library, Berkeley, California
   John Coffee Hays Correspondence and Papers, 1850–54
   "Sketch of John C. Hayes, the Texas Rangers, Incidents in Texas and Mexico,
      etc., from Materials Furnished by Col. Hayes and Major
      John Caperton," n.d. MS
University of New Orleans Library, Archives and Special Collections,
New Orleans, Louisiana
   School Board, Second Municipality, Minutes, June 3, 1843–Sept. 4, 1847,
      Orleans Parish
University of North Carolina at Chapel Hill, Southern Historical Collection,
Chapel Hill, North Carolina
   Charles W. Bradbury Papers, collection 3011

PERIODICALS
Bee / L'Abeille de la Nouvelle-Orléans, New Orleans
Brother Jonathan, New York
Call, San Francisco
Daily Alta California, San Francisco
Daily Delta, New Orleans
Daily Picayune, New Orleans
Native American, New Orleans
New Orleans Commercial Bulletin
Wide West, San Francisco

CONTEMPORARY WORKS
Andersen, Hans Christian. *The Improvisatore; or, Life in Italy.* Trans. Mary
   Howitt. London, 1845.
Bremer, Frederika. *The Comforter.* Boston: Reading and Co., 1844.
———. *The Neighbours: A Story of Everyday Life.* 2 vols. New York: Harper and
   Bros., 1843.

————. *New Sketches of Every-Day Life: A Diary Together with Strife and Peace.* Trans. Mary Howitt. New York: Harper, 1844.

Briddens, R. P. *Map of San Francisco.* Philadelphia, 1854.

Clapp, Theodore. *Autobiographical Sketches and Recollections, During a Thirty-five Years' Residence in New Orleans.* Boston: Phillips, Sampson and Co., 1857.

————. *Theological Views, Comprising the Substance of Teachings During a Ministry of Thirty-five Years, in New Orleans.* Boston: Abel Tompkins, 1859.

Cohen's New Orleans and Lafayette Directory . . . for 1851. New Orleans: Daily Delta, 1851.

Cohen's New Orleans Directory . . . for 1853. New Orleans: Daily Delta, 1852.

Cohen's New Orleans Directory . . . for 1854. New Orleans: Daily Delta, 1853.

Combe, George. *The Constitution of Man Considered in Relation to External Objects.* New York: William H. Colyer, 1844.

Dick, Thomas. *Complete Works of Thomas Dick, LL.D.* 10 vols. in 5. Philadelphia, 1843.

Ellis, Sarah Stickney. *Look to the End; or, The Bennets Abroad.* New York, Harper, 1845.

————. *The Poetry of Life.* 2 vols. Philadelphia: Carey, Lea and Blanchard, 1835.

Fardon, G. R. *San Francisco in the 1850s: 33 Photographic Views.* 1856; New York: Dover, 1977.

Hall, Harvey. *The Cincinnati Directory for 1825.* Cincinnati: Samuel J. Browne, 1825.

Journal de la Première Municipalité. New Orleans, n.d.

Kimball, Charles P. *The San Francisco City Directory, Sept. 1, 1850.* San Francisco: Journal of Commerce Press, 1850.

LeCount, Josiah J. *LeCount and Strong's San Francisco City Directory, for the Year 1854.* San Francisco: San Francisco Herald, 1854.

Leovy, Henry J. *The Laws and General Ordinances of the City of New Orleans.* Rev. ed. New Orleans: E. C. Wharton, 1857.

New Orleans City Directories. 1831–80.

Norman, Benjamin Moore. *Norman's New Orleans and Environs: Containing a Brief Historical Sketch of the Territory and State of Louisiana, and the City of New Orleans, from the Earliest Period to the Present Time . . . .* New Orleans: B. M. Norman, 1845.

Ordinances Ordained and Established by the Mayor & City Council of the City of New Orleans. New Orleans: J. C. de St. Romes, 1817.

The Pictorial Bible; Being the Old and New Testaments According to the Authorized Version; Illustrated with More Than One Thousand Engravings, Representing the Historical Events, After Celebrated Pictures; the Landscape Scenes, from Original Drawings, or from Authentic Engravings; and the Subjects of Natural History, Costume, and Antiquities, from the Best Sources. 2 vols. New York: J. S. Redfield, 1843–44.

Ripley, Eliza. *Social Life in Old New Orleans: Being Recollections of My Girlhood.* New York: Appleton, 1912.

The San Francisco Directory, for the Year 1852–53: Embracing a General Directory of Citizens; a Street Directory; a New and Complete Map of the City; and an Appendix of General Information, an Almanac, etc. San Francisco: James M. Parker, 1852.

Stranger of the Valley; or, Louisa and Adelaide, an American Tale, by a Lady. New York, 1825.

Van Buren, Martin. *Letter of Mr. Van Buren: Texas.* Columbus, Ohio, 1844.

Volney, Constantin-François. *The Law of Nature; or, Principles of Morality, Deduced from the Physical Constitution of Mankind and the Universe.* Pittsfield, Mass.: Seymour and Smith, 1807.

Walker, Alexander. *Woman Physiologically Considered, as to Mind, Morals, Marriage, Matrimonial Slavery, Infidelity and Divorce.* New York, 1843.

[Walker, Robert J.] *Letter of Mr. Walker, of Mississippi, Relative to the Annexation of Texas: In Reply to the Call of the People of Carroll County, Kentucky, to Communicate His Views on That Subject.* Washington, D.C.: Globe, 1844.

Williams, C. S. *Williams' Cincinnati Directory, City Guide and Business Mirror; or, Cincinnati in 1856.* Cincinnati: C. W. Williams, 1856.

Secondary Sources

Acklen, Jeannette Tillotson, comp. *Tennessee Records: Tombstone Inscriptions and Manuscripts Historical and Biographical.* Nashville: Cullom and Ghertner, 1933.

Baym, Nina. *Novels, Readers, and Reviewers: Responses to Fiction in Antebellum America.* Ithaca, N.Y.: Cornell University Press, 1984.

———. *Woman's Fiction: A Guide to Novels by and about Women in America, 1820–1870.* 2d ed. Urbana: University of Illinois Press, 1993.

Bender, Thomas. "The 'Rural' Cemetery Movement: Urban Travail and the

Appeal of Nature." In *Material Life in America, 1600–1860*, ed. Robert B. St. George, 505–18. Boston: Northeastern University Press, 1988.

Booth, Andrew B., comp. *Records of Louisiana Confederate Soldiers and Louisiana Confederate Commands*. 3 vols. 1902; Spartanburg, S.C.: Reprint Co., 1984.

Bowman, Alan P., comp. *Index to the 1850 Census of the State of California*. Baltimore: Genealogical Publishing Co., 1972.

Bynum, Victoria E. *Unruly Women: The Politics of Social and Sexual Control in the Old South*. Chapel Hill: University of North Carolina Press, 1992.

Censer, Jane Turner. " 'Smiling Through Her Tears': Ante-Bellum Southern Women and Divorce." *American Journal of Legal History* 25, no. 1 (Jan. 1981): 24–47.

Cisco, Jay Guy. *Historic Sumner County, Tennessee, with Genealogies of the Bledsoe, Cage, and Douglass Families, and Genealogical Notes of Other Sumner County Families*. 1909; Nashville: Charles Elder, 1971.

Collins, Peter. *Changing Ideals in Modern Architecture, 1750–1950*. London: Faber, 1965.

Conrad, Glenn R., ed. *A Dictionary of Louisiana Biography*. New Orleans: Louisiana Historical Association, 1988.

Corbett, Mary Jean. *Representing Femininity: Middle-Class Subjectivity in Victorian and Edwardian Women's Autobiographies*. New York: Oxford University Press, 1992.

Davidson, Cathy N. *Revolution and the Word: The Rise of the Novel in America*. New York: Oxford University Press, 1986.

Doriani, Beth Maclay. "Black Womanhood in Nineteenth-Century America: Subversion and Self-Construction in Two Women's Autobiographies." *American Quarterly* 43, no. 2 (June 1991): 199–222.

Duffy, John, ed. *Parson Clapp of the Strangers' Church in New Orleans*. Baton Rouge: Louisiana State University Press, 1957.

Durham, Walter T. *The Great Leap Westward: A History of Sumner County, Tennessee, from Its Beginnings to 1805*. Gallatin, Tenn.: Sumner County Public Library, 1969.

———. *Old Sumner: A History of Sumner County, Tennessee, from 1805 to 1861*. Gallatin, Tenn.: Sumner County Public Library, 1972.

Erffa, Helmut von, and Allan Staley. *The Paintings of Benjamin West*. New Haven, Conn.: Yale University Press, 1986.

Fisher, Roger A. *Tippecanoe and Trinkets Too: The Material Culture of Ameri-*

can Presidential Campaigns, 1828–1984. Urbana: University of Illinois Press,
    1988.

Fossier, Albert E. *New Orleans, the Glamor Period, 1800–1840: A History of the
    Conflicts of Nationalities, Languages, Religions, Morals, Cultures, Laws, Poli-
    tics, and Economics During the Formative Period of New Orleans.* New Orleans:
    Pelican, 1957.

Fox-Genovese, Elizabeth. *Within the Plantation Household: Black and White
    Women of the Old South.* Chapel Hill: University of North Carolina Press,
    1988.

Garvey, Joan B., and Mary Lou Widmer. *Beautiful Crescent: A History of New
    Orleans.* New Orleans: Garmer Press, 1982.

Giddens, Anthony. *A Contemporary Critique of Historical Materialism.* Vol. 1.
    Berkeley: University of California Press, 1981.

———. "Time, Space and Reginalisation." In *Social Relations and Spatial
    Structures,* ed. Derek Gregory and John Urry, 265–95. London: Macmil-
    lan, 1985.

Groce, George C., and David H. Wallace. *The New-York Historical Society's Dic-
    tionary of Artists in America, 1564–1860.* New Haven, Conn.: Yale University
    Press, 1957.

Grossberg, Michael. *Governing the Hearth: Law and the Family in Nineteenth-
    Century America.* Chapel Hill: University of North Carolina Press, 1985.

Gunderson, Robert Gray. *The Log Cabin Campaign.* Lexington: University
    Press of Kentucky, 1957.

Haskins, Charles Warren. *The Argonauts of California, Being the Reminiscences
    of Scenes and Incidents that Occurred in California in Early Mining Days.* New
    York: Fords, Howard, and Hulbert, 1890.

Hodder, Ian. *Reading the Past: Current Approaches to Interpretation in Archae-
    ology.* 2d ed. Cambridge: Cambridge University Press, 1991.

Holliday, J. S. *The World Rushed In: The California Gold Rush Experience.* New
    York: Simon and Schuster, 1981.

Hutchinson, J. R. *Reminiscences, Sketches, and Addresses Selected from My Papers
    During a Ministry of Forty-five Years in Mississippi, Louisiana, and Texas.* Hous-
    ton: E. H. Cushing, 1874.

Kelley, Mary. *Private Woman, Public Stage: Literary Domesticity in Nineteenth-
    Century America.* New York: Oxford University Press, 1984.

Lebsock, Suzanne. *The Free Women of Petersburg: Status and Culture in a South-
    ern Town, 1784–1860.* New York: Norton, 1984.

Levine, Lawrence W. "Clio, Canons, and Culture." *Journal of American History* 80, no. 3 (Dec. 1993): 849–67.

Lucas, Silas Emmett, Jr., ed. *Marriages from Early Tennessee Newspapers, 1794–1851.* Easley, S.C.: Southern Historical Publications, 1978.

Lucas, Silas Emmett, Jr., and Ella Lee Sheffield, eds. *35,000 Tennessee Marriage Records and Bonds, 1783–1870.* 3 vols. Easley, S.C.: Southern Historical Publications, 1981.

Merk, Frederick, and Lois Bannister Merk. *Fruits of Propaganda in the Tyler Administration.* Cambridge, Mass.: Harvard University Press, 1971.

Morphy, Edward A. " 'San Francisco's Thoroughfares,' Published in the *San Francisco Chronicle* from January 1919 to July 1920." 5 vols., n.d. Typescript. San Francisco History Room, San Francisco Public Library.

Murray, Joyce Martin. *Sumner County, Tennessee, Deed Abstracts, 1793–1805.* Wolfe City, Tex.: Henington Publishing Co., 1988.

Nussbaum, Felicity A. "Eighteenth-Century Women's Autobiographical Commonplaces." In *The Private Self: Theory and Practice of Women's Autobiographical Writings,* ed. Shari Benstock, 147–71. Chapel Hill: University of North Carolina Press, 1988.

Pease, Jane H., and William H. Pease. *Ladies, Women, and Wenches: Choice and Constraint in Antebellum Charleston and Boston.* Chapel Hill: University of North Carolina Press, 1990.

Peterson, Alma Hobbs. "The Administration of Public Schools in New Orleans, 1841–1861." Ph.D. diss., Louisiana State University, 1964.

Proctor, William A. "Location, Regulations, and Removal of the Cemeteries in the City and County of San Francisco." San Francisco Planning Department, 1950. Mimeo. Copy in San Francisco History Room, San Francisco Public Library.

Reilly, Timothy F. "Parson Clapp of New Orleans: Antebellum Social Critic, Religious Radical, and Member of the Establishment." *Louisiana History* 16, no. 2 (Spring 1975): 167–91.

———. "Religious Leaders and Social Criticism in New Orleans." Ph.D. diss., University of Missouri, 1972.

Riess, Karlem. *John Leonard Riddell, Scientist-Inventor; Melter and Refiner of the New Orleans Mint, 1839–1848; Postmaster of New Orleans, 1859–1862.* New Orleans: Louisiana Heritage Press, 1977.

Rosenberg, Charles E. *The Cholera Years: The United States in 1832, 1849, and 1866.* Chicago: University of Chicago Press, 1987.

Ryan, Mary P. *Women in Public: Between Banners and Ballots, 1825–1880*. Baltimore: Johns Hopkins University Press, 1990.

Sahlins, Marshall. *Historical Myths and Mythical Realities: Structure in the Early History of the Sandwich Islands Kingdom*. Ann Arbor: University of Michigan Press, 1981.

———. *Islands of History*. Chicago: University of Chicago Press, 1985.

Schafer, Judith K. " 'Open and Notorious Concubinage': The Emancipation of Slave Mistresses by Will and the Supreme Court in Antebellum Louisiana." *Louisiana History* 28, no. 2 (Fall 1987): 165–82.

Schuyler, David. "The Evolution of the Anglo-American Rural Cemetery: Landscape Architecture as Social and Cultural History." *Journal of Garden History* 4, no. 3 (Sept. 1984): 291–304.

Sloane, David Charles. *The Last Great Necessity: Cemeteries in American History*. Baltimore: Johns Hopkins University Press, 1991.

Soulé, Frank, John H. Gihon, and James Nisbet. *The Annals of San Francisco*. New York: Appleton, 1855.

Stansell, Christine. *City of Women: Sex and Class in New York, 1789–1860*. Urbana: University of Illinois Press, 1987.

Sullivan, Edmund B. *Collecting Political Americana*. Hanover, Mass.: Christopher Publishing House, 1991.

Tamalpais Chapter, Daughters of the American Revolution, comp. *San Francisco Cemetery Records, 1848–1863*. N.p., 1938.

Toledano, Roulhac, and Mary Louise Christovich. *New Orleans Architecture*. Vol. 6, *Faubourg Tremé and the Bayou Road*. Gretna, La.: Pelican, 1980.

"Vital Records from the *Daily Alta California:* Including Records from the *Golden Era* and the *Wide West*, 1854." Comp. El Palo Alto, San Francisco, Tamalpais, and California chapters, California State Society, Daughters of the American Revolution, 1955. Typescript. California State Library, Sacramento.

Waldo, John F. C. *Historical Sketch of the First Unitarian Church of New Orleans, La.* [New Orleans: First Unitarian Church], 1907.

Whitley, Edythe Rucker, comp. *Marriages of Sumner County, Tennessee, 1787–1838*. Baltimore: Genealogical Publishing Co., 1981.

———. *Sumner County, Tennessee: Abstracts of Will Books 1 and 2 (1788–1842)*. Baltimore: Genealogical Publishing Co., 1978.

Wilson, Samuel, Jr. *The First Presbyterian Church of New Orleans: Its Buildings and Its Ministers*. New Orleans: Louisiana Landmarks Society, 1988.

Index

Adams, John B., 75, 78, 211, 236, 340 (n. 16)

Adelle (H. J. Budington's lover), 21, 215, 216, 235, 239, 242, 243, 247, 248, 249, 261

African Americans, 10, 107, 121, 122, 148, 149, 258; sexual relationships with whites, 19–20; MSE's views on, 37–38, 221, 258, 337 (n. 79). *See also* Slavery; Slaves

Alexandria, La. *See* Red River, La.

All Saints' Day. *See* Ceremonies, public

Andersen, Hans Christian, 39; *Improvisatore*, 268, 269

Anelli, Francesco, 255, 327; *Opening of the Seventh Seal*, 255, 326, 327

Astronomy, 1, 34, 69, 99, 153, 154, 224, 322, 323, 325, 337 (n. 73)

Baym, Nina, 44

Boze, Jean, 19

Bradbury, Charles W.: meets MSE, 8, 313; sued by MSE, 10, 21, 46, 317–18; breaks with MSE, 11, 24, 301–17; biography of, 14, 16–19, 333 (n. 33); business of, 16, 94, 268, 333 (n. 33); residence of, 16, 320; relationships with women, 16–19, 109; marriage of, 17–18; as MSE's audience, 41, 44; financial status of, 54, 203, 333 (n. 35); birthday of, 92, 93; trip north of, 94, 102, 105–6, 262; dreams of, 103, 241; poetry of, 233, 234; death of, 320, 330 (n. 2)

Bradbury, Cornelius, 16, 17–18

Bradbury, James Anson, 20, 21, 118, 122, 135, 136, 137, 147, 148, 152, 154, 274; biography of, 14

Bradbury, Marcus, 17

Bradbury, Mary Ann Taylor Hamilton, 25–26, 29, 49, 51, 54, 72, 94, 95–96, 100, 134, 148, 190, 192, 194, 211, 226, 236, 248, 249, 252, 267, 270, 317, 334 (n. 38); marriage of, 17–18

Bradbury, Sarah, 18

Breedlove, James Waller, 16, 22–24, 275, 276, 279, 293, 306–7, 309, 318; biography of, 22

Breedlove, Maria Ellen Winchester, 22, 274–75, 276, 325

Bremer, Frederika, 39, 91, 92, 93, 94, 103, 123, 134. Works: *New Sketches of Every-Day Life*, 91, 92, 93, 94; *Comforter*, 103; *Neighbours*, 134, 135

Brother Jonathan, 231

Brown, Angelica Eugenia, 21

Budington, Henry J., 11, 18–19, 20–
    21, 71–109 passim; 117, 118, 120,
    121, 123, 133, 135, 136, 137, 145,
    147, 149, 154, 155, 182, 184, 185,
    200, 203, 213, 214, 215, 216, 230,
    231, 238, 239, 244, 245;
    biography of, 14; and affair with
    Adelle, 21, 242, 243, 247, 248,
    249, 261

Budington, Margaret, 14

Byron, George Gordon, Lord, 40,
    116, 157, 163, 257, 276–78, 325

Cage (MSE's brother), 4, 331 (n. 6)

Cage, Albert (MSE's brother), 4, 5,
    137, 253, 325

Cage, Eliza. *See* Coleman, Eliza D.
    Cage

Cage, Fanny (MSE's sister), 4, 80,
    235

Cage, Lofton (MSE's father), 4, 5, 6,
    8, 75, 81, 105, 108, 153, 235, 253,
    254, 259, 312

Cage, Naomi (Nabury) Gillespie
    (MSE's mother), 4, 5, 71

Cage, William, Sr. (MSE's
    grandfather), 4

Cage, William, Jr. (MSE's uncle), 4

Cage's Bend, Tenn., 4, 346 (n. 16)

Carrollton, La., 252, 267

Cemeteries: Yerba Buena, xi, 319,
    320; Girod Street, 21, 209–10;
    Jewish, 82, 340 (n. 30); Lafayette
    No. 1, 102, 117, 123, 124 (illus.),

125–27; MSE on, 123, 125–32,
    204–10, 322; Cypress Grove
    (Firemen's), 124 (illus.), 125, 232,
    342 (n. 11); St. Louis No. 2, 125,
    204–10, 206 (illus.), 324; Laurel
    Hill (Lone Mountain), 320;
    Cypress Lawn, 320

Ceremonies, public: 262; Fourth of
    July, 38, 118–20, 267; Eighth of
    January, 69, 230; Washington's
    Birthday, 69, 240–41; St. Patrick's
    Day, 72; All Saints' Day, 193, 344
    (n. 3); Whig torchlight parade,
    193–94; Native American
    Artillery banner presentation,
    262–63, 263–64; Jackson funeral,
    264–65, 265–67; New Year's Day,
    344 (n. 1)

Chapman, John Gadsby, 255

Christ Healing the Sick (West), 255,
    322

Christian Philosopher (Dick), 76, 77

Clapp, Rev. Theodore, 17, 30–33, 31
    (illus.), 40, 61, 64–68, 71, 79, 92,
    118, 132, 134, 136, 138, 145, 153,
    183, 189, 202, 210, 211, 225, 231,
    234, 247, 261, 267, 274, 277, 292,
    301, 311, 339 (n. 3), 348 (n. 3);
    sermons of, 28–29, 30, 34, 66–68,
    70, 72, 76, 78, 80, 81, 82, 83, 86–
    91, 94, 95–98, 103, 104, 106, 120,
    154–55, 184, 185, 188, 200, 229,
    235, 237, 241, 248, 249, 251, 252,
    254, 260, 263, 264, 278, 322;
    biography of, 30; theology of, 30,
    33, 148, 337 (n. 73); MSE's views